The Postwar International Money Crisis – an Analysis

The Postwar International Money Crisis – an Analysis

VICTOR ARGY
Professor of Economics, Macquarie University

London
GEORGE ALLEN & UNWIN
Boston Sydney

First published in 1981

GEORGE ALLEN & UNWIN LTD
40 Museum Street, London WC1A 1LU

British Library Cataloging in Publication Data

Argy, Victor
The post-war international money crisis.
1. International finance—History
I. Title
332.4'5 HG3881

ISBN 0-04-332075-9
ISBN 0-04-332076-7 Pbk

Library of Congress cataloging number 80-70240

Set in 10 on 11 point Times by Typesetters (Birmingham) Ltd.
and printed in the United States of America.

Contents

PART FOUR Managed Floats – 1973 to 1978

PART FIVE Choice of Exchange Rate Regime

PART SIX Macro-Policy

This book is dedicated to
Renate, Jacqueline and Frederick

Preface

The book has two principal aims. First, to provide a description of the major international monetary developments in the industrial world in the postwar years. Second, to evaluate and analyse these developments by reference to a theoretical framework and, in addition, to look at the key policy issues in the context of the new environment of the last decade.

Part One of the book reviews the history of exchange rate regimes from the gold standard to the breakdown of Bretton Woods. At the same time, it describes the growth of the Euro-currency market and examines the implications of that market for world liquidity, world reserves, capital mobility and exchange rate instability. It also looks at the financial aspects of the oil price shock of late 1973.

Part Two is unavoidably technical. It provides a representative survey of macro models of open economies which have been in use in the literature in the postwar years. These include a neo-Keynesian model, the monetarist expectations-augmented Phillips curve model and a monetarist two-sector model. Its objective is to arm the reader with the basic macro-theoretical foundations with which to attack many of the problems and issues that emerge in the subsequent chapters.

Part Three deals with theories of global inflation and the empirical evidence that bears on these theories. It also examines the reasons for the global plunge into recession in the mid-1970s.

Part Four provides the theoretical framework for an understanding of how spot and forward rates are jointly determined in a relatively free market. At the same time, it reviews the empirical evidence, from the most recent period, for the theories presented.

Part Five examines, in some detail, the considerations that enter into the choice between fixed and flexible exchange rate regimes. In particular, it looks at the relative effectiveness of macro-policy, the relative insulation of the domestic economy from random disturbances, the relative effects on world inflation and unemployment, the relative effects on the demand for reserves as well as trade and the relative potential for the generation of vicious spirals of devaluation (revaluation) and inflation (deflation). Finally, it looks at the costs and benefits of a monetary union and reviews the EEC experience with a monetary union.

Part Six reviews traditional macro-policy, identifies the ways in which the economic environment has changed and then looks at a range of policy issues posed by the new environment. Chapters 30 and 31 deal specifically with policies directed at stagflation. Finally, Chapter 32 presents a framework for macro-policy that focuses on counteracting specific disturbances to which an economy is exposed.

ACKNOWLEDGEMENTS

I am indebted to many people for help and encouragement in the production of this work. In particular, I would like to acknowledge helpful comments from the following on earlier drafts of the book: J. R. Artus, A. Blundell-Wignall, A. R. Braun, J. C. Chouraqui, K. W. Clements, W. M. Corden, R. Dornbusch, D. I. Folkerts-Landau, J. Horne, P. D. Jonson, W. D. McClam, J. M. Parkin, J. O. N. Perkins, J. J. Polak, M. G. Porter, J. Salop, E. Spitaeller and L. Stein.

I also wish to acknowledge research assistance from the following: my wife, Renate, my daughter, Jacqueline, Sean Manefield, Tracey Sparks, Wendy Filewood, Muthi Semudram and John Davies.

Finally, I owe a very special debt to my secretary, Miss Lydia Miceli, who worked long tedious hours with great skill, accuracy and patience at earlier drafts.

The author thanks the publishers of the *Australian Economic Review* and *Management Forum* for permission to publish extracts from articles which appeared in those journals.

A Summary Perspective on the Issues

Exchange Rates Regimes – the last hundred years

In the last hundred years the industrial world has seen three principal types of international monetary regimes. First, the gold standard regime, which operated between 1880 and 1914 and again between 1925 and 1931. Second, the managed float regime, which operated between 1918 and 1925 and again from 1973 to date. Third, the IMF (Bretton Woods) type regime which functioned between 1946 and 1973.

These three regimes are distinguishable, principally, by their differing prescriptions on exchange rates and the adjustment mechanism. At one extreme, in the gold standard regime exchange rates are permanently fixed and adjustment occurs by allowing deficits/surpluses to act on the volume of money. At the other extreme – the managed float regime – exchange rates are principally determined by market forces and serve to equilibrate the demand and supply for foreign exchange. The IMF regime represents, in intention, the intermediate case. It allows exchange rate flexibility in the long term to correct fundamental disequilibria but, at the same time, there is an obligation on participant countries to maintain the exchange rate fixed, within a narrow band, in the short term.

The events of the last hundred years have shown that a fixed rate type regime will be viable only if certain conditions are met. First, the key country, which is placed at the centre of the financial system, must provide a reasonably stable environment. Second, the adjustment mechanism to correct or avert emerging disequilibria in the balance of payments must be relatively painless. Third, the underlying world social and political conditions must not be too disruptive.

If these conditions are not met a fixed rate regime tends to break down and is, in due course, replaced by a regime that allows a greater degree of exchange rate flexibility. At the same time, with conditions now inherently unstable a more flexible rate regime tends to perform in ways that are widely felt to be unsatisfactory. As a result a reaction eventually sets in and moves are initiated to restore a greater degree of exchange rate stability.

These points can easily be demonstrated by reference to the last hundred years. There were two periods when fixed rate regimes flourished and when the basic preconditions were, in large part, met. These were the first gold standard period, when the key country was the UK, and the IMF period between 1950 and the mid-1960s, when the key country was the USA.

In the aftermath of the First World War, with conditions still very unsettled, there was a first experiment with managed floats; this was widely viewed at the time as a transitional and unsatisfactory arrangement. The world returned, in 1925, to the gold standard with something of a relief; this time, however, the gold standard was a failure because by then conditions had dramatically changed: sterling was overvalued, the adjustment mechanism worked unsatisfactorily, the political and economic environment had become much more unstable and London was encountering increasing competition as a financial centre. It took, finally, the Great Depression in 1930/31 to bring the second gold standard regime to an end.

There followed a period of considerable uncertainty, marked by competitive devaluations and restrictions on trade. The dissatisfaction with the workings of the exchange rate regime led once again to a reaction. This came in 1936 with the signing of the Tripartite Agreement (between the USA, the UK and France), which endorsed moves in the direction of stabilising exchange rates.[1]

The IMF system emerged as a reaction to the interwar experience. Up to the mid-1960s, despite some strains, the system was able to function reasonably well. In those years US conditions were stable and its rate of inflation low. However, by the second half of the 1960s conditions in the USA and Europe began to move unfavourably. There were social and political tensions and wage explosions in several European economies, while, at the same time, US economic conditions, in the wake of the Vietnam War and the social programmes of the Johnson years, had steadily deteriorated. The US inflation rate accelerated significantly while US monetary conditions became very unstable. This led to several years of stress which came to a head with the oil price shock of 1973, which then brought to an end the Bretton Woods era.

The world recession that followed, the continuing uncertainties surrounding the oil price situation, the differences in inflationary experience and in cyclical positions, the inexperience in coping with flexible rates, all combined to produce considerable exchange rate uncertainty. Inevitably, there was a reaction to this exchange rate instability. This manifested itself in several ways. First, the Jamaica Agreement of January 1976 pledged countries to 'promote a stable system of exchange rates' and to 'seek to promote stability by fostering orderly underlying economic and financial conditions and a monetary system that does not tend to produce erratic disruptions'. Second, by late 1977 growing dissatisfaction with the workings of the exchange rate regime led to moves within the EEC to inject new life into a monetary union. These negotiations came to a head in December 1978 with the resolution to implement a new European Monetary System, Third, with exchange rate instability reaching new heights during 1978 and 1979, these years saw a succession of arrangements on intervention and financial aid, aimed at securing greater exchange rate stability. Fourth, there is evidence (see later) that increasingly macro-policy has been directed at securing exchange rate objectives. Fifth, there is even some nostalgia for, and indeed some talk of returning to, the international gold standard system.

To summarise, just as there was a reaction to the post-First World War experience with managed floats (as manifested in the return to the gold standard) and to the exchange rate uncertainties of the 1930s (as manifested in the Tripartite Agreement of 1936), so we observe, in 1978/79, growing discontent with the workings of the exchange rate regime and moves towards stabilising exchange rates. At the same time, there is widespread recognition that, given current conditions, a return on a large scale to a fixed rate regime is, realistically, out of the question. This feeling of frustration was aptly represented recently by Emminger[2] who, adapting one of Churchill's sayings, concluded that 'floating may be the worst system, except for all the other available ones'.

World Inflation, Unemployment in the 1970s and the Conservative Reaction

Several factors combined to generate the acceleration in world inflation in the late 1960s and the first half of the 1970s. First, in several European countries, notably France, the UK and Italy, there were some sociological factors at work. Second, in the second half of the 1960s, the US rate of inflation started accelerating and this was transmitted to the rest of the world; also, more importantly, in 1970/71 US monetary expansion was excessive and this led to huge outflows of capital, which, in turn, contributed to the acceleration in monetary growth in the rest of the world. Third, there were the commodity price shocks of 1973.

As with inflation, the downturn into recession in 1974 was a global phenomenon. The recession can be accounted for by the combined influences of the oil price shock, the associated policy stances at the time (principally on the monetary front) and the transmission of deflation across frontiers.

By 1975/76 most industrial countries were following conservative policy stances. These were reflected, first, in the switch to monetary targets which themselves were relatively modest, and second, in the fiscal policies which were very moderate, in the light of the prevailing unemployment.

Exchange Rate Instability (1973–1978)

In the wake of the switch to managed floats in early 1973 there has been a renewed interest in previous experiences with managed floats (notably in the period immediately after the First World War) and, also, a proliferation of new ideas and analyses aimed at explaining exchange rate fluctuations.

A useful starting point in trying to understand exchange rate movements is to identify three sets of influences: the underlying conditions, the structural relations and exchange rate expectations.

It is now widely recognised (and was so explicitly at Jamaica) that if underlying conditions are unstable, this will be reflected in unstable exchange rates. This no doubt has played a principal part in accounting for recent exchange rate instability.

There is, too, recognition that, given the instability in the underlying conditions, structural responses in the economy can contribute to exchange rate instability. In this context, three sources of potential exchange rate instability are particularly worthy of note. First, if asset markets adjust first and real markets later (a notion which is intuitively appealing), monetary changes are likely to lead to exaggerated movements in exchange rates. Second, there is evidence that the trade balance adjusts with a considerable lag to changes in exchange rates and that for several industrial countries the initial effects of exchange rate changes (over, say, six months to a year) are actually perverse, leading, in the absence of stabilising capital flows, to exaggerated exchange rate movements. Third, with real wages and interest rates fixed, sustained disturbances to the balance of payments can lead, under flexible rates, to a vicious (virtuous) circle of devaluation–inflation–devaluation (revaluation–deflation–revaluation).

Finally, despite considerable research, little is really known about the determination of exchange rate expectations and their contribution to exchange rate instability. It is evident, however, that, given the underlying conditions and the structural relations, exchange rate expectations also have the potential for dampening or aggravating exchange rate fluctuations.

An Evaluation of Managed Floats

After some six to seven years of managed floats, are we now in a position to evaluate their performance, particularly in the light of the claims made by their protagonists as well as their critics?

During the 1950s and 1960s the principal theoretical claims made by the protagonists of the flexible exchange rate were: that it is easy to administer; that it secures continual balance of payments equilibrium and so frees macro-instruments for the achievement of other targets; that it allows individual countries to choose their optimal combination of inflation and unemployment; that monetary policy becomes more effective; that it allows monetary independence; that it provides insulation from external disturbances; that it eliminates the need for reserves; that, relative to fixed rates, the effects on trade are not necessarily harmful but, in any case, small; and, finally, that speculation will be based on longer-term movements in the underlying economic conditions and, hence, will tend to be stabilising.

Critics of managed floats contend that on most of these counts and others flexible rates have been a disappointment. First, under certain, not unrealistic, conditions (for example, if capital mobility is imperfect, if the effects of the exchange rate on the trade balance are initially perverse, if one allows for the price effects of exchange rate changes), monetary policy may not be more effective under flexible rates. Second, monetary policy is now increasingly directed at stabilising exchange rates. This was strikingly in evidence during 1978/79. For example, in 1978 the USA was forced twice to raise its discount rate for external reasons while Germany, by intervening heavily in the foreign exchange market and refusing to sterilise, allowed its monetary growth to exceed its target. Also, in late 1979 US interest rates rose sharply, as they had done in 1968/69; again, as in 1968/69, this led to competing increases in interest rates. Third, with more flexible rates, there is now greater uncertainty surrounding macro-policy. Fourth, flexible rates, particularly in a world where there is wage indexation, are likely to lead to a greater amplitude of price fluctuation, which itself imposes a cost on the community. Fifth, in a world where there is no trade-off between inflation and unemployment, the case for flexible rates has been substantially weakened. Sixth, some intervention has been necessary, requiring the continuing use of international reserves. Seventh, while it is true that exchange rate flexibility allows greater insulation from inflation in the rest of the world and from changes in output in the rest of the world, it does not insulate the economy from changes in interest rates overseas; moreover, flexible rates, in general, tend to be poor insulators for disturbances originating within the economy. Eighth, there are (previously largely unsuspected) sources of substantial exchange rate instability inherent in the system. Ninth, long-run stabilising speculation has not been forthcoming.

Protagonists, however, contend that flexible exchange rates have actually performed well. They argue that conditions have remained unstable, making it difficult for exchange rates to be stabilised; that fixed rates would not have been feasible in the conditions; that the experience is still relatively new; that trade has not been adversely affected; that intervention may well have served to destabilise exchange rates; that monetary authorities have been over-concerned about exchange rate instability, whose costs, in any case, tend to be small.

The New Policy Environment

In the last decade or so the economic environment has changed in a number of ways which have important implications for policy. The principal changes have been (1) the shift to more flexible exchange rates, (2) the high rate of inflation combined with historically high rates of unemployment (including a higher natural rate of unemployment), (3) the larger government sector, (4) the increased importance of supply shocks to the economy, (5) the large budget deficits combined with the large global current account deficits (for the oil-consuming countries), (6) the greater interdependence in the world economy and (7) the secular fall in the rate of growth of productivity in several industrial countries.

In the current (1979) economic environment there is a sharp division of opinion about the appropriate macro-policy. Typically, Conservative–Monetarists believe that the attack on inflation should be given priority, that attention should also focus on correcting serious structural imbalances in the economy and that expansionary policies in current conditions would be quickly dissipated in higher prices and, hence, would be self-defeating. By contrast, Liberal–Keynesians attach more importance to the social and economic costs of unemployment. They contend that the costs of fully anticipated inflation are small and that there are policies available that are designed to reduce unemployment without increasing inflation.

Neither school has the answers to the serious policy predicaments posed by today's world. Although traditional macro-policy, derived from Keynes, Meade, Tinbergen and Mundell, is largely irrelevant, nothing has replaced it and the search for new policies remains in its infancy.

With inflation continuing high and with regular oil price shocks a feature of today's world, many industrial countries must make the choice between allowing unemployment rates to continue to rise, with the attendant serious social and economic losses, or living with rates of inflation that are high by recent historical standards. The resolve on the part of most governments to bring inflation down to moderate levels, even in the face of sustained supply shocks, is perhaps all the more surprising when one considers that a solid body of economic theory continues to proclaim that industrial economies can live comfortably with inflation rates of the order of 10–20 per cent, provided they are prepared to make the necessary institutional changes (for example, introduce widespread indexation). In the author's view, continuing frustration, as well as political and social pressures, will force governments sooner or later to take this route.

Notes: Introduction and Summary

1 See S. V. O. Clarke (1977a, 1977b).
2 O. Emminger (1979).

Part One

International Monetary Regimes and the Euro-Dollar System

Chapter 1

The Gold Standard Regime[1]

General Principles

The gold standard regime has, conventionally, been associated with three rules of the game. The first rule is that in each participating country the price of the domestic currency must be fixed in terms of gold. The second rule is that there must be a free import and export of gold. The third rule is that the surplus country, which is gaining gold, should allow its volume of money to increase while the deficit country, which is losing gold, should allow its volume of money to fall.

The first two rules together ensure that exchange rates between participating countries are fixed within fairly narrow limits. With the price of any two currencies fixed in terms of gold the implied exchange rate between the two currencies is also fixed and any significant deviation from this fixed rate would be rapidly eliminated by arbitrage operations. Suppose, for example, the two currencies concerned are the US dollar and the franc and suppose that $40 exchange for an ounce of gold in the USA while 160 francs exchange for an ounce of gold in France. This fixes the bilateral exchange rate at 4 francs to $1. Suppose, too, to begin with, that arbitrage (that is, the converting and shipping of gold) is costless. Now consider the case where France is running a deficit. The excess demand for the dollar cannot produce an exchange rate such that more than 4 francs would sell for $1. At that rate no one would want to sell francs because it would be cheaper to sell francs for gold, ship the gold to the USA and convert the gold there into US dollars. In other words, traders could get more US dollars per franc by transacting in gold than by selling francs for dollars in the foreign exchange market. By the same token if France were in surplus the exchange rate could not be such that fewer than 4 francs would sell for $1; for, in that case, no one would want to sell US dollars at that rate since it would be cheaper to convert US dollars into gold, ship the gold to France and convert it into francs at the official rate.

In reality, of course, there are costs associated with the buying and shipping of gold (for example, a service charge by the central authority, a shipping charge, insurance costs and a loss of interest during transit). This means that deviations from the implicit exchange rate are quite possible so long as these deviations are equal to or less than the costs of transacting in gold. Suppose that these costs amount, roughly, to 5 per cent; then the exchange rate could fluctuate within the range, say, of $1 for 3.8–4.2 francs (the so-called gold points) without any shipment of gold. The rate of $1 for 3.8 francs is, from the point of view of France, its gold import point while the rate of $1 for 4.2 francs is its gold export point. In other words, if the French franc is weak and the exchange rate is being pushed beyond 4.2 francs to the dollar, France will lose gold to the USA, while if the US dollar is weak and the exchange rate is being pressed below 3.8 francs to the dollar the USA will lose gold to France.

The third rule, requiring the volume of money to be linked in each participating country to balance of payments developments, provided an 'automatic' mechanism of adjustment which ensured that, ultimately, any balance of payments disequilibria would be corrected. There are several potential mechanisms by which changes in the money supply serve to correct the disequilibria. One mechanism is through the variations in the interest rate which induce corrective movements of capital; for example, the surplus country would lower its interest rate while the deficit country would raise its interest rate and capital would flow from the former to the latter. Another mechanism, through the goods markets, operates more slowly. Deflation and inflation of the money supplies will lead to relative changes in prices and/or real output that will correct the imbalances. The adjustment through prices is associated with the classical price–specie flow mechanism while the adjustment through output is associated with (later) Keynesian thinking.

The precise operation of the three rules will vary depending on the institutional arrangements. Consider, first, a primitive monetary system represented by a gold specie standard, where money is made up only of gold coins with a fixed gold content and the national mint will always supply gold by melting down gold coins or coin gold supplied to it by the public. In these conditions adjustment is simple and automatic. The exchange rate cannot move outside the gold points; gold will flow out (after being melted down) at the gold export point and will flow in at the gold import point.

Next consider the simplest gold bullion standard where money is made up of notes only, which are themselves backed 100 per cent by gold. In this case the outcomes and method of adjustment are effectively the same. For example, instead of melting coins for payment notes are presented for conversion into gold. Suppose, however, that notes in circulation are not backed 100 per cent by gold but, initially, by, say, only 50 per cent gold and there is no legal reserve requirement. The balance of the backing is assumed to be in loans to the private sector (commercial banks are assumed, at this point, to be non-existent). The central bank balance sheet in its simplest form would now have the note issue in its liabilities (say 100 units) and half of that (50 units) as loans (the fiduciary issue) and the other half (50 units) as gold in its assets. Now suppose that a payment of 5 units needs to be made overseas. Notes and gold will now both drop by 5 units so gold reserves will have fallen by 10 per cent while the volume of money will have fallen by only 5 per cent. Partial backing, therefore, may weaken the corrective mechanism of the gold standard, and threaten the reserve position. The smaller this backing the greater the danger that the corrective mechanism might not work before reserves are severely depleted. By contrast, with 100 per cent backing the corrective process cannot fail since the volume of money cannot be reduced 100 per cent.

Suppose, now, that a legal reserve ratio of the order of 40 per cent is imposed while the central bank, de facto, holds 50 per cent. (It is necessary to hold excess reserves if the strict letter of the law is not going to be broken since with notes and gold falling by equal amounts the reserve ratio falls.) Clearly, to restore the reserve ratio of 50 per cent a reduction in gold of 10 per cent must be associated with a reduction in notes of 10 per cent as well and hence loans, in our example, must also fall by 10 per cent. The reduction in gold will then also be associated with a reduction in the domestic assets of the central bank. How much of this process is automatic and how much is discretionary depends, of course, on the legal reserve requirement and the margin of excess reserves.

Now consider the case where commercial banks exist and suppose that money is made up of notes as well as bank deposits. (To place this in historical perspective, in Britain the proportion of money held in the form of demand deposits had increased from some 35 per cent in 1885 to some 60 per cent in 1913.) The non-bank private sector now holds notes as well as deposits while the banks hold, say, a proportion of their deposit liabilities as deposits with the central bank. In turn the central bank has domestic assets as well as gold. Now central bank reserve ratios may apply only to the note liability or may extend as well to the deposit liabilities or may be different for the two forms of liabilities. Clearly, in this more complicated system the possible slippages are greater; how the total volume of money will respond to a change in gold reserves will clearly depend not only on central bank legal reserve requirements but also on cash/deposit and notes/deposit conventions by commercial banks and the private sector, respectively. The adjustment will now be automatic, proportionate and predictable only so long as the relevant ratios (of the commercial banks, central banks and private sectors) are all rigidly defined and exactly observed.

Suppose, finally, that the system in force is a gold exchange standard, where one country's currency (the reserve currency) is held as 'reserves' by the rest of the world while the reserve currency itself is backed by gold. To take the simplest case, if central banks hold their foreign exchange as deposits with the commercial banks in the reserve currency country, settlement of disequilibria may be effected by changes in the ownership of deposits with the commercial banks without any change in the total volume of their deposits or in their cash reserves. For example, if sterling were the reserve currency, a British deficit might be financed by the switch in the ownership of a deposit from, say, a British resident to a foreign central bank. In this case there would be no automatic adjustment. There would also be an asymmetry in that the full burden of adjustment would now fall on the rest of the world. The automaticity of a gold standard regime in this case (with a reserve currency) would be thus further weakened.

The First Gold Standard Period 1880–1914

Reasons for Survival

Although by 1819–21 Britain was already on a full-fledged gold standard, it was not until about 1880 that most of the industrial world joined Britain in meeting the conditions of the gold standard. This regime was to endure until the outbreak of the First World War.

How is it possible to account for the survival of the gold standard fixed rate regime over a 35-year period? Several reasons may be advanced. First, the world economy was relatively stable: there were no major wars or disturbances; governments and their budgets were relatively small and hence were not a volatile element in the economy; monetary conditions and the financial environment tended to be relatively stable; the period was also distinguished by powerful long-term expansionist influences while, more important, output growth was relatively steady. Second, economic cycles of participating countries were highly synchronised, thus averting the emergence of large disequilibria. Third, it is likely, as Triffin has argued,[2] that substantial discrepancies in cost competitiveness were not allowed to surface because participating countries exercised ex ante constraint in the conduct of their monetary policies.

Fourth, sterling's dominant role at the centre of the world financial scene considerably facilitated the workings of the gold standard system. For almost every year in the 35 years of the gold standard Britain had a current account surplus. Indeed her basic economic strength is evidenced by the fact that these surpluses actually grew over the time period. This surplus tended to fluctuate by only small margins over economic cycles and this meant that Britain's task became essentially one of tailoring her lending overseas to the fluctuations in her current account; this she managed with considerable success. This is so despite the fact that Britain had, in fact, relatively meagre international reserves. For example, if we take the ratio of reserves to imports as a very rough measure of a country's reserve adequacy, Bloomfield[3] found that the UK's ratio was very low in a sample of ten countries. Also, although Britain's sterling liabilities to foreigners exceeded her gold holdings (by 1913 they were over twice as much) sterling was never under speculative attack in those years.

Fifth, the adjustment mechanism appeared to have worked relatively painlessly and without undue strain on the system. In general, an outflow (inflow) of gold tended to be associated with an increase (decrease) in the central bank discount rate.[4] In turn, these variations in the discount rate acted to correct the external position. For the UK at least, the Bank Rate mechanism worked so quickly and effectively that any changes did not have to be sustained for too long. Much of the evidence now suggests that the adjustment came about largely through changes in the flow of capital which was particularly sensitive to changes in the UK Bank Rate.[5] Economic activity and employment, it appears, were only marginally affected by the Bank Rate. The effects on relative prices, to the extent they occurred, would have been considerably delayed and, with early reversals of policies, dispersed over time. Indeed the evidence suggests that movements in price levels were predominantly in the same rather than in the opposite direction in participating countries.

Sixth, and finally, over the period as a whole the supplies of gold accruing to central authorities were adequate to meet the needs of the regime. Ford,[6] in summarising the role of monetary gold stocks in this period, asserts: 'the main role of the increasing gold supplies was to facilitate the workings of the international payments system, so that as trade and payment flows expanded the system was never permanently braked by sharply rising interest rates through shortage of cash . . .'.

The Second Gold Standard Period 1925–1931

Background

The dislocation of the war had made it impossible to return immediately to the gold standard. Its enormous success, however, in the prewar years and the absence of clearly defined alternatives left no doubt in the minds of policy-makers and the financial community about the desirability of a return to the gold standard as soon as conditions rendered it appropriate. This attitude is most clearly reflected in the views of the UK's Cunliffe Committee set up in January 1918 to examine currency issues in the years after the war. Its report presented a glowing picture of the workings of the prewar gold standard and concluded that the objective of policy was to restore the gold standard along traditional lines at prewar parity as soon as feasible.[7]

In the years immediately following the war exchange rates for the major currencies were allowed to move more or less in line with market forces. Indeed, in the period 1920–24 the sterling–dollar exchange rate fluctuated with very little official intervention. Its prewar parity had been $4.86, but by early 1920 it had dropped to a low $3.18, 35 per cent below par. Intent on restoring prewar parity and strengthening the currency, the British authorities responded by implementing severe deflationary policies in 1920/21. This led to a sharp drop in wages and prices (the latter falling by as much as 50–60 per cent from their peak levels in 1920); at the same time unemployment rose substantially. In the event, the exchange rate rose to about $4.2 by early 1922. Policy reversals in 1922/23, which now gave greater priority to domestic over external considerations, were successful in bringing down the rate of unemployment. Prices, however, remained relatively stable in the two years between March 1922 and March 1924. The exchange rate moved roughly in line with relative prices in the UK and the USA, strengthening as US prices rose between 1922 and 1923 and then weakening as US prices fell again in the year to 1924. Then, in the year that followed, US prices rose more rapidly than British prices and, at the same time, foreign exchange markets began to anticipate a return to gold at parity. The combination of influences forced the rate up to 4.78 by early 1925, only 1½ per cent below parity.

The Chamberlain–Bradbury Committee, set up in June 1924 to take up once again the issues originally raised by the Cunliffe Committee, was now sufficiently impressed by the strength of sterling to recommend an immediate return to gold at parity. Winston Churchill, who was then Chancellor of the Exchequer, announced in his Budget Speech in April 1925 that Britain would immediately return to gold. Most countries followed and by 1927 the gold standard had, in fact, been restored. This time, however, it did not have the endurance of the prewar phase. After a few turbulent years, including the world collapse into the Great Depression after 1929, Britain left the gold standard in September 1931. She was subsequently followed by other countries, notably the USA in 1933 and the French Bloc in 1936.

Reasons for Collapse

We now turn to an examination of the changing environment under which the postwar gold standard operated, and the fundamental reasons for its disintegration.[8]

First, it is almost certain that sterling was overvalued at its prewar par rate when Britain returned to gold in 1925.[9] The war had transformed Britain's current account adversely in a number of ways. There was some decline in her export markets, due to increased competitiveness, at the same time that there was an increase in her import needs. There was also a loss of property income, an increased war indebtedness, some loss of earnings from the switch in financial services from London to New York as well as from her merchant shipping losses. In addition, the structure of her trade had changed significantly, creating greater uncertainty in her trade position. Finally, purchasing power parity calculations suggested a probable overvaluation of sterling of something of the order of 10 per cent.[10]

Second, a widely held view was that the adjustment mechanism worked unsatisfactorily during the restored gold standard. One argument supporting this view was that the stock of monetary gold was poorly distributed among participating countries.[11] Concern centred on the excessive gold holdings in the USA and France and the inadequate gold stocks in the UK. On the one hand, the USA and France came under criticism for allegedly failing to adjust by allowing credit to expand in line with their accrual of gold; on the other hand, the UK came under criticism for continuing to expand credit even in the face of stable or declining gold stocks.[12]

Another widely held view was that the adjustment mechanism in the postwar gold standard had become costlier because wages and prices had become more rigid, and hence the burden of adjustment would be more likely to fall on employment than on prices. This was sometimes combined with the view that in the postwar environment, with a deteriorating employment position and increased domestic political pressures, priorities by governments had shifted away from external towards domestic targets. Triffin[13] is one of the few to question the view that wages had become more rigid. He points to the fact that in the 50 years or so preceding the First World War there were very few instances of actual declines in money wages and these declines in any case were moderate, while, on the other hand, there were very sharp drops in wages in the 1920–22 recession and some (less severe) wage cuts in the first years of the Depression. As against this, however, it could be asserted that the employment situation was considerably less favourable in the postwar period, and hence that wages should have shown even greater flexibility. For example, in the UK the unemployment rate averaged 10.5 per cent in the interwar period as against 4.5 per cent in the prewar period. Moggridge[14] has also argued that 'The General Strike (1926) removed the possibility of widespread reductions in money wages and costs, if only because attempts at reductions were too expensive socially and economically'.

Third, the political and economic environment had become much more hostile towards the efficient functioning of the gold standard. The postwar years saw cycles less synchronised. Economic conditions, in general, deteriorated and the structure of external payments was radically transformed. There was, too, a possible intensification of hot money flows as capital markets may have become more united.[15] Reparations and war debts not only dramatically altered the current account positions of a number of individual countries (for instance, Germany as a donor and France as a recipient) but also contaminated the political environment, making co-operation more difficult.

Fourth, the gold exchange standard system in operation in the restored gold standard exposed the reserve currencies to risks of speculative attack. The Genoa Conference of 1922 had, in fact, recommended the increased holding of foreign exchange in reserves as a means of economising on gold, which was then thought to be in short supply. Whether in fact foreign exchange had increased in relative importance during the restored gold standard remains a matter for debate. Lindert[16] asserts that whereas in 1924/25 foreign exchange represented some 17 per cent of reserves, in 1913 the roughly comparable figure was some 16 per cent. But the figures for the prewar gold standard are those at the very end of the period, which are larger than those prevailing through most of the earlier period. Lindert also asserts that Britain's vulnerability (as measured by the ratio of her liquid liabilities to her reserves) may have been no worse on the eve of the 1931 crisis than it had been in, say, 1913. There are, however, several points that make this argument somewhat unconvincing. There is little doubt about Britain's basic payments weakness in the postwar years, and with the more volatile political and economic environment in those years her need for reserves was surely greater. Moreover, the sharp fluctuations in foreign exchange holdings in those years added to the vulnerability of the reserve currencies. For example, Yeager[17] reports that Germany's foreign exchange ratio fell from 63 per cent in December 1924 to 18 per cent in December 1928. France's conversions or threats of conversions posed a continuing danger to the system.

Fifth, another major development in the postwar environment, unfavourable to the gold standard, was the weakened position of London as the financial centre of the industrial world. New York and, to a lesser extent, Paris were now vying with London as a financial centre. This not only rendered the system less efficient (in so far as international clearing operations had now become more complex) but also exposed it to more 'hot money' flows between centres. Also the USA was ill-equipped to assume the dominant role that Britain had played in the management of the international financial system: reasons for this included parochialism, isolationism, immaturity, some hostility to US foreign investment, which was less dependable, and a central banking structure too decentralised and complex.

Finally, all the difficulties associated with the restored gold standard were further vastly accentuated by the onset of the Great Depression in 1930. Britain's earnings from overseas investments began to fall promptly. American lending abroad declined drastically; the Smoot–Hawley Tariff of 1930 in the USA added to the uncertainties of trade. The immediate reasons for the collapse of the gold standard and Britain's withdrawal were a succession of crises beginning with the announced weakness of the powerful Austrian Credit–Anstalt Bank in May 1931. This frightened foreign creditors and led to withdrawals from Austrian banks. These economic difficulties, as well as the (earlier) political tensions created by Austria's proposal for an economic union with Germany,[18] began to shake confidence across the Continent. In Germany, whose official financial standing was, in any case, weak (her short-term foreign liabilities being about twice her short-term assets), a run on German banks ensued, while her official reserves fell by about a third in June. Despite official help extended to both Austria and Germany, confidence did not return.

It was now Britain's turn to be in difficulties. Britain had been liberal in her advances to German banks and industry, and when the collapse occurred in Germany and the Berlin banks closed, her German assets were frozen. Britain's own financial weaknesses were now exposed and there was a run on sterling. Between July and September her reserve losses were huge and in September 1931 the Bank of England finally announced that it would no longer support the gold standard.

The years that followed were marked by rising protectionism and by a succession of competitive exchange rate adjustments. Britain's devaluation of 1931 put pressure on the USA which then in 1933 also left the gold standard and herself devalued. The US devaluation in turn put pressure on the French gold bloc which itself devalued in 1936. In that year, too, France withdrew from the gold standard. Interestingly, the end result of all these competitive devaluations was to more or less restore the 1930 relationships.

Notes for Chapter 1

1 General references are: J. E. Meade (1951), Chapter 14; L. B. Yeager (1976), especially Chapters 15–18; A. G. Ford (1962); D. E. Moggridge (1972); W. A. Brown (1940); R. G. Hawtrey (1931); M. Palyi (1972); S. Pollard (ed.) (1970); C. P. Kindleberger (1973).

2 R. Triffin (1964), p. 10.

3 A. Bloomfield (1963), pp. 31–5.

4 A. Bloomfield (1959), pp. 30–40. Bloomfield's finding (pp. 47–51), that for eleven countries, for the years 1880–1913, there was quite often a negative association between year-to-year changes in international assets and in domestic assets discounts, advances, securities), is frequently cited as evidence that the third rule was not consistently observed and, therefore, that the adjustment mechanism did not function well. Bloomfield's results are, in fact, open to two interpretations. They may be evidence that exogenous changes in domestic assets were being offset by changes in foreign assets or they may be evidence that changes in foreign assets were being sterilised. On the latter interpretation it is important to note that sterilisation, if it occurred, was only partial in the sense that the change in international assets was larger than the opposite change in domestic assets. This suggests that base money was allowed to change in response to changes in international assets, thus allowing some adjustment in the appropriate direction.

5 A. G. Ford (1962), Chapter 3; P. Lindert (1969), pp. 42–51; A. Bloomfield (1959), pp. 40–4.

6 A. G. Ford (1962), pp. 24–7.

7 W. Reddaway (1970).

8 See W. A. Brown (1940); T. Gregory (1925); H. F. Fraser (1933); A. Gayer (1935), Chapter 4; R. G. Hawtrey (1931); J. Viner (1951), p. 134; D. Moggridge (1972).

9 For a good discussion of this see: D. Moggridge (1972), Chapters 2 and 4; L. Yeager (1976), pp. 321–4.

10 D. Moggridge (1972), p. 105.

11 L. Robbins (1934), pp. 22–7; A. Gayer (1935), pp. 98–118; H. F. Fraser (1933), pp. 64–90.

12 For an evaluation of these arguments see L. Robbins (1934), pp. 22–7.

13 R. Triffin (1964), p. 4.

14 D. Moggridge (1972), p. 235. See also G. Haberler (1976), p. 6.

15 This is a recurrent theme in the literature. See L. Yeager (1976), p. 132; A. Gayer (1935), p. 22. See also: D. McCloskey and J. Zecher (1976); O. Morgenstern (1959), Tables 83 and 84.

16 P. Lindert (1969), p. 14.

17 L. Yeager (1976), p. 331.

18 France withdrew credit from Austria and Germany in response to the threatened economic union which France viewed as a violation of the post-war treaties.

Chapter 2

The IMF System

Background

Already by 1941 plans were being prepared in both the UK and the USA to set up a new postwar international monetary order. In the UK it was Keynes, as adviser to the Treasurer, who was assigned the task of formulating the outlines of a new monetary system, while in the USA it was Harry Dexter White, from the US Treasury, who was given responsibility in the area. In 1942 the original Keynes and White Plans surfaced, setting in motion a series of bilateral talks between the two countries based on these plans.

The British and American negotiations began with some common ground. Both sides were opposed to a system of freely fluctuating exchange rates, which they judged to have had adverse effects on the world economies in the years immediately after the First World War but also again in the 1930s.[1] At the same time, the unfavourable experience during the restored gold standard argued against absolutely fixed exchange rates. There was, in addition, a measure of concensus that unregulated and competitive restrictions on trade for balance of payments purposes (as practiced during the 1930s) were not in the best interest of the international community. By contrast, both countries also agreed, in principle, that countries should be relatively free to control certain capital transfers,[2] particularly those at the short end.

At the same time, there were differences in the attitudes of the two negotiating parties. The UK was very internationally minded and dedicated to the resolution of world divisions through international institutions and co-operation. The USA for its part was still somewhat isolationist and retained some suspicion about international organisations. (It had, in fact, refused to join the interwar League of Nations.) The USA was at the time anti-imperialist in its pronouncements, opposing the formation of economic blocks, preferential trade agreements and direct control over trade,[3] while emphasising multilateralism. The British, on the other hand, were anxious to retain Commonwealth economic and financial ties, arguing, too, that British relaxation of exchange controls and restrictions on trade would only be feasible if US aid and credit were very liberal.

Britain had, virtually, a 'fixation' about full employment and was determined to avoid repeating her experience during the restored gold standard when her overvalued currency had proved costly in terms of output and employment. Keynes insisted that there should be the 'least possible interference with internal national policies'[4] and that governments should be left relatively free to determine their desired levels of employment, while the exchange rate should be set so as to make possible those levels of employment. As Keynes put it, the external value of sterling should be altered 'to conform to whatever de facto internal value results from domestic policies which themselves shall be immune from criticism'.[5] So Keynes's emphasis was on the ability to change the exchange rate. The USA, on the other hand, (whose experience with the gold standard had not been nearly as unfortunate as Britain's) tended to emphasise the stability of exchange rates and wanted them changed only in circumstances that they visualised as occurring quite infrequently (for example, to meet a fundamental disequilibrium). Britain, too, felt that adjustment to correct balance of payments disequilibria was required by both surplus and deficit countries, while the USA took the view that the burden of adjustment should fall largely on the deficit countries.

If Britain was particularly concerned with the risks of unemployment attendant on an inappropriate exchange rate regime, the USA was somewhat more concerned with the possible risks of inflation which it felt attached to Britain's proposals. Again, if Britain was anxious to avoid political interference the USA appeared to have few reservations about this.[6]

Britain also wanted to retain some role for sterling as a reserve currency in the postwar years[7] while the USA did not envisage a major reserve currency role for the dollar. Britain, as a potential debtor, whose financial needs were expected to be enormous after the war, visualised an institution providing relatively generous credit to member countries while the USA, the potential creditor, had in mind a more modest scale of financing. Britain's approach to an international institution was somewhat radical while the USA was more conservative, emphasising sound 'banking principles' in the lending operations. Finally, Britain was quite firm on the need to allow countries to assert control over their capital movements, while the USA seemed anxious to define more explicitly the circumstances in which countries should be allowed this right[8] (for example, in the face of disequilibrating short-term capital as against the movement of productive capital which should not be restricted).

In the event, what finally emerged was (not surprisingly, given the dominance of the USA at the time) much closer to the US than to the Keynes Plan, although the USA did, at several points in the negotiations, make a number of concessions to British objections. The

Joint Statement by Experts on the Establishment of an International Monetary Fund, which was released in April 1944, embodied the basic principles and outlines for the setting up of the International Monetary Fund (IMF), which actually then became operative in 1946.

The IMF System – Principles and Regulations

The original Articles of Agreement of the IMF spell out the purposes of the IMF, the obligations and responsibilities of its members and the administrative duties as well as the organisational structure of the institution.[9]

Its purposes are admirably described in Article 1.

(i) To promote international monetary co-operation through a permanent institution which provides the machinery for consultation and collaboration on international monetary problems.
(ii) To facilitate the expansion and balanced growth of international trade, and to contribute thereby to the promotion and maintenance of high levels of employment and real income and to the development of the productive resources of all members as primary objectives of economic policy.
(iii) To promote exchange stability, to maintain orderly exchange arrangements among members, and to avoid competitive exchange depreciation.
(iv) To assist in the establishment of a multilateral system of payments in respect of current transactions between members and in the elimination of foreign exchange restrictions which hamper the growth of world trade.
(v) To give confidence to members by making the Fund's resources temporarily available to them under adequate safeguards, thus providing them with opportunity to correct maladjustments in their balance of payments without resorting to measures destructive of national or international prosperity.
(vi) In accordance with the above, to shorten the duration and lessen the degree of disequilibrium in the international balances of payments of members.

Each member country[10] is assigned a quota which is calculated largely on the basis of a formula that takes account of a country's national income, its trade and its international reserves. Twenty-five per cent of the quota is payable by a member country in gold or US dollars and the balance in its own (non-interest-bearing) currency. Article III Section 2 also provides for a quinquennial review of quotas and for their revision (with the approval of four-fifths of the voting power). Voting power on the Board of Governors and the Directorate (unlike the UN) is based on quotas – those with the largest quotas having the largest share of the votes. For example, at its inception some of the principal shares were: USA 27.93, UK 13.33, France 5.54 and India 4.28. Thus the USA and the UK – the two principal negotiators, as we have seen, of the IMF Agreement – together absorbed over 40 per cent of the total vote.[11]

The principal functions of the IMF fall conveniently into two categories: one relating to provisions on the adjustment mechanism, the other relating to provisions bearing on the supply of credit to member countries. Articles IV, VII, VIII and XIV carry the principal provisions bearing on the adjustment mechanism to correct balance of payments disequilibria.

Article IV requires each member country to establish a par value for its currency to be expressed in terms of gold as a common denominator or in terms of the US dollar of the weight and fineness in effect on 1 July 1974.[12] Maximum and minimum rates for exchange transactions between currencies of members are not to differ from parity by more than 1 per cent. At the same time, these par values may be changed but only to correct a fundamental disequilibrium in the balance of payments. (The term fundamental disequilibrium is not defined in the Articles.) If the proposed change will not move the exchange rate by more than 10 per cent from its initial parity the IMF may not object to the adjustment, but larger changes require the approval of the Fund. Section 4, however, makes it clear that in general these changes would be expected to be relatively infrequent and that a country has an obligation 'to promote exchange stability, to maintain orderly exchange arrangements with other members'. Article IV also allows the Fund to propose uniform percentage changes in par values of all member countries, thus revaluing gold in terms of all currencies.

The objectives of multilateral trade, currency convertibility and non-discrimination, to which the Americans attached so much importance, are embodied in some of the provisions of Article VIII, which bars member countries from imposing, without approval of the Fund, restrictions on the making of payments and transfers for current international transactions. At the same time, members were to avoid discriminatory currency practices and their currencies were to be freely convertible into one another at official rates.[13] In deference, however, to the abnormal conditions expected to prevail in the years immediately after the war, Article XIV does recognise a transition period of five years during which countries would be given the opportunity to gradually dismantle their controls over current transactions. Interestingly, the Articles do not prohibit resort to controls over capital movements;[14] indeed 'in the face of a large or sustained outflow of capital the Fund may request a member to exercise (such) controls'.[15]

One issue that divided Britain and the USA, as we have seen, had to do with the relative obligations of deficit and surplus countries in the adjustment process. Article VII (on scarce currencies) makes some concession to the principle of symmetry in adjustment by permitting various kinds of discrimination against payments to a country whose currency had been so much in demand that it would be declared 'scarce'. Thus the objective of multilateral free trade is compromised, in this case, but the intention of the provision is to put pressure on the surplus country to undertake some adjustment.

Since members are required to maintain their par value within a small margin they would need to intervene regularly in foreign exchange markets as their currencies approached the upper and lower limits as defined in Article IV. Intervention requires the ready availability of a stock of international reserves, comprising gold or foreign exchange with which to support an exchange rate. If a country in deficit needs to strengthen its reserve position, it may seek aid from the IMF, which may provide financial assistance under certain conditions, as defined in Article V.

A member obtains access to Fund resources by supplying its own currency in exchange for the currency of a member country whose reserve position is relatively strong. A member enjoys automatic access to borrowings up to 25 per cent of its quota (originally the gold tranche, now the reserve tranche). Beyond that a member has drawing rights equal to its quota. In other words, a member may borrow up to the point where the Fund is holding currency equal to 200 per cent of the member's quota. These additional drawing rights are referred to as credit tranches, which are divided into four equal parts, each representing again a quarter of its quota. The first credit tranche is made available relatively easily but borrowings beyond the first credit tranche are subject to increasingly restrictive conditions. These must 'support a program aimed at establishing or maintaining the enduring stability of the member's currency at a realistic rate of exchange'. For these borrowings the Fund negotiates a 'stabilisation program' with the member country aimed at ultimately correcting its deficit.[16] The Fund imposes an interest and service charge on its sales of foreign exchange; this charge increases with the member's scale of borrowing.

How do transactions with the IMF by member countries affect the total stock of international reserves? The IMF includes in reserves what it calls 'reserve positions in the Fund' which is defined as a country's quota less the Fund's holdings of that country's currency, disregarding a negative figure. To demonstrate how changes in reserve positions can come about we take a number of illustrations (and assume a borrowing of 100 units).

Case 1

A borrower draws on its gold tranche only and receives US dollars from the IMF. In this case, the borrower extinguishes its reserve position as defined above and receives an equivalent amount of 100 units of US dollars, so its net reserve position is unchanged. On the other hand, the USA, the supplier of the currency, enjoys an equivalent increase in its reserve position of 100 units (its quota having remained unchanged but the Fund's holding of its currency has now fallen by 100 units).[17] World reserves, therefore, increase by 100 units.

Case 2

A borrower draws on its first credit tranche and receives US dollars. In this case (since we disregard a negative reserve position) the borrower's reserve position has now increased by 100 units. At the same time, the USA's reserve position also increases by 100 units. Hence, in this case, world reserves increase by 200 units.

Case 3

A borrower draws on its gold tranche, this time receiving German marks. In this case, the borrower's reserve position is unchanged but, assuming Germany is required to convert the marks into US dollars for use by the borrower, Germany's net reserve position also remains unchanged, exchanging, in this case, an improved reserve position in the Fund for a reduction in its own stock of reserves. Hence, world reserves now remain unchanged by the transaction.

Case 4

A borrower draws on its first credit tranche and receives German marks. In this case, the borrower's reserve position will have improved by 100 units while Germany's reserve position will again be unchanged. World reserves will now have increased by 100 units.

It is clear, therefore, that transactions with the Fund may alter the stock of international reserves; by how much will depend on the currency that a member obtains and its own standing with the IMF.

What provision was made in the original Articles of Agreement for the long-term growth in the stock of world international reserves to accommodate the growth in world trade? We will return to this issue later when we evaluate the failings of the IMF, but, at this point, we may note that no explicit allowance was made for this. In general, it was thought (if at all) that IMF lending and an increased supply of gold would in combination probably meet the world's needs; there was, as well, one provision that could have been invoked to raise world liquidity and that was the section in Article IV allowing the IMF to recommend uniform changes in par values (that is, raise the price of gold).

Finally, mention needs to be made of the fact that in addition to overseeing the Articles of Agreement and supplying credit to member countries, the Fund also supplies technical assistance to some members, regularly consults with them and provides a forum for the discussion of monetary and exchange rate issues of common interest to members.

The Keynes Plan[18]

Reference was made earlier to a Keynes Plan, Britain's alternative to the White Plan, the latter ultimately providing the basis for the IMF Agreement. It is interesting, from this distance, to look again at the principal ways in which Keynes's plan differed from the IMF Agreement.

Keynes called his international institution a Clearing Union. Members would hold deposits (a new international currency which he called Bancor) with the Union. These deposits could only be used for transfers to the accounts of other central banks and could be obtained in exchange for gold, but gold could not be obtained in exchange for Bancor.[19] The price of Bancor would be fixed (although alterable) in terms of gold, while par values would be fixed (although again alterable) in terms of Bancor.

Each member of the Union would be assigned a quota that determined the limits of its drawings (overdraft) from the Union. The quota was to be determined by the sum of a country's exports and imports, on average, over the previous 3–5 years. Periodic revisions to the quotas would be made as foreign trade increased. A country suffering a deficit in excess of its credit balance could draw on its overdraft facility to make payment. There was to be a charge of 1 per cent per annum if the debit balance exceeded one quarter of its quota, and an additional 1 per cent on balances exceeding one half of the quota. Keynes limited the rights to accumulate a debit balance in any one year to one quarter of the quota. Creditors were also required to pay charges of 1 per cent if their credit balance exceeded one quarter of their quota, and an additional 1 per cent on balances over one half of the quota.

Keynes laid down detailed actions that would be required in the event that debit or credit balances exceeded one half of the quota. For deficit countries the Union would have powers to require members (1) to devalue, (2) to control outward capital transactions and (3) to surrender a suitable proportion of any separate gold or other liquid reserves in reduction of its debit balance. For surplus countries measures included (1) the expansion of domestic credit and demand, (2) appreciation, (3) the reduction in tariffs or other barriers against imports and (4) development loans.

An interesting and important feature of the scheme is that members could escape the charges by recycling funds to one another. In other words, debtors could borrow directly from creditors after consulting with the Union.

How different was this Keynes Plan in essentials from the IMF Agreement, as finally ratified? First, the Keynes Plan, while in some ways somewhat more radical, had the advantage of simplicity in its administration. The creation of a single international currency would have replaced the complicated schemes of transactions in multiple currencies. Second, the Keynes Plan was considerably more generous than the IMF scheme. The latter provided some $8–$9 billion, while Keynes had in mind some $26 billion. As Gardner has noted, had the USA negotiated on the basis of the Keynes Plan it might have accumulated a very large credit balance in the earlier postwar years which it could have used in later years to finance its own deficits; at the same time, it might have reduced the volume of aid it eventually provided by way of the Marshall Plan.[20] Third, Keynes clearly had in mind not only a more flexible exchange rate regime but also provided in some detail for the possible triggering of exchange rate changes for both deficit and surplus countries. In this respect, it is reminiscent of much more recent proposals for presumptive indicators to trigger exchange rate changes.[21] Fourth, Keynes was explicit about the need for symmetry in the treatment of deficit and surplus countries, providing a mechanism by which penalties for non-adjustment would fall on surplus as well as deficit countries. In the Articles of Agreement, only the scarce currency provision deals explicitly with this. Fifth, Keynes did play down the role of gold in his scheme; Bancor, not gold, was at the centre of his scheme and his numeraire was Bancor, not gold, although the price of Bancor itself was determined by gold. Sixth, his scheme to permit the recycling of funds among members was novel and interesting and indeed is reminiscent of some features of the Eurodollar market in today's world.

Seventh, neither scheme really provided for the secular growth of international reserves. Perhaps surprisingly in retrospect the question of providing for the future growth of reserves did not assume any importance in the minds of the negotiators at the time. In Keynes's scheme new international reserves are created by the exercise of a member's overdraft facilities. (We have already seen how reserves are created by parallel IMF credit transactions.) If Country A overdraws the volume of Bancors in the world increases. With quotas revised upwards as the volume of foreign trade increases it is likely that the stock of international reserves would increase over time; but the counterpart of the increase would be an increased volume of debit balances, which presumably would have a somewhat depressing influence on world trade. Thus the stock of owned reserves would not be increasing over time. This failing, so to speak, in the Keynes Plan is perhaps all the more surprising when one recalls the third of the so-called objects of his plan. To quote Keynes:

> We need a quantum of international currency which is neither determined in an unpredictable and irrelevant manner as, for example, by the technical progress of the gold industry not subject to large variations depending on the gold reserve policies of individual countries; but is governed by the actual current requirements of world commerce and is also capable of deliberate expansion and contraction to offset deflationary and inflationary tendencies in effective world demand.[22]

It is worth noting, in this connection, that his Union was entitled also to reduce the quotas of members if it was necessary to correct 'an excess of world purchasing power'.[23]

Notes for Chapter 2

1 R. Nurkse (1944), Chapter 9. Nurkse's unsympathetic conclusion about this experience was said to have been influential.
2 J. Gold (1977), pp. 7–9.
3 There is little doubt that given US strength in the postwar years it was in its own economic interest to remove barriers to its own penetration of markets.
4 J. K. Horsefield (1969), p. 19.
5 R. Gardner (1975), p. 207.
6 A. Acheson, J. Chant and M. Prachowny (1972), Introduction.
7 This, however, was not true of Keynes himself. See R. Gardner (1975), p. 208. Gardner notes that there were hints, which Britain did not take up, about the funding of sterling balances.
8 J. Gold (1977).
9 All changes in the Articles and changes in the responsibilities of the IMF will be noted in subsequent discussions of developments in the postwar years. This section is predominantly concerned with the original regulations.
10 The only non-members at present are the Communist bloc countries (with the exception of Yugoslavia) and Switzerland. Both Czechoslovakia and Poland were original members but Czechoslovakia was expelled in 1953 while Poland withdrew in 1950.
11 This has since been considerably reduced.
12 This provision was later amended to allow the par value to be expressed in terms of an intervention currency such as the US dollar or sterling. In practice, then, although official par values were in terms of gold these par values would be defended by buying and selling a particular nominated intervention currency. The USA itself maintained its par value by directly buying and selling gold.
13 See J. Gold (1971).
14 J. Gold (1977).
15 Article VI, Section 1(a) (Capital Transfers).
16 For a description of these stabilisation programs see J. K. Horsefield (1969), Vol. 2. See also: M. De Vries (1976), Chapter 18; T. A. Connors (1979). For a critical evaluation of the IMF stabilisation programs see C. Payer (1974).

17 This is referred to as its super-gold tranche.
18 For more details of the Keynes–White Plans see: J. K. Horsefield (1969), Vol. 1; A. E. Eckes (1975); J. Robertson (1943); J. Robinson (1943); J. Viner (1943).
19 Keynes visualised that monetary reserves would be made up largely of gold and Bancor. The exception was the holding of currencies within currency blocs (for example, the sterling bloc).
20 R. Gardner (1975), p. 209.
21 See the discussion in Chapter 10.
22 J. K. Horsefield (1969), Vol. 3, p. 20.
23 J. K. Horsefield (1969), Vol. 3, p. 25.

Chapter 3

The Postwar Experience – 1946 to 1967

US Dominance (1946–1959)

Europe and Japan emerged from the war badly incapacitated, with their international reserves very low, their industrial capacity and export potential crippled and their import needs enormous. The USA, on the other hand, was very strong both financially and economically. Her industrial capacity was relatively unaffected, she owned some 60 per cent of the gold reserves in the world and her allies were heavily indebted to her.

Impressed by the tremendous needs for reconstruction in Europe and, in the Cold War environment that rapidly developed, determined to resist the implantation of communism on European soil the USA embarked on a massive aid programme (the Marshall Aid). In the four years of the programme, from mid-1948 to mid-1952, the USA disbursed some \$11.6 billion in grants and another \$1.8 billion in loans to the countries in Europe. These huge handouts put the USA in a position from which it could exercise considerable leverage over those countries that it assisted; at the same time there is little doubt that the aid contributed greatly to the rehabilitation and reconstruction of Europe, as well as to the payments adjustment.

In the early postwar years, particularly from 1946 to 1949, the US balance of payments was very strong, notwithstanding extensive discrimination against her imports.[1] In those years the USA had a surplus in goods and services averaging some \$8 billion (see Table 3.1, Line 1) and, despite annual grants averaging over \$5 billion, these same years saw the US gold stock actually increase and foreigners run down their dollar reserves (see Table 3.1, Lines 8 and 9).

In September 1949, encouraged by the USA, sterling devalued by some 30 per cent against the US dollar. She was followed by some thirty other countries. This massive realignment in exchange rates, combined with the beginnings of European recovery and the Korean War, brought about a major change in the US balance of payments by

Table 3.1 US balance of payments – 1946 to 1958 (in billions of US dollars)

	1946	*1947*	*1948*	*1949*	*1950*	*1951*	*1952*	*1953*	*1954*	*1955*	*1956*	*1957*	*1958*
1 Balance – goods & services	+7.74	+11.53	+6.44	+6.15	+1.80	+3.72	+2.35	+0.44	+1.86	+2.06	+3.88	+5.81	+2.27
2 Net military expenditure	−0.49	− 0.45	−0.80	−0.62	−0.58	−1.27	−1.96	−2.34	−2.42	−2.62	−2.80	−2.79	−3.11
3 Private remittances & government pensions	−0.63	− 0.72	−0.62	−0.63	−0.52	−0.46	−0.55	−0.62	−0.62	−0.59	−0.67	−0.70	−0.72
4 Government grants & capital transactions (net)	−4.98	− 5.80	−4.92	−5.65	−3.64	−3.19	−2.38	−2.06	−1.55	−2.21	−2.36	−2.57	−2.59
5 Private capital transactions (net)	−0.76	− 1.08	−1.08	−0.43	−1.2	−0.88	−1.0	−0.16	−1.4	−0.9	−2.5	−2.8	−2.82
6 Errors & omissions	+0.20	+ 0.94	+1.2	+0.78	−0.03	+0.47	+0.51	+0.30	+0.17	+0.45	+0.64	+0.75	+0.38
7 Overall (1+3+4 balance +5+6)	+1.57	+ 4.9	+1.0	+0.21	−3.6	−0.34	−1.1	−2.1	−1.5	−1.1	−1.0	+0.5	−3.48
8 Changes in short-term and liquid liabilities to foreigners[a]	+0.96	+ 2.0	−0.52	+0.05	−1.9	−0.40	−1.5	−0.94	−1.2	−1.1	−1.3	−0.33	−1.20
9 Changes in monetary gold stock[b]	+0.62	+ 2.9	+1.5	+0.16	−1.7	+0.05	+0.40	−1.2	−0.30	−0.04	+0.31	+0.80	−2.28

Source: Adapted from S. Harris (ed.) (1961). Appendix.
[a] + = decrease.
[b] + = increase.

1950. In that year the surplus on goods and services dropped dramatically while the overall balance went into deficit by some $3.5 billion. This marked the beginnings of overall US deficits, which indeed were to persist into the 1970s.

The years 1950–58 saw a steady increase in US military expenditures abroad and (from 1956) a sharp increase in net foreign investment; at the same time, these years also saw a gradual winding down in Government grants. In 1958, largely as a result of a turn-around in the trade balance, the size of the overall deficit increased dramatically. This large deficit, of the order of $3.5 billion, was financed by a large increase in US liabilities to foreigners ($1.2 billion) as well as by a huge drain on her gold reserves ($2.3 billion).

The persistent overall deficits in those years (1950–58) were not, however, viewed with any alarm. On the contrary, the USA encouraged the European governments to use their surpluses to build up their reserves; the redistribution in reserves that took place between 1949 and 1958 (see Table 3.2) was generally considered to be highly

Table 3.2 World reserves and their distribution – 1949 and 1958 (in billions of US dollars)

	1949	*1958*
Gold	33.5	37.4
Reserve position IMF	1.7	2.6
Foreign exchange	10.4	17.2
TOTAL	45.6	57.3
OF WHICH		
USA	26.0 (56.5%)[a]	22.5 (39.2%)[a]
Rest of world	19.6 (43.5%)[a]	34.8 (60.8%)[a]

Source: International Monetary Fund, *International Financial Statistics.*
[a]Figures in brackets = share of world.

desirable. At the same time, these years marked the beginnings of the US dollar as a major reserve currency. From 1950 onward US deficits were mainly financed by the creation of liabilities against herself. Nearly all of the increase in the foreign exchange component of reserves between 1950 and 1958 of nearly $7 billion took the form of US dollars. This method of increasing world reserves emerged more or less by default (that is, in the absence of any other mechanism for reserve creation) and because of the basic strength of the US dollar.

Despite the continuing increase in her liquid liabilities the USA still had more than enough gold by the end of 1958 to meet any demand for convertibility. By then the ratio of her total liquid liabilities to her gold reserves had risen from nearly 0.3 in 1949 to over 0.8 in 1958 (see

Table 3.3 US gold reserves and external liabilities (in billions of US dollars)

Year	Gold Reserves (1)	External Liquid Liabilities (2)	Official Liabilities (3)	Ratio (2):(1) (4)	Ratio (3):(1) (5)
1949	24.56	6.94	3.36	0.28	0.14
1950	22.82	8.89	4.89	0.39	0.21
1951	22.87	8.85	4.16	0.39	0.18
1952	23.25	10.43	5.56	0.45	0.24
1953	22.09	11.36	6.47	0.51	0.29
1954	21.79	12.45	7.52	0.57	0.35
1955	21.75	13.52	8.26	0.62	0.38
1956	22.06	15.29	9.15	0.69	0.41
1957	22.86	15.83	9.14	0.69	0.40
1958	20.58	16.85	9.65	0.82	0.47

Source: International Monetary Fund, *International Financial Statistics.*

Table 3.3). Her real position, however, in 1958 was even stronger than suggested by this ratio. Although all liquid liabilities were potentially convertible into gold (since private dollar holdings could find their way into official hands) only official liabilities, which were much smaller (see Table 3.3, column 3), were legally convertible; moreover, a good portion of the dollar liabilities were immobilised in the sense that they were required as working balances by the monetary authorities and for trade by the private sector.

To sum up, then, it is probably fair to say that in those years the growth in world reserves, originating in the continuing US deficits, was largely demand induced, in the sense that it was needed to allow the rest of the world to build up their reserves and also to keep up with the rapid growth in trade in those years.

Beginning in 1950/51 continental Europe recovered rapidly. Several factors contributed to her performance: a sustained high level of demand as well as a steady growth of demand, high investment ratios, the absorption of disguised unemployment (which allowed labour productivity to grow), the reduction in trade barriers and the exploitation of the productivity gap between the USA and Europe. At the same time, her balance of payments strength provided conditions for self-perpetuating export-led growth. By contrast, the UK's growth performance in those years was poor, her growth was frequently interrupted by deflationary action to improve her external position and her investment ratio was lower than in the continental economies.

In those years, at least until 1956, borrowings from the IMF were very slight and the IMF's role was very largely passive. There were several reasons for this. First, and most important, the early postwar years were almost totally dominated by the USA. A recipient of US Marshall Aid, for example, was expected to desist from the use of Fund resources. Second, other institutions were created to assume functions that might otherwise have been the concern of the IMF. Notable among these institutions were the Organisation for European Economic Co-Operation (OEEC),[2] created in 1948, which became active in the field of general economic policy, and the European Payments Union (EPU), formed in 1950 to assist in multilateral payments clearing among European countries.

Third, the IMF was ill-equipped and her resources inadequate to deal with the early postwar world, whose problems had clearly been under-rated. As we have seen, too, the IMF had envisaged a transition period of some five years, to 1952, after which member countries' currencies would become convertible and trade would be on a multilateral basis. As it happened, except for a very brief flirtation with convertibility by the UK in 1947 (under pressure from the USA), convertibility by the developed countries had to wait until the end of 1958.

In 1956 the IMF began to come into its own. In that year, there was a big loan to the UK following the Suez crisis and this was followed by loans to France in 1957 and 1958 (when France devalued). At the same time, its prestige began to build up. Spurred by its increasing role, negotiations got under way in 1958 for an increase in Fund quotas. (A 50 per cent increase was implemented in 1959.)

The period under review (1946–59) can now be summarised in the following terms:

(1) There was a radical transformation in the US balance of payments from sizeable surpluses to sustained deficits. The period ended with a huge US deficit and some muted concern about the health of the US dollar. The US dollar began to assume (by accident) the dominant role as a reserve currency and as the supplier of the world's reserves.
(2) Europe, rapidly recovering its economic strength, took the first tentative steps to unification (the Treaty of Rome was signed in 1957) and began to provide some countervailing power to the USA.
(3) The IMF began to find its feet and assume an increasing role, just as the role of the USA was slowly diminishing.
(4) There were very few exchange rate adjustments by the currencies of the developed countries after 1949; the exceptions being France in 1957/8 and Canada's float beginning in 1950 (despite its illegality under the IMF Articles of Agreement).

The System under Stress (1959–1967)

The most important features of these years were the following.[3] First, by January 1959 the developed world had switched to convertibility of their currencies after a transition period which, in the event, was to last thirteen years. This was to have a major impact in the years that followed on the ease with which capital flowed across the frontiers. Second, the system was under more or less continuing and severe stress. The major crises were associated initially with the US dollar and the German mark in the years 1960/61 and later with sterling in the years 1964–67. These years also saw a succession of US measures directed at correcting the US deficits.

Third, the continuing difficulties with the dollar and sterling forced government and academic economists increasingly to recognise certain difficulties with the monetary system and to offer diagnoses of the problems. These years were also marked by a proliferation of plans for reform, some mild, some radical, originating from academic as well as official sources. Fourth, Europe's economic strength consolidated and we see the beginnings of challenge to US supremacy. Fifth, IMF resources were substantially increased by the General Arrangements to Borrow (GAB) which came into force in October 1962. Under the Agreement ten industrial countries undertook to lend to the Fund, on request, in their own currencies a total sum of $6 billion.[4]

The US deficit continued to be very high in both 1959 and 1960. While, however, in 1959 the deficit was financed largely by the creation of official liabilities to foreigners, with only a small reduction in the gold stock, in 1960 the bulk of the financing fell on gold stocks, which now dropped by a further $2 billion (see Table 3.4). The reasons for the continuing large deficit in 1960 were of particular interest. Nineteen sixty was a year that saw the USA drift into recession; this, combined with further liberalisation of imports from the USA as well as continuing very high activity in Europe, brought about a dramatic improvement in the trade balance. At the same time, however, to combat the recession, monetary policy became expansionary and with US interest rates now relatively less attractive the first fruits of convertibility manifested themselves in large outflows of capital from the USA, more or less undoing the improvements in the trade balance. By 1960, then, the acute dollar shortage of the earlier postwar years had been transformed into what was now beginning to look like a dollar glut.

Some anxiety over the US dollar was beginning to surface by 1959. The OEEC Report in 1959, the IMF Annual Report in 1960, and the Economic Report of the US President in 1960 all expressed some concern over the continuing US deficits.[5] Stirred by official concern over the dollar and amid some rumours of a possible dollar devaluation, speculative activity pushed the gold price in the London gold market to over $40 in October, a substantial premium over the official price of $35.[6] However, after some sales by the USA and some reassuring statements by Kennedy (the then Presidential Candidate), the London price fell back to some $36 by November. This experience led, in November 1961, to the formation of the Gold Pool, an agreement between the USA, the UK and six continental countries to provide sufficient gold to the private market to ensure that the price remained close to $35.[7]

The USA responded to the first dollar crisis in 1959/60 in a number of ways. First, the restrictive monetary and fiscal policies in 1959 and the caution in providing stimulus in 1960/61 were partly inspired by the state of the balance of payments. Second, after the 1960/61 recession, faced with both a deficit and considerable unemployment, the USA implemented a policy mix (Operation Twist) which involved keeping short-term interest rates relatively high to attract short-term capital from overseas but long-term rates relatively low to stimulate investment spending and relieve the unemployment.[8] In the same spirit, in 1961, President Kennedy proposed an investment tax credit again to stimulate investment spending without the need to lower domestic interest rates, which might be damaging to the balance of payments. (The investment tax credit was not enacted until late 1962.) Third, in late 1960 the Eisenhower Administration announced a number of (small) measures: these included reducing the number of dependents abroad of military personnel, reducing Defence Department procurement abroad and some tying of the US Aid to exports. These measures were later strengthened by the Kennedy Administration.

Meanwhile, in Germany, the combination of dollar weakness, balance of payments strength, convertibility and the relative restrictiveness of Germany's monetary policies, all conspired to produce the first postwar German crisis in 1960/61. Germany's problem was the exact opposite of the US problem. With the exception of 1959 (when there was an exceptionally large outflow of long-term capital) her basic balance (the sum of the current account and the long-term capital account) had recorded a continuing and significant surplus since 1951 and her reserves rose rapidly in the decade 1950–60 (see Table 3.5). At the same time, by mid-late 1960 she was faced with an overheated economy which she tried to counteract by implementing a restrictive monetary policy. As a result, the interest differential favouring Germany began to rise sharply by the second quarter of 1960.

The large inflows of capital that followed led the monetary authorities, by the middle of the year, to take a number of counter-

Table 3.4 US balance of payments summary 1959 to 1976 (in billions of US dollars)

(Credit +; Debit −)	*1959*	*1960*	*1961*	*1962*	*1963*	*1964*	*1965*	*1966*	*1967*	*1968*	*1969*	*1970*	*1971*	*1972*	*1973*	*1974*	*1975*	*1976*
1 Trade balance	0.91	4.89	5.57	4.52	5.22	6.80	4.95	3.82	3.80	.64	.61	2.16	− 2.72	− 6.99	.62	− 5.88	9.0	− 9.3
2 Current account balance	−2.14	1.80	3.07	2.46	3.20	5.79	4.29	1.94	1.54	− .96	−1.63	− .32	− 3.91	− 9.81	.67	− 4.03	11.9	− 1.4
3 Long-term capital	−2.0	−3.20	−3.11	−3.69	−5.04	−6.19	−6.19	−4.12	−5.36	−1.08	−2.27	−3.02	− 6.27	− 1.67	−2.52	− 6.55	−10.5	
4 Basic balance (2+3)	−4.1	−1.40	− .04	−1.23	−1.84	− .40	−1.91	−2.18	−3.81	−2.05	−3.90	−3.34	−10.18	−11.47	−1.85	−10.58	1.4	− 9.1[d]
5 Short-term balance + other balances	0.3 [a]	−2.00	−1.31	−1.42	−0.09	−1.13	0.62	2.40	.39	3.69	6.64	−6.50	−19.58	1.12	−3.45	2.51	− 3.9	
6 Official reserve transactions (4+5) (overall balance)	−3.8 [b]	−3.40	−1.35	−2.65	−1.93	−1.53	−1.29	.22	−3.42	1.64	2.74	−9.84	−29.75	−10.35	−5.30	− 8.07	− 2.5	−10.5
7 Financed by reserve assets (+ = drop)	+0.7	2.14	.61	1.53	.38	.17	1.22	.57	.05	− .88	−1.19	2.48	2.35	.03	.21	− 1.43	− 0.5	− 2.5
8 Reserve liabilities (+ = increase)	+3.1[c]	1.26	.74	1.12	1.55	1.36	.07	− .79	3.37	− .76	−1.55	7.36	27.41	10.32	5.10	9.50	3.0	13.0
US government military transactions (net)	−2.79	−2.75	−2.60	−2.45	−2.30	−2.13	−2.12	−2.94	−3.23	−3.14	−3.34	−3.38	− 2.91	− 3.60	−2.20	− 2.1	− 0.8	0.4
US government grants (excluding military)	−1.62	−1.66	−1.85	−1.92	−1.92	−1.89	−1.81	−1.91	−1.81	−1.71	−1.65	−1.73	− 2.04	− 2.17	−1.93	− 5.44	− 2.8	− 3.1

Source: US Department of Commerce, *Survey of Current Business.*

[a]Non-liquid short-term capital. Note Lines 5, 6, 7, 8 for 1959 are not strictly comparable with later years.

[b]Liquidity basis.

[c]Increase in official and private official liabilities.

[d]Total capital − long-term and short-term.

Table 3.5 Germany's balance of payments summary 1950 to 1967 (in billions of deutsche marks)

	1950	*1951*	*1952*	*1953*	*1954*	*1955*	*1956*	*1957*	*1958*	*1959*	*1960*	*1961*	*1962*	*1963*	*1964*	*1965*	*1966*	*1967*
1 Current account	−0.4	2.3	2.5	3.9	3.7	2.2	4.4	5.9	6.0	4.1	4.7	3.2	−1.5	0.9	0.5	−6.2	0.5	10.0
2 Long-term capital	0.5	−0.1	−0.4	−0.4	−0.4	−0.2	−0.4	−0.4	−1.4	−3.6	0.0	−4.1	−0.2	1.8	−0.9	1.1	−0.3	− 2.9
3 Short-term capital	0.1	−0.5	0.4	−0.3	0.3	−0.4	0.2	−2.3	−0.9	−2.8	1.4	−1.0	−0.4	−1.2	−0.4	1.0	−0.3	− 8.9
4 Errors/omissions	−0.8	0.3	0.4	0.5	−0.6	0.3	0.7	1.9	−0.2	0.5	2.0	1.0	1.3	1.1	+1.2	2.8	2.1	1.7
Overall balance (1+2+3+4)	−0.6	2.0	2.9	3.6	2.9	1.9	5.0	5.1	3.4	−1.7	8.0	−0.8	−0.9	2.7	0.4	−1.3	2.0	− 0.1

Source: Monthly Report of the Deutsche Bundesbank (June 1976).

acting measures.[9] These included raising reserve requirements against increases in foreign owned bank deposits and barring banks from paying interest on foreign owned demand and time deposits and, as well, from selling money market paper to non-residents. Nevertheless, the inflows persisted and during the second half there was, in fact, a premium on the forward mark in the open market, indicating some speculation in favour of the mark. Ultimately, the authorities decided that the attempt to maintain a restrictive stance, superimposed on a strong payments position, was becoming self-defeating so, from November 1960, the stance of monetary policy changed. External rather than domestic considerations were allowed to dominate interest rate policy: the discount rate was lowered and the rate of growth in the money supply was allowed to accelerate. It became possible to reassert the role of monetary policy only when the German authorities revalued the deutsche mark in March 1961.

With convertibility now established on the continent and with the rise in EEC tariff barriers, long-term outflows into Europe from the USA accelerated rapidly after 1962, offsetting improvements in the current account balance in the years 1963–65 (see Table 3.4). With the US deficit thus persisting, the USA introduced a succession of measures to restrict the outflows of capital. In July 1963 the Interest Equalisation Tax (IET), designed to discourage portfolio investment by US residents abroad, became effective. It imposed a tax on purchases of foreign securities by US residents to offset the higher yields abroad.[10] Then, in March 1965 the US authorities introduced a voluntary balance of payments programme, made up of the Voluntary Foreign Credit Restraint Programme (VFCR) and the Foreign Direct Investment Programme (FDI). The first imposed ceilings on loans to foreigners by US financial institutions while the second restricted the availability of funds from US non-financial corporations to their overseas affiliates. Also, the IET was extended to include long-term bank loans to foreigners (which had been a loophole under the original regulations).[11]

In 1963 and 1964 there were also sales of Roosa Bonds to foreign central banks; these were medium-term US government bonds denominated in foreign currencies and designed to 'freeze' some of the official dollar liabilities. In the same spirit, during the 1960s, the USA also appealed to allied countries to exercise restraint in converting official dollars into gold, an appeal that was largely heeded by most countries, except France. Table 3.6 shows the continued deterioration in the US external position in the years 1959–67. For example, whereas in 1959 her external liabilities were roughly equal to her gold reserves, by 1967 they were three times as large. Also, her official liabilities were about half as large as her gold reserves in 1959, but about one and a half times her gold reserves in 1967.

Table 3.6 US gold reserves and external liabilities (in billions of US dollars)

End of year	*Gold Reserves (1)*	*Total Reserves (2)*	*External Liquid Liabilities (3)*	*Official Liabilities (4)*	*Ratio (3):(1) (5)*	*Ratio (4):(1) (6)*
1959	19.51	21.51	19.43	10.12	1.0	0.5
1960	17.80	19.36	21.03	11.09	1.2	0.6
1961	16.95	18.75	22.94	11.83	1.4	0.7
1962	16.06	17.22	24.27	12.91	1.5	0.8
1963	15.60	16.84	26.39	14.43	1.7	0.9
1964	15.47	16.67	29.36	15.78	1.9	1.0
1965	14.07	15.45	29.57	15.82	2.1	1.1
1966	13.24	14.88	31.02	14.89	2.3	1.1
1967	12.07	14.83	35.67	18.19	3.0	1.5
1968	10.89	15.71	38.47	17.34	3.5	1.6
1969	11.86	16.96	45.91	15.99	3.9	1.4
1970	11.07	14.49	46.96	23.77	4.2	2.1
1971	11.08	13.19	67.81	50.64	6.1	4.6

Source: International Monetary Fund, *International Financial Statistics.*

Britain's external situation had been precarious for some time, but her position had almost certainly deteriorated by the mid-1960s, giving strong indications of a fundamental disequilibrium. Her large and increasing official commitments[12] (see Table 3.7), a declining competitive position, inadequate reserves[13] and official liabilities that far exceeded her reserves (see Table 3.8), and a sharp turn for the worse beginning in 1964[14] all combined to produce a particularly difficult situation when the Labour Party went into office in October 1964.[15] What followed was a succession of crises. These were met by some official borrowing, some IMF-inspired restrictive demand–management policies and various attempts at implementing an incomes policy.[16] The crises finally came to a head in November 1967 with the 14 per cent devaluation of sterling.[17]

During these years Japan was not a source of friction in the world economy. In the very early 1950s, Japan's overvalued currency was buttressed by extensive controls over imports. With her exchange rate fixed from 1950 onward, Japan's growing strength manifested itself in the gradual relaxation of these controls. Although her reserves steadily improved her reserve levels, in fact, remained relatively meagre into the mid-1960s. At the same time, her current account showed no clear trend until about 1965/66, when large surpluses began to surface. It was not, however, until about 1968/69 that evidence of a fundamental disequilibrium became manifest. Until then Japan's monetary policy had been largely geared to her current

Table 3.7 UK balance of payments summary 1955 to 1966 (in millions of sterling)

	1955	*1956*	*1957*	*1958*	*1959*	*1960*	*1961*	*1962*	*1963*	*1964*	*1965*	*1966*
1 Current account	−155	208	233	347	149	−258	5	127	116	−402	−110	−59
2 Long-term capital	−122	−187	−106	−196	−255	−192	68	−98	−155	−374	−232	−116
3 Basic balance	−277	21	127	151	−106	−450	73	29	−39	−776	−342	−175
4 Adjusted basic balance[a]	−141	57	51	−10	−136	−244	37	−204	−64	−551	−253	−393
5 Short-term capital – errors and omissions	121	42	80	64	−28	292	−34	60	−71	45	104	−1
6 Overall balance	−156	63	207	215	−134	−158	39	89	−110	−731	−238	−176
7 Government (net)	−138	−175	−144	−219	−227	−282	−332	−359	−381	−432	−446	−460

Source: R. Cooper (1968), p. 161.

[a] Adjusted for variations in unemployment – assumed steady unemployment rate of 1.6% of labour force.

Table 3.8 UK external liabilities and reserves 1960 to 1966 (in billions of US dollars)

Year	Reserves (1)	External Liabilities (2)	Official Liabilities (3)	Ratio (2):(1) (4)	Ratio (3):(1) (5)
1960	3.7	10.9	7.1	2.9	1.9
1961	3.3	9.9	7.1	3.0	2.2
1962	3.3	11.2	6.2	3.4	1.9
1963	3.1	11.9	6.5	3.8	2.1
1964	2.3	12.4	6.9	5.4	3.0
1965	3.0	12.7	7.1	4.2	2.4
1966	3.1	13.3	7.8	4.3	2.5

Source: International Monetary Fund, *International Financial Statistics* (1971 Supplement).

account positions, tightening when the current account deteriorated and relaxing as it improved. This policy turned out to be remarkably successful in correcting any emerging deficits in her current account.[18]

France's external position improved dramatically after the 1957/58 devaluations, allowing her to gradually relax some of her restrictions. Her current account surpluses were substantial, though diminishing, over the period while her reserves grew very rapidly. By contrast, Germany's strength and her fundamental disequilibrium were clearly in evidence in the late 1950s; it is, however, arguable whether she continued to be in fundamental disequilibrium between 1961 and 1967 (see Table 3.5).

Notes for Chapter 3

1 The so-called dollar shortage of those years has been extensively diagnosed. See L. Yeager (1976), Chapter 27 and the references cited therein.
2 Embracing countries in receipt of US Marshall Aid.
3 See M. De Vries (1976).
4 In addition, there were the mutual assistance arrangements as embodied in the Swap Agreements beginning in 1962 and the 'Basel Arrangement' in 1961. For a detailed description of these see P. Rushing (1972).
5 R. Solomon (1977), pp. 27–8.
6 Central banks had previously purchased some gold in the London market but they ceased to buy (and indeed were legally bound not to buy) when the price exceeded the official price.
7 The formal arrangement was that the US contribution to any net gold sale was to be 50 per cent. Technically, however, any loss of gold outside the USA could always be offset by official conversions of dollars into gold, so the USA could be made to bear the brunt, if not the whole, of the gold losses.
8 For an estimate of the success of Operation Twist and its effects on capital flows (which were probably relatively minor), see D. Rowan (1974).

9 See V. E. Argy and Z. Hodjera (1973), pp. 69–70.

10 Direct investments, investment in developing countries and in Canadian obligations and bank loans by foreign branches of US banks to foreign residents were all exempt from the tax.

11 For details of these measures and an evaluation of their effectiveness see: J. Hewson and E. Sakakibara (1975).

12 See W. Manser (1971).

13 The ratio of her reserves to her imports averaged about 0.17 in 1964–66 compared to an average for all industrial countries in those years of 0.45.

14 This was brought on largely by the Conservative 'push for growth' in that year (to avoid the stop–go policies of the past). Some commentators have argued that the pace of expansion then produced a permanent increase in imports. See F. Brechling and J. Wolfe (1965); R. Bacon and W. Eltis (1978).

15 Thirwall also contends that the income elasticity of UK's exports is about 1 while its own income elasticity for imports is of the order of 2.6, presenting Britain with a serious long-run balance of payments constraint. See A. Thirwall (1978).

16 See Chapter 31 for details of the incomes policies.

17 For details of the crises see S. Brittan (1971).

18 OECD (1972); R. Komiya and Y. Suzuki (1977).

Chapter 4

Reform Proposals – Mark I: The Early 1960s

Introduction

Outside official circles, beginning in 1959, proposals for reform came to be directed at correcting three alleged weaknesses in the international monetary system. The first was a weakness in the adjustment mechanism to deal with payments disequilibria. The second was a weakness in the arrangements for the provision of a continuing and dependable growth in world international reserves. The third was a weakness inherent in a reserve currency system (the gold exchange standard), which exposed the reserve currency to lapses of confidence, leading to demands for conversion into gold.

These three weaknesses, adjustment, liquidity and confidence, were not, of course, unrelated. It was recognised, for example, that the quicker and more effective the adjustment mechanism the less would be the need for liquidity to accommodate potential disequilibria. At the same time, the reverse also held in that the larger (smaller) the volume of international reserves the slower (quicker) would tend to be adjustment. In the debate of the early 1960s there was a clear division between those who emphasised the adjustment problem and those who emphasised the liquidity problem. Triffin also drew attention to the important connection between liquidity and confidence.[1] In the longer run, a reserve currency can continue to provide for the secular growth in reserves, through sustained deficits, only at the cost of a rise in the ratio of its official liabilities to its gold supplies (see Tables 3.3 and 3.6). A point would then clearly be reached when confidence in the viability of the reserve currency would be shaken. This would provoke shifts from the reserve currency into gold. These shifts would maintain intact the rest of the world's reserves but would lower the reserves of the reserve currency country, forcing the reserve country to take measures to correct its position, measures that could be harmful to world trade, employment and confidence in the international monetary system.[2] If, on the other hand, confidence in the reserve currency was restored by the elimination of the deficits, world reserves would cease to rise and this would have the effect of braking world trade and growth. Ultimately, therefore, the system, as it operated, was doomed since either the reserve currency (the dollar) continued to provide the needed reserves, in which case the system was exposed to increasing crises of confidence, or it ceased to be the source of reserves, in which case the system would be imperilled by a shortage of reserves.

An improvement in the adjustment mechanism, which, say, corrected the US deficit, would also directly affect both world liquidity and confidence in the reserve currency. At the same time, the creation of new sources of world liquidity would not only have some bearing on adjustment but would also tend to reinforce the position of the dollar.

Adjustment

Of the proposals for the improvement in the adjustment mechanism the two most radical were at once at opposite poles and also the most thoroughgoing and comprehensive, in the sense that they claimed to solve all problems simultaneously. At one extreme was the proposal for the introduction of flexible exchange rates.[3] If exchange rates were determined entirely by market forces and there was no intervention by the monetary authorities then the proposal would, at the same time, solve all three problems. Adjustment would always be complete, reserves would be unnecessary (hence a liquidity problem could not arise) and, finally, the reserve currency would no longer become vulnerable since its backing in gold could not deteriorate over time.

At the other extreme was the proposal to return to a semi-automatic gold standard.[4] Briefly the proposal was to (1) raise the price of gold sufficiently to allow the removal (redemption) of all reserve currencies from the system (leaving only gold as a reserve asset), at the same time ensuring that world reserves were adequate to meet the needs of trade; (2) fix exchange rates virtually once and for all; (3) arrive at an international agreement by which countries would allow their money supply to respond to deficits or surpluses in their balance of payments, thus providing explicitly for a corrective mechanism (which, in the historical gold standard, had been only implicit). The restored gold standard would again solve all three problems: the adjustment mechanism would become effective through the rule that linked the volume of money to disequilibria; the liquidity problem would also be solved, initially by ensuring that liquidity was adequate by raising the price of gold and, in the longer run, by an in-built self-correcting mechanism which linked incentives to produce gold with world prices (for example, with world prices rising (falling) the real price of gold would fall (rise) thus discouraging (stimulating) the production of gold); finally, the vulnerability of the gold exchange regime would vanish with the removal of all reserve currencies from the system.

There were also several proposals for an improvement in the exchange rate mechanism of adjustment. One proposal was for exchange rates to be allowed to fluctuate within a wider 'band' (for example, 2 per cent or 5 per cent on each side of parity) than the range (of 1 per cent) permitted under IMF rules.[5] Another proposal was to replace large 'discrete' changes in parity (with their associated sharp speculative bursts) by very small and frequent changes in parity (the crawling peg or gliding parity).[6] Another proposal combined these two into a 'crawling band', permitting not only greater short-run flexibility within a wider band but also more frequent and smaller changes in parity in the longer run. Still another proposal was to establish currency blocs (geographical regions linked closely by trade and culture) with exchange rates fixed within the bloc but flexible between blocs.[7]

Liquidity

Most of the huge reform literature focused not on the improvement in the adjustment mechanism but rather on the issue of liquidity. It was widely recognised, in the years following Triffin's statement of the problem, that, whether or not there was a liquidity shortage in the early 1960s, the US dollar could not continue indefinitely to supply world reserves; hence the need, at the least, for a contingency plan to create another source of liquidity. Proposals here ranged from relatively minor changes in existing institutional arrangements to complex and radical changes in the monetary system.[8] First, there were the suggestions to strengthen existing sources of liquidity and credit. Second, there was the proposal for an increase in the price of gold. Third, there was the proposal to multiply the numbers of reserve currencies or to consolidate a number of key currencies into a composite reserve unit. Fourth, there was the proposal to set up a world central bank, whose liabilities (deposits) would serve as a new international currency.

At the most conservative level there were proposals to extend the volume of unconditional borrowing from the IMF beyond the gold tranche (for example, to the other 75 per cent of the quota), to increase Fund quotas annually or to reinforce the loan arrangements among the industrial countries.

Another proposal was to implement one of the provisions in the Articles of Agreement which permits, under certain conditions, a rise in the price of gold vis-à-vis all currencies. The proposal (to double or triple the price of gold) came, as we saw, from the proponents of a return to a semi-automatic gold standard; it also found support among economists who saw it simply as a device for raising liquidity and for restoring confidence in the reserve currencies, but who, in fact, were opposed to the restoration of the gold standard.[9] The advantages of the proposal were its extreme simplicity in implementation (in effect by the stroke of a pen) and its ability, at the same time, to secure any needed increase in world liquidity and to improve the liquidity position of the US dollar by lowering the ratio of her liabilities to her gold reserves. The proponents also argued that with the increase in the price some gold would flow out of private hoards and production of gold would be stimulated, thus increasing the stocks of physical gold in the hands of the monetary authorities.

The proposal, however, was opposed on several grounds. There was the argument that, having raised the price of gold this time the expectation would be created that it would happen again, thus inviting a fresh burst of instability some time in the future. Many felt, too, that as a device to raise liquidity it would, in any case, need to be used again if reserves were to grow at the appropriate rate. Infrequent (but large) jumps in the price of gold might then be inflationary or, at least, highly disruptive. There was also some concern about the fact that the US would be reneging on its promises and assurances that the price of gold would be maintained. Much was made of the argument, too, that the distribution of the benefits would be most uneven as well as politically unacceptable. The beneficiaries would be the official gold hoarders (for example, France),[10] the producers of gold (South Africa and Russia) and the private gold speculators. At the same time, the smallest benefits would accrue to the less developed countries whose share of gold in their reserves was relatively low.[11]

A more interesting variation was the proposal to raise the price of gold gradually by, say, 2 per cent a year.[12] The rise in the price of gold would thus be known with certainty, while the return on gold would be held below the prevailing interest rate in money markets. This variation meets many of the objections mentioned above to the rise in the price of gold.

A third set of proposals centred on an extension of the reserve currency system (rather than its abolition). The underlying idea here was to encourage central banks to hold, and count as part of their reserves, the currencies of some developed countries, other than the USA and the UK.[13] In turn, these countries, whose currencies would serve as reserves, would have to offer acceptable financial instruments and would have to accept, in principle, an asymmetry between their new official liabilities and their reserves, largely discounting the former in the calculation of their own reserve positions. To illustrate how the scheme can create new reserves, consider the case where two continental economies, say, Germany and France, were in deficit while the USA was in surplus. Instead of Germany and France now financing their deficits by reducing their dollar reserves (thus reducing the stock of world reserves) they would create official mark and franc liabilities against themselves, without depleting their reserves, while the USA would now hold these currencies in her portfolio of official reserves, in this way raising world reserves. An even simpler way of visualising the addition to world reserves is to suppose that some holders of dollar reserves sell these to a number of European countries in exchange for these countries' currencies. Then European reserves would rise while the rest of the world's reserves would be unchanged.

The multiple currency proposal would have had three advantages. First, it would have contributed to world reserves. Second, in so far as it took the strain off the US dollar, permitting the US balance of payments to go into equilibrium or into surplus, confidence in the US dollar would have been restored. Third, it would also have met the criticism that the USA had been advantaged by having a reserve currency.[14]

The scheme had, however, a number of problems. First, it was advantageous to the richer industrial countries, who would now share the privileges of reserve currency status. Second, multiplying the numbers of reserve currencies might not secure stability in the system but might, in fact, destabilise it further by increasing the menu of choice, thus encouraging disruptive shifts between key currencies.[15] Third, it is not easy to see how the scheme would have provided for a steady, controlled growth of reserves over time. Fourth, adjustments would have been needed in the location as well as the financing of deficits. Presumably, too, ultimately all key currencies would have reached their 'limits', when they would have become vulnerable.

A better conceived variation of the multiple reserve currency scheme was the composite reserve unit (CRU).[16] Each country in a group (for example, the Group of Ten plus Switzerland) would deposit agreed amounts of its currency into a pool with the IMF. The quotas or contributions would be based on the country's gold holdings in relation to the group's total holdings of gold or on the country's importance in trade or its reserve levels. The currencies would be collected in the specified proportions, 'composite reserve units' (each, say, equal in value to $1), and would then be created and credited to the participating countries in proportion to (or somewhat less than) their contributions. The CRUs would earn interest and (in one variation at least) would be held in a fixed proportion to gold. Each of the currencies making up the reserve unit would also carry a gold guarantee.

The CRU proposal had some advantages over the looser multiple-currency reserve proposals. It avoided the clumsiness of direct holdings of key currencies and hence was administratively simpler. It probably also had less potential for instability. It allowed better (although far from complete) control over the growth of reserves. Its 'elitism' might also be attenuated by the retention of some portion of the contributions for use, say, by the LDCs.

The most radical proposals centred around the creation of a world central bank, a variation of Keynes's Clearing Union. The best known of these schemes was that proposed by Triffin.[17] A new international currency (which he also called Bancor) would be created in the form of deposits with an X.IMF (expanded IMF). Initially, at least 20 per cent of total reserves would have to be held as Bancor deposits, which would be used for international settlements. Some gold and foreign exchange would be turned into the X.IMF in exchange for Bancor whose value would be fixed in terms of gold. Currencies would also be fixed (but not unalterably) in terms of Bancor. Ultimately, the aim was to remove from circulation all reserve currencies, which would be replaced by Bancors.

Keynes (as we saw) had made no provision for the long-term growth of reserves. By contrast, an important element in Triffin's scheme was to ensure that Bancor deposits grew at 3 per cent to 5 per cent a year to accommodate the needs of trade. This was to be achieved by means of loans and investments by the X.IMF. For example, some securities issued by Development Banks could be purchased; some investments would also be made in the major financial markets;[18] some long-term loans would be made to member countries.

Confidence

As already indicated, many of the proposals to ensure better adjustment or more liquidity had a very direct bearing on the problem of 'confidence'. There were, however, also suggestions for directly attacking the problem of confidence in the US dollar as a reserve currency. These included the offering of a gold guarantee on official US liabilities, which would have removed the incentives to switch into gold, the complete abandonment of convertibility of the US dollar, which would have effectively placed the world on a pure dollar standard, and the funding of official liabilities into longer-term debt.

Official Negotiations and the Decision to Create SDRs

Thus far we have focused on academic discussions of weaknesses in the monetary system and proposals for reform. Although, as indicated, there were official expressions of concern from 1959 onward, it was not until 1963 that official multilateral negotiations actually got under way and continued for several years. At the IMF Annual Meeting of that year the Group of Ten announced that they would 'undertake a thorough examination of the outlook for the functioning of the international monetary system and of its probable future needs for liquidity'. Beginning in 1963/64, too, the IMF carried out intensive studies of alternative approaches to liquidity creation, of the adequacy of world reserves and of reserve needs for the future. The explicit assumption underlying the work of the Group of Ten as well as of the IMF was that fixed exchange rates would continue to be the basis of the international monetary system; thus at the official level there was, in those years, no serious attention given to exchange rate reforms.

National positions surfaced soon after negotiations started. The French began by supporting their own variant of a CRU but by 1965 had effectively abandoned that position and were advocating a return to a gold standard. The USA, on the other hand, began by taking a conservative stance, endorsing only extensions to existing institutional arrangements (for example, more liberal drawing rights within the Fund); but by July 1965 the US position had changed with the announcement that it now 'stands prepared to attend and participate in an international monetary conference that would consider what steps we might jointly take to serve substantial improvements in international monetary arrangements'.[19] Not long after, the USA came to support a dual scheme: a CRU with restricted participation and a more universal arrangement that involved an expansion in automatic drawing rights in the IMF, open to all members.[20] Many European countries (including Germany, Italy, the Netherlands and Belgium) were supporting, by 1966, some variant of the CRU proposal. The IMF put up two proposals for reserve creation, both involving universal rather than restricted participation. One was to extend automatic rights within the Fund. In the other, more radical, proposal 'members would acquire claims (reserves) on the International Reserve Fund (IRF) (an affiliate of the IMF) expressed in IRF units of gold weight and the IRF would acquire corresponding claims on the member. The exchange of claims between the IRF and participants would be in amounts broadly proportionate to IMF quotas'.[21]

This phase of the negotiations effectively came to a head in 1967 when the decision to create a new reserve asset, the Special Drawing Right (SDR), was finally approved. The SDR, which will be described in some detail in the next chapter, evolved from the many schemes proposed in the previous years and represented a compromise of various positions. First, the SDR was to be a universal scheme open to all members. Thus, the IMF view, that schemes ought to be universal rather than restrictive (as with the European CRU proposal), came, in due course, to prevail. Second, the SDR evolved directly from the CRU proposals and the proposals to extend automatism. An interesting feature of the SDR, as distinct from the CRU proposal, was that it was to have no backing. It was, in effect, to be an accounting creation in the books of the IMF without any backing. In this respect, it was radical compared to its rival schemes. Third, the SDR emerged as something of a compromise between the views of the French, who insisted that it should be a credit scheme, and the views of the Americans and others, who wanted to create additional owned reserves. Fourth, the SDR represented, at this point, a contingency plan to be activated only as the need should arise; indeed, as we will see, some evidence was beginning to surface that suggested that world reserves were becoming inadequate after 1964. Fifth, the SDR scheme was an ad-hoc, patchwork scheme in the sense that, although it created a new reserve asset, it did not represent a comprehensive reform intended to correct all the ills that were besetting the international monetary system; it did not provide complete control over the growth of reserves; nor did it address itself to adjustment problems; nor, again, did it directly attack the problem of confidence.

Notes for Chapter 4

1 R. Triffin (1960).
2 Evidence of this instability is to be found in: H. Hagemann (1969). Hagemann found that a decline in the ratio of US gold to external liabilities induced conversions of dollars into gold.
3 Notable exponents here were: M. Friedman (1953); E. Sohmen (1961); J. Meade (1955).
4 The most articulate academic exponent of this was M. Heilperin (1963). See also F. Machlup and B. Malkiel (1964). The French of course were also supporters of this at the official level. See J. Rueff (1961).
5 G. Halm (1965).
6 J. Williamson (1965); G. Halm (1969).
7 R. Mundell (1961).
8 The most thorough review of the proposals appeared in: F. Machlup (1966), Part 4. See also H. Grubel (1963).
9 For example, R. Harrod (1965).
10 In 1958 gold represented some 70 per cent of France's reserves. In 1966 it was over 90 per cent.
11 Some of these arguments were countered in the following way. It was said that gold mining was a progressive industry in South Africa and that the gains would pass on to its labour force (of whom a large part was black). It was also argued that it would have been easy to arrange for some of the benefits accruing to the developed countries to be redistributed to the LDCs.
12 P. Wonnacott (1963).
13 Leading advocates here were F. Lutz (1963) and X. Zolotas (1961).
14 See Chapter 9 for a discussion of this issue.

15 See J. Williamson (1963).
16 Leading advocates of this scheme were: E. Bernstein (1963); R. Roosa (1965).
17 See R. Triffin (1959).
18 This also meant that those countries would be acquiring the Bancor deposits. Problems of 'equity' and 'need' immediately presented themselves.
19 Statement by the Secretary of the Treasury, Fowler.
20 S. Cohen (1970), pp. 89–90.
21 See S. Cohen (1970), pp. 110–11. See also M. De Vries (1976), Chapter 3, for details of positions and the IMF proposals.

Chapter 5

Special Drawing Rights (SDRs)

The previous chapter provided the historical background to the decision to create a new reserve asset called SDR. This chapter looks at the principal characteristics of the SDR (as originally conceived) and the thinking and analysis underlying its activation in 1970.

Characteristics[1]

The SDR is essentially an accounting creation that has no currency or gold backing. Its value was, initially, fixed at 1/35th of an ounce of gold, equal, at the time, to one US dollar. A decision to create SDRs is normally made for a basic period extending to five years (but the duration of the basic period may be altered by the IMF). Member countries may, if they choose, opt out of the scheme, so in that sense participation is voluntary, but if more than 15 per cent (measured in terms of quotas) do so, the allocation cannot take place. After a decision is taken to create SDRs in a given amount the SDRs are distributed to participants in proportion to their quotas in the IMF. The SDRs acquired in this way represent 'owned' reserve assets; but, at the same time, there are complicated rules governing their use and acceptance.

The Articles describe the circumstances in which participants would be permitted to use SDRs. A participant would be expected to 'use SDRs only to meet balance of payments needs or in the light of developments in its official holdings of gold, foreign exchange and SDRs and its reserve position in the IMF and not for the sole purpose of changing the composition of the foregoing as between SDRs and the total of gold, foreign exchange and reserve position in the Fund'. Reconstitution rules also impose some constraints on the use of SDRs. 'A participant shall so use and reconstitute its holdings of Special Drawing Rights that, five years after the first allocation and at the end of each calendar quarter thereafter, the average of its total daily holdings of Special Drawing Rights over the most recent five-year period will not be less than thirty per cent of its daily net cumulative allocation of Special Drawing Rights over the same period.'

When a participant decides to use SDRs the IMF must then designate another participant who will accept these SDRs and provide, in return, foreign exchange.[2] The Articles prescribe the conditions under which countries might be designated. 'A participant shall be subject to designation if its balance of payments and gross reserve position is sufficiently strong, but this will not preclude the possibility that a participant with a strong reserve position will be designated even though it has a moderate balance of payments deficit. Participants shall be designated in such manner as will promote over time a balanced distribution of holdings of Special Drawing Rights among them.' Just as there are limits placed on the use of SDRs, so, in this case, a participant cannot be required to hold more SDRs than three times its net cumulative allocation.

Interest, which was initially determined at 1½ per cent, is paid on the amount of holdings of SDRs. Charges, at the same rate, are paid on the amount of net cumulative allocation of SDRs. A participant who has used some of its SDR allocation continues to pay charges on its original allocation but receives interest on its (depleted) holdings. A participant designated to holds SDRs in excess of its original allocation receives interest on its holdings of SDRs but pays charges only on its original allocation.

There are several differences between creating reserves by supplying additional amounts of a reserve currency, such as the US dollar, and creating reserves by distributing a new reserve asset such as SDRs. First, seignorage in the case of SDRs accrues to participants in the scheme while seignorage in the case of a reserve currency accrues to the issuer of the reserve currency (see Chapter 9). Second, the acquisition of SDRs has no initial impact on the money supply; it accrues to the monetary or government authorities and appears as a balance sheet adjustment. On the other hand, the official acquisition of a reserve currency in the foreign exchange market normally involves the creation of domestic base money (which may or may not, of course, be sterilised by the monetary authorities). Third, reserve creation through a reserve currency is 'earned' in the sense that it requires an 'overall' surplus in the balance of payments. At the same time, assuming the reserve currency is convertible, the reserve creator's liquidity position deteriorates. On the other hand, SDRs are not earned and their acquisition does not create a liability against another member. Hence there is greater 'reserve ease' from SDRs than from an equivalent creation of reserve currency. In this respect, of course, SDRs are similar to liquidity creation through an increase in the volume of gold.

Fourth, a legally convertible reserve currency, such as the US dollar until 1971, has a backing in gold, while SDRs have no legal backing in the sense that they are 'covered' by counterpart member currencies. Fifth, owned reserve currency can be freely used while owned SDRs are subject to a number of regulations governing their use and acquisition (as indicated above). Sixth, reserve creation by a reserve currency is the result of a deficit in the reserve centre, which, in turn, depends on monetary and real conditions in the reserve centre vis-à-vis the rest of the world. On the other hand, reserve creation by SDRs is determined by an international decision-making body and its growth is controlled.

Activation

Article XXIV Section 1 (b) lays down those considerations that must be taken into account before SDRs can be activated. First, there must be a 'collective judgement that there is a global need to supplement reserves'. Second, there must be evidence of the 'attainment of a better balance of payments equilibrium'. Third, there must be evidence of a 'likelihood of a better working of the adjustment process in the future'.

The Fund adopted an eclectic approach to the question of global reserve adequacy.[3] First, it looked at the recent trends in a number of summary measures of global reserve adequacy. These were essentially three: the rate of growth of world reserves, the ratio of reserves to imports or its variation, the ratio of the change in reserves to imports, and the ratio of reserves to aggregate imbalances. Second, it looked for manifestations of a global reserve shortage.

Table 5.1 shows reserve growth in the period 1952–77. Whereas reserve growth had averaged some 3.8 per cent a year in the years 1962–65, growth slowed to some 2.7 per cent in the years 1966–69. There was a marked slowing down in the growth rate in late 1968 and 1969 (associated with the improvement in the US balance of payments).

Table 5.2 shows the trend in the ratio of reserves to the trend value of imports. Including the USA, there is a continuing sharp fall in the ratio in the years 1954–68, but, if the USA is excluded, the fall is substantially less pronounced. It was not clear, however, whether this necessarily indicated an increasing shortage of reserves. First, imports may be a poor indicator of the 'need' for reserves, which are more likely to be geared to 'imbalances' than to the level of imports. Second, to the extent that there are economies of scale in the holding of reserves the decline in the ratio may simply reflect these economies. Third, global reserves may well have been excessive in the earlier years so the decline in the ratio may simply reflect the adjustment process at work.[4]

Table 5.1 International reserves 1952 to 1977 (in billions of SDRs)

End of Year (1)	*Gold* (2)	*SDRs* (3)	*Reserve Positions in Fund* (4)	*Foreign Exchange* (5)	*Total Reserves* (6)	*Percentage Change in Total Reserves* (7)
1952	33.5		1.8	14.0	49.3	–
1953	33.9		1.9	15.4	51.2	3.8
1954	34.6		1.8	16.5	52.9	3.3
1955	35.0		1.9	16.8	53.7	1.5
1956	35.7		2.3	17.8	55.8	3.9
1957	36.9		2.3	17.1	56.3	0.9
1958	37.6		2.6	17.1	57.3	1.8
1959	37.6		3.3	16.1	57.0	– 0.5
1960	37.7		3.6	18.5	59.8	4.9
1961	38.5		4.2	19.2	61.9	3.5
1962	38.9		3.8	19.9	62.6	1.1
1963	39.9		3.9	22.7	66.5	6.2
1964	40.5		4.2	24.2	68.9	3.6
1965	41.5		5.4	24.0	70.9	2.9
1966	40.7		6.3	25.7	72.7	2.5
1967	39.4		5.7	29.3	74.4	2.3
1968	38.7		6.5	32.5	77.8	4.6
1969	38.9		6.7	33.0	78.7	1.2
1970	37.0	3.1	7.7	45.4	93.2	18.4
1971	35.9	5.9	6.4	75.1	123.2	32.2
1972	35.6	8.7	6.3	96.2	146.8	19.2
1973	35.6	8.8	6.2	101.7	152.2	3.7
1974	35.6	8.9	8.8	126.7	180.1	18.3
1975	35.5	8.8	12.6	137.4	194.3	7.9
1976	35.4	8.7	17.7	160.3	222.1	14.3
1977	35.5	8.1	18.1	200.7	262.4	18.1

Source: International Monetary Fund, *International Financial Statistics.*

Table 5.2 Ratio of reserves to trend values of imports (selected years)

	1954	*1958*	*1961*	*1964*	*1968*
All countries (60)	0.73	0.59	0.51	0.45	0.35
All countries excluding USA	0.48	0.40	0.41	0.40	0.34

Source: International Monetary Fund (1970a), p. 473.

Similar trends were in evidence for the ratio of reserves to payments imbalances (the sum of surpluses and deficits without regard to signs). For example, over the period 1954–68 reserves had grown at an annual rate of 2.2 per cent while global payments imbalances had grown at an annual rate of 4.2 per cent.

The second approach to judging reserve adequacy focuses on the overt manifestations of a reserve shortage. Consider, for example, the case where global reserve needs exceed the global supply of reserves. How would this assumed reserve shortage manifest itself? First, to attract additional reserves, countries may change their monetary–fiscal mix, easing fiscal policy at the same time that they restrict their monetary policies. This particular manifestation would lead to competitive increases in interest rates. Second, adjustment may take the form of worldwide deflation, resulting in a fall in economic activity. Third, there may be widespread resort to restrictions on imports. Fourth, there may be competitive devaluations, leading to an effective increase in the price of gold and hence in world liquidity.

These overt manifestations of a reserve shortage also serve to justify the creation of a new reserve asset. For example, in the circumstances assumed, the creation and distribution of a new reserve asset will benefit the world economy in one of several ways. First, it may prevent a decline in investment associated with the global rise in interest rates (corresponding to the first adjustment). Second, it may increase world output (corresponding to the second adjustment). Third, it may improve the allocation of resources (corresponding to the third adjustment). Fourth, it may eliminate the uncertainties associated with competitive devaluations (corresponding to the fourth adjustment).

After reviewing all the available evidence the Managing Director of the IMF concluded in 1969 that, in the 1950s and early 1960s, global reserves were adequate. After 1964, however, he asserted that the 'signals were conflicting'.[5] On the one hand, world output and international trade had expanded rapidly in an environment where exchange rates had been reasonably stable. On the other hand, there was some evidence of reserve inadequacy from 'the increased reliance on restrictions on international transactions and the increased recourse to international financial assistance'. The Fund took the view that those last developments were sufficiently significant to justify the judgement that reserves had, in fact, become inadequate.

As for the other two considerations that had to be taken into account, the significant transformation in the US balance of payments in 1968 and 1969 was taken as evidence of a better balance of payments equilibrium as well as of a better working of the adjustment process.

Having concluded that there was a need to activate SDRs there was still the question of the volume of SDRs to be created. This clearly was an extremely complex exercise involving, essentially, two steps. First, there was a need to evaluate reserve needs over a basic period. Second, there was a need to estimate the growth of other reserves.[6]

Projecting reserve needs on the basis of various summary measures outlined above, the Fund concluded that reserve needs fell between $4 and $5 billion a year. At the same time, they judged that other reserve growth would amount to $1–$1.5 billion a year (made up of dollar accruals from US deficits of $0.5–$1 billion and another $0.5 billion from gold and reserve positions in the Fund). This suggested a figure of $3–$3.5 billion a year to meet reserve needs by the creation of SDRs. The final proposal, which was accepted and implemented, was to distribute $3.5 billion in 1970 and $3 billion in each of the following two years.

Notes for Chapter 5

1 See *IMF – Articles of Agreement of the IMF* (Articles XXI–XXXII). Quotes are from these Articles. Changes to the original provisions on SDRs are discussed in Chapter 10. J. J. Polak (1971); J. Gold (1970), pp. 23–6.
2 SDRs cannot be used in transactions with private parties.
3 International Monetary Fund (1969).
4 A more general criticism of the ratio as a measure of reserve adequacy is that where reserves decline relative to imports and countries respond to the reserve shortage by restricting imports or by deflation, the reserve/import ratio will show no decline at the same time that there is evidence of a reserve shortage.
5 Proposal by the Managing Director (P. P. Schweitzer) on the Allocation of SDRs to the First Basic Period in International Monetary Fund (1970a).
6 This method of presenting the problem assumes that the creation of a new reserve asset does not affect the growth of other reserves. Of course, to the extent that reserves are predominantly demand determined this assumption would clearly not hold.

Chapter 6

Continuing Crises and the Breakdown of Bretton Woods

The Crises between 1968 and mid-1971

The Gold Crisis of 1968

It was the dollar's turn to come under attack after the sterling devaluation in November 1967. Now, anticipating a possible dollar devaluation (a rise in the official price of gold), there was massive buying of gold in the private gold market. The Gold Pool (minus France who had withdrawn in June 1967) accommodated this demand from official gold stocks.[1] This crisis reached a head in March 1968 when the Gold Pool finally decided to withdraw support. In the meantime, the crisis had proved costly to the monetary authorities in terms of gold losses. Altogether, in the six months from the end of September 1967 to the end of March 1968, these losses mounted to about \$3.5 billion of which the US share was about \$2.4 billion (nearly 20 per cent of her gold reserves at the end of September 1967).

At the same time that official support was withdrawn, an agreement was reached that there was to be no change in the official price of gold and that monetary authorities were to refrain from either selling gold to the private market or buying gold from that market.[2] The arrangement effectively established a two-tier gold market – a private market whose price was to be determined by demand and supply and an official market (for official transactions between monetary authorities) whose price would continue at \$35 an ounce.

The Franc–Mark Crisis (1968–69)

No sooner had the gold crisis been resolved than a new crisis exploded in France. The French 'events' of May 1968 had major repercussions on the economy: there was a huge exodus of capital, production was severely disrupted and there was a wage explosion. France drew heavily on her credit facilities, despite which her reserves in the succeeding six months fell by some $3 billion. With the franc under attack,[3] the dollar relatively subdued and sterling recovering from the devaluation, there was now a new burst of speculation in favour of the German mark. The franc–mark 'war' was to continue for over a year during which the French and German authorities doggedly resisted any change in their exchange rates.

Germany's recession in 1966/67 had considerably strengthened her trade balance and, despite her rapid recovery in 1968, the trade balance continued to show considerable strength. The huge current account surplus in 1968 was, however, almost exactly offset by a massive outflow of long-term capital (see Table 6.1).[4] Interestingly, this coincided with huge speculative inflows of short-term capital, which turned this account from a 9 billion mark deficit in 1967 to a 5 billion mark surplus in 1968.[5] In the event, Germany entered 1969 in a very strong reserve position. At the same time, all indicators were pointing to a vigorous expansion and an accelerating inflation. Policy, therefore, became oriented towards maintaining a restrictive monetary policy as well as discouraging short-term capital inflows.

Table 6.1 Balance of payments – Germany (in billions of deutsche marks)

	1968	*1969*	*1970*	*1971*	*1972*	*1973*	*1974*
1 Current account	11.9	7.5	3.2	3.1	2.5	11.5	25.1
2 Long-term capital	–11.2	–23.0	– 0.9	6.3	15.5	12.9	– 5.8
3 Short-term capital	5.1	4.4	16.0	4.3	– 3.5	0.3	–19.1
4 Errors/omissions	1.3	0.9	3.6	2.7	1.2	1.7	– 2.2
5 Overall balance (1+2+3+4)	7.1	–10.2	21.9	16.4	15.7	26.4	– 2.0

Source: Monthly Report of the Deutsche Bundesbank (June 1976).

The strength of the mark during 1969 is indicated by the fact that while the uncovered interest differential continued to favour the Euro-dollar the covered differential tended to favour the domestic market. In the first three quarters there was a large non-monetary inflow, a very large part of which would have been speculative. These inflows reached a peak in early May when in a matter of a few days some $4 billion entered the country.

The other side of the mark's strength was the weakness of the French franc, which continued to be under attack in 1969. The first exchange rate adjustment in the franc–mark 'war' came in August 1969 when France devalued by some 11.1 per cent.[6] Then, in October, Germany, after a brief float, established a new par value, representing a revaluation of some 9.5 per cent.

US Monetary Policy Swings (1968–71) and the New Mark–Dollar Crisis (1970–71)

In the meantime, most important developments were taking place in the US economy. With demand rapidly expanding in 1968 and most of 1969 and some loss in price competitiveness, the US trade surplus fell dramatically in these two years (see Table 3.4). At the same time, as had happened in 1966, with monetary policy tightening short-term inflows of capital increased sharply. Now net inflows were of the order of $3.7 billion and $6.6 billion in 1968 and 1969, respectively (as against $2.4 billion in 1966). The massive inflows were responsible for converting a long succession of overall deficits (or near balance as in 1966) into surpluses of the order of $1.6 billion and $2.7 billion in 1968 and 1969, respectively.

Monetary restriction in the USA in 1968/69 led to very sharp increases in interest rates in the Euro-dollar market. For example, interest rates rose from a trough of about 6 per cent in August 1968 to a peak of over 11 per cent a year later. In many European countries, domestic conditions, which were moderately expansive, did not justify increases in local interest rates of that order. Many European economies responded to the situation, in part by tightening their own domestic monetary policies, in part by trying to sterilise the effects of outflows on domestic liquidity and in part, too, by directly restricting the outflow of short-term capital. Despite some of these measures there was a large outflow of capital from Europe and into the USA in those years.

By the end of 1969 the US economy had slid into a recession. By 1970 US monetary policy had become expansionary and US and Euro-dollar interest rates began to tumble. The short-term capital account now recorded huge outflows. In 1970 the outflows were of the order of $6.5 billion, virtually reversing the 1969 inflows (see Table 3.4); but, in 1971, when monetary policy continued to be expansionary outflows were huge, reaching nearly $20 billion in that year alone. The counterpart of these outflows were inflows into the rest of the world, increasing their money supply and laying the foundation for the acceleration in their inflation.[7] The huge US deficits (nearly $10 billion in 1970 and $30 billion in 1971) swelled world reserves, which increased by about 18 per cent and 32 per cent in 1970 and 1971, respectively (see Table 5.1). At the same time, by 1971, US gold reserves represented less than one quarter of her official liabilities (see Table 3.6).

In most industrial countries outside the USA domestic activity continued to be high during 1970; on domestic grounds, therefore, policy would have been directed at moderating rather than stimulating demand. Now with Euro-dollar rates falling very sharply the policy dilemma was the exact opposite to the one that presented itself in

1968/69; and the response was similar to 1968/69. In general, the other industrial countries allowed their interest rates to drop and they tried to sterilise the effects of inflows on domestic liquidity; at the same time, they reversed their capital controls, imposing restrictions on the inflow of capital. Again, despite some of the measures, the inflows into Europe in 1970/71 were, as we saw, huge.

The case of Germany is again particularly interesting. Economic activity remained high throughout 1970 and into the first half of 1971. The current account, still in surplus, had weakened, however, during 1970, in contrast to 1969, and with outflows on the long-term capital account the basic balance remained roughly in balance through 1970 and early 1971. However, with Euro-dollar and US rates beginning to drop early in 1970, the interest differential swung sharply in favour of Germany from the first quarter of the year and persisted into 1970 and the first half of 1971. The inducements to import short-term capital were aggravated in 1971 by speculation, as indicated by a premium on the forward deutsche mark, coinciding with a favourable interest differential. The strong inflows persisted despite special measures to resist them. Then, in May 1971, the German authorities ceased to maintain the exchange rate for the deutsche mark within the established margins.

The Smithsonian Agreement and the Collapse of Bretton Woods

Background

With the mark floating by May 1971 (now joined by the Netherlands) and the USA running a huge deficit, the dollar was once again under severe attack by mid-1971. There were reports of large conversions of official dollars into gold. Then, on 15 August, the USA announced a number of new measures to try and retrieve the situation, which had become critical. On the domestic front, a price freeze was imposed; on the international front the most significant measure was the formal suspension of dollar convertibility into gold.[8] Additionally, a 10 per cent surcharge on imports was imposed, imported capital equipment was excluded from the proposed investment tax credit, tax advantages were given for exports through domestic sales corporations and foreign aid expenditures were cut.

The blunt announcement of those measures was accompanied by demands for the removal of certain specific trade barriers in Europe, for some contribution by the Europeans towards US defence costs on the continent and, finally, and most important, for other countries to revalue their currencies. The surcharge and the investment tax credit exclusion were intended as temporary measures until a satisfactory response became forthcoming.

With expectations, now, of a dollar devaluation threatening further massive inflows into stronger currencies, other major currencies were, in due course, forced to join Germany and the Netherlands in a float. Then followed protracted negotiations, which came to a head in the Smithsonian Agreement in December 1971.

In those negotiations, the USA argued for an improvement in her full-employment current account of some $13 billion. The current account deficit expected in 1972 was $4 billion, while expected capital and aid outflows were some $7 billion. This gave an expected overall deficit of some $11 billion; to transform this into a targeted $1–$2 billion surplus required a turnaround of something of the order of $13 billion. The current account deficit would thus be turned into a $9 billion surplus. To achieve this, the USA wanted a substantial revaluation from the rest of the world vis-à-vis the dollar averaging out at something like 15 per cent, as well as some trade liberalisation and some sharing of defence burdens. On the other side, the other members of the Group of Ten argued for a smaller net realignment, to be effected by some change in their own par value but, as well, by some contribution from the USA in the form of an increase in the official price of gold, and also for restrictions on US direct investment overseas.

A substantive difference, therefore, arose over the relative contributions to the net realignment, the USA insisting that it would not alter its own official par value, while the rest of the world wanted some devaluation of the US dollar in terms of gold. In part, this was a political issue, with the rest of the world arguing that the USA must be seen to be 'contributing' to the realignment, in this way, facilitating, domestically, the political acceptance of the change. But there were also some real economic issues involved. One had to do with differing implications for the real value of world liquidity. Consider, for example, two extreme alternatives: one involving a revaluation of 10 per cent by the rest of the world vis-à-vis the dollar while the dollar retains its par value, and the other involving a 10 per cent devaluation of the US dollar vis-à-vis gold, while the rest of the world retain their official par value vis-à-vis gold (revaluing vis-à-vis the dollar by 10 per cent). In both cases, there is the same net exchange rate realignment; but, in the first case, the purchasing power of both gold and the US dollar reserves will fall vis-à-vis the rest of the world while, in the second case, the purchasing power of the dollar will fall vis-à-vis the rest of the world but the purchasing power of gold will now increase vis-à-vis the US dollar. Hence, the larger the US contribution the greater would be real global reserves and the better off would be the rest of the world.[9] Another technical difference had to do with the location of the changes in par values. Suppose a 10 per cent net realignment is required: to take an extreme case, it is, presumably, administratively simpler for the USA to announce a change in its par value while the rest of the world retain their par value vis-à-vis gold (but alter their intervention points vis-à-vis the dollar)[10] than to have each other country announce a change in its own par value. There were also issues of equity. Countries with the largest share of gold in their reserves would benefit most the larger the US contribution.

The Agreement

The final result, the Smithsonian Agreement, was a compromise. The realignments are shown in Table 6.2. The US dollar revalued vis-à-vis gold by 7.89 per cent (raising the price of gold to $38 an ounce). Most other currencies either maintained their gold par values (for example, France and the UK) or revalued upwards vis-à-vis gold, the largest revaluations being by Japan and Germany. The effective (trade weighted) devaluation of the dollar vis-à-vis other currencies was of the order of 6.5–7.5 per cent. Calculations by the IMF also suggested that the realignment had, on balance, increased world reserves.[11]

Three other decisions were taken at the time. The first was to increase the permissible margins for exchange rate movements around parities from 1 to 2.25 per cent. The second was to permit countries to declare central rates rather than parities. The difference lay in the fact that while the latter could be expressed only in terms of gold the former could be expressed in terms of gold, SDRs or another member's currency. Countries opting for central rates rather than par values could also change these central rates without IMF approval but the IMF had to be notified and could challenge a decision. Most industrialised countries, in fact, chose to declare central rather than par values. The third decision was the agreement that 'discussions should be promptly undertaken particularly in the framework of the IMF to consider reform of the international monetary system in the longer run'.[12]

The Aftermath

Despite President Nixon's representation of the Smithsonian Agreement as 'the conclusion of the most significant monetary agreement in the history of the world', it became suspect within a few weeks and totally collapsed in just over a year. With the US trade and capital accounts worsening, doubts about the new exchange rate realignment began to surface in the early months of 1972. There were, again, huge inflows into Germany in February 1972 with the Germans now responding by the imposition of the Bardepot – a 40 per cent deposit requirement on business borrowing from abroad.[13] By mid-year, with the UK's current account now weakening and accelerating inflation menacing, sterling came under attack and after huge reserve losses (of the order of $2.6 billion in six days) sterling began to float

Table 6.2 Exchange rate relationships after the Smithsonian Agreement – 18 December 1971[a]

Country	*Percentage Change in Par Value*	*Percentage Change in terms of the US dollar*
Belgium	+2.76	+11.57
Canada	(floating continued)	—
France	—	+ 8.57
Germany	+4.61	+13.58
Italy	−1.00	+ 7.48
Japan	+7.66	+16.88
Netherlands	+2.76	+11.57
Sweden	−1.00	+ 7.49
United Kingdom	—	+ 8.57
United States	−7.89	—

Source: M. De Vries (1976), p. 555.
[a] + indicates revaluation; − indicates devaluation.

on 23 June. The situation deteriorated over the next two weeks with massive inflows once again entering Europe and Japan.

Calm returned to the scene in the later months of 1972 with a sharp improvement in the US balance of payments position and the reactivation of swap operations by the Federal Reserve. In January 1973 Nixon announced Phase 3 of his wage–price controls, a looser more voluntary arrangement than the mandatory Phase 2. Italy soon afterwards joined France in the establishment of a two-tier (dual) exchange rate regime.[14] The Swiss followed with a float and a new foreign exchange crisis ensued in early February with massive inflows yet again entering Germany. On 12 February the USA announced a 10 per cent devaluation of the dollar (with the new official price of gold up to $42.22 an ounce). After this all major currencies began to float. This effectively put an end to the Bretton Woods System. The regime of managed floats has continued since then.

Notes for Chapter 6

1 In January 1968, too, with the dollar weak, the USA announced new controls over the outflows of capital. The scope of IET was widened and the FDI guidelines became mandatory (all these controls were finally abandoned in January 1974). See J. Hewson and E. Sakakibara (1975).

2 R. Solomon (1977, p. 122) notes that the obligation to refrain from selling was stronger than the obligation to refrain from buying.

3 France's balance of payments, as we saw, had shown considerable strength in the early-mid 1960s but, in the face of weakening international competitiveness, had already begun to turn around before the 1968 events.

4 Possible reasons were the US restrictions on outflows (which made borrowing in Germany more attractive) and low German interest rates. See L. Yeager (1976), p. 506.
5 In November adjustments made to import and export taxes were tantamount to an effective revaluation of some 5 per cent.
6 Despite the crisis and the decline in France's balance of payments position, many observers did not believe that the franc at the time was overvalued; in any event, the 11 per cent devaluation was widely thought to be excessive.
7 It will be recalled that the IMF, in projecting reserve needs for these years as the basis for the activation of SDRs, had figured US deficits in these years to be of the order of \$0.5–\$1 billion a year.
8 For something like a decade, although the dollar had remained de jure convertible, considerable restraint had been exercised and, for practical purposes, convertibility had been limited. The move meant that the USA was abandoning its obligations under the IMF Articles of Agreement to maintain its par value within a 1 per cent margin by buying and selling gold. It effectively put the world on a dollar standard and ended one important provision of the Bretton Woods System.
9 Had the US dollar continued to be convertible there would have been another significant difference. A rise in the price of gold would have destabilised the US dollar vis-à-vis gold.
10 One complication, however, here was that a rise in the official price of gold required Congressional consent in the USA.
11 See IMF *Annual Report* (1972), p. 22.
12 Smithsonian Communique.
13 The aim was to close a loop-hole that existed in the earlier regulation, which had acted predominantly on the banking system.
14 France had been on a two-tier exchange rate system since August 1971. A two-tier regime is one where the exchange rate on commercial transactions is fixed while that on most other transactions is allowed to float.

Chapter 7

The Growth of the Euro-Currency System [1]

Introduction

A Euro-currency is a deposit held in a bank and denominated in a specific currency, its distinguishing feature being that it is located outside the country of that currency's origin. A Euro-dollar, for example, is a special case of a Euro-currency; it is a dollar deposit in a bank located outside the USA. A Euro-mark would be a mark deposit in a bank outside Germany. Since Euro-dollars make up the bulk of the Euro-currency market, we will limit ourselves in the main to the functioning of that market.

There are many estimates of the Euro-currency market, the best known being those by the Bank for International Settlements (BIS) (in their *Annual Reports*) and the Morgan Guaranty Trust Company of New York (in their *World Financial Markets*). Excellent coverage of the UK-based component of the market (which represents some one half of the total) is also regularly provided in the Statistical Annex of the Bank of England *Quarterly Bulletin*.

Since BIS data is easily the most widely used and quoted we will draw, in the main, on their own estimates of the size of the market. Table 7.1 shows these estimates on a gross and on a net basis. The estimates[2] are derived from the external liabilities in foreign currencies of banks in eight European countries: Belgium–Luxembourg, France, Germany, Italy, the Netherlands, Sweden, Switzerland and the UK. They thus exclude all foreign currency liabilities located outside this region (for example, in the Bahamas, Singapore, Hong Kong, Canada, Japan, Panama and the Cayman Islands), where growth has, in fact, been fairly rapid in the 1970s. The difference between the gross and the net figures is that the latter exclude inter-bank deposits among the eight European countries.

By way of comparison Table 7.1 also shows the Morgan Guaranty estimates of the net size of the Euro-currency market. This estimate includes the foreign currency liabilities of the non-European banks, so

Table 7.1 Estimates of the size of Euro-currency market (in billions of US dollars)

Year (1)	Gross (BIS) (2)	Dollar (Component) (BIS) (3)	Net Euro-currency (BIS) (4)	Net Euro-currency (Morgan Guaranty) (5)	Net % Increase in Size of Market (BIS) (6)	% Increase in World Money Supply (7)
1964	12		9	14		
1965	14		12	17	33.3	9.0
1966	18		15	21	25.0	8.1
1967	23		18	25	20.0	7.7
1968	34	27	25	34	38.9	9.7
1969	57	46	44	50	76.0	8.8
1970	75	59	57	65	29.5	7.6
1971	98	71	71	85	24.6	12.1
1972	132	97	92	110	29.6	13.3
1973	191	131	132	160	43.4	14.0
1974	221	156	177	215	34.1	10.5
1975	259	189	205	250	15.8	12.9
1976	305	224	247	310	20.5	15.0
1977	385	268	300	380	21.4	13.2
1978	502	340	375	485	25.0	14.1

Sources: Bank for International Settlements, *Annual Reports.*
Morgan Guaranty Trust Company of New York, *World Financial Markets.*
International Monetary Fund, *International Financial Statistics* (world money supply).

its coverage is broader than that of the BIS. It will be seen that the share of the European banks in the total business has dropped somewhat in the 1970s, with Euro-currency business outside the BIS area now running to the order of some $100 billion.[3]

Table 7.1 column (6) also shows the rate of growth of the market since 1965. Interestingly, growth has continued to be rapid into the 1970s. For example, in the years 1965–78 the market (as measured by the BIS) grew at an annual rate of something like 30 per cent, with no apparent tendency for the growth to slow down. By way of comparison, the last column shows the rate of growth of money for the world as a whole (as calculated by the IMF). It will be seen that the Euro-currency market grew on average at something like three times the growth in the world money supply.

The BIS also reports the sources and uses of funds in the Euro-currency markets by region. This is shown in Table 7.2 for the years 1969–76. The table should be interpreted in the following way. If a country's net position (sources less uses) is positive in any one year this means that it is supplying more funds to the market than it is drawing from the market (in other words, its claims on the market exceed its

Table 7.2 Estimated sources and uses of Euro-currency funds (in billions of US dollars)

			REST OF WORLD							
USES	*Reporting European Area*	*United States*	*Canada Japan*	*Other Developed*	*Eastern European*	*Offshore Banking Centres*	*Oil-Exporting Countries*	*Developing Countries*	*Un-allocated*	*Total*
1969	15.0	16.8	(. . .		12.0			. . .)	0.2	44.0
1970	24.0	13.1	(. . .		19.0			. . .)	0.9	57.0
1971	32.8	8.3	(. . .		28.9			. . .)	1.0	71.0
1972	38.9	9.6	(. . .		43.1			. . .)	0.4	92.0
1973	49.0	13.5	12.7	14.7	7.4	18.7	3.3	11.0	1.7	132.0
1974	61.5	18.2	18.2	20.4	10.1	26.7	3.5	15.7	2.7	177.0
1975	63.0	16.6	20.2	25.8	15.9	35.5	5.3	19.5	3.2	205.0
1976	75.1	18.3	21.6	33.0	20.8	40.7	9.6	24.7	3.2	247.0
SOURCES										
1969	21.7	4.1	(. . .		17.6			. . .)	0.6	44.0
1970	27.7	4.5	(. . .		24.0			. . .)	0.8	57.0
1971	32.4	6.1	(. . .		31.4			. . .)	1.1	71.0
1972	35.2	6.9	(. . .		47.9			. . .)	2.0	92.0
1973	50.8	9.5	9.8	17.7	3.7	12.5	10.0	14.6	3.4	132.0
1974	67.8	11.9	8.7	18.5	5.1	17.8	29.1	15.5	2.6	177.0
1975	79.5	15.4	8.3	19.9	5.4	21.8	34.6	16.2	3.9	205.0
1976	87.6	18.8	10.5	21.3	6.4	30.1	45.2	21.3	5.8	247.0

Source: Bank for International Settlements, *Annual Reports*.

liabilities to the market). On this basis, for most of the years 1969–76 the Reporting European Area was a net supplier of funds to the market while the USA was a net user of funds from the market. From 1973 the data is available on a more disaggregated basis. The huge increase in the supply of funds to the market from the oil-exporting countries, after 1974, is striking.

Table 7.3 also indicates the degree of maturity transformation in the Euro-currency market.[4] The Bank of England has for some years been publishing data on the maturity structure of the banks located in London and engaged in Euro-currency business. The data is most revealing. It shows that in the years 1971 and 1974, for example, the Euro-banks did not engage in any significant 'maturity transformation'; in other words, the maturity structure of their liabilities tended to match fairly closely the maturity structure of their assets. In 1977, however, the position had changed significantly. For example, in May 1977 the liabilities maturing in three months or less amounted to 66 per cent of their total liabilities while their assets maturing in three months or less represented only 53 per cent of their assets. At the same time, while some 7 per cent of their liabilities matured in a year or longer, 24 per cent of their assets fell in this category. The implications of these facts will be examined later.

Table 7.3 Maturity structure of claims and liabilities of all UK-based Euro-banks (percentage of total)

	CLAIMS			*LIABILITIES*		
	October 1971	*May 1974*	*May 1977*	*October 1971*	*May 1974*	*May 1977*
Less than 8 days	20	18	17	18	21	21
8 days to 3 months	41	41	36	51	47	45
3 months to 1 year	25	25	23	26	26	27
1 year to 3 years	6	5	10	3	2	5
3 years and over	8	11	14	2	4	2

Source: Bank of England, *Quarterly Bulletins.*

Notation used in this chapter

C, C_1 = relevant deposits in US banks less the cash deposits of the Euro-banks

De = net Euro-dollar deposits

Hd, H_1 = relevant deposits in US banks (base money of Euro-system)

Mo = relevant money supply

R = cash deposits of Euro-banks

Rw = world international reserves

Reasons for Growth of the Market

How is one to account for the existence and rapid growth of the market? The fundamental reason lies in the fact that, for a variety of reasons, to be noted shortly, Euro-currency banking transactions can be undertaken more cheaply in the offshore centres than in the countries of origin. Consider the case of the Euro-dollar and suppose that there are no differences in risk/liquidity in the two markets and, additionally, no restrictions on arbitrage between the markets. Figure 7.1 shows the position in the offshore Euro-dollar market and the 'home' market (the USA). Suppose *re* represents the interest rate paid

Figure 7.1 *The Euro-Dollar Market – demand and supply*

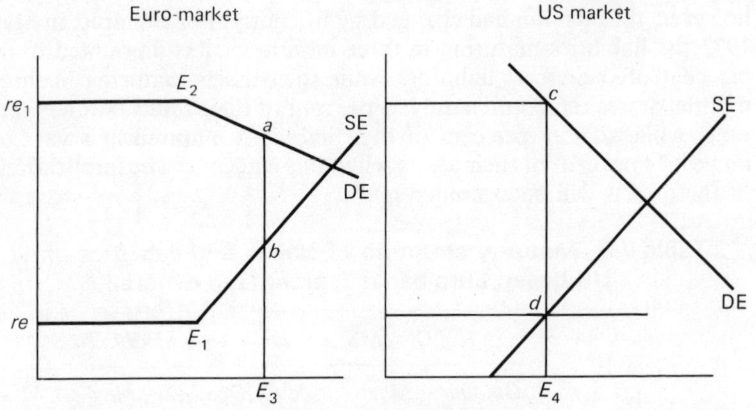

on deposits in the US market. Now, if the Euro-market were to offer the same interest rate, the volume of dollars supplied to the market would be E_1. This can be explained in terms of convenience and political considerations. European residents or businesses will, for example, find it more convenient to hold their dollar deposits in a bank in Europe than in a US bank. At the same time, some groups (for example, Eastern European or some oil-exporting countries) will also prefer, for political reasons, to hold their dollar deposits outside of the USA. A higher deposit rate in the Euro-dollar market would now attract additional deposits (for example, out of the US banking system). This is shown by the upward slope of the supply schedule in the market (SE).

At the loan rate in the US market re_1 the demand for loans in the Euro-market would be E_2 for reasons that are somewhat similar to the case of deposits. The profit margin in the US market (that is, the difference between the borrowing and lending rates) is *cd*. If, in fact, the margin in the Euro-dollar had to be the same then the size of the Euro-market would be limited to E_1. However, as we have noted, they are able to function with significantly smaller margins (for example, more recently of the order of ⅜ per cent), hence they can simultaneously offer a higher deposit rate and a lower loan rate.[5] If the margin in the Euro-market is *ab* as against *cd* then the size of the market will be E_3. At a loan rate represented by *a* and a deposit rate represented by *b* the 'supply' of deposits will be equal to the 'demand' for loans.[6]

The key question then is to explain why the Euro-markets are able to operate with a significantly lower margin than in the home markets. The two principal reasons for this are: the lack of legally imposed (non-interest bearing) reserve requirements and the very large transactions undertaken, which hold down their operating costs.[7]

Within this framework the size and growth of the Euro-dollar market could be explained along the following lines.[8] There would be an initial phase of rapid growth, during which the market would gradually become better known, more widely used and accepted. It would then grow at roughly the same rate as their counterparts in the home markets (or at the rate of growth of wealth in these markets). The settling-in phase would, in normal circumstances, have come to an end by the middle 1960s, say, in 1965/66: Table 7.1, however, shows that market growth continued at a rapid rate beyond that point. To explain this, one needs to invoke special factors. These are not hard to identify. First, there were the US capital controls; second, the credit squeeze in the USA in 1968/69; third, the huge OPEC surpluses beginning in 1974.[9]

US capital controls beginning in 1965 restricted the transfer of funds by Americans to the Euro-market at the same time that they provoked an increase in the demand for Euro-dollar loans by American and foreign borrowers. In 1968 and 1969 when US financial conditions became tight US banks borrowed heavily from their foreign branches operating in the Euro-dollar market.[10] Finally, the large deposits by the OPEC countries beginning in 1974 further helped to sustain the growth in the market.[11]

Freedman notes that these special factors can be broken down into demand shifts or supply shifts or combinations of the two. The US capital controls and the heavy US borrowings in 1969 can be represented as demand shifts[12] while the OPEC depositing represents a supply shift. A demand shift, given the Euro-margin required, will increase the size of the market while raising the interest rate on both loans and deposits relative to the domestic market. On the other hand, a supply shift will also increase the size of the market, but now interest rates on loans and deposits will fall relative to the domestic market. (This is clearly demonstrable in terms of Figure 7.1.)[13]

Conflicting Views about the Euro-dollar Market

There are very few areas in economics that have aroused so much controversy and such sharp disagreements. At one extreme are those economists who blame the Euro-dollar market for many of the ills that have beset the industrial world in recent years. The list of charges is impressive:

(1) The growth of the market and the alleged associated acceleration in the growth of world liquidity has been held responsible, in part at least, for the acceleration in inflation in the early 1970s.
(2) The market has been held largely responsible for the alleged increase in the degree of capital mobility and, hence, for the loss of monetary independence, which, in part at least, led to the collapse of Bretton Woods (see Chapter 9).
(3) The market has been seen as a major source of funds for speculation and hence as a source of destabilising and disruptive capital movements across national frontiers.
(4) The workings of the market are mysterious and not properly understood, creating fears that its superstructure of credit (like a house of cards) may all collapse one day bringing serious financial crises in its trail. In recent years, particularly, special concern has been expressed over the financial health of these Euro-banks in the light of their increasing involvement in longer-term lending, while continuing to rely on relatively shorter-term borrowing.
(5) Its capacity for creating international reserves poses not only a threat to world liquidity but also means that the international monetary authorities lose all control over the growth of world reserves.

Over the years, all these various concerns had led to demands for controls over the Euro-dollar market.

At the other extreme are those economists who have come to view the Euro-dollar market in a far more favourable light (indeed in many cases seeing it as having been of some net benefit to the world) and who are opposed to any control over the market. These economists would argue that:

(1) The capacity of the Euro-market for creating liquidity is really very limited indeed.
(2) Its contribution to capital mobility is, at most, marginal or, to the extent that it has made a significant contribution, this has been to the advantage of the world in that it has facilitated the free flow of capital.
(3) The market has proved invaluable in recent years in recycling

funds from surplus to deficit countries, thus helping in the adjustment process attendant on the oil price shock.

Our own analysis will lean a little more towards the latter than the former view of the Euro-market.

The analysis that follows examines the effects of the Euro-dollar market on world liquidity, world reserves and (briefly) capital mobility. We then (again briefly) look at the case for exercising some official control over the market.

The Euro-dollar Market and Liquidity Creation – the Fixed Multiplier Approach

Multiplier Analysis

Much of the theoretical literature on the Euro-dollar market has tended to centre on the capacity of the market to create additional global liquidity. We deal with this issue by looking, first, at 'fixed multiplier' models, analogous to a domestic banking system and, second, at the work of those who reject the concept of a fixed multiplier and prefer a more flexible general equilibrium, portfolio approach, as manifested in the writings of J. Hewson, J. Niehans and E. Sakakibara.

Consider a shift of a deposit (100 units) out of a US bank and into a Euro-bank and assume that:

(1) Central banks sterilise the liquidity effects on the balance of payments.
(2) Central banks do not deposit any of their dollar reserves in the Euro-market.

We also disregard any monetary effects in the USA associated with different reserve requirements on demand and time deposits and different preferences by central banks and the public for financial assets. In what follows, too, we define the dollar component of the world money supply to include private sector holdings of Euro-deposits and exclude Euro-banks' holdings of cash in the US banking system.

The initial position of the Euro-bank is as follows:

POSITION 1

Euro-bank

Deposit 100	Cash (in US Bank) 100

At this point, there is simply a change in the ownership of the deposit in the US banking system from the original depositor to the Euro-bank. Also, world money supply, as defined, has not changed since we include Euro-deposits but exclude Euro-bank cash.

Of course, the Euro-bank will not hold all that cash but will lend out a large proportion of it. Suppose it wishes to hold some 5 per cent of deposits in cash alone. It will then lend out 95 units. Initially, this will show up as a private deposit in a US bank so the position is now:

POSITION 2

Euro-bank

Deposit 100	Cash 5
	Loan 95

Now the world money supply has increased by 95 units. If nothing more happened the initial deposit in the Euro-dollar bank will have increased world money supply by 95 units. This, however, may not be the end of the process; much of the controversy has centred on how to represent the next stages. There are several possibilities. The proceeds of the loan:

(1) may stay in private hands in a US bank;
(2) may be converted into another currency, in which case the deposit will be held by a foreign central bank;
(3) may be redeposited in the Euro-bank.

If (1) holds, as we have seen, nothing further happens. If (2) holds, given our assumptions about sterilisation and redepositing by a central bank, again nothing further happens. If (3) holds then the process will start again. Let us suppose that some proportion of the loan proceeds is, in fact, redeposited in the Euro-bank. If r is the cash/deposit ratio, d the proportion of the loan proceeds redeposited, the multiplier is:[14]

$$\frac{\Delta Mo}{A} = \frac{1-r}{1-d(1-r)}$$

How is this result altered if we relaxed our two assumptions about sterilisation and redepositing by central banks? If the loan proceeds were converted into a foreign currency and there was no sterilisation then the cash base of the country concerned would increase, leading to domestic money creation. If, moreover, the central bank were to redeposit some of its additional reserves the 'leakages' would be reduced and the multiplier would now be larger. In effect, this would be tantamount to raising the value of d in the above multiplier analysis.

As an alternative, we can suppose that the original deposit to the

Euro-market came from a foreign currency. In other words, there is, initially, a shift out of a foreign currency into a dollar deposit (at which point, the ownership of the deposit will change from the central bank to private hands) and then into a Euro-bank. Now if our original assumptions held the outcomes and sequence would be the same as in our previous example. If, however, the assumptions did not hold then there would be: (1) some initial reduction in the case base: and (2) some initial withdrawal of central bank depositing in the Euro-market. Both of these factors would tend to reduce the ultimate liquidity creation.

Returning to our basic multiplier above, it is clear that much depends on the size of d. For example, if $d=0$, the multiplier would be $(1-r)$ which is less than 1. At the other extreme, if $d=1$ (there was 100 per cent redepositing), the multiplier would be

$$\frac{1-r}{r}$$

which, with $r=0.05$, is as high as 19. Many economists have argued that the return flow is large and has increased over the years, with the wider acceptance of the Euro-market. Others insist that redepositing is very low and there is no real analogy with a domestic banking system whose demand deposits are a medium of exchange and hence tend to be automatically returned to the banking system.[15]

Empirical Estimates of the Multiplier

In what follows, we look at two empirical attempts, by B. Lee and R. McKinnon,[16] to estimate the size of the multiplier, within the framework of a fixed-multiplier model.

Lee draws an analogy between the domestic money multiplier process and Euro-dollar liquidity creation.

$$Mo = De + C \tag{7.1}$$

$$Hd = C + R \tag{7.2}$$

$$C = cDe \tag{7.3}$$

$$R = rDe \tag{7.4}$$

Equation (7.1) is the definition of the relevant money supply which is taken to be the sum of deposits in the Euro-banks and foreigners' deposits in the US banking system (excluding the cash of the Euro-bank). Equation (7.2) is the definition of the cash base of the system. Its counterpart in a domestic banking system would be currency holdings plus banks' cash base. Equation (7.3) assumes that foreigners hold a proportion c of their Euro-deposits in the US banking system while Equation (7.4) asserts that a proportion r of the Euro-banks' deposits is held as cash reserves.

These four equations yield a familiar multiplier:

$$\frac{\Delta Mo}{\Delta Hd} = \frac{1+c}{c+r} \qquad (7.5)$$

To determine the size of the multiplier all that is needed is an estimate of r and c. For the period covered by Lee's study r is estimated to have fallen from around 10–11 per cent in 1963 to 4–5 per cent in 1968/69. c is estimated at around 3 in 1963 and around 1 in 1969, implying a very sharp drop in the ratio of cash in US banks to Euro-deposits. With $r=0.1$ and $c=3$ the multiplier is about 1.3; with $r=0.05$ and $c=1$ the multiplier is about 1.9. So according to Lee's calculations the lower cash deposit ratio and the higher redepositing in the later period raised the multiplier from 1.3 to about 1.9.

Using this framework it can be seen that the difference between the Euro-multiplier and the multipliers in a domestic banking system lies largely in the size of c, which is very roughly of the order of 0.1 in a domestic banking system. With leakages of that order the multiplier would be considerably larger.[17]

McKinnon's estimates are based on a somewhat different framework. His definition of the money supply (Mo_1) is net Euro-deposits (De) (as in Lee) plus adjusted US deposits (C_1), now defined as all US deposits (H_1) less Euro-reserves. McKinnon is interested in the effects of shifts of deposits out of the US banking system into a Euro-dollar (as in our own original illustration) and assumes that the public holds a proportion of its total money supply (as defined) in the form of Euro-deposits. The system is now represented as:

$$Mo_1 = De + C_1 \qquad (7.1a)$$

$$H_1 = C_1 + R \qquad (7.2a)$$

$$De = eMo_1 + A \qquad (7.3a)$$

$$R = rDe \qquad (7.4a)$$

where A is the shift component (the exogenous change in the demand for Euro-dollars). Solving this system with H_1 assumed fixed yields a multiplier:

$$\frac{\Delta Mo}{\Delta A} = \frac{1-r}{1-e(1-r)} \qquad (7.6)$$

McKinnon estimates $r=0.033$ and $e=0.16$. The multiplier is then 1.15.

The multiplier for the change in the base, instead of an exogenous change in the demand for Euro-deposits, is:

$$\frac{\Delta Mo}{\Delta H_1}=\frac{1}{1-e(1-r)} \tag{7.7}$$

which, for the values of e and r assumed, is about 1.2.

What are the more substantive differences between the two multipliers? First, and less important, is the assumed source of the additional deposit in the Euro-bank. Lee assumes that it comes from an increase in the base of the system, while McKinnon assumes that there is an exogenous change in the propensity to hold Euro-dollars. In terms of a domestic banking system the difference is between a change in base money and a shift out of currency into a bank deposit. McKinnon's has more relevance for evaluating the effects of a change in preference favouring Euro-dollars (for example, in the earlier phases of growth in the market or when the OPEC invest a portion of their surplus in the market), while Lee's has more relevance for longer-term analysis (that is, the effects of changes in the base of the system). It needs to be noted in this connection that so long as the multiplier is stable (has settled down to a given value), the rate of growth of broadly defined money (including Euro-dollars) will be roughly the same as the growth of the domestic money supply.

The second difference is more significant and has to do with the definition of the base in the system. Lee's base is foreigners' deposits in the US banking system; McKinnon's is all US deposits, including those held by US residents. McKinnon's base is, therefore, broader. Clearly, the broader the base the larger is the assumed 'leakage' from the system and hence the smaller will tend to be the multiplier. If only foreigners transacted in the Euro-markets, as depositors and borrowers, Lee's base would be the more appropriate one. To the extent that US residents also transact in the Euro-market, Lee's base is too narrow. In fact, until January 1974 US residents were prohibited from depositing in the Euro-market, but there was, no doubt, considerable evasion. Since then there have been no restrictions. This is not to say that McKinnon's base is now the more appropriate one; McKinnon's base includes a (large) component which simply does not transact in the Euro-market (because, for example, minimum transactions are very large). Hence, the truth lies somewhere between the two.[18]

To conclude, then, the multiplier is unlikely to be very much in excess of 1 and almost certainly would be (well) below 2. Even if we include net Euro-dollars in the (world) money supply what appears to

Table 7.4 Growth of Euro-dollars and US money supply (in billions of US dollars)

Year	Gross Euro-Dollar Liabilities (1)	US Money Supply (Broad) (2)	Total (3)	% Change in (2) (4)	% Change in (3) (5)
1968	27	406	433		
1969	46	403	449	− 0.7	3.7
1970	59	451	510	11.9	13.6
1971	71	507	578	12.4	13.3
1972	97	570	667	12.4	15.4
1973	131	634	765	11.1	14.7
1974	156	693	849	9.3	11.0
1975	189	739	928	6.6	9.3
1976	224	789	1013	6.8	9.2

Sources: International Monetary Fund, *International Financial Statistics.* Bank for International Settlements, *Annual Reports.*

be relevant in the end is the rate of growth of dollar liquidity (including Euro-dollars) in relation to the rate of growth of the US (broad) money supply. Column (4) in Table 7.4 shows the rate of growth in the US money supply in the years 1968–76, while column (5) shows the rate of growth of dollar liquidity, which includes (gross) Euro-deposits.[19] This gives some rough indication of how (at most) Euro-dollars might have accelerated the rate of growth of dollar liquidity. The difference between the two columns is of the order of 2 per cent or over on average. Thus, at the very maximum Euro-dollars might have accelerated the rate of growth of liquidity by some 2 per cent a year.[20]

Liquidity Creation – The Hewson–Niehans–Sakakibara Approach

The Hewson–Niehans–Sakakibara writings[21] reject the fixed multiplier approach, believing that a more relevant framework of analysis is the theory of non-bank intermediaries rather than banking theory. Their contributions are twofold. First, they identify what they call a gross deposit multiplier, derived from a more general equilibrium framework that allows for portfolio considerations. Second, they argue that whatever the gross deposit multiplier is, what is relevant in evaluating the contribution of the Euro-market to liquidity is its net contribution to private sector liquidity which in turn depends on the degree of maturity transformation by the market.

Consider the Euro-dollar market as represented in Figure 7.2. Now,

Figure 7.2 *Effects of a deposit shift to the Euro-Market*

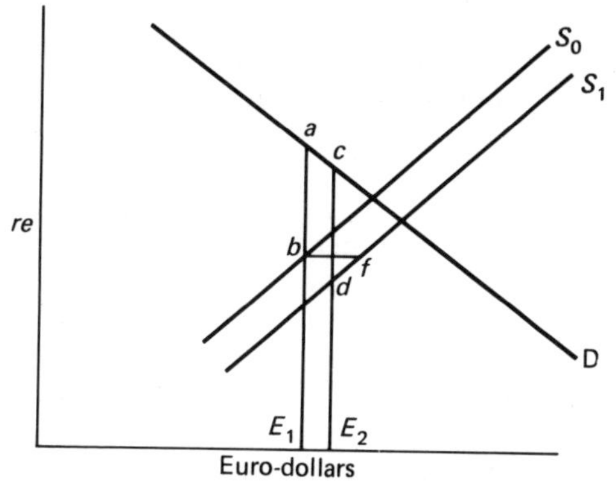

suppose that there is a shift in deposits from the USA to the market and again assume sterilisation and abstract from central bank depositing in the market. At the initial deposit interest rate there is an inflow represented by *bf*. The inflow will now lower Euro-rates (from *a* to *c* for loans and from *b* to *d* for deposits) and this will serve to reduce the supply of deposits from all regions (there will be a movement down the supply schedule) and to increase the demand for loans (again from all regions). The Euro-market will grow by $E_1 E_2$. If we define the multiplier as the increase in deposits (loans) divided by the initial inflow we have:

$$\frac{E_1 E_2}{bf} < 1$$

According to this analysis, then, given the assumptions made, the multiplier is bound to be less than 1 and will approximate 1 only if the supply schedule had zero interest sensitivity or the demand schedule had infinite interest sensitivity.

To sum up, the contributions here extend the analysis of the previous section by at least allowing for the effects of inflows into the Euro-market on the demand and supply of funds.

Niehans–Hewson also argue that whatever the gross multiplier, as determined above, the true measure of the impact on liquidity is the degree of maturity transformation. If maturity transformation is close to zero then the Euro-banks' contribution to the net liquidity of the private sector is effectively zero. Since, in fact, until very recently there was close matching of the maturity structures of their liabilities and assets, Niehans–Hewson concluded that the net liquidity effect of the Euro-market is very small. As we have seen, however (see Table

7.3), there has been some (considerable) maturity transformation more recently; hence, even if one accepted their theoretical position one would have to conclude that they have now made some contribution to net liquidity. For example, Little,[22] drawing on the work of Niehans–Hewson, applies specific liquidity weights to the liabilities and assets of the UK Euro-banks and finds that whereas in 1973 the moneyness of the banks' liabilities exceeded the moneyness of the banks' assets by some 16 per cent, by 1977/78 the banks' net liquidity creation had reached some 40 per cent.

Their theoretical position, interesting as it is, is probably too extreme. Even if maturity transformation were zero in so far as the Euro-dollar market provokes a shift out of US deposits (for reasons already noted) the world supply of funds and, hence, world liquidity will increase. As in the theory of non-bank financial intermediaries, any reduction in the net demand for money provoked by the entry of a new intermediary is expansionary, whatever its maturity structure.

Implications of Official Use of the Euro-dollar Market

Official Placements in the Euro-Market and Reserve Creation

Beginning in the late 1960s central banks, attracted by the higher interest rates in the market, began to place some of their dollar reserves in the Euro-dollar market. We examine here the view that official deposits of dollar reserves can lead to the creation of further dollar reserves; in other words, that there is a multiplier mechanism for reserves at work.[23]

Consider a deposit in a Euro-bank by a European central bank of some of its dollar reserves. A large portion of these will be lent out to non-banks. As in our previous analysis, if the proceeds of the loan are held as dollar deposits, the end result would be that US official liabilities would fall while, at the same time, international dollar reserves would have remained unchanged (but their location will have switched from the USA to Europe). In effect a transaction of this kind opens up an asymmetry between reported holdings of official dollar reserves and official liabilities to foreign central banks against the USA, but new reserves are not created in the process.

The result is different if the proceeds of the loan are converted into a foreign currency, so that they find their way into central banks as additional dollar reserves. Now the original deposit has resulted in the creation of additional dollar reserves which, in part, can be deposited once again, possibly creating further reserves. Again, in this case, official liabilities will be smaller than official reported dollar reserves.

How far can the process go and how many new reserves would be created? A fixed multiplier model would set the process in motion by an exogenous deposit by a central bank (A). As we saw previously, the proceeds of the loan can be (1) returned, (2) held in a US bank or (3) converted into a foreign currency. In the latter case, some proportion of the new reserves may now be returned to the Euro-dollar market. The sequence is clearly very complicated but the multiplier can be shown to be:[24]

$$\frac{\Delta Rw}{A} = \frac{\alpha_3(1-r)}{1-(1-r)[\alpha_2(1-\alpha_3)+\alpha_4\alpha_3]}$$

where

α_3 = proportion of loan proceeds converted into foreign currency

$\alpha_2(1-\alpha_3)$ = proportion of loan proceeds redeposited by the private sector

α_4 = proportion of new reserves redeposited by central bank.

To illustrate, suppose $r=0.05$, $\alpha_3=0.2$, $\alpha_2=0.3$ and $\alpha_4=0.6$, then the multiplier would be very close to 0.3, which is very low indeed. In other words, it would take an initial deposit of 10 units by the central bank to create three additional units of reserves.

Table 7.5 shows the scale of depositing by central banks. The proportion of foreign exchange reserves placed in the Euro-currency market has risen sharply in recent years. In 1970 particular concern was expressed over the effects of placements not only on the total volume of reserves (which meant that control over global reserves was

Table 7.5 Official holdings of Euro-currencies (in billions of SDRs)

	1969	*1970*	*1971*	*1972*	*1973*	*1974*	*1975*	*1976*
1 Total reserves	78.7	93.2	123.2	146.8	152.6	180.2	194.3	222.1
2 Total official holdings of foreign exchange	33.0	45.4	75.1	96.2	102.0	126.9	137.4	160.4
3 Total identified holdings Euro-dollars of which:	4.7	10.5	10.4	18.0	21.1	32.3	38.7	46.0
3a Industrial countries	2.2	5.1	3.4	5.6	7.3	6.5	7.0	7.8
3b Major oil exporting countries	0.8	1.6	2.8	3.9	4.0	15.6	21.0	24.1
4 Total identified other Euro-currencies	N.A.	0.4	1.1	3.2	5.0	5.6	6.8	7.0
3+4 as % of 1	–	11.7	9.3	14.4	17.1	21.0	23.4	23.8
3+4 as % of 2	–	24.0	15.3	22.0	25.6	29.9	33.1	33.0

Source: International Monetary Fund, *Annual Reports.*

being made even more difficult) but also on the world money supply; in other words, in so far as changes in reserves affected the money supply, the addition to reserves would have further added to world liquidity. In 1971 the authorities of the Group of Ten and Switzerland agreed to refrain from placing additional deposits in the market. (This is reflected in a drop in industrial countries' holdings in 1971.) After 1974 the pace of official placements accelerated, when the OPEC countries showed a preference for depositing in the Euro-market.

Official Borrowing from the Euro-Market

An even more recent development following the oil crisis and the large deficits associated with it is the big increase in official or semi-official borrowings from the Euro-currency market for balance of payments purposes. Table 7.6 gives some indication of the scale of these borrowings. These borrowings reached a peak in 1974 following the

Table 7.6 Publicly announced, medium-term Euro-currency credits to governments and public financial institutions[a] 1971 to 1976(1) (in billions of US dollars)

Year	*Total Government*	*Developed Countries*	*LDCs*
1971	1.5	.2	1.3
1972	2.4	1.0	1.4
1973	8.8	4.8	4.0
1974	14.5	8.9	4.5
1975	10.3	1.1	6.4
1976 (first half)	6.2	0.6	3.4

Source: J. S. Little (1977).
[a]Loans with a maturity of at least one year.

oil crisis and slowed down in recent years as the recession improved the balance of payments position of the industrial countries. These borrowings and their potential availability may have had the effect of reducing the need to hold owned international reserves.

The Euro-dollar Market and Capital Mobility

A case can be made for the view that the Euro-dollar market, by providing a focal point for the transmission of funds as well as convenience of location, may have increased the degree of capital mobility across national frontiers. However, this contribution is certain to be only a marginal one. Without the Euro-market funds would have flowed directly rather than through the intermediary of the Euro-market. The large increase in capital mobility in the 1960s is due not to the growth of the Euro-market but rather to the relaxation of exchange controls and, to a lesser extent, the growth of multinationals.

Any change in capital mobility induced by the Euro-dollar market has, itself, potential implications for the conduct of monetary policy and, as well, for the demand to hold international reserves. Increased capital mobility in a fixed rate world renders it more difficult to implement independent monetary policies.[25] By contrast, the implications of increased capital mobility for the demand to hold reserves is, on balance, ambiguous. On the one hand, increased mobility exposes the country to larger flows of capital, which are destabilising to reserves and hence there is an increased need to hold reserves. On the other hand, the existence of the Euro-dollar market serves to facilitate the financing of deficits and hence reduces the need for reserves.

A Case for Controls?

In dealing with controls over Euro-currency operations there are two questions that need to be asked. First, the rationale for controls; second, assuming controls were justified, the particular techniques to be used.

Controls have been urged on three principal grounds: first, the inflationary potential of the market; second, the prudential concern; third, the potential contribution of the market to exchange rate instability.

The first has been discussed in some detail and we concluded that it was probably not serious and this now appears to be the consensus. The second has assumed considerably more importance since 1974. Since that date the maturity transformation has significantly lengthened and, at the same time, it is contended that the quality of credit in the market has deteriorated. This has led to charges that it is now exposed to the risks of a liquidity crisis and also the potentially serious defaulting of debtors. Given, however, the available safeguards[26] these charges may be exaggerated.[27] As to the third ground, it is extremely difficult to evaluate the Euro-currency's contribution to exchange rate instability; at most, however, its contribution would have been marginal.

Even if there were a strong case for control it would appear difficult to secure agreement on the best technique to be used. The most widely discussed method is the imposition of reserve requirements on the Euro-banks. For this to be successful, however, it would have to be universally implemented (otherwise the funds would simply shift towards centres that are uncontrolled), but universal agreement would be particularly hard to secure given that existing centres (London, Singapore, Luxembourg and the Bahamas) reap significant benefits (in the form of foreign exchange earnings, tax revenues and some employment) from these activities.[28]

Notes for Chapter 7

1 General references here are: G. Bell (1974); G. Dufey and I. Giddy (1978); J. Hewson (1975); F. Klopstock (1968); J. Little (1975); A. Swoboda (1968).
2 There are numerous conceptual difficulties in measuring the size of the Euro-currency market. For a detailed examination of the BIS estimates see: H. Mayer (1976). See also G. Dufey and I. Giddy (1978), pp. 21–34.
3 To obtain some idea of the size of the Euro-dollar market relative to its nearest counterpart in the USA (bank time deposits) we may note that in recent years it has represented something like half the US market.
4 See J. Hewson (1975), Chapter 3.
5 For evidence of this in periods when there were virtually no restrictions on arbitrage in the markets see G. Dufey and I. Giddy (1978, p. 56) and Morgan Guaranty, *World Financial Markets* (monthly issues). For example, during 1974 the Euro-dollar loan rate was some 0.5–1 per cent below the US rate while the Euro-dollar deposit rate was some 0.5–1 per cent above the corresponding US rate.
6 We do not represent reserve requirements on the figure.
7 G. Dufey and I. Giddy (1978), pp. 133–5; C. Freedman (1977). Other reasons are (1) the lower regulatory expenses in the Euro-markets (for example, there are no Federal Deposit Insurance Corporation fees on their deposits), (2) the fact that they are not forced to direct credit to certain borrowers, (3) the absence of ceilings on interest rates on deposits or loans, (4) market efficiency and competitiveness and (5) low tax locations.
8 The line of argument taken here follows C. Freedman (1977).
9 See C. Freedman (1977), pp. 471–2; J. Hewson (1975), pp. 151–3; G. Dufey and I. Giddy (1978), pp. 57–9.
10 Until August 1969 there were no reserve requirements on these borrowings. There were similar borrowings but on a smaller scale in the 1966 squeeze.
11 J. Hewson (1975) also mentions the European (particularly German) capital controls in the early 1970s as a further stimulus to growth in the market.
12 While the US capital controls also restricted the supply of funds, Freedman argues that the dominant effect was on the demand side.
13 Freedman demonstrates that these anticipated movements in Euro-rates vis-à-vis domestic rates are actually borne out by the evidence.
14 Derived from the series

$$\Delta Mo = (1-r)A + d(1-r)^2A + d^2(1-r)^3A + d^3(1-r)^4A \ldots$$

15 For a discussion of these issues see: J. Hewson (1975), pp. 10–16; G. Dufey and I. Giddy (1978), Chapter 3; F. Klopstock (1970); M. Friedman (1969); G. Bell (1974), Chapter 5.
16 B. Lee (1973); R. McKinnon (1977).
17 Of course, r will tend to be lower in the Euro-market for reasons already discussed.
18 A different and more sophisticated 'fixed multiplier' model is developed by A. Swoboda (1978).
19 Because gross deposits are used this exaggerates the weight of the Euro-deposits.

20 For a discussion of some of these issues see R. J. Sweeney and T. Willett (1977).
21 J. Hewson (1975); J. Niehans and J. Hewson (1976); J. Hewson and E. Sakakibara (1974).
22 J. Little (1979).
23 See G. Dufey and I. Giddy (1978), pp. 169–77; J. Little (1977).
24 If $(1-r)\,A$ is the amount of the loan, $\alpha_3(1-r)\,A$ would be the proportion of the loan converted into foreign currency and hence the initial increment to reserves.
Now $\alpha_2(1-\alpha_3)(1-r)\,A$ would represent the redeposit by the private sector while $\alpha_4\alpha_3(1-r)\,A$ would be the redeposit by the central bank so the total redeposit in the second round would be:

$$\alpha_2(1-\alpha_3)(1-r)A+\alpha_4\alpha_3(1-r)A$$

and the second round accrual of reserves would be:

$$\alpha_3(1-r)[\alpha_2(1-\alpha_3)(1-r)A+\alpha_4\alpha_3(1-r)A]$$

The sum total of the increase in reserves (ΔRw) then observes a geometric series which takes the following form:

$$\begin{aligned}\Delta Rw = {} & \alpha_3(1-r)A+\alpha_3(1-r)[\alpha_2(1-\alpha_3)(1-r)A \\ & +\alpha_4\alpha_3(1-r)A]+\alpha_3(1-r)[\alpha_2(1-\alpha_3)(1-r)A \\ & +\alpha_4\alpha_3(1-r)A]^2 \ldots\end{aligned}$$

25 See Chapter 14.
26 The internal strength of the larger banks, the support that would be forthcoming from the central banks and the potential for official international support.
27 D. Kern (1979); Morgan Guaranty, *World Financial Markets* (March 1979).
28 At the time of writing (late 1979) there are new moves and negotiations aimed at imposing controls. For example, the USA has proposed minimum reserve requirements on a worldwide basis. See 'Euro-Markets: Has the US–German Initiative Run Out of Steam?', *The Banker*, October 1979, pp. 51–5.

Chapter 8

The Oil Price Shock of 1974 – Financial Impacts

Introduction

The quadrupling of the price of oil between late 1973 and early 1974 had major effects on the world economy in three distinct areas. First, there were the macro-economic effects on world employment and inflation in the oil-importing countries. Second, there were the problems posed by the financing of the unprecedented current account deficits, and the implications of alternative forms of financing for world reserves, the world money supply and exchange rates. Third, there were the effects on the distribution of real world income amongst the world economies. In this chapter we deal only with the effects on the current accounts and the associated financing problems.[1]

Table 8.1 shows the current accounts in 1973 and 1974 for select industrial countries and the increased burden of net oil payments for the same countries during 1974. An interesting feature of the table is that for most countries, including the OECD as a whole, the deterioration in 1974 was less than the net increase in oil payments. This is most striking in the cases of the USA and Germany. For example, the USA increased its net oil payments by some $14 billion yet her current account deteriorated by only some $2 billion. Germany's net oil payments increased by some $5 billion yet her current account actually improved by about the same amount. By contrast, the deterioration for both the UK and Italy in 1974 marginally exceeded the increased oil commitments. For all of the OECD, increased oil payments of some $55 billion substantially exceeded the deterioration in the combined current account of some $37 billion.

What happened, then, was that the OECD current account balance significantly improved in relation to other regions. For example, oil payments by the non-oil LDCs increased by about $10 billion, yet their current account deteriorated by nearly $18 billion (see Table 8.2). This shift against the non-oil LDCs is even more striking in the

Table 8.1 Current account balances OECD and impact of higher oil prices (in billions of US dollars)

Country	Current Account 1973 (1)	Current Account 1974 (2)	Change in Current Account (2)–(1) (3)	Net Increase in Oil Payments (-) 1974[a] (4)
Canada	0.1	– 1.5	– 1.6	0.8
France	–0.7	– 6.0	– 5.3	– 5.8
Germany	4.3	9.8	5.5	– 5.5
Italy	–2.7	– 8.0	– 5.3	– 4.3
Japan	–0.1	– 4.7	– 4.6	–11.0
UK	–2.6	– 8.6	– 6.0	– 5.3
USA	6.9	4.5	– 2.4	–14.3
Total OECD	9.6	–27.6	–37.2	–55.5

Source: OECD Economic Outlook (December 1978).
[a]Increased oil payments less increase in exports to OPEC in 1974 – estimates by OECD.

following year when the OECD countries, as a whole, were actually able to eliminate their 1974 deficit while, in sharp contrast, the non-oil LDCs suffered a further deterioration of some $14 billion.

Theoretical Analysis

This section will examine how, in theory, the financing of the huge current account deficits can influence world reserves, world money supply and exchange rates. We will then see how the current account deficits were actually financed during 1974 and how reality conformed to the theoretical framework.

Case 1

Our first case assumes that the whole of the OPEC surplus is held in the form of short-term liquid US government securities. We consider, to begin, the case where exchange rates are fixed.

Suppose oil-importing countries (OICs) increase their current account deficit with the OPEC countries by $60 billion. Suppose, too, that the US share of this deficit is $10 billion and that all other oil-importing countries (OOICs) only draw on reserves located in the USA (that is, they do not use Euro-dollar deposits). Then OOICs would reduce their reserves by $50 billion while OPEC countries would increase their reserves by $60 billion, so world reserves will have risen by $10 billion (the US oil deficit).

What happens to the privately held volume of money in the OICs?

Table 8.2 World current account (including official transfers) (in billions of US dollars)

	1973	*1974*	*1975*	*1976*	*1977*	*1978*
OECD	9.5	−27.5	0.3	−18.8	−27.5	− 0.8
OPEC	8.0	59.3	27.3	37.0	31.5	11.0
Non-oil LDCs	− 7.0	−24.5	−38.5	−26.0	−24.0	−34.0
Other (including discrepancies)	−10.5	− 7.3	10.9	7.8	20.0	23.8

Source: OECD Economic Outlook (December 1978).

In both the USA and the OOICs the current account deficit represents a reduction in wealth, which may take the form of a reduction in deposits or a reduction in other financial assets. For example, in the OOICs if there is no sterilisation, the associated fall in base money is the counterpart of the fall in wealth. If, however, the monetary authorities attempt to sterilise the impact on base money by purchases of government securities, the fall in wealth will manifest itself in a fall in private holdings of government securities. By contrast, in the USA the situation is different. If US residents sold short-term government securities to make the additional oil payments, then the US drop in wealth will also show up in a drop in privately held government securities, while the interest rate on government securities would be unchanged. If, however, they ran down their deposits to make the payments and OPEC then invest in US government securities (as assumed), privately held government securities would fall but the interest rate on government securities would also fall.

Suppose now, to make the case more realistic, that the OOICs sought finance from the USA and suppose that the government of each OOIC borrowed exactly enough from the USA to cover its additional oil deficits. Then reserves of OOICs would remain unchanged and world reserves would increase by $60 billion.

The outcomes would be still more complicated if we assumed that no loans were made by the USA and that OOICs' reserves were now, partly at least, withdrawn from the Euro-dollar market. Euro-banks would now call in some of their loans, so privately held world money supply would drop. At the same time, OOICs' reserves could now fall (marginally) by more than their withdrawals from the Euro-dollar market since loans could be repaid from reserve holdings.[2]

What would happen if exchange rates were flexible? Reverting to our simplest original case, the net outcome would be that the US currency would appreciate vis-à-vis OOICs to the point where the OOICs' current account deficit of $50 billion would be eliminated. The US current account deficit would increase by $60 billion (the aggregate oil deficit) and this would be offset by a matching inflow of capital represented by the OPEC investments in the US short-term capital market. The USA, in other words, would bear the burden of the whole current account deficit and world reserves would increase by $60 billion.

Case 2

Our second case assumes that OPEC countries place all their additional reserves ($60 billion) in the Euro-dollar market and that $50 billion are then diverted to OOICs exactly in proportion to their oil deficits.

OOICs initially run down their US reserves by $50 billion and OPEC countries acquire these reserves, in addition to the $10 billion reserves obtained from the USA to cover her oil deficit. The $60 billion are now placed in the Euro-market.[3] $50 billion then go to OOICs allowing them to restore their reserve position. If these borrowings from the Euro-market are by governments, which place the funds in their central banks, domestic base money would, initially, drop by the $50 billion.[4]

Suppose that the additional $10 billion placed in the Euro-dollar market are lent out to the private sector and suppose that they do not find their way into OOICs' central banks. Then, privately held money supply will have risen by $10 billion, offsetting, in part, any monetary deflation in the OICs. With OOICs' reserves unchanged and OPEC reserves up by $60 billion, world reserves will have increased by the world oil deficit.

If the additional $10 billion Euro-loans find their way into OOICs central banks, which hold them within the USA, then world reserves will have risen by $70 billion.

Case 3

Now, suppose that OPEC invest, long-term, their increased reserves in the OICs exactly in proportion to these countries' oil deficits. These long-term investments would no longer be treated as international reserves. OPEC, OOICs' and US reserves would all remain unchanged, so world reserves would be constant.

As a variation, suppose that these long-term investments are equally divided between the UK ($30 billion) and the USA ($30 billion). Suppose, too, that the UK oil deficit were $5 billion. Then OPEC reserves remain unchanged. OOICs' (less the UK) reserves are down by $45 billion. US reserves are unchanged while UK reserves rise by $25 billion ($30 billion minus $5 billion). World reserves will now have fallen by $20 billion.

By way of summary, then, it is clear that the issues are complex and depend very much on the assumptions made. The outcome will clearly depend on the weight attaching to each of the cases examined.

Table 8.3 The OPEC surplus and its disposition (in billions of US dollars)

	1974	*1977 (first half)*
Current account balance	65	17.5
Adjustment for lag between oil exports and payments	−10	0.7
Financial surplus	55	18.2
Investments in US	11.1	4.2
Bank deposits	4.2	—
Treasury securities	5.5	0.4
Other bonds	0.9	2.6
Equities	0.4	0.6
Direct loans	0.1	0.6
Investments in UK	7.2	0.6
Bank deposits (in pounds)	1.7	0.5
Government securities (in pounds)	3.6	−0.1
Equities and property (in pounds)	0.7	0.2
Direct loans (foreign currency)	1.2	—
Euro-currency bank deposits	22.8	7.3
International organisations	4.0	0.1
IMF oil facility	1.9	0.1
World bank and others	2.1	—
Grants and loans to developing countries	2.5	2.8
Direct loans to developed countries other than the USA and the UK	4.5	1.0
Other Investments, including Euro-bonds, other portfolio investments, direct investments, local currency bank deposits in countries other than the USA and the UK	3.0	2.2

Source: Morgan Guaranty Trust Company of New York, *World Financial Markets* (October 1975) and (November 1977).

Financing the Deficits – 1974

We first look at the disposition of the OPEC surplus and subsequently examine how these funds were ultimately recycled amongst the OICs. Table 8.3 shows where the OPEC surplus was invested during 1974 and, by way of contrast, the first half of 1977. Out of a financial surplus of $55 billion in 1974, about 20 per cent was invested directly in the USA, another 13 per cent was invested in the UK, while just over 40 per cent was invested in the Euro-currency market. The balance went into other developed countries (8 per cent), grants and loans to developing countries (5 per cent), multilateral aid (7 per cent) and other investments (6 per cent). The table also reveals that the

Table 8.4 Financing the current account deficits 1974 select industrial countries (in billions of US dollars)

Country	*Current Account*	*OPEC Deposits, Loans and Investments*	*Publicised Euro-currency Credits*	*Borrowings from US Banks*	*Official IMF EEC Other Governments*	*Balance on Official Settlements*	*Change in Gross Reserves*
United States	4.5	11.0	1.4	—		−8.1	1.5
Germany	9.8	0.5	—	0.3	−2.0[a]	−0.7	−0.2
United Kingdom	−8.6	6.0	5.7	0.7		−2.9	0.3
France	−6.0	1.2	3.2	0.1		−0.6	−0.1
Italy	−8.0	1.2	2.2	—	6.2[b]	−4.8	0.5
Japan	−4.7	1.0	0.2	6.0		1.4	1.3

Sources: Morgan Guaranty Trust Company of New York, *World Financial Markets* (October, 1975). Organisation for Economic Co-Operation and Development, *OECD Economic Outlook* (July, 1975). G. Pollack (1975).

[a]Bundesbank loan to Italy included in $6.2 billion for Italy.

[b]Includes borrowing from EEC Support Fund ($1.9 billion), IMF ($1.6 billion) and Bundesbank ($2 billion).

OPEC countries had a very strong preference for risk-free liquid investment: just over 50 per cent of their financial surplus was directed into bank deposits, including Euro-currency deposits, while about 70 per cent went into liquid risk-free investments. This position was largely sustained in the first half of 1977.

We now consider how the OICs managed to finance their deficits during 1974. Table 8.4 provides some data, for select industrial countries, bearing on this. Four of the countries (the UK, France, Italy and Japan) had large current account deficits reflecting in large part the (net) additional oil payments. For the UK the additional oil payments ($5.3 billion) were more than covered by direct OPEC investments ($6 billion), borrowings (chiefly government) on the Euro-currency market ($5.7 billion) and some minor borrowings from US banks. Additionally, OPEC countries increased their foreign exchange reserves in sterling by over $5 billion. On balance, UK

Table 8.5 Non-OPEC LDC external financing (in billions of US dollars)

	1973	*1974*
Gross requirements:		
Current account	– 9	–26
Amortisation of external debt	– 8½	– 9
Total requirements	–17½	–35
Gross sources:		
Official	15.1	21.2
OECD bilateral	8.5	10.3
Communist bilateral	2.1	2.3
OPEC bilateral	0.9	2.5
Multilateral development institutions (eg IBRD, IADB)	3.2	4.3
IMF drawings	0.4	1.8
International reserve changes[a]	– 8.3	– 2.8
Private direct investment (net)	3.6	3.6
Commercial credits	10.3	16.5
Eurocurrency loans	4.6	6.3
International bond issues	0.6	0.2
US bank credits (net)	1.0	4.8
Export credits[b]	4.1	5.2
Other[c]	– 3.2	– 3.5
Memorandum:		
Gross international reserves at year-end	29.5	32.3

Source: Morgan Guaranty Trust Company of New York, *World Financial Markets* (January, 1976).

[a]Minus sign indicates reserve increase.

[b]Includes suppliers credits and credits (other than Euro-loans) by non-US banks.

[c]Includes short-term capital outflows plus errors and omissions.

reserves rose marginally in 1974. France's additional oil payments ($5.8 billion) were largely covered by OPEC investments ($1.2 billion) and Euro-currency borrowings ($3.2 billion), while Italy's additional oil payments ($4.3 billion) were more than covered by OPEC investments ($1.2 billion), Euro-currency borrowings ($2.2 billion) and very large official borrowings ($6.2 billion). Japan relied very heavily on borrowings from US banks to cover a large part of her increased oil payments. To sum up, the Euro-currency market functioned efficiently in transmitting funds to deficit countries; official financing came into play, notably in the case of Italy, and finally those countries with stronger current accounts or with large inflows of OPEC money (Germany and the USA) played their part in the recycling of funds to the deficit countries.

Table 8.5 reveals that the non-oil developing countries financed their large deficits during 1974 by additional aid, some borrowings from the Euro-currency market, some official borrowing and some considerable commercial credit (notably from US banks). Reserves actually rose in 1974 although to a lesser extent than in 1973, when the high level of activity in industrial countries and the commodity price boom had combined to swell their export receipts.

Table 8.6 International reserves (end of period) (in SDRs)

	1972	*1973*	*1974*
All countries	146.84	152.61	180.47
Industrial countries	97.46	95.75	97.94
Oil-exporting countries	10.34	12.38	39.22
Western hemisphere	7.26	9.65	8.98
Other Middle East	2.61	3.50	3.89
Other Asia	7.55	8.79	10.42
Other Africa	1.96	2.22	2.42

Source: International Monetary Fund, *International Financial Statistics* (December, 1975).

Table 8.6 shows the total as well as the distribution of international reserves. Consistently with our theoretical discussion, world reserves increased substantially in 1974. OPEC reserves, however, did not increase by the full extent of their current financial surplus because some of this surplus went into aid, some was invested long and some again was invested in financial markets outside the USA and the UK.[5]

Later Developments – 1975–1978

Three developments since 1974 are worthy of note. First, the rate at which the OPEC current account surplus fell between 1974 and 1978 (see Table 8.2). For example, whereas this surplus was of the order of $60 billion in 1974, it had, against all expectations, dropped to around $10 billion by 1978. Several factors combined to bring about this result. One factor was the rate at which the OPEC countries increased their imports. This was due, in part, to their high absorptive capacity and, in part, again, to the fall in OPEC terms of trade (by something like 20 per cent, between 1974 and 1978). Still another factor was the slowdown in the growth of imports by the OICs. There were three reasons for this: the recession in the years that followed, the conservation measures and the increased availability of oil outside the OPEC (from the North Sea, Mexico and Alaska).

Second, the recycling process continued to be efficient after 1974. One major original source for concern was the enlarged indebtedness of the non-oil LDCs and the implications of this for their ultimate solvency and for their real growth. In the event, most of these countries were, in fact, able to finance their current account deficits but their external debt (net of international reserves) as a percentage of GNP did increase significantly. For example, for twenty non-OPEC LDCs it rose from about 13 per cent in 1973/74 to around 18 per cent in 1977/78.[6]

Third, following the Iranian crisis in 1978, a significant new situation had begun to develop. In 1979 the price of oil increased by at least 50 per cent. This was expected to lead to an increase of some $30–$50 billion in the OPEC surplus, with financial implications similar to those previously discussed. While this increase was very much more moderate than the 1974 increase, the world environment had, in the interim, become more precarious and more delicately poised while the level of indebtedness, notably of the non-oil LDCs, had now deteriorated further.

Notes for Chapter 8

1 The effects on inflation and unemployment are dealt with in Chapters 15, 17 and 18. The effects on real income and consumption are dealt with briefly in Chapter 32.

2 This, of course, is the reverse of the case where reserves are placed in Euro-markets when world reserves may multiply. See Chapter 7.

3 In what follows we simplify by abstracting from cash holdings of Euro-banks.

4 The original current account deficit would reduce base money by $50 billion but the borrowings would not increase base money. The central bank balance sheet would show an increase in government deposits and a matching increase in its reserves. On balance, central bank reserves would be unchanged but liabilities to the banking system would be down by $50 billion while liabilities to the government sector would be up by $50 billion.

5 A number of financial agreements were negotiated by the oil-importing countries

to facilitate the recycling and financing of oil generated deficits. For details of the IMF oil facility (which lapsed in 1976 when Fund quotas were raised), the EEC Plan and the $25 billion OECD Financial Support Fund see: Bank for International Settlements, *Annual Report* (1975); Organisation for Economic Co-Operation and Development, *OECD Observer* (March–April, 1975).

6 Morgan Guaranty Trust Company of New York, *World Financial Markets* (May 1979), p. 8.

Chapter 9

Deficiencies of the IMF System and Reasons for its Collapse

Introduction

This chapter examines the deficiencies of the IMF system and the reasons why it ultimately collapsed. It will also serve to summarise many of the points already made in previous chapters.

It is useful to distinguish five reasons for the collapse of the IMF. These are (1) the failure of the exchange rate adjustment mechanism, (2) the asymmetries in the system, (3) the difficulties associated with the provision for the secular growth in reserves, (4) the importance of capital flows and the constraints they placed on monetary independence and (5) the increasing global instability. In essence, then, the system collapsed because of its inherent deficiencies (the first four reasons) and, most importantly, because it became increasingly exposed to stresses which made it difficult to function effectively.

The Failure of Adjustment

The failure of exchange rate adjustment in the years 1949 to 1967–69 can be attributed to two factors. First, there were the ambiguities and weaknesses in the original Articles of Agreement. These, as we saw, did not define the concept of 'fundamental disequilibrium';[1] nor did they provide real pressures, particularly on surplus countries, to bring about exchange rate changes.[2] Second, there was the, de facto, failure to adjust (within the spirit of the IMF system) in the face of emerging evidence of fundamental disequilibria. Examples would be the UK by 1963/64, Germany and Japan by 1967/68 and, possibly, France in the mid-1960s. A case could also be made for the view that the USA, despite its special position in the world monetary order, was in fundamental disequilibrium by the early-mid 1960s.

The major sources of imbalances, then, were Japan and West Germany on the one hand, with strong currencies, and the UK and the USA on the other, with weak currencies. Japan and Germany, with strong entrenched interests in their export sectors and a belief in the 'virtuous circle' of export-led growth, were hesitant to force a structural adjustment away from their export and import-competing sectors by a revaluation and were content to allow their international reserves to rise.

On the other side, the USA and the UK hesitated to devalue for reasons that were far more complex. In the case of the UK massive financial assistance helped postpone the decision to devalue. In both cases, considerations of national pride, no doubt, played a part. There were, too, unique problems associated with a devaluation of a reserve currency. With reserves held in the devalued currency falling in value, countries might become more hesitant about holding reserves in that currency, prompting potentially destabilising shifts out of those currencies.[3]

The case of the USA was special for a number of reasons. First, the USA could, de jure, initiate a change in its par value by unilaterally changing the price of gold. The rest of the world would then be left to determine whether their intervention points in respect of the US dollar would be changed. If, for example, the rest of the world chose to retain their intervention points in the face of an official dollar devaluation, then the rest of the world would have effectively devalued (changed their par value) vis-à-vis gold in the same proportion as the US dollar, and the USA would not have succeeded in securing a change in its currency vis-à-vis the rest of the world. Second, as we have seen, there were many objections raised to a rise in the official price of gold. Third, with US deficits the principal means (until 1970) by which new international reserves were being created, any exchange rate adjustment that effectively eliminated the deficits could have left the world with a reserve shortage. Fourth, so long as there was little pressure on her gold stocks the USA was, in any case, largely free from the discipline imposed on a deficit country to take corrective measures.

The Asymmetries of the IMF System

There were also a number of asymmetries in the IMF system.[4] First, there were the asymmetries associated with the scope, and initiative, for exchange rate changes and with the maintenance of exchange margins. With the US as the principal intervention currency and intervention points determined in relation to the US dollar, the maximum possible change in the US dollar vis-à-vis another currency was effectively half the change possible between any two non-dollar currencies. Trivial as this point might appear, it had, in fact, become a source of some irritation to the USA. Also, while most of the rest of the world met their obligations on exchange rate margins by buying and selling their intervention currency (notably the dollar) in the foreign exchange markets, the USA met its obligation (until 1971) by buying and selling gold in exchange for dollar reserves. In effect, then, the USA played a predominantly passive role in securing the exchange margins for the US dollar vis-à-vis other currencies.

Second, there tended to be more pressure, potentially, on deficit countries than on surplus countries to initiate exchange rate changes and, with the US dollar at the centre of the system, this could create a devaluation bias against the US dollar.[5]

Third, with the failure of the exchange rate adjustment mechanism, more of the adjustment burden fell on demand management policies and direct import controls. The charge was made that with deficit countries having to do most of the adjusting a 'deflationary bias' would be injected into the world economy while the use of direct import controls would have an adverse effect on the allocation of world resources. The UK admirably illustrates the kinds of strains that developed. Determined to defend an exchange rate that had become inappropriate, the UK was forced, periodically, to resort to import restrictions and to deflationary measures which, on occasion, created stagnating conditions and growing unemployment. But, at the other extreme, West Germany, anxious to keep its own rate of inflation below the rate prevailing in the rest of the industrial world, and, at the same time, determined to hold the exchange rate, was intermittently threatened with imported inflation.

Fourth, there was the asymmetry associated with the reserve currency role of the dollar. The principal charge here was that the USA was in a privileged position in that it could extract benefits, from the official use of the US dollar, in the form of seignorage.[6] This seignorage accrues to the issuer of a currency when the resources obtained by the issuer exceed the cost of producing the currency. To illustrate, consider the case of one year's deficit which is liquidated after *n* years. Then, the present value of the future net returns on that deficit can be presented as:

$$S=\left[\frac{RI-r-c}{1+d}+\frac{RI-r-c}{(1+d)^2}+\ldots+\frac{RI-r+c}{(1+d)^n}\right]DU$$

where S is the present value, RI is the return on investment overseas by the USA, r is the interest payment on obligations, c represents the costs per annum of administering the reserve currency system, d is the discount rate, n is the redemption year and DU is the deficit.[7]

In the simplest case where $n \rightarrow \infty$ and $c=0$, the present value is $[(RI-r)/d]\,DU$. Alternatively, the annual flow benefit accruing to the USA would be $(RI-r)\Sigma DU$ (that is, the net interest differential earned on that year's reserve liability – which is the sum of all previous deficits).

The benefits, therefore, are represented, basically, as due to the difference between the rate of interest the reserve country pays on its obligations and the long rate it can earn by investing overseas. In other words, the seignorage accruing to the USA stems essentially from its role as a financial intermediary in the transmission of funds. Consider, as an extreme case, a 5 per cent differential in interest rates. Then, at the end of 1976, when US reserve liabilities amounted to about $92 billion the benefit to the USA would have been of the order of about 0.3 per cent of GNP. On the other hand, in sharp contrast, it may be contended that in a highly competitive market these net benefits would be very small, since they would effectively be arbitraged away, with the differential covering operating costs only.[8]

Whatever these benefits, there may, at the same time, be some costs borne by the issuer of a reserve currency. The contention here is that a reserve centre does not have the freedom to use the exchange rate as a method of adjustment and that, in general, it has fewer instruments of policy than a non-reserve centre.[9] For example, in so far as a reserve centre has a balance of payments target, it may, in the face of a persistent deficit, have to endure some deflation or it may have to take second best measures to alleviate the situation. The argument is almost certainly of considerable importance for the UK. It has, however, somewhat less significance for the USA. There are only two possible instances (in 1960/61 and in 1970) when US policy may have been somewhat more restrictive than was required by domestic conditions. On the other hand, for the USA, the proliferation of measures restricting capital outflows may not have been a 'first best'. Moreover, the holders of dollar reserves (especially on the Continent) had, by the mid-late 1960s, begun to exercise some political leverage over the USA.

We must conclude, therefore, that whatever the social benefits, in terms of status and prestige, the material benefits flowing from a reserve currency are probably, on balance, fairly negligible.[10]

Providing for the Secular Growth in Reserves

Another difficulty associated with the IMF system was the lack of a systematic method for providing for the longer-run growth in global reserves. This issue was, as we have seen, the principal preoccupation of the negotiations that took place in the mid-1960s. These came to a head with the creation of SDRs, which were then activated in 1970. SDRs, however, in themselves did not permit a controlled growth in world reserves. The principal continuing problem resided in the fact that there was no control over the creation of other sources of reserves. For example, with an inconvertible dollar, after 1971, there was even less constraint on dollar creation. Moreover, the low return and method of valuation of SDRs acted to constrain the acceptance of SDRs as the principal reserve asset.

The role of gold, too, as a reserve asset had become increasingly ambiguous. With the two-tier market in operation after 1968 the true valuation of gold became an issue. As the price advantage in the free market started growing, central banks increasingly hoarded their gold rather than trade it at the relatively low official price. The gold component of reserves, therefore, had become effectively frozen.

Capital Mobility

Another important reason for the collapse of the IMF system had to do with the mobility of capital. As we saw, after 1958, barriers to the free movement of capital were relaxed. Furthermore, the growth of the multi-nationals and the Euro-dollar markets meant that huge sums were available to move from one country to another in search of profit. Any suggestion, therefore, that a currency was overvalued (undervalued) tended to trigger the movement of huge sums out of (into) that currency. These 'speculative flows' made it increasingly difficult for central banks to hold the line on exchange rates. It also made it difficult for industrial countries to maintain relatively independent monetary policies. An attempt to set interest rates above (below) world levels, for example, would tend to result in the movement of capital into (out of) the country.

Many developed countries, as we saw, experienced difficulties of this kind in the years 1968–71. In 1968/69, for example, when interest rates were very high in the USA, the huge outflows of capital from Europe made it difficult for these countries to hold their interest rates down. In 1970/71, when US interest rates were very low and European interest rates were relatively high, capital flooded into these countries, expanding their money supply and frustrating, in varying degrees, their attempts to implement relatively restrictive policies. Despite a growing resort in those years to restrictions on capital movements as a means of attaining greater independence for monetary policy, it proved extremely difficult to regulate the flow of funds across nations.

Global Instability

Finally, it is possible to argue that, apart from inherent deficiencies in the system, it had come under increasing stress because of increased divergence in economic conditions as well as increased global instability. Interest differentials rose sharply in the late 1960s and early 1970s; there were huge reversals in reserve movements; reserve growth was very large and unprecedented in the early 1970s; wage explosions erupted in several countries in the late 1960s and early 1970s; the upsurge in inflation in these years added to the difficulties; the commodity price boom in 1972/73 and, most important of all, the oil price shock in 1974 dealt the final blows to the system.

Notes for Chapter 9

1 This looseness emerged as a compromise between the Keynes and White views.

2 Despite the scarce currency provision, which was, in any case, never invoked.

3 Given the weakness of the dollar, the UK also hesitated to devalue out of fear that pressures would then be diverted to the dollar. The events in early 1968 bear this out.

4 For a discussion of these asymmetries see: M. Posner (1972); R. Cooper (1972); M. v. Whitman (1974).

5 For a discussion of this issue see S. Katz (1972).

6 This was sometimes put in the form that the USA was able to finance its long-term investments and its defence expenditures overseas (its so-called imperialist role) by effectively borrowing short from the rest of the world. The literature on seignorage is very large. See: J. Karlik (1968); W. Salant (1964); H. Grubel (1964); R. Aliber (1964); B. Cohen (1971); H. Goldstein (1965); H. Grubel (1972); E. Kirschen (1974); R. Cooper (1975).

7 This follows H. Grubel (1972).

8 Indeed, the only net benefit might then be the USA would be in a position to hold fewer reserve assets with the dollar as a reserve currency.

9 Of course, in so far as non-reserve centres did not use the exchange rate instrument this argument would not hold. The argument would not, of course, hold for a reserve centre whose currency is inconvertible (for example, in the case of a pure dollar standard).

10 Seignorage apart, there was also the argument that the USA, as a substantial debtor to the rest of the world, was in a position where it could impose an 'inflation tax' on its official and private holders of the US dollar. For example, if the USA inflated its currency at a rate that was unanticipated (so that it was not fully reflected in the interest rate) there would be some real losses imposed on these foreign holders. These benefits would be very small again, but, in any event, it is difficult to believe that the USA would deliberately impose this tax as an instrument of policy.

Chapter 10

Reforms and Reform Discussions – Mark II: 1968 to 1978

Background

Whereas official negotiations on reform in the earlier period focused very largely on alternative methods of providing additional liquidity, now, as the crises deepened, these negotiations were increasingly directed at more comprehensive reform of the international monetary system. Two distinct phases in these new negotiations can be identified. An earlier phase was largely concerned with correcting the weaknesses of the Bretton Woods Agreement while, at the same time, preserving the par value system. By late 1973, however, and particularly after the oil price shock, when it became evident that a par value regime was no longer viable, attention began to focus on 'how to live' with managed floats, on developing rules of the game in the new environment and on resolving a number of problems carried over from the previous regime.

In January 1969 the Executive Directors of the IMF agreed to a thoroughgoing review of the exchange rate adjustment mechanism and in September 1970 they produced a first Report.[1] This Report explored three proposals for reform of the exchange rate regime: (1) quicker and possibly smaller adjustments in par value, (2) wider margins and (3) 'transitional floating' as a means of establishing a new par value. The Report favoured the first, reached no agreement on the second but treated the third with some sympathy.

Deliberations continued within the IMF and in August 1972 the IMF released its study on the Reform of the International Monetary System.[2] This study was broader than the 1970 Report, dealing now not only with the exchange rate mechanism but also with much broader issues. These included the question of convertibility and the settlement of imbalances, the role of various assets in reserves, the problem of disequilibrating capital movements and reform in relation to the developing world. The Report was more concerned with spelling out the available options than with putting forward firm proposals for reform.[3]

One of the decisions taken at the Smithsonian Agreement was that negotiations should be undertaken to review ways of reforming the international monetary system. To give effect to that decision the Governors of the IMF created the Committee of Twenty (C20) in July 1972; the membership of this Committee was broader than the Group of Ten,[4] now including representation from the less developed areas. The ground that was to be covered by the C20 was very much the same as that encompassed by the 1972 IMF Report.

The Deliberations of the C20 and the Negotiating Stances

In evaluating the deliberations of the C20 and the stances adopted by individual countries, it is useful to distinguish three negotiating blocs. The first was the USA, the second was Europe and Japan and the third was the LDCs.[5]

The key to the US stance was its emphasis on a symmetrical system of adjustment. To give effect to that it proposed a reserve indicator system, under which countries would be subject to increasing pressures to adjust as their reserves progressively passed certain defined points. The precise form of adjustment would be left to the discretion of the individual country, although the USA had a definite preference for the prompt and frequent use of the exchange rate. Refusals to adjust outside the prescribed limits would invite sanctions of various kinds: suggestions here included the loss of a scheduled SDR allocation, discrimination against the country's exports (the activation of the scarce currency clause) or a tax on excessive reserve holdings. This emphasis by the USA on symmetrical adjustment reflected its view that the principal weakness of the IMF system was the lack of adjustment by the surplus countries which had forced the USA into continuous deficits.

To the USA, too, symmetry in adjustment also meant that she should have the same capacity to initiate par value changes, as well as the same margin of flexibility (see pp. 99–100).

It is most interesting to note that the US emphasis on greater exchange rate flexibility, reserve indicators and symmetry in adjustment parallels Keynes's position at the Bretton Woods negotiations. The irony is that in those negotiations the USA was advancing the cause of the prospective surplus country, while within the C20 she was now pleading the cause of a country persistently in deficit (which Britain had expected to be after the war).

The USA did not oppose, in principle, the return to on-demand convertibility but took the view that convertibility would have to be placed under some constraint (for instance, if dollar holdings went outside certain limits) and would, in any event, only be feasible again when the US balance of payments had improved. The USA aimed at a surplus not only as a condition for the restoration of convertibility but also as a means of creating jobs, removing controls over capital exports, and relieving herself of the irritations and pressures originating in Europe. The USA also opposed mandatory asset settlement, which would have required the USA to settle all its payments deficits in reserve assets other than the dollar, and any scheme that involved the removal of the dollar as a reserve currency (for example, by replacing the dollar overhang with SDRs). Finally, the USA opposed the proposal to link the distribution of SDRs with aid, which would have given a larger share of any new allocation of SDRs to the LDCs than an allocation based on Fund quotas (the so-called 'link' proposal).

There was considerable common ground in the negotiating stance of Europe and Japan, although there were, of course, notable differences in the vigour with which certain views were held. In general, this bloc was less favourable to exchange rate flexibility, continuing to lean towards an adjustable peg regime. France and Japan (as well as Austria and Belgium) were particularly averse to flexible rates. France, indeed, had a long history of attachment to a fixed rate regime, based on gold, while Japan favoured a regime that had, in fact, served it well in the past and had allowed it (and it was thought would continue to allow it) to maintain an undervalued currency. Europe tended, therefore, to place more emphasis on demand management than on exchange rate management in the adjustment process. At the same time, she (notably Germany) wanted a monetary order which encouraged discipline against irresponsible financial policies leading to excessive inflation (for instance, of the kind that led to the vast expansion of global reserves in 1970–72). Europe, and particularly France, wanted to remove the privileged role of the USA in the monetary order. To give effect to this it favoured restoration of convertibility and asset settlement and supported the ultimate removal of all reserve assets and their replacement by SDRs. She also opposed the reserve indicator system, partly on technical grounds but also because she saw it as a means by which the USA would be securing adjustment by the rest of the world rather than by herself. Finally (with the exception of Germany), she supported the link proposal.

The LDCs pressed very hard for implementation of the link proposal. They also favoured relatively fixed exchange rates (on grounds that may not have been very rational)[6] and freedom of reserve composition, hence opposing moves to consolidate reserves. So in some respects (the link and fixed rates), they tended to follow Europe and Japan while, in one other at least (reserve composition), they took the US line.

It is also worth stressing that there was some common ground among all blocs: first, the universal recognition of the advantages of multilateral co-operation and consultation; second, that SDRs should play a larger role in the future monetary order as a reserve asset and in securing the growth in global reserve needs; third, that vast movements of short-term capital across frontiers were destabilising and needed to be offset or controlled in some ways; fourth, that trade should be liberal and that competitive exchange rate policies should be avoided; and fifth, that in an environment where exchange rates had become more flexible countries ought to ensure that the fluctuations in exchange rates were not 'undue' or 'excessive'.

The international environment had begun to change dramatically by early 1973 just as negotiations were warming up. While the negotiators were preoccupied with the reconstruction of a new par value regime, by early 1974 such a regime had, in fact, proved unworkable for some time. The C20 published their report in June 1974.[7]

Part I of the Report reviewed the principal features of a reconstructed system, expressing a belief that 'the exchange rate mechanism will remain based on stable but adjustable par values and countries should not make inappropriate par value changes'. It examined the adjustment mechanism, convertibility, consolidation and the management of currency reserves, the role of primary reserve assets and the link proposal. These were areas in which there continued to be disagreement, as we have seen.

Part II outlined the immediate steps that the Committee agreed should be taken. The principal actions recommended, and officially endorsed, were:[8]

(1) the creation of an Interim Committee to advise the Board of Governors of the IMF on continuing reform of the system (in effect, to carry on the unfinished work of the C20 which ceased to exist after June 1974);
(2) the adoption of guidelines for floating;[9]
(3) a new method of valuation of the SDR and of determining the interest rate on the SDR.

The last change was designed to make the SDR more attractive both as a reserve asset and as a numeraire in the world economy, as a step towards placing it at the centre of the new monetary order.

Until then, the SDR had been based on gold, one SDR being equal to 1/35th of an ounce of gold. There were several reasons why this had now become inappropriate. The official price of gold had changed twice since (in December 1971 and in February 1973) while, at the same time, there continued to be large differences between the official and market price of gold, creating some uncertainty about the 'true' value of the SDR. There was, too, a general desire to de-emphasise the role of gold in the international monetary system. Also, with widespread floating the value of the SDR (its purchasing power) in terms of all currencies became increasingly volatile and uncertain. The (interim) solution adopted was to value the SDR in terms of a 'basket' of sixteen currencies.[10] One SDR would now be equal to the sum of the following currency components:

US dollar	0.40	Belgian franc	1.6
Deutsche mark	0.38	Swedish krona	0.13
Pound sterling	0.045	Australian dollar	0.012
French franc	0.44	Danish krone	0.11
Japanese yen	26	Norwegian krone	0.099
Canadian dollar	0.071	Spanish peseta	1.1
Italian lira	47	Austrian schilling	0.22
Netherlands guilder	0.14	South African rand	0.0082

The implied weights attaching to each currency were intended to reflect the commercial and the financial importance of the currency: for example, the US dollar carried a weight of 33 per cent, the German mark a weight of 12.5 per cent, the pound sterling a weight of 9 per cent, and the French franc and Japanese yen each a weight of 7.5 per cent, with other currencies sharing a weight of about 30 per cent.[11]

At the same time, with rising market interest rates in the industrial countries, the interest rate on SDRs of 1½ per cent had also become inappropriate. Hence, it was decided that the interest rate on SDRs would now be a weighted average of short-term interest rates in the USA, Germany, the UK, France and Japan with the same relative weights for each of these countries as in the 'basket'. The precise formula is complicated. At the time, the interest rate on the SDR was raised to 5 per cent. Then the weighted average for the five countries was 10 per cent. So long as this average remained in the 9–11 per cent range there would be no change in the interest rate on the SDR. If the average fell below 9 per cent, the interest rate on the SDR would adjust downward by three-fifths of the shortfall, while if it rose above 11 per cent the interest rate would adjust upward by three-fifths of the excess.

This decision to hold the interest rate on SDRs below a weighted average of the interest rates in five major centres effectively means that countries designated by the IMF continue to be penalised by losing on interest earnings while countries that are net users continue to be effectively subsidised. The reason, it will be recalled, is that the users pay interest only on the short fall below allocation; the cost to them, then, is less than the cost of running down, say, US dollar reserves. By contrast, countries designated earn an interest rate on their excess holdings that is below the interest rate on the foreign exchange they have to give up.[12]

A Reformed Par Value Regime

We have already outlined, in earlier chapters, the major weaknesses of the old system. Negotiations in the years 1971–74 were aimed at comprehensive reform to remove those specific weaknesses. We now indicate the elements of a reformed par value system, drawing on the work of the C20 and the literature associated with their deliberations.

First, a reformed system would have provided for symmetrical adjustment based on presumptive or mandatory objective indicators. A considerable literature developed over the use of objective indicators.[13] Four types of objective indicators were widely discussed. The first was some variation of a member's reserve position (or changes in its position). The second was the cyclically adjusted basic balance. The third was the position of the spot or forward rate. The fourth was based on relative rates of inflation (purchasing power parity).[14]

There are at least five problems posed by a reserve indicator. First, how to define a norm (or target range) for each member country. There are big differences between countries in their reserve positions in relation to their reserve needs, however measured. For example, Germany has a relatively strong reserve position while the UK has a relatively weak reserve position. How would these historical-institutional differences be taken into account? Clearly, too, different measures of reserve needs (for example, imports, past imbalances and their volatility, money supply) would yield different indications of reserve adequacy. Second, the possibilities of disguising true reserve positions (for example, by offical borrowing or by, say, requiring changes in net foreign exchange holdings of the commercial banks). To overcome some of these possibilities reserve positions may have to be defined in terms of the net official foreign asset position or in terms of the net foreign asset position of the banking system as a whole. Third, there are the risks of disruptive speculative capital flows as limits were approached. Fourth, the distinct possibility that in a highly integrated world very large movements in reserves need not be associated with changes in underlying economic conditions (for instance, when financial conditions change). Fifth, there is the problem of translating a situation of 'excessive' or 'deficient' reserves into an appropriate exchange rate package that will return the country to a normal position.

Basic balance indicators and purchasing power parity indicators are intended to capture longer-run economic conditions. The basic balance is a 'flow' indicator and there would be a need to indicate a time horizon over which sustained deviations from a basic balance norm would require adjustment. Moreover, if the basic balance and reserve indicators point in conflicting directions (for instance, because there are more than offsetting trends in the short-term capital account), the issues may be difficult to resolve. As for purchasing power parity indicators, their principal limitations are discussed in subsequent chapters to which the reader is referred.[15]

A spot or forward rate that was consistently at its 'ceiling' or 'floor' would be suggestive of a need for a change in the par value. This assumes no intervention within the band or manipulation of reserves to avoid (or assist in) reaching the limits. Indeed, the last four objections to reserve indicators would also apply to exchange rate indicators.

In general, then, we can sum up by saying that a single objective indicator tends to be too simplistic; if a single objective indicator were used, if exchange rate changes were the principal means of adjustment and, moreover, if these changes were mandatory, the risks of disruptive speculation might be serious. This argues for a more eclectic approach, drawing on all the available information and allowing more flexibility in the form of adjustment.

One matter that emerged from the deliberations was that if a par value system was to function efficiently there must be reasonable stability in the underlying economic conditions. Policy co-ordination, the absence of large disruptive changes in financial conditions, as well as exogenous shocks were seen as minimal conditions for the survival of a par value system.

Second, the reformed par value system would have elevated the SDR to the status of (1) the numeraire for the establishment of par values and (2) the principal reserve asset as well as the principal source of growth in global reserves.

Par values would be expressed in terms of the SDR. In turn the valuation of the SDR would be based, say, on a basket of currencies (as above). To ensure symmetry in the treatment of reserve centres and the rest of the world, mandatory asset settlement would be introduced. The total of reserve currencies would be fixed at a point in time and thenceforth settlements would be in other reserve assets (gold, SDRs and reserve positions in the IMF). The USA would thus be subject to the same discipline as non-reserve centres, adding to its reserves when it was in surplus and losing reserves when it was in deficit.[16]

Asset settlement would have the additional advantage that it would greatly facilitate the control over the growth in international reserves through SDR creation. A disadvantage is that it restricts the freedom of monetary authorities to hold additional reserve currencies.

A more radical scheme, which would eliminate all possibilities of destabilising shifts between reserve assets and provide even greater control over the growth in international reserves, would be the mandatory replacement of all other reserve assets by SDRs. This would be achieved through the creation of a Substitution Account in the IMF that would buy those reserve assets in exchange for a special issue of SDRs.[17] This arrangement would, however, restrict even further the freedom of monetary authorities to hold their preferred portfolio of reserve assets.

Assuming SDRs would not be privately held (as now), monetary authorities would normally continue to need to hold currencies for intervention. These, however, need only be minimal working balances. Moreover, they need not be restricted to dollars. With the SDR as the numeraire, intervention to maintain parities could be in multiple currencies.

All these reforms, or their somewhat less radical version, would ensure not only that the USA was subject to some discipline in adjustment but also that the USA could both initiate par value changes and enjoy the same margin of flexibility as other currencies.[18]

Third, the reformed par value system would have attempted to restore some degree, at least, of monetary independence and to offset or recycle disruptive movements of capital. Wide margins around par values could have provided some degree of monetary autonomy; while disruptive capital movements would have had to be countered by (1) tighter controls, (2) recycling and (3) sterilisation. Moreover, it was thought that if exchange rates adjusted promptly and reflected underlying economic conditions, hot money flows might be minimised.

The Second Amendment to the IMF Articles of Agreement

The Interim Committee continued the discussions on reform. Those negotiations reached a head in the Jamaica Agreement in January 1976, which endorsed draft amendments to the IMF Articles of Agreement. The Second Amendment, as these came to be called,[19] came into effect in March 1978. Those amendments and associated documents/agreements embrace several aspects.[20]

Under the new provisions, members may follow any one of several exchange rate arrangements. They may, for example, float or they may maintain the value of their currency in terms of the SDR or some other denominator, but not in terms of gold. Thus floating is finally legalised in the new Articles while gold, which was the numeraire under the old Articles, is now dethroned. Members, too, have an obligation to promote stable exchange rates by fostering orderly underlying economic, financial and monetary conditions. There is also a provision to restore a par value system, if endorsed by an 85 per cent weighted majority.

The most interesting innovations deal with IMF surveillance and exchange rate policies. The new Article 10 provides that the IMF shall 'exercise firm surveillance over the exchange rate policies of members and shall adopt specific principles for the guidance of all members with respect to these policies'. Following extended deliberations, a document setting out the Principles and Procedures for Surveillance was approved in April 1977 and came into effect in March 1978. This replaced the older guidelines for floating.

Members have an obligation to provide the IMF with information required for surveillance and to consult with the IMF on exchange rate policies. There are three principles for the guidance of members. Principle A provides that 'a member shall avoid manipulating exchange rates or the international monetary system in order to prevent effective balance of payments adjustment or to gain an unfair competitive advantage over other members'. Principle B provides that 'a member should intervene in the exchange market if necessary to counter disorderly conditions which may be characterized inter alia by disruptive short-term movements in the exchange value of its currency'. Principle C provides that in their intervention policies, members 'should take into account' the interests of other members.

There are also principles for the guidance of the IMF in its evaluation of a member's exchange rate policies. Five indicators are put forward as possible pointers 'to an inappropriate exchange rate policy: protracted intervention in one direction in the exchange market, undue official or quasi-official borrowing, restrictions on, or incentives for, current and capital transactions, the use of monetary/financial policies to stimulate or discourage capital flows, exchange rate behaviour that appears to be unrelated to underlying economic and financial conditions including factors affecting competitiveness and long-term capital movements'.

These indicators are intended to be merely suggestive; firmer conclusions would need to wait on a more careful study by the IMF. Clearly, the exercise would be a most difficult one. If, however, the Managing Director is not satisfied that a member's exchange rate policies are appropriate he is required to formally advise the Executive Board.

Under the new provisions, too, the official price of gold was abolished, allowing member countries to write up their gold reserves to market values. This decision was inevitable since, with the free market price many times the official price (of $42.2 an ounce after February 1973), there were no transactions at the official price. Already in November 1973 the 1968 Agreement prohibiting the sale of gold in the private market had terminated and members were then free to sell gold on the private market so long as the free price remained above the official price.[21] It was this decision that had effectively ended the dual price. In June 1974, too, a decision had been taken to allow countries in balance of payments difficulties to pledge their gold stocks at free market prices as backing for foreign loans.[22]

Also, one-sixth of the Fund's own holdings of gold (amounting to some 25 million ounces) was to be sold in the free market for the benefit of the less developed countries, while another one-sixth was to be sold back at the official price to members in proportion to their quotas. Certain obligations by members to use gold in transactions with the Fund were eliminated.[23] Over a two-year period, action to peg the price of gold was prohibited while the total stock of gold in the hands of the Fund and the Group of Ten countries would not be allowed to increase (the latter to prevent joint action to push up the price of gold or support its price in a weak market).

Do these decisions and developments bearing on gold effectively demonetise gold in the international monetary order? The dethronement of gold as the numeraire, the large fluctuations in the price of gold which effectively diminish its role as a liquid reserve asset, the sales of gold and the termination of transactions in gold, all point in that direction. On the other hand, the restitution of gold, the freedom to transact officially in gold, the abolition of the gold price and the revaluation of gold in reserves go some way towards reinstating gold in the monetary system. On balance, though, it is probably true that concrete steps have now been taken which may ultimately have the effect of demonetising gold.

The Second Amendment also provided for changes in the role and characteristics of the SDR. The changes here are intended to contribute to the objective of making the SDR the 'principal reserve asset' in the international monetary system. The method of valuing the SDR may be determined by the Fund with a weighted 85 per cent majority approving. The regulations surrounding the uses of SDRs are now much freer. Members may now add to their SDRs without designation and may sell SDRs without showing a balance of payments need. This means members will now be relatively free to trade in SDRs by mutual agreement and, thus, will be able to alter the composition of their reserves if they so wish. The Fund may also broaden the categories of other holders of SDRs but these must continue to be official entities. The SDR also now replaces gold in many of the functions previously assumed by the latter.

Despite these provisions, the SDR is still a very long way from being the 'principal reserve asset'; its effective rate of return remains relatively low, while in 1978 it represented only a tiny proportion of total reserves (about 3 per cent). In the absence of large future allocations or a scheme to replace reserve currencies by SDRs, it is difficult to see how this objective of the new Articles is to be realised.[24]

Notes for Chapter 10

1 IMF (1970b).
2 IMF (1972).
3 It did, however, put forward new ideas on asset settlement and on the substitution of reserve currencies and gold for SDRs. See J. Williamson (1977), pp. 61–6.
4 The C20 was a Ministerial Committee. There was also a committee at deputy level, charged with formulating proposals for review by the Ministerial Committee.
5 J. Williamson (1977), Chapter 4. Williamson also identified a bloc whom he calls the 'heretics', made up of Canada, South Africa and Australia.
6 R. Cooper (1975); J. Williamson (1977), pp. 92–3.
7 IMF (1974a).
8 The establishment of an oil facility also came out of the work of the C20. The arrangements involved borrowing the equivalent of 2.8 billion SDRs for the period ending December 1975.
9 See also Chapter 26.
10 For a discussion of the alternative methods of valuing SDRs, see J. Polak (1974).
11 From June 1978 Iran and Saudi Arabia were included in the basket, while Denmark and South Africa were dropped. The weights were also changed (for example, the UK's share dropping from 9 per cent to 7½ per cent).
12 K. Chrystal (1978) argues that if capital markets were perfect and the interest rate on the SDR were also the same as the market interest rate the SDR stock would be irrelevant, except to those LDCs who would find it difficult to borrow at market rates. In other words, a market interest rate on SDRs would correct the asymmetry between 'users' and 'designated' but since at that rate, by assumption, most countries could borrow in international capital markets the cost would be the same as using SDRs; hence SDRs would become irrelevant.
13 IMF (1974a), pp. 24–30; J. Williamson (1977); T. Underwood (1973); U. Sacchetti (1972).
14 This was an early proposal by the German Council of Experts. See T. Underwood (1973), p. 108.
15 See Chapter 20.
16 The mechanics of such a scheme are lucidly described in IMF (1972), Chapter 3.
17 For a discussion of this proposal, which in late 1979 was being seriously negotiated see: *IMF Survey*, March 19, 1979; D. M. Sobol (1979); Morgan Guaranty Trust Company, *World Financial Markets* (September 1979); IMF (1974a), pp. 41–2. The objective of the proposed scheme is to neutralise some part of the 'dollar overhang' and so prevent official shifts out of the US dollar, which might destabilise currency markets.
18 For a discussion of this see: IMF (1974a), pp. 31–3; J. Williamson (1977), pp. 80–2, 126–30, 192–4.
19 The First Amendment was made in 1969 when the SDR scheme was adopted.
20 See *IMF Survey*, April 3, 1978. See also the articles by J. Gold (1978a, b, c) and E. M. Bernstein *et al.* (1976).

21 In fact, they did not sell on any large scale, presumably partly out of fear of lowering the price in a relatively thin market but also because they wished to hold on to their gold reserves.

22 Italy exercised this option soon afterwards.

23 Under the new provisions on quotas, members now have the option to pay the entire increase in their own currency or 25 per cent of the increase in SDRs or in the currencies of other members specified.

24 Two recent changes should be briefly noted. First, in January 1979 the interest rate on the SDR was increased from 60 per cent to 80 per cent of the weighted interest rates. Second, new SDR allocations of SDR 4 billion were to be made in each of the three years 1979, 1980 and 1981.

Part Two

The Analytical Framework for an Open Economy

Chapter 11

A Neo-Keynesian Model of Aggregate Demand and Aggregate Supply

Introduction

The aim of the first three chapters in this part is to underpin the theoretical framework for much of the analysis that follows in the subsequent chapters. This chapter presents a model that is basically neo-Keynesian in spirit while the two chapters that follow present models which, by contrast, are monetarist in spirit. These three chapters together serve to provide a representative sample of the kinds of macro-models that have been variously used in the postwar years. Chapter 14 then looks at issues arising out of the models and some evidence bearing on the choice between some of these models.

Notation used in this chapter

Ar = real absorption
B = balance of payments
D = domestic assets of the central bank
E = exchange rate (units of domestic currency per unit of foreign currency)
edm = elasticity of demand for imports
edx = elasticity of demand for exports
FC = value of foreign assets in foreign currency held by residents
Gr = real government expenditure
K = net capital flows
M = volume of imports
Mo = money supply
P = overall price level (composed of domestic and foreign-produced goods)
Pd = domestic price level
Pf = foreign prices denominated in foreign currency
r = domestic interest rate

rf = foreign interest rate
W = nominal wage rate
We = domestic wealth
X = volume of exports
Yf = foreign real GNP
Yr = real GNP
Yr_d = real aggregate demand for domestic goods

General Structure of Model

The model in this chapter is composed of two parts: an aggregate demand sector and an aggregate supply sector. The aggregate demand sector is in the tradition of Fleming–Mundell[1] which, in turn, is basically Keynesian in spirit. The aggregate supply sector is in the neo-classical tradition. Its key feature is that it assumes that real wages are fixed. The complete model then jointly determines domestic prices as well as output.

Three different monetary regimes are represented in the model. The first of these is a gold-standard-type regime, which we represent by the letters GR. The second is an IMF-type regime, which we represent by the letters MR. The third is a flexible rate regime, which we represent by the letters FR. These three regimes correspond in effect to the three prototype regimes which the industrial world has experienced, as we have seen, since 1870.

The model accommodates several key differences between these three regimes. First, in the MR and GR regimes the monetary authorities are assumed to intervene in the foreign exchange market to maintain a fixed exchange rate. By contrast, in the FR regime the monetary authorities do not intervene, allowing the exchange rate to move in line with market forces so as to remove any potential disequilibria in the balance of payments. Second, in the GR regime it is assumed that the monetary authorities allow changes in the balance of payments to influence the volume of money which, it will be recalled, was one of the rules of the game. By contrast, in the MR regime it is assumed that they sterilise the effects of the balance of payments on the volume of money. This corresponds to the spirit of the IMF system where balance of payments disequilibria in the short term are financed by movements in reserves, without, at the same time, allowing these reserves to influence the volume of money. Third, the FR and GR regimes are both 'equilibrium' regimes, in the sense that they provide an automatic mechanism of adjustment for the balance of payments. At the same time, the method of reaching equilibrium in the balance of payments is quite different. With FR, equilibrium is continuous; with GR, it emerges only after the adjustment mechanism has been set in motion and changes in the volume of money have taken effect on the domestic economy. By contrast, the MR regime is a disequilibrium regime, sustained in the short term by sterilisation operations.

The Aggregate Demand Sector of the Model

The aggregate demand sector is composed of three markets: a market for domestically produced goods, a market for money and a market for foreign exchange. This section will describe each of these markets and show how they interact with one another.

The Goods Market

The goods market identifies the determinants of real aggregate demand for domestically-produced goods and shows how production must change to accommodate variations in real demand.

Consider, first, the gross national product and its components:

$$Yr.Pd = Ar.P + X.Pd - M.Pf.E \tag{11.1}$$

In this equation, gross national product (*Yr.Pd*) is the sum of nominal absorption (*Ar.P*) and the surplus in the current account of the balance of payments (*X.Pd* − *M.Pf.E*).

Deflating this equation throughout by domestic prices (*Pd*), we can derive the components of the real demand for domestically produced goods, Yr_d:

$$Yr_d = \left(\frac{P}{Pd}\right)Ar + X - \left(\frac{Pf.E}{Pd}\right)M \tag{11.2}$$

Real absorption, *Ar*, is composed of real consumption, real investment and real government expenditure. It is assumed that real consumption and investment combined are determined (positively) by real output and (negatively) by the interest rate, while real government expenditure is exogenous. So we can write:

$$Ar = \alpha_1 Yr - \alpha_3 r + Gr \tag{11.3}$$

The volume of exports, *X*, is assumed to be determined by the ratio of the foreign price in domestic currency to the price of domestic goods (a substitution effect) and, also, by foreign output. So we now have:

$$X = \alpha_8 \frac{Pf.E}{Pd} + \alpha_{20} Yf \tag{11.4}$$

The volume of imports, M, is determined by the same price ratio and now, also, by domestic output. Thus:

$$M = \alpha_9 Yr + \alpha_{10} \frac{Pd}{Pf.E} \qquad (11.5)$$

If the goods market is to be in equilibrium, production of domestically produced goods must equal the demand for these goods. So to represent equilibrium in the goods market we write:

$$Yr_d = Yr \qquad (11.6)$$

Now substituting Equations (11.3), (11.4), (11.5) and (11.6) into Equation (11.2), differentiating and rearranging, allows us to represent the goods market in a summary form:[2]

$$\Delta r = -\left(\frac{1-\alpha_1+\alpha_9}{\alpha_3}\right)\Delta Yr + \frac{1}{\alpha_3}\Delta Gr + \frac{X(edx+edm-1)}{\alpha_3}(\Delta E - \Delta Pd + \Delta Pf) + \frac{\alpha_{20}}{\alpha_3}\Delta Yf \qquad (11.7)$$

where $edx + edm - 1$ is the Marshall–Lerner condition.

This equation can be represented graphically in the form of a conventional *IS* schedule, which traces the relationship between the interest rate and output that preserves equilibrium in the goods market, holding constant, at the same time, *Gr, E, Pd, Pf* and *Yf* (see Figure 11.1).

Figure 11.1 *Equilibrium in goods, money and foreign exchange markets*

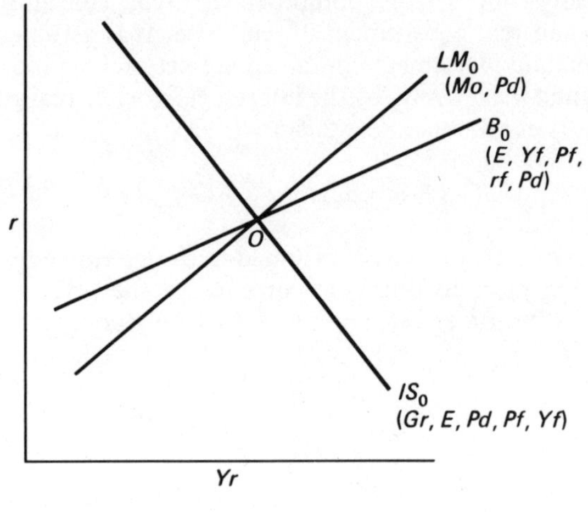

This *IS* schedule will shift to the right (left) if government expenditure (*Gr*) increases (decreases) or if foreign output (*Yf*) increases (decreases). Again, the *IS* schedule will shift to the right (left) if the exchange rate (*E*) weakens (strengthens), if foreign prices (*Pf*) increase (decrease) or if domestic prices (*Pd*) fall (rise), provided, in these cases, the Marshall–Lerner condition holds (that is, the sum of the two demand elasticities exceeds unity).[3]

The Money Market

It is assumed here that the public's holdings of real money balances are determined (positively) by real output and (negatively) by the interest rate. So we have:

$$\left(\frac{Mo}{P}\right)d = \alpha_4 Yr - \alpha_6 r \qquad (11.8)$$

If the money market is in equilibrium, the demand for real money balances must equal the supply of real money balances. So:

$$\left(\frac{Mo}{P}\right)d = \frac{Mo}{P} \qquad (11.9)$$

We can now combine Equations (11.8) and (11.9) to represent equilibrium in the money market:[4]

$$\Delta r = \frac{\alpha_4}{\alpha_6}\Delta Yr - \frac{1}{\alpha_6}\Delta Mo + \frac{1}{\alpha_6}Mo\Delta Pd \qquad (11.10)$$

This equation can be represented graphically in the form of an *LM* schedule, which now shows the combinations of the interest rate and output that preserve equilibrium in the money market, while, at the same time, holding the volume of money and domestic prices fixed (see Figure 11.1). This *LM* schedule will shift to the right (left) if the volume of money increases (decreases) or if domestic prices decrease (increase).

In the MR and FR regimes, the volume of money is treated as exogenous and hence as an instrument of policy. However, in the GR regime, the volume of money is allowed to be influenced by the balance of payments. We need, therefore, for this regime, an equation that explains the determination of the volume of money. Assuming, for simplicity, that the money multiplier is 1, the change in the volume of money will then be composed of the change in net foreign assets of the central bank (the overall balance of payments) and the change in the domestic assets of the central bank. We have, then:

$$\Delta Mo = B + \Delta D \qquad (11.11)$$

Exogenous monetary policy is implemented in the GR regime by changing the central banks' holdings of domestic assets.

The Foreign Exchange Market

The overall balance of payments, which represents the net pressure on the foreign exchange market, is composed of a current account and a capital account:

$$B = X.Pd - M.Pf.E + K \tag{11.12}$$

The volume of exports and imports has already been explained. We now need to explain capital movements. We assume that net capital flows are determined by the interest rate differential (that is, the difference between the domestic and foreign interest rates) as in:

$$K = \alpha_{12}(r - rf) \tag{11.13}$$

This asserts that the higher the domestic interest rate relative to the foreign rate, the larger will be the net capital inflows. α_{12} represents the degree of capital mobility.[5]

If we substitute Equations (11.4), (11.5) and (11.13) into Equation (11.12) and differentiate,[6] we can derive a balance of payments equation:

$$\Delta B = X(edx + edm - 1)(\Delta Pf + \Delta E - \Delta Pd) - \alpha_9 \Delta Yr + \alpha_{20}\Delta Yf + \alpha_{12}\Delta r - \alpha_{12}\Delta rf \tag{11.14}$$

It will be recalled that in the MR regime, the overall balance of payments is not necessarily in equilibrium (so ΔB need not be zero). By contrast, in the other two regimes, the foreign exchange market (the balance of payments) is assumed to reach equilibrium. For these regimes then we can set $\Delta B = 0$ and derive a summary equation, which now represents equilibrium in the foreign exchange market:

$$\Delta r = \frac{X(edx + edm - 1)}{\alpha_{12}}(\Delta Pd - \Delta E - \Delta Pf) + \frac{\alpha_9}{\alpha_{12}}\Delta Yr - \frac{\alpha_{20}}{\alpha_{12}}\Delta Yf + \Delta rf \tag{11.15}$$

This equation can be represented graphically in the form of a B schedule which shows the combinations of the interest rate and output that preserve overall balance of payments equilibrium, holding constant, at the same time, *Pd, E, Pf, Yf* and *rf* (see Figure 11.1).

The schedule is positively sloped because as income increases and the current account deteriorates a rise in the interest rate, which induces an inflow of capital, is required to restore equilibrium to the overall balance of payments. The slope of this schedule α_9/α_{12} reflects the degree of capital mobility. When capital is completely immobile (that is, insensitive to interest rate changes so $\alpha_{12}=0$), the *B* schedule is vertical. At the other extreme, when the degree of capital mobility is infinite (that is, when the domestic interest rate cannot diverge from the foreign interest rate $\alpha_{12}\rightarrow\infty$), the schedule is horizontal. Hence, as *B* moves in a clockwise direction the slope decreases and the degree of capital mobility increases, requiring a progressively smaller rise in the interest rate to offset a given current account deficit.

This *B* schedule will shift to the right (left) if foreign output increases (decreases) or if the foreign interest rate falls (rises). Again, the schedule will shift to the right (left) if there were a devaluation (revaluation), if foreign prices increase (fall) or if domestic prices fall (increase), provided, in all these cases, the Marshall–Lerner condition holds.

The area to the right (left) of the *B* schedule will represent an overall deficit (surplus) in the balance of payments because, in that area, the level of output is too high (low) and/or the interest rate too low (high) relative to the levels of output and the interest rate required to secure overall balance of payments equilibrium.

Figure 11.1 represents a situation where there is equilibrium in all three markets at point *O*.

For GR and FR full equilibrium always requires that all markets be in equilibrium, so for any disturbance a new equilibrium will be located at the intersection of all three schedules. With GR any disequilibrium in the balance of payments will force shifts in the *LM* schedule until full equilibrium is restored. With FR any disequilibrium in the balance of payments will be removed by appropriate exchange rate changes which shift, now, the *IS* and *B* schedules. For the MR regime equilibrium is located at the intersection of *LM* and *IS* but not necessarily on *B*, so equilibrium is consistent with a surplus or deficit in the overall balance of payments.

For regime MR the solutions for output and the interest rate are obtained from Equations (11.7) and (11.10). Equation (11.14) then allows us to determine the overall balance of payments, given the exogenous variables. For regime GR the solutions for output and the interest rate are obtained at the points of intersection of the *IS* and *B* schedules from Equations (11.7) and (11.15). Having determined output and interest rate, Equation (11.10) then determines the required volume of money (which is endogenous in this system). For regime FR Equations (11.7), (11.10) and (11.15) are required to determine, jointly, output, the interest rate and now, in addition, the exchange rate.[7]

The Aggregate Demand Schedule

To obtain an aggregate demand function we combine Equations (11.7) and (11.10) (the *IS* and *LM* schedules). This yields a relationship between output and domestic prices of the form:

$$\Delta Yr = \frac{\alpha_3}{D1}\Delta Mo - \left(\frac{\alpha_3 Mo + \alpha_6 ML}{D1}\right)\Delta Pd + \frac{\alpha_6}{D1}\Delta Gr + \frac{\alpha_6 ML}{D1}(\Delta E + \Delta Pf) + \frac{\alpha_6\alpha_{20}}{D1}\Delta Yf \qquad (11.16)$$

where

$$D1 = \alpha_3\alpha_4 + \alpha_6(1 - \alpha_1 + \alpha_9)$$

and

$$ML = X(edx + edm - 1)$$

Graphically, the aggregate demand schedule is derived in the following way. We want to trace the effects of changes in domestic prices on real aggregate demand, given all the exogenous variables. Figure 11.2 shows the *IS* and *LM* schedules for three price levels Pd_0, Pd_1 and Pd_2.

As the price level increases from Pd_0 progressively to Pd_2 both the *IS* and *LM* schedules shift to the left, the first (assuming the Marshall–Lerner condition holds) because of a substitution effect, the second because of a real balance effect. A, B, C trace the (progressively lower) levels of real demand corresponding to the (progressively higher) levels of prices. The prices and levels of real demand are then traced on an aggregate demand schedule (*AD*) shown in Figure 11.3.

The Aggregate Supply Sector

The Labour Market

We now explicitly introduce a relatively simple labour market into the model.[8] Assuming production is subject to diminishing marginal productivity, the demand for labour and hence the supply of output are assumed to be an inverse function of the real wage rate, defined as the nominal wage rate deflated by the price of domestic output. The nominal wage rate, in turn, is assumed to adjust fully to changes in the overall price level, represented by a weighted average of domestic and import prices, so as to maintain the real purchasing power of a unit of labour.

Figure 11.2 *Derivation of an aggregate demand schedule*

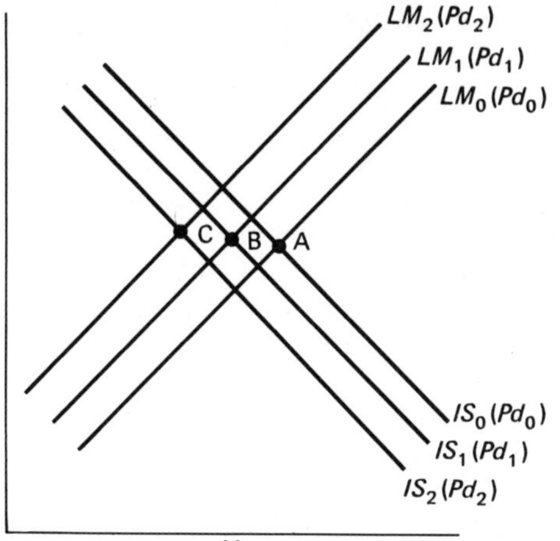

Figure 11.3 *The joint determination of prices and output – aggregate demand and aggregate supply*

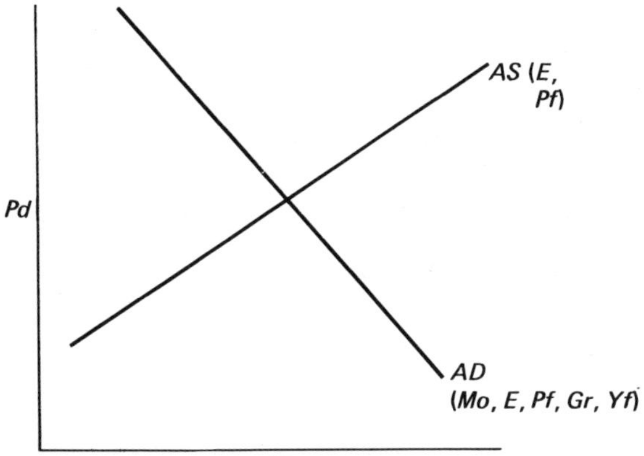

More formally, we may write the aggregate supply of output first as a function (linear for simplicity) of the real wage rate:

$$Yr = -\alpha_{15}\frac{W}{Pd} \tag{11.17}$$

The real wage rate which is held fixed W/P is defined in terms of the overall price level:

$$P = \alpha_{14} Pd + (1 - \alpha_{14})(Pf.E) \tag{11.18}$$

This then generates an aggregate supply function of the form:

$$\Delta Yr = \alpha_{15}(1 - \alpha_{14})(\Delta Pd - \Delta E - \Delta Pf) \tag{11.19}$$

This is shown as *AS* in Figure 11.3.

Output in this formulation is determined by the terms of trade. With the exchange rate and foreign prices fixed an increase in domestic prices will now induce some increase in output. The reason is that since the overall price level, to which wages fully adjust, is composed of a weighted average of domestic and foreign prices, wages will increase proportionately less than domestic prices, allowing a reduction in real wages to the employers and hence an inducement to expand production.

The Complete Model with Four Markets

Mathematically, we now have a complete model composed of four markets which can be solved for a number of endogenous variables. For flexible exchange rates (FR), Equations (11.7), (11.10), (11.15) and (11.19) jointly determine domestic prices, real output, the interest rate and the exchange rate. For fixed rates without sterilisation (GR), Equations (11.7), (11.15) and (11.19) determine output, prices and the interest rate, while Equation (11.10) determines the volume of money. For fixed rates with sterilisation (MR), Equations (11.7), (11.10) and (11.19) determine output prices and the interest rate while, then, Equation (11.14) determines the balance of payments. Finally, Equation (11.16) (the aggregate demand equation) and Equation (11.19) (the aggregate supply equation) together determine output and prices.

Annex 1 The Stock Theory of Capital Movements

Our Equation (11.13) in the model asserted that if the domestic interest rate increased to a new higher level, there would be a permanently higher flow of capital into the economy. An alternative (stock) representation of capital movements[9] argues, by contrast, that there would be a portfolio readjustment by domestic and foreign residents leading to an inflow of capital in the initial period; at the same time, however, the higher domestic interest rate will provoke a continuing inflow of capital in subsequent periods, but at a more modest rate.

To illustrate this, suppose domestic residents held foreign assets (but, for simplicity, foreigners did not hold domestic assets). Suppose *FC* represents the value of foreign assets in foreign currency held by residents, while *We* represents domestic wealth. Then, in its simplest form:

$$\frac{E.FC}{We} = \alpha_{12}(rf - r) \tag{11A.1}$$

This asserts that the proportion of wealth held in the form of foreign assets (denominated in domestic currency) increases as the foreign interest rate increases relative to the domestic interest rate. Differentiating this equation yields:

$$\Delta FC = -K = \alpha_{12} We(\Delta rf - \Delta r) + \alpha_{12}\Delta We(rf - r) - FC\Delta E \tag{11A.2}$$

The capital inflow following an increase in the domestic interest rate is represented by $\alpha_{12} We$; this inflow, however, is not sustained since Δr becomes zero in subsequent periods. The continuing flow is represented by $\alpha_{12}\Delta We$ which says that so long as home wealth is growing a larger share of the increased wealth will be absorbed in domestic, as against foreign, assets. The sustained flow is, therefore, $\alpha_{12}\Delta We$, while the initial stock adjustment, by contrast, is $\alpha_{12} We$. The ratio of the flow to the stock adjustment is $\Delta We/We$, which is the rate of growth of wealth. In other words, if wealth grows at 5 per cent the (sustained) flow effect will be 5 per cent of the (initial) stock effect.

For relatively short-term analysis we may disregard the change in wealth, so $\Delta We = 0$; if we also disregard valuation effects ($FC\Delta E$), this reduces the new capital flow equation to:

$$K = \alpha_{12} We(\Delta r - \Delta rf) \tag{11A.3}$$

We will, occasionally, in subsequent chapters, refer to this alternative formulation of capital flows as the 'stock' version of capital movements, in contrast to the 'flow' version embodied in the original model.

The stock model may be better founded in theory and in practice. At the same time, the flow model is much more widely used in macro-models, particularly those derived from Fleming–Mundell. Also, over a short-term horizon of, say, six months to a year the two models have rather similar implications. In the long run we have seen that with wealth growing there is a lasting flow effect, albeit at a lower level. Hence, for the analysis of the long run the basic model should still be useful but the capital mobility coefficient should be reinterpreted to represent the flow that is sustainable.

Annex 2 The Special Case of Perfect Capital Mobility

This Annex addresses itself to some technical aspects of the case where capital mobility is perfect ($\alpha_{12} \rightarrow \infty$). In this case, as we have already indicated, the *B* schedule is horizontal and the domestic interest rate is exogenously determined by the foreign interest rate. With the interest rate exogenous the volume of money can no longer be treated as within the control of the monetary authorities, so the two regimes MR and GR become identical. How is the model solved in this case for the three regimes?

For MR and GR, Equations (11.7) and (11.19) together determine prices and output while Equation (11.10) determines the volume of money. The current account is then determined by prices and output. Given the current account and given that the balance of payments must be in equilibrium, the capital account is then determined as a residual. For FR, Equations (11.7), (11.10) and (11.19) together determine prices, output and the exchange rate. These in turn determine the current account. Given the current account and given, again, the requirement that the balance of payments be in equilibrium, the capital account is then determined as the residual.

Notes for Chapter 11

1 See: J. Fleming (1962) and R. A. Mundell (1963).

2 The solution is derived by totally differentiating the equations, assuming all initial prices are unity and the current account is initially in equilibrium, while α_8, α_{10} are replaced by *X.edx* and *M.edm*, respectively. Also, for simplicity, the terms of trade effect on real absorption is disregarded.

3 If the Marshall–Lerner condition did not hold the *IS* schedule would shift, in each case, in the opposite direction.

4 We, again, deliberately, simplify by disregarding the terms of trade effect in the money market so $P = Pd$.

5 See, however, Annex 1 for an alternative representation of capital flows.

6 Again assuming initial current account balance.

7 The special case where capital mobility is perfect is explained in Annex 2.

8 See V. Argy and J. Salop (1978, 1979). The basic insight here was first developed in J. Salop (1974). See also F. Casas (1977).

9 See Z. Hodjera (1973); W. H. Branston and R. Hill (1971).

Chapter 12

Monetarist Models – I:

The Expectations-Augmented Phillips Curve and the Natural Rate of Unemployment

Introduction

The expectations-augmented Phillips curve (EAPC) derives from the work of Friedman and Phelps in the late 1960s and represents an important extension to the traditional Phillips curve, which originated in the work of Phillips himself, and others.[1]

There are three reasons why we need to deal with the analytics of the EAPC: first, because of its central role in discussions of inflation in the postwar years; second, because, inevitably, we intend to draw on its foundations at several points in subsequent chapters; third, and most importantly, because it provides an analytical alternative to the aggregate supply schedule presented in our basic model.[2]

Notation used in this chapter

$\dot{E}$ = rate of change in the exchange rate
$\dot{Mo}$ = rate of growth in the money supply
$\dot{P}$ = overall rate of inflation
$\dot{Pd}$ = rate of change in domestic prices
$\dot{Pe}$ = expected overall rate of inflation
$\dot{Pf}$ = rate of change in foreign prices
$\dot{Q}$ = long-run rate of growth of productivity
U = unemployment rate
UN = natural unemployment rate (NRU)
$\dot{W}$ = rate of change in wages
Yc = full employment output
$\dot{Yr}$ = rate of growth in real GNP

The Analytics of the EAPC

The EAPC can be represented by a set of four equations:

$$\dot{P} = b_{12}\dot{P}d + (1 - b_{12})(\dot{P}f + \dot{E}) \qquad (12.1)$$

$$\dot{P}d = \dot{W} - \dot{Q} \qquad (12.2)$$

$$\dot{W} = b_{13}\dot{P}e - b_{15}(U - UN) + \dot{Q} \qquad (12.3)$$

$$\dot{P}e = \dot{P}_{-1} \qquad (12.4)$$

Equation (12.1) says that the overall rate of inflation is a weighted sum of the domestic and the foreign rate of inflation (adjusted for the exchange rate). Equation (12.2) asserts that the rate of inflation of domestic goods is equal to the rate of growth of long-run unit labour costs, while Equation (12.3), which captures the essence of the EAPC, asserts that the rate of change in wages is a function of the expected rate of inflation, the long-run productivity growth and the difference between the actual unemployment rate and the natural (full employment) unemployment rate. Finally, Equation (12.4) asserts that the expected rate of inflation is determined, for simplicity, by the previous period's rate of inflation.

It is important, from the start, to distinguish two versions of the EAPC – one distinctly neoclassical, the other with some Keynesian elements. Although both yield identical outcomes their underlying assumptions are different.[3] The neoclassical version assumes, in effect, that all unemployment is essentially voluntary (search unemployment), while the alternative, more Keynesian, version recognises the existence of some (temporary) involuntary unemployment (for example, layoffs).

The distinction can be highlighted by looking again at the key equation (12.3) of the model. Given the rate of growth of productivity ($\dot{Q}$) and assuming no money illusion ($b_{13} = 1$), the neoclassical version would view this equation as essentially a supply of labour equation, with unemployment (search unemployment) voluntarily responding (negatively) to the expected growth in real wages (that is, $\dot{W} - \dot{P}e$) in excess of $\dot{Q}$. In this version the unemployment rate is the dependent variable, and the expected change in the real wage rate the independent variable. In the alternative version, the unemployment rate is a proxy for the degree of excess demand; now causation runs from excess demand to the expected change in the real wage rate rather than the reverse. This alternative version is consistent with the existence of variations in involuntary unemployment. For reasons that will become evident as our discussion progresses the second version appears to be more internally consistent as well as more realistic.

In order to highlight some key issues associated with the EAPC we will now manipulate this simple model in a number of ways, making, on the way, various assumptions about some of the relationships identified in the model. The economics underlying these manipulations will be examined in more detail subsequently.

Let us begin by assuming that the expected rate of inflation is exogenous. (In other words, Equation (12.4) is put to one side for the moment.) Then, we can easily substitute Equation (12.3) into Equation (12.2) and Equation (12.2) into Equation (12.1) to obtain:

$$\dot{P} = b_{12}b_{13}\dot{P}e - b_{12}b_{15}(U - UN) + (1 - b_{12})(\dot{P}f + \dot{E}) \qquad (12.5)$$

This equation represents the short-run trade-off between the rate of inflation and the rate of unemployment, given the expected rate of inflation. The slope of this short-run Phillips curve is $b_{12}b_{15}$, while $\dot{P}e$ and $(\dot{P}f + \dot{E})$ represent shift variables. In other words, when $\dot{P}e$ or $(\dot{P}f + \dot{E})$ changes, the whole of the short-run Phillips curve will shift. This short-run Phillips curve is shown in Figure 12.1.

Figure 12.1 *The Phillips curve*

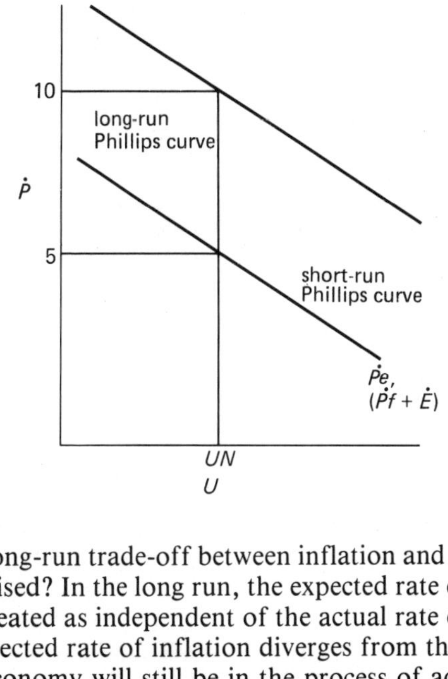

How is the long-run trade-off between inflation and unemployment to be characterised? In the long run, the expected rate of inflation can no longer be treated as independent of the actual rate of inflation. So long as the expected rate of inflation diverges from the actual rate of inflation the economy will still be in the process of adjusting. Long-run equilibrium must, therefore, be characterised by a situation where $\dot{P}e = \dot{P}$. If we impose this condition on Equation (12.5) we have:

$$\dot{P} = -\frac{b_{12}b_{15}}{1-b_{12}b_{13}}(U-UN) + \frac{1-b_{12}}{1-b_{12}b_{13}}(\dot{P}f+\dot{E}) \qquad (12.6)$$

The slope of the long-run Phillips curve is, now, $b_{12}b_{15}/1-b_{12}b_{13}$. Since $b_{12}b_{13}<1$ this expression is clearly larger than the short-run Phillips trade-off, whose slope was $b_{12}b_{15}$. The long-run Phillips curve is, therefore, steeper than the short-run Phillips curve.

Under what conditions will this long-run Phillips curve assume a vertical shape? The two key conditions required for this are that there be no money illusion (that is, that wages fully adjust to changes in inflation $b_{13}=1$) and that the difference between the domestic and foreign rate of inflation be exactly offset by a change in the exchange rate ($\dot{P}d = \dot{P}f + \dot{E}$) (that is, purchasing power parity, PPP, holds). If we impose those two conditions on Equation (12.6), the trade-off disappears altogether (the denominator of the new slope coefficient assumes a value of infinity).

What is the likelihood of these two conditions holding? Suppose, for example, that PPP did not hold in the long run. Then, clearly, there would be a continuing change in the country's competitive position, with serious implications for employment and the country's international reserve situation. Later, in Chapter 21, we show that the evidence, in fact, supports PPP in the long run. Again, it is not realistic to suppose (after adjusting for productivity growth) that wages can grow, say, at a slower pace than the rate of inflation, for, in this case, the profit margin would rise indefinitely.

We have established, it seems, that the long-run Phillips curve must be vertical since the two key conditions required for this are almost certain to hold. This long-run vertical Phillips curve is also shown in Figure 12.1.

Suppose, now, that $b_{13}=1$ and also that PPP holds. Then Equation (12.5) can be rewritten as:

$$\dot{P} - \dot{P}e = -b_{15}(U-UN) \qquad (12.7)$$

This is an important result which asserts that, given our assumptions, any departure of the unemployment rate from its long-run (natural) unemployment rate is due to a difference between the existing rate of inflation and the rate of inflation that is anticipated.

This result also allows us to demonstrate another important implication of the EAPC, the so-called accelerationist hypothesis. If we substitute $\dot{P}_{-1}$ for $\dot{P}e$ (Equation 12.4) in Equation (12.7) we have:

$$\dot{P} - \dot{P}_{-1} = -b_{15}(U - UN) \tag{12.8}$$

This result says that if the unemployment rate is held below the NRU ($U<UN$), the rate of inflation must continually accelerate. On the other hand, if the unemployment rate is held above the NRU ($U>UN$), the rate of inflation must continually decelerate.

The Response of Inflation and Unemployment to a Change in Monetary Growth

We want, now, to use the model to look at the dynamics of adjustment of inflation and unemployment following a sustained increase in the rate of growth in the volume of money, assuming no money illusion and also, for simplicity, that PPP holds.[4]

We carry over, then, from the model:

$$\dot{P} = \dot{P}d = \dot{W} - \dot{Q} \tag{12.9}$$

$$\dot{W} = \dot{P}e - b_{15}(U - UN) + \dot{Q} \tag{12.10}$$

$$\dot{P}e = \dot{P}_{-1} \tag{12.4}$$

To enable us to carry out the aims of the exercise, two additional equations are required to complete the model. First, we introduce a primitive monetarist aggregate demand equation:

$$\dot{P} = \dot{M}o - \dot{Y}r \tag{12.11}$$

This simply asserts that the rate of inflation is determined by the rate of growth of money per unit of output. Second, we need some link between output growth, which appears in Equation (12.11), and the unemployment rate, which appears in Equation (12.10). We assume:

$$U - U_{-1} = b_{21}(\dot{Q} - \dot{Y}r) \tag{12.12}$$

This asserts that when output growth exceeds (is less than) long-run capacity growth in the economy (assumed, for simplicity, to be equal to productivity growth here),[5] the unemployment rate will fall (rise). This equation represents what has come to be known as Okun's Law.[6]

We can now put this simple model to work by taking plausible values of the coefficients. We assume that $b_{15} = 1$ and $b_{21} = 0.4$,[7] and that the economy is initially in equilibrium with the following values: $\dot{M}o = 10$, $\dot{P} = 5$, $\dot{W} = 10$, $\dot{Y}r = 5$, $U = UN = 4$ and $\dot{Q} = \dot{W} - \dot{P} = 5$.

Suppose that monetary growth accelerates to 15 per cent and is sustained at this new rate. Table 12.1 shows how the key variables in

Table 12.1 The effects of an acceleration in monetary growth on inflation and unemployment

Period	$\dot{M}o$ (1)	$\dot{P}$ (2)	$\dot{W}$ (3)	$\dot{Y}r$ (4)	$\dot{U}$ (5)	$\dot{W}-\dot{P}e$ (6)
1	10	5	10	5	4	5
2	15	6.45	11.45	8.55	2.55	6.45
3	15	8.51	13.51	6.49	1.94	7.06
4	15	10.40	15.40	4.60	2.11	6.89
5	15	11.62	16.62	3.38	2.78	6.22
6	15	12.01	17.01	2.99	3.61	5.39
7	15	11.70	16.70	3.30	4.31	4.69
8	15	10.98	15.98	4.02	4.72	4.28
9	15	10.17	15.17	4.83	4.81	4.19
10	15	9.53	14.53	5.47	4.64	4.36
11	15	9.20	14.20	5.80	4.33	4.67
12	15	9.19	14.19	5.81	4.01	4.99
13	15	9.41	14.41	5.59	3.78	5.22
14	15	9.73	14.73	5.27	3.68	5.32
15	15	10.03	15.03	4.97	3.70	5.30
16	15	10.23	15.23	4.77	3.80	5,20
17	15	10.30	15.30	4.70	3.93	5.07
18	15	10.26	15.26	4.74	4.04	4.96
19	15	10.15	15.15	4.85	4.11	4.89
20	15	10.02	15.02	4.98	4.13	4.87

the model will respond over the first 20 periods. Consider, first, what happens in period 2. There is an excess demand for labour, pushing up the growth of wages and lowering the unemployment rate. In the neoclassical version, unemployment (search activity) falls because expected real wages ($\dot{W}-\dot{P}e$) are now growing faster. At the same time, the increased wages will be passed on while output will now be growing faster than long-run productivity growth ($\dot{Y}r>\dot{Q}$), which is consistent with the fall in unemployment. At this point, we are observing a movement to the left along a short-run Phillips curve.

In period 3 workers will seek compensation for the higher rate of inflation in period 2, so wages and prices will both rise further. With inflation accelerating, the growth in real money balances and, hence, output will slow down but it will still exceed capacity growth, so excess demand for labour persists and unemployment falls further. Again, in the neoclassical representation, expected real wages are growing still faster and this is consistent with a willingness to supply additional labour. In this period, with the expected rate of inflation now adjusting upwards, the short-run Phillips curve will have shifted upwards to the right.

As wages and prices adjust, the acceleration in inflation will be such that the growth in real money balances will fall below long-run capacity growth and so the trend in unemployment will reverse itself (this happens in period 4). Unemployment will, in due course, overshoot its natural rate (in period 7) and then fall below it again (in period 13). Ultimately the system will come to rest when the natural rate of unemployment is restored, the inflation rate has settled at 10 per cent, wages are growing at 15 per cent and output at 5 per cent. In the long run, then, the economy will settle down on a higher point in its (vertical) Phillips curve (see Figure 12.1). At the same time, there will be a new short-run Phillips curve corresponding to the new higher rate of inflation (which is equal to the anticipated rate of inflation).

The path of adjustment, shown in Table 12.1, is most revealing. At first (periods 1 to 3), the economy traces something like a traditional Phillips curve, with unemployment falling and inflation accelerating. In the second phase (periods 4 to 6), unemployment is rising but the inflation rate continues to accelerate (we have a perverse Phillips curve). In the third phase (periods 7 to 9), the traditional Phillips curve reappears while in the fourth phase (periods 10 to 12), it is perverse again, with both unemployment and inflation now falling. The important point to be made here is that the relationship between inflation and unemployment is very complicated, with a single sustained monetary shock capable of generating traditional as well as perverse relationships over the shorter run.

The Accelerationist Hypothesis

We indicated earlier that, if purchasing power parity held and if there were no money illusion, the only way in which the unemployment rate could be held below the natural unemployment rate would be by allowing the rate of inflation to accelerate from period to period (in effect endlessly).

Perhaps the simplest way to visualise this is in terms of a step-wise process, illustrated in Figure 12.2 by arrows. Suppose the economy is initially at A and monetary growth accelerates. The economy moves as we have seen to B and then back to C. To restore the (desired) lower rate of unemployment U_1 the monetary authorities will have to accelerate monetary growth further. The economy will move to D but then again to *UN* at a still higher rate of inflation at E. Again, monetary growth must accelerate further to restore U_1 so the economy will move to F and from there back to G. The process, theoretically, is endless. Of course, sooner or later, under these same conditions, the public will come to a realisation that expected real wages are not rising; with a better understanding of the underlying mechanics the speed of adjustment will accelerate and it will, then, no longer be possible to secure much of a reduction in unemployment.

Figure 12.2 *The accelerationist hypothesis*

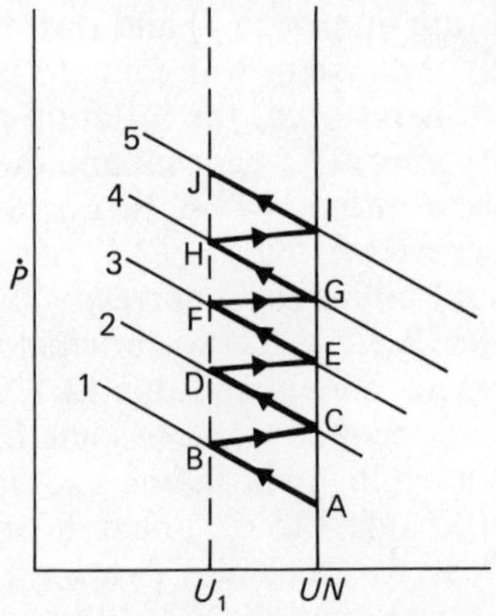

Of course, the economy need not move in this step-wise fashion. In theory, at any rate, the moment there is any reversal in unemployment the monetary authorities can 'offset' this by accelerating monetary growth. Then the economy might move along the path BDFHJ.

Determinants of the Natural Rate of Unemployment (NRU)

We have shown that, according to the EAPC, given certain realistic assumptions, there is a NRU to which the economy returns in the long run. What determines this NRU? The brief discussion which follows is not intended to be exhaustive but merely illustrative of the kinds of factors that may influence this NRU.[8]

First, the real value of unemployment benefits may alter the NRU in so far as it influences the amount of search activity on the part of those seeking work. Second, the NRU will be influenced by the availability and speed of transmission of information about job vacancies. Third, demographic factors may influence the NRU. For example, the larger the proportion of the labour force represented by youth and females, the larger will tend to be the NRU, because this segment of the labour force has a relatively high turnover rate. Fourth, the existing capital stock, at any point in time, imposes something of a constraint on the amount of labour that can be employed and, hence, on the NRU. Fifth, structural change may create a mismatch between the skills in demand and the available skills from those seeking work, in this way influencing the NRU. Sixth, an inappropriate real wage rate for a particular group (for example, youth) may influence the unemployment rate for that group and, in turn, the NRU.

It is evident that the NRU can change over time. This itself has implications for macro-policy. Suppose that there were an unanticipated increase in the NRU while the monetary authorities continued to have the same (original) target unemployment rate. Then, under these conditions, the economy might be exposed to accelerating inflation.

The EAPC as a Representation of the Aggregate Supply Sector

The EAPC can be used to represent the aggregate supply sector of an economy, providing an alternative to the aggregate supply equation we derived in the neo-Keynesian model.

To derive an aggregate supply equation from our EAPC model, all we need now, as an addition to the model, is a relationship between the unemployment rate and the level of output:

$$U - UN = -b_{20}(Yr - Yc) \tag{12.13}$$

This equation says that the gap between the actual and the natural unemployment rates is related to the gap between actual output, Yr, and full employment output, Yc.

Setting $b_{13} = 1$, the model can now easily be manipulated to obtain:

$$Yr = Yc + \frac{1 - b_{12}}{b_{15}b_{20}}(\dot{P}d - \dot{P}f - \dot{E}) \tag{12.14}$$

Equation (12.14) represents the aggregate supply equation derived from the EAPC and it bears comparison with the aggregate supply equation (Equation 11.19) of our own model.

One difference is that in Equation (11.19) the level of output is determined by the terms of trade while in Equation (12.14) the level of output is determined by the rate of change in the terms of trade. Also our own representation of the EAPC assumes mark-up pricing over costs. In the neo-Keynesian model we have an explicit demand for labour function which is, itself, dependent on the real wage rate. With the renewed emphasis, in recent years, on the role of the real wage rate in determining employment our own formulation would appear to have some advantage.

The neoclassical version of the EAPC explicitly allows for a supply of labour function while unemployment is voluntary. By contrast, our own version assumes real wages are exogenously given, while employment is determined by the employers on the basis of the trend in the real wage rate (as it is relevant to them). There is no labour supply function and unemployment can be involuntary. In this respect, it is more analogous to the alternative version of the EAPC.

Summary Points on EAPC

It is convenient, at this point, to summarise the more important points made in this chapter.

(1) The two key conditions necessary to generate a vertical Phillips curve in the long run are zero money illusion and PPP. We have argued that these two conditions are almost certain to hold in the long run.
(2) A long-run vertical Phillips curve suggests that, ultimately, the economy will return to its NRU. There is, therefore, an automatic mechanism of adjustment that will restore the economy to its full employment, albeit after a time lapse which may be very long indeed.
(3) Once the economy has settled at a given mean (long-run) rate of inflation it may be able to exploit its short-run Phillips curve and move along it around its NRU (without bias).[9]
(4) It is not possible to secure a permanent reduction in the rate of unemployment without exposing the economy to ever accelerating inflation.
(5) The speed of adjustment in the labour market determines how quickly the economy will move from one position to another. The speed of adjustment depends on the response of wages (and prices) to variations in excess demand, on how quickly expectations adjust to changes in inflation and, as well, on the extent to which institutional conditions allow changes in expectations to be translated into changes in wages.
(6) Within the framework of the EAPC, given the NRU,[10] the aim of macro-policy would be to direct the economy towards its NRU. However, if the NRU is not known or if it changes in an unpredictable way over time, macro-policy will be very difficult to conduct.
(7) The neoclassical version of the EAPC, notably its emphasis on voluntary unemployment and the implied labour supply function, is almost certainly in conflict with the evidence.[11] It would seem, therefore, that to the extent that the EAPC has any plausibility the alternative version would be more acceptable.
(8) The EAPC can serve to provide an aggregate supply equation, as one component of a complete macro-model.

Notes for Chapter 12

1 M. Friedman (1968); E. Phelps (1968); A. W. Phillips (1958). See also R. Gordon (1976); D. Laidler and J. Parkin (1975); H. Frisch (1977); A. M. Santomero and J. J. Seater (1978).

2 The aggregate supply sector remains without doubt the more difficult and controversial component of any macro-modelling.

3 This distinction is made in R. E. Brinner (1977).

4 For other models which integrate a Phillips curve with a primitive (aggregate demand) monetary sector see: D. Laidler (1973); J. Vanderkamp (1975).

5 Strictly, of course, it is the sum of productivity growth and the growth in the labour force (the latter assumed to be zero in the text).

6 A. Okun (1962); J. Tatom (1978).

7 For empirical evidence bearing on b_{15} see, for example, E. Spitaeller (1971). For evidence on b_{21} see J. Tatom (1978).

8 See also the discussion of this in Chapter 29.

9 See, however, the criticisms of the 'rational expectations' theorists in Chapter 29.

10 Of course, the NRU, at any point in time, need not be optimal. Longer-term policy (for instance, manpower policy) may be directed at altering the NRU.

11 The search–voluntary unemployment model has difficulties grappling with layoffs – dismissals. The model also suggests that in periods of declining unemployment search activity falls off, yet the evidence is that search activity (for instance, the quit rate) actually increases as economic activity accelerates. See A. M. Santomero and J. J. Seater (1978) and R. E. Brinner (1977).

Chapter 13

Monetarist Models – II: A Two-Sector Model

Introduction

The monetarist model to be presented in this chapter represents an approach whose origins reach back to the writings of D. Hume in the eighteenth century. The approach was revived and refined during the 1950s and 1960s in the writings of the IMF (notably by Polak and Prais), R. Mundell, H. Johnson, J. Frenkel and R. Dornbusch.[1]

Its key features are the following.[2] First, it is assumed that there is sufficient wage and price flexibility in the economy to ensure that the aggregate level of production is fixed at full employment, at least in the longer run. Second, the economy is assumed to be divided into two sectors of production: a traded goods sector and a non-traded goods sector. Traded goods are assumed to be highly competitive with similar goods produced overseas and hence sell at the same price when expressed in a common currency (the so-called 'law of one price' applies). Non-traded goods, by contrast, are sheltered from overseas competition and their price is determined by demand and supply.

Third, it is assumed that capital markets are highly integrated. In a world where exchange rates are relatively free to move, this means that interest rate differences will reflect expectations of a change in the exchange rate (for instance, if the domestic interest rate is higher than the foreign interest rate this must reflect an expectation that there will be a sufficient devaluation to offset any incentive to move funds into the country). In a world with firmly fixed exchange rates, highly integrated capital markets imply that comparable interest rates must be the same across countries.

Fourth, it is assumed that the monetary authorities do not sterilise the effects on domestic liquidity of developments in the balance of payments.

The monetarist model embodying these features will now be presented in two steps. First, we abstract from capital movements and assume that all adjustment is real (that is, through changes in real expenditure and the trade balance).[3] Second, we then explicitly allow for integrated capital markets.

Notation used in this chapter

AB = private sector expenditure (in nominal terms)
CA = current account of the balance of payments
D = domestic assets of the central bank
Dh = real private sector demand for non-traded goods
DT = real private sector demand for traded goods
E = exchange rate (units of domestic currency per unit of foreign currency)
Gh = real government sector demand for non-traded goods
GT = real government sector demand for traded goods
Mo = money supply
P = overall price level
Pd = price of non-traded goods
Pf = foreign prices denominated in foreign currency (of traded goods)
r = domestic interest rate
Sh = production of non-traded goods
ST = production of traded goods
Y = nominal GNP
Yc = full employment output

The Model without Capital Movements

The model can be represented in full by the following ten equations:

$$DT = \alpha_4 \frac{Pd}{Pf.E} + \alpha_5 \frac{AB}{P} \tag{13.1}$$

$$ST = -\alpha_6 \frac{Pd}{Pf.E} \tag{13.2}$$

$$\frac{Y}{P} = Yc = \frac{Pf.E}{P} ST + \frac{Pd}{P} Sh \tag{13.3}$$

$$\frac{AB}{P} = \frac{Pf.E}{P} DT + \frac{Pd}{P} Dh \tag{13.4}$$

$$Sh = Dh + Gh \tag{13.5}$$

$$CA = Pf.E.ST - Pf.E.DT - Pf.E.GT \tag{13.6}$$

$$\frac{AB}{P} = -\alpha_1 r + \alpha_2(\frac{Y}{P}) \qquad (13.7)$$

$$\Delta Mo = CA + \Delta D \qquad (13.8)$$

$$\frac{Mo}{P} = -\alpha_7 r + \alpha_{10}(\frac{Y}{P}) \qquad (13.9)$$

$$P \ = \alpha_8 Pd + (1 - \alpha_8) Pf.E \qquad (13.10)$$

Equation (13.1) asserts that the real demand for traded goods is determined by the relative price of traded and non-traded goods and, as well, by real private expenditure on both traded and non-traded goods. Equation (13.2) assumes that the supply of traded goods is a function of the relative price of traded and non-traded goods. Equation (13.3) says that aggregate domestic production, which is assumed to be fixed, is composed of traded as well as non-traded goods. Equation (13.4) says that real private expenditure is composed of private expenditure on traded as well as on non-traded goods. Equation (13.5) represents the assumption that the market for non-traded goods is in equilibrium, with the production of non-traded goods equated to the demand for non-traded goods. The demand for non-traded goods, in turn, has a private component as well as an exogenous government component (*Gh*).

Equation (13.6) is derived directly from the definition of the current account and from the assumption that the market for non-traded goods is in equilibrium. The current acccount is:

$$CA = (Pf.E.ST + Pd.Sh) - (Pf.E.DT + Pf.E.GT + Pd.Dh + Pd.Gh)$$

The first bracketed expression is GNP and the second is total absorption (made up of private and government expenditure). Since $Pd.Sh = Pd.Dh + Pd.Gh$ (Equation (13.5) multiplied through by *Pd*), the expression reduces to Equation (13.6). The current account, then, is represented as the difference between the supply of and the demand for traded goods.

Equation (13.7) explains real private expenditure in terms of the domestic interest rate and real income (which is fixed). Equation (13.8) represents the familiar breakdown of the money supply into its foreign and domestic components. Equation (13.9) explains the demand for real money balances (assumed equal to the supply) in terms of the interest rate and real income. Finally, Equation (13.10) asserts that the overall price level (the money demand deflator)[4] is composed of a weighted average of domestic and foreign prices.

The complete model can be conveniently reduced to three markets a market for traded goods, a market for non-traded goods and a money market. We can deduce equilibrium conditions for each of these markets and then represent each of these in graphical form.

The Market for Traded Goods (The Foreign Exchange Market)
Equilibrium in the market for traded goods requires that the current account be in balance. Setting $CA = 0$ in Equation (13.6), substituting Equations (13.1), (13.2) and (13.7) into the equation and differentiating throughout yields:

$$\Delta r = \left(\frac{\alpha_6 + \alpha_4}{\alpha_1 \alpha_5}\right)\Delta Pd - \left(\frac{\alpha_6 + \alpha_4}{\alpha_1 \alpha_5}\right)(\Delta Pf + \Delta E) + \frac{1}{\alpha_1 \alpha_5}\Delta GT \quad (13.11)$$

Given foreign prices, the exchange rate and government expenditure on traded goods, we can now derive a positive relationship between the interest rate and domestic prices which preserves equilibrium in the market for traded goods. The equation asserts that if the domestic price level increases there will be some substitution in consumption in favour of traded goods (see Equation 13.1) and a substitution in production in favour of non-traded goods (see Equation 13.2) which, in combination, will lead to an excess demand for traded goods; so to eliminate this excess demand for traded goods and restore equilibrium the domestic interest rate must rise (see Equations 13.7 and 13.1).

This equilibrium relationship for the traded goods market is represented in Figure 13.1 by *TB*. This *TB* schedule will shift to the right if the currency devalues or the foreign price increases, and to the left if government expenditure on traded goods increases. For

Figure 13.1 *Equilibrium in the Markets for traded, non-traded goods and money*

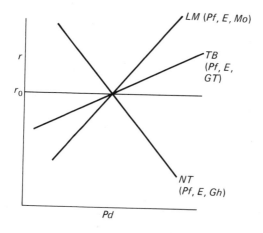

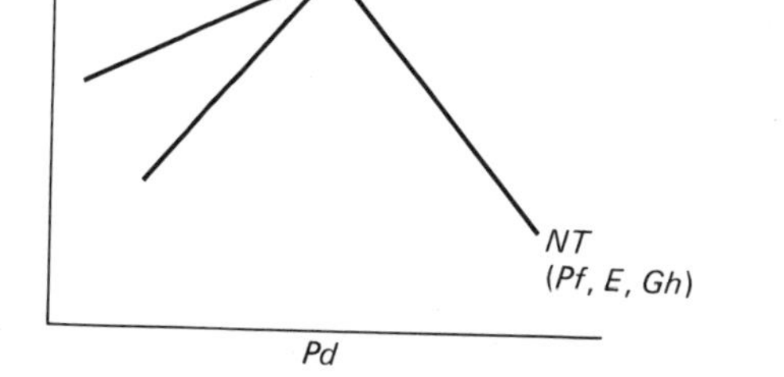

example, with a devaluation or an increase in the foreign price level the excess supply of traded goods has to be offset by an increase in the domestic price level and/or a reduction in the interest rate. Also, if government expenditure on traded goods increases there must be an offsetting reduction in the demand for traded goods, requiring an increase in the interest rate and/or a fall in the domestic price level.

The area to the right (left) of the *TB* schedule will represent a current account deficit (surplus) because, with domestic prices relatively high (low) and/or the interest rate relatively low (high), there will be an excess demand for (supply of) traded goods.

The Market for Non-Traded Goods

Equilibrium in the market for non-traded goods is defined by Equation (13.5). The supply function for non-traded goods (*Sh*) is secured, implicitly, from Equation (13.3), which takes output as fixed. At the same time, the real private demand for non-traded goods (*Dh*) is secured implicitly from Equation (13.4). In other words, both the supply of and the demand for non-traded goods are, as one would expect, the 'mirror image' of the demand for and the supply of traded goods. After making the appropriate substitutions, equilibrium in the non-traded goods market is defined by:

$$\Delta r = -\left\{\frac{\alpha_6+\alpha_4}{\alpha_1(1-\alpha_5)}\right\}\Delta Pd + \left\{\frac{\alpha_6+\alpha_4}{\alpha_1(1-\alpha_5)}\right\}(\Delta Pf+\Delta E) + \frac{1}{\alpha_1(1-\alpha_5)}\Delta Gh \qquad (13.12)$$

This equation asserts that, given foreign prices, the exchange rate and the government demand for non-traded goods, an increase in the price of non-traded goods will lead, through substitution in consumption and production, to an excess supply of non-traded goods which needs to be offset by a fall in the domestic interest rate to restore equilibrium to the market.

Equation (13.12) is represented graphically as *NT* in Figure 13.1. The schedule will shift to the right (left) if foreign prices increase (fall), if the currency devalues (revalues) and if expenditure by the government on non-traded goods increases (decreases). For example, an increase in foreign prices or a devaluation will lead to an excess demand for non-traded goods which needs to be offset by a rise in the interest rate and/or an increase in the price of non-traded goods to secure equilibrium in the market.

The Money Market

Equilibrium in this market is derived directly from Equations (13.9) and (13.10) holding output fixed:

$$\Delta r = -\frac{1}{\alpha_7}\Delta Mo + \frac{\alpha_8}{\alpha_7} Mo\Delta Pd + \frac{(1-\alpha_8)}{\alpha_7} Mo(\Delta Pf + \Delta E) \qquad (13.13)$$

This equation is represented in Figure 13.1 by the *LM* schedule, which will shift when the volume of money, foreign prices or the exchange rate changes.

Equilibrium in all Three Markets

In full equilibrium in this model all three markets, represented by Equations (13.11), (13.12) and (13.13), must be in balance. The model as a whole, summarised by these three equations, allows us to evaluate the effects of various disturbances on the system, again for different exchange rate regimes. Mathematically, we have three equations that will solve for three endogenous variables, given changes in the exogenous variables. If the exchange rate is fixed and, by assumption, there is no sterilisation, the three equations determine the price of non-traded goods, the domestic interest rate and, as well, the volume of money. In effect, Equations (13.11) and (13.12) jointly determine the interest rate and the price of non-traded goods while Equation (13.13) determines the volume of money. Equilibrium, then, for any given disturbance, is determined by the intersection of *TB* and *NT* while *LM* then shifts to accommodate the new equilibrium.[5] For a flexible rate regime the volume of money is treated as exogenous. Now the three markets together determine the domestic interest rate, the price of non-traded goods and also the exchange rate.

For a fixed rate regime, we can thus evaluate the effects of changes in fiscal policy (increases in expenditure on traded or non-traded goods), changes in exogenous monetary policy (represented by the domestic assets of the central bank) or changes in foreign prices or exchange rates. For a flexible rate regime we can evaluate the effects of changes in the volume of money but not, of course, independent changes in the exchange rate. In the chapters that follow some, at least, of these exercises will be carried out and the precise mechanisms of adjustment will be spelt out in more detail.

The Model with Capital Movements

As already pointed out, monetarists are predisposed to assume that capital markets are highly integrated. We now show how the model needs to be amended to accommodate the case where capital mobility is perfect. Since at this point we are only interested in the longer-run properties of the model we can take the domestic interest rate as given (that is, determined by the comparable interest rate overseas).

In the model with capital movements the trade balance need not be in equilibrium. A surplus or deficit may now be offset by a capital movement, so Equation (13.11) which defines equilibrium in the market for traded goods may not hold. In terms of Figure 13.1 equilibrium must be located on the horizontal line r_0 but not necessarily along *TB*. With the interest rate now predetermined, Equations (13.12) and (13.13) provide the solutions for the system. For fixed rates these two equations determine the price of non-traded goods and the volume of money. In effect, Equation (13.12) independently determines the price of non-traded goods and Equation (13.13) the volume of money. For flexible rates these two equations jointly determine the price of non-traded goods and the exchange rate.

The two models, with and without capital movements, correspond to quite different mechanisms of adjustment. For example, in the first model, with fixed rates, an excess demand for money will lead to a reduction in real private expenditure which, in turn, will improve the trade balance, increase the volume of money and thus accommodate the excess demand. With flexible rates the potential improvement in the trade balance leads to a revaluation which lowers the price level, relieving the excess demand. By contrast, with capital movements an excess demand for money under fixed rates leads directly to an accommodating inflow of capital; under flexible rates the excess demand leads to a potential inflow and a revaluation, relieving the excess demand.

The two models may also correspond to different time horizons. If capital markets are assumed to adjust first, in the longer run the real sector must come into play since any borrowings/lendings will need to be serviced or repaid.

Notes for Chapter 13

1 See J. Frenkel and H. Johnson (eds) (1976); IMF (1977).

2 See: V. Argy (1978); R. Boyer (1975); R. Dornbusch (1975); W. M. Corden (1977), Chapters 1–3; P. Jonson and H. Kierzkowski (1975); R. McKinnon (1976a); A. Swoboda (1977); R. Dornbusch (1973).

3 For examples of monetarist models which focus on the real side only see R. Dornbusch (1973); A. Swoboda (1977).

4 Now money demand is deflated by the overall price level whereas in the Keynesian model we deflated it by the domestic price level. In the context of a monetarist model, where the price of all tradables is included in the overall price level, this is much more important.

5 This, of course, has an almost exact parallel in the neo-Keynesian model of aggregate demand without sterilisation where the *IS* and *B* schedules determine equilibrium and the *LM* schedule shifts to accommodate the new equilibrium.

Chapter 14

The Choice of Model – Issues and Evidence

Introduction

In the three previous chapters we presented three models, one neo-Keynesian, two essentially monetarist in spirit. In this chapter we intend to focus on the key features that divide the neo-Keynesian model from the two-sector monetarist model and to look at a number of issues posed by these models and at some evidence which bears on their usefulness and appropriateness.[1]

Our presentation of these two models reveals that there are several differences in their analytical approaches. First, Keynesians are more flexible in their approach to capital market integration; Keynesian models are able, as we have seen, to accommodate a whole range of assumptions about the degree of capital mobility. Monetarists, on the other hand, tend to be committed to the assumption of perfect capital mobility.[2]

Second, monetarists tend to assume that monetary authorities are unable or unwilling to sterilise the monetary effects of balance of payments developments, when exchange rates are fixed. Keynesians, on the other hand, while predisposed to assume that sterilisation is possible over the time horizon relevant to macro-analysis, do not have a strong commitment here and their models, as we saw, can easily accommodate all the possibilities.

Third, and most important, monetarists assume that the law of one price applies to traded goods while Keynesians assume that the price of traded goods, produced domestically, is largely determined by domestic costs, independently of exchange rate and foreign price changes. Typically, for example, if there is a devaluation a monetarist would argue that the domestic price of the traded goods would increase in the same proportion (while, of course, the foreign price would be unchanged) even though, initially at any rate, the domestic cost of producing these goods is unchanged. A Keynesian, on the other hand, would assume that the foreign currency price of the goods is (initially) lowered in the same proportion while the domestic price remains unchanged.

Fourth, Keynesian models assign a key role to Marshall–Lerner conditions, as we have seen, while monetarist models assign key roles to substitution elasticities in consumption and production for traded and non-traded goods within the domestic economy. These differences reflect the different theoretical constructs of the underlying model. It is easily demonstrable, for example, that in a neo-Keynesian model, a devaluation or a change in foreign prices can have perverse effects while in a monetarist model a devaluation or a foreign price change cannot have perverse effects.

Fifth, and also very important, Keynesians take the view that, typically, labour markets adjust with a considerable lag, so real and monetary disturbances tend to affect, first, output and, subsequently, prices. International monetarists, on the other hand, tend to be more comfortable with the assumption that output is exogenous and prefer to trace the effects of real and monetary changes on prices, contending that labour markets and prices, in fact, adjust fairly quickly.

These, then, are the issues to which this chapter will address itself.

Notation used in this chapter

B = balance of payments (Δ in net foreign assets of the central bank)
CA = current account of the balance of payments
D = domestic assets of the central bank
K = net capital flows
m = money multiplier
Mo = money supply
r = domestic interest rate
rf = foreign interest rate
Y = nominal GNP

Financial Integration and Sterilisation with Fixed Exchange Rates

To illustrate some key relationships that exist between financial integration and sterilisation in a fixed rate world, we begin with a very simple model of the financial sector of an open economy.[3] We consider, first, the case where there is no sterilisation.

The Model

$$Mo = eY - rf \tag{14.1}$$

$$\Delta Mo = m(B + \Delta D) \tag{14.2}$$

$$B \quad = CA + K \tag{14.3}$$

$$K \quad = g(\Delta r - \Delta rf) \tag{14.4}$$

Equation (14.1) is a money demand equation, where the demand for money is assumed equal to the actual volume of money. The change in the volume of money in Equation (14.2) is a multiple m of the change in base money which in turn is composed of the change in domestic assets and the change in net foreign assets of the central bank. Equation (14.3) is the balance of payments identity while Equation (14.4) explains capital flows in terms of changes in interest rate differentials (our stock version).[4]

If we assume that, in the short run, the level of income and the current account are exogenous, the solution to this model for capital flows is:

$$K = \frac{eg}{f+mg}\Delta Y - \frac{mg}{f+mg}CA - \frac{mg}{f+mg}\Delta D - \frac{fg}{f+mg}\Delta rf \tag{14.5}$$

The equation asserts that capital flows are determined by a change in the level of income, the current account, a change in domestic assets and a change in foreign interest rates. An increase in income will increase the demand for money and draw capital in from overseas; an improvement in the current account will result in an excess supply of money that will encourage an outflow of capital; an open market purchase (in the form of an increase in D) will also lead to an excess supply of money which will induce an outflow, offsetting at least part of the original excess supply; finally, an increase in the foreign interest rate will directly induce an outflow of capital.

Our immediate concern is with the coefficient attaching to ΔD. g represents the responsiveness of capital flows to interest rate differentials and, hence, the mobility of capital. If $g=0$ then this coefficient reduces to zero. At the other extreme, if $g\rightarrow\infty$ (there is perfect capital mobility), the coefficient approaches unity. This means that the more mobile the capital the closer the coefficient for ΔD will approach 1. This coefficient is known as the offset coefficient.[5] It represents, in effect, the degree to which an exogenous change in monetary policy is offset by a movement in capital.

To simplify, Equation (14.5) can be rewritten as:

$$K = b_1\Delta Y - b_2CA - b_2\Delta D - b_3\Delta rf) \tag{14.5a}$$

where b_2 represents the offset coefficient.

We now extend the model to allow for the possibility of sterilisation.[6] Suppose the monetary authorities attempt to sterilise the monetary effects of the balance of payments by changes in their domestic assets. Then:

$$\Delta D = A - a_1(CA + K) \tag{14.6}$$

where a_1 represents the extent of sterilisation and A is the 'autonomous' component of domestic monetary policy.

The system can be solved for capital flows and the volume of money. The solutions are:

$$K = \frac{b_1}{1 - a_1 b_2}\Delta Y - \frac{b_2(1 - a_1)}{1 - a_1 b_2}CA - \frac{b_2}{1 - a_1 b_2}A - \frac{b_3}{1 - a_1 b_2}\Delta rf \tag{14.7}$$

and

$$\Delta Mo = \frac{m(1 - b_2)}{1 - a_1 b_2}A + \frac{b_1 m(1 - a_1)}{1 - a_1 b_2}\Delta Y + \frac{m(1 - a_1)(1 - b_2)}{1 - a_1 b_2}CA - \frac{mb_3(1 - a_1)}{1 - a_1 b_2}\Delta rf \tag{14.8}$$

These results show that the larger is a_1 (the greater the attempt to sterilise) the larger is the coefficient for A in Equation (14.8), that is, the more successful independent monetary policy is in securing control over the volume of money. Where $a_1 = 1$ the coefficient is m, or in other words, there is complete control over the money supply. At the same time, the coefficient for A in Equation (14.7) increases as a_1 increases, that is, the effect on capital flows and reserves is even stronger. Where, however, $a_1 = 1$ and $b_2 = 1$ (in other words, there is complete sterilisation and perfect capital mobility), sterilising will result in an infinite change in reserves and unstable effects on the volume of money.

One or two examples will serve to illustrate the economic meaning of these findings. Suppose, first, that the offset coefficient is 0.5 and that there is no sterilisation. Then if the domestic assets are allowed to increase by 10 units (if, for example, there is an open market purchase), the interest rate will fall and there will be an outflow of capital of 5 units, allowing base money, on balance, to increase by 5 units only. Suppose, however, the monetary authorities wished to add 10 units to base money, then in the face of an 'offset' of 5 units they would need to sterilise by buying a further 5 units of domestic assets. This, however, will result in a new outflow of 2.5 units. To secure a net increase in base money of 10 units they must now purchase 2.5 additional domestic assets. This will lead to a further outflow and further sterilisation.

In Equation (14.7) if $b_2=0.5$ and $a_1=0$ (that is, there is no sterilisation) the coefficient for A is 0.5. If $a_1=1$, however, the coefficient becomes 1. In other words, the reserve loss will be twice as large. In Equation (14.8) if $m=3$, $b_2=0.5$ and $a_1=0$, the coefficient for A is 1.5, that is, the volume of money will have increased by three times the increase in base money, which, in this case, is half the initial open market operation. If $m=3$, $b_2=0.5$ and $a_1=1$ the coefficient is 3 and base money will have increased by the initial open market operation.

If the offset coefficient were 1, then, without sterilisation, any initial injection of base money would all leak overseas because in this case the domestic interest rate could not depart from the foreign interest rate. If the monetary authorities, nonetheless, wished to secure an independent change in base money they would have to keep sterilising indefinitely. The reserve loss, in this case, would be infinite.

We arrive, then, at the important conclusion that, in theory, as long as $b_2<1$ (capital mobility is imperfect) control over the money supply, and hence independent monetary policy, is possible. It is, however, also evident that attempts to sterilise to secure an independent monetary policy in conditions where the degree of capital mobility is high will run up against a serious foreign reserve constraint. For example, an attempt to persist with a restrictive policy, by sterilisation of inflows, will so build up reserves that speculation might then set in, at which point control over the money supply will almost certainly be lost.

Before concluding this section it is worth noting that Equation (14.6) may be viewed as a reaction function for the monetary authorities where A would represent such variables as inflation and/or the rate of unemployment. What we have, then, is two equations, (14.5) and (14.6), that can be jointly estimated to determine simultaneously the offset coefficient (b_2) and the sterilisation coefficient (a_1).[7]

Evidence of Financial Integration

How does one go about seeking evidence of financial integration? Studies in this area fall, neatly, into four categories.[8]

First, there are studies that look at the interest rate dispersion among select industrial countries and its trend over time. Second, there are studies that look at the degree of covariation and the trend in the covariation in interest rates among select industrial countries. Third, there are the studies that focus on the covered interest differential (that is, the interest differential adjusted for the forward premium or discount) and again its trend over time. Fourth, there are the studies that concentrate on the offset coefficient (and its trend).

Table 14.1 Standard deviation short-term interest rates – industrial countries – to 1973

Year	Standard Deviation Six Countries[a]	Year	Standard Deviation Six Countries[a]
1952	1.58	1963	0.60
1953	1.10	1964	0.64
1954	1.03	1965	0.90
1955	0.99	1966	0.73
1956	1.27	1967	0.98
1957	1.25	1968	1.89
1958	1.93	1969	1.51
1959	1.26	1970	1.21
1960	2.22	1971	1.11
1961	1.02	1972	1.08
1962	0.84	1973	2.20

Source: International Monetary Fund, *International Financial Statistics.*
[a]Six countries include USA, Canada, Belgium, France, Germany, UK.
Canada, USA, UK: Treasury Bill Rates.
Belgium, France, Germany: call money rates.

Data on interest rate dispersion is provided in Table 14.1. Taking the table at its face value it suggests (as one would expect) a significant jump in the degree of financial integration in the early 1960s but (surprisingly) some possible reversal in this trend in the late 1960s. Several limitations, however, attach to this test. First, changes in interest rate dispersion may be the result of changes in the degree of cyclical co-ordination in the group of countries. For example, if business cycles become more synchronised one might expect less interest rate dispersion.[9]

Second, in an adjustable peg regime, there are periods (as in the late 1960s) when exchange rate expectations are unstable and firm expectations are held about changes in exchange rates. Under these conditions, interest rate levels will tend to become more dispersed without implying any diminution in the degree of financial integration. Also levels of interest rates tend to be affected by rates of inflation; hence a change in the dispersion in inflation rates could have a significant effect on the dispersion of interest rates. In this case, it is the change in integration in the market for goods that is responsible for the change in interest rate dispersion.[10]

Third, a change in financial integration need not necessarily manifest itself in interest rate harmonisation; it may simply manifest itself in larger movements of capital. Fourth, the test is clearly inapplicable for periods when flexible exchange rates are in force. In this case, interest rates will tend to be more widely dispersed, reflecting the wider differences in rates of inflation made possible by flexible exchange rates. A more relevant test here might be the dispersion in real interest rates.[11]

Studies that look at the covariation in interest rates tend to find significant positive correlation coefficients for links between domestic and foreign interest rates, but these coefficients are not usually close to unity.[12] Moreover, the correlation coefficients are well below unity when the exercise is carried out in first difference form. These studies, however, are subject to limitations very similar to those raised against the first test.[13]

The covered differential is clearly the most direct measure available of the degree of integration. If the covered differential, appropriately measured, is small enough to cover costs of transactions only, that would be an indication that all potential profits from arbitrage have been fully exploited and, therefore, that integration is 'perfect'. Some of the evidence bearing on this is reviewed in a subsequent chapter pp. 223–4.[14] To anticipate, there is some evidence, for some markets, that there is little in the way of unexploited profits, at least in normal (non-crisis) periods.

Finally, there is the offset coefficient. The advantage of the offset coefficient is that it appears to provide a precise measure of the degree of financial integration. At the same time, it allows comparisons across countries in the degree to which they are integrated and, moreover, in principle, it can be used as a means of evaluating trends in integration. On the other hand, there are serious econometric problems in measuring this offset coefficient[15] and, of course, it is only appropriate for fixed rate regimes. By contrast, the covered differential can be applied to any exchange rate regime but, while it need not require the use of econometrics, there are very difficult data limitations associated with the test. Nor does it provide a precise measure of the degree of integration as a basis for comparison across countries.

There have been numerous studies of the offset coefficient for several countries. A summary of these studies by Kreinin and Officer[16] concluded that 'The clear majority of estimates result in offset coefficients that are negative and statistically significant but distinctly below unity in absolute value'.

We can now summarise our review of the state of the evidence on financial integration. Much depends on the capital markets tested[17] and the time horizon covered. At the same time, on the face of it the evidence does appear somewhat conflicting. Focusing on the last two tests, the test using the covered differential suggests a very high degree of integration in the more advanced capital markets while the test using the offset coefficient suggests a somewhat lesser degree of integration.

The apparent contradiction might be reconcilable in the following way. Suppose financial integration were perfect. An open market purchase will lower domestic interest rates, lead to an outflow and, in due course, to an offsetting increase in the forward premium on the domestic currency. This allows some interest differential and, hence, the open market purchase will not have been fully offset by an outflow even though financial markets are fully integrated. In other words, an offset coefficient significantly less than one may be consistent with perfect integration.[18]

Kreinin–Officer themselves summarise some of the evidence in these terms. 'While international integration in the bond market may have increased over time the evidence indicates that it is far from complete, contrary to the monetarist hypothesis of perfect capital mobility.'[19]

Evidence on Sterilisation

There are several studies[20] that have attempted to evaluate, by means of an estimated reaction function, the degree to which the monetary authorities tried to sterilise the effects of the balance of payments on the volume of money.

These studies have also been summarised by Kreinin and Officer[21] who conclude:

> Results of estimating sterilization coefficients uniformly . . . run counter to the monetarist theory. In 4 of the 6 relevant studies statistically significant sterilization coefficients appear in all equations indicating the presence of sterilization. . . . In most cases over all 6 studies, the estimated sterilization coefficient is negative, significant and below unity in absolute value. On occasion, the coefficient is not significantly different from −1 suggesting full sterilization. . . .[22]

The Law of One Price for Traded Goods

Does the law of one price hold at all times for traded goods as monetarists contend? Several types of tests may be undertaken. One common test is to regress export prices of a single country against home unit labour costs (or domestic prices) as well as foreign prices (in a common currency). The law of one price hypothesises that foreign prices could tend to be the dominant influence rather than unit labour costs. This test was carried out by Dornbusch–Krugman and the OECD.[23]

The evidence can be summarised as follows. For both studies, in virtually every country, domestic costs play a significant role in determining export prices. In the OECD study, competitors' prices also made a contribution to export prices; however, this element tended to be more important in the smaller countries (the Netherlands, Norway, Sweden and Austria) than in the larger industrial countries (Germany, the UK and the USA). In the Dornbusch–Krugman study, competitors' prices appeared to play a significantly lesser role, particularly in the large countries.

A careful study of export pricing of different countries for a number of products was also undertaken by Kravis and Lipsey[24] who found evidence of substantial differences in prices. Similar results were obtained by Isard who also found that changes in exchange rates had significant effects on relative prices for a whole range of manufacturing goods.[25]

The evidence strongly suggests that the law of one price, in the strict sense in which the term is interpreted in the literature, does not in general hold for heterogeneous manufacturing goods; it would be more applicable to economies whose export goods, for example, tend to be predominantly agricultural. However, there is evidence that the prices of goods traded in competitive world markets do tend to adjust, in part at least, to competitors' prices independently of movements in unit labour costs in the home economy. Moreover, this tendency is more powerful the smaller the economy, which is more likely to be a price taker in world markets. The state of the art on this issue is best summarised in the words of Kravis and Lipsey[26] who, in their latest work, concluded: 'We think it unlikely that the higher degree of national and international commodity arbitrage that many versions of the monetarist theory of the balance of payments contemplate is typical of the real world.'

Speed of Adjustment of Output and Prices

Finally, what is the speed of adjustment of labour markets? The evidence (at least until the early 1970s) strongly suggests that there are long lags in the adjustment of wages and prices to changes in real demand in the economy. The evidence comes from simulations of large scale econometric models of several economies – large as well as relatively small ones.[27] For example, for an increase in government expenditure nearly all these models show a deterioration in the real output multiplier after two years or so, many showing virtually complete real crowding out after a period varying from 4 to 10 years. In short, output typically adjusts first, and over a time horizon of, say, at least a year and a half output effects are dominant; subsequently price effects become progressively more important, becoming over-riding after say three years or so.

Summary of Conclusions

What, then, are we to conclude from our general review? The degree of financial integration will vary across countries, across markets and over time, but, on balance, the evidence, for most economies, is probably against the strong monetarist hypothesis of perfect capital mobility. The evidence on sterilisation also appears to be contrary to the monetarist hypothesis while the evidence is largely against the law of one price in commodity markets. Finally, labour markets appear to adjust fairly slowly.

Recalling that our neo-Keynesian model can accommodate a variety of assumptions about capital mobility and sterilisation our conclusion would have to be that for short-term analysis at least the neo-Keynesian model is the more appropriate and relevant one. For short-term analysis the aggregate demand sector of the Keynesian model would appear to represent more realistically the real world, and in the chapters that follow we will frequently draw on this model, although we will also occasionally, even for short-term analysis, make reference to the monetarist model.

However, for longer-term analysis when, say, labour markets have adjusted, the complete neo-Keynesian model is the more relevant one and we will use it for that purpose. But, for longer-term analysis, the monetarist model also has valuable insights to offer. As it happens, and this is important, although the mechanism and dynamics of adjustment are quite different in the two models, they typically yield very similar longer-term outcomes.

It may be useful before we complete this chapter to provide some illustrations of the last point. In both models with fixed exchange rates and no sterilisation monetary expansion will have no effect on prices or output in the long run, whatever the assumption about capital mobility. In both models too with flexible exchange rates monetary expansion will lead to a proportionate devaluation and a proportionate increase in domestic prices while leaving both output and the interest rate unchanged. Finally, as we demonstrate in Chapter 15, without sterilisation a devaluation or an increase in foreign prices will lead to a proportionate increase in domestic prices, again leaving both output and the interest rate unchanged. At the same time, in the two models, there will be a once-for-all increase in reserves.

Notes for Chapter 14

1 The rationale for disregarding the EAPC is that we have already argued that it can be viewed as providing an alternative aggregate supply sector. In other words, it can be used to supplement the aggregate demand sector of the neo-Keynesian model.

2 At the same time, as we indicated, they do sometimes abstract altogether from capital movements and focus on real adjustment only.
3 This is based on a simplified version of Kouri–Porter. See P. Kouri and M. Porter (1974).
4 See the Annex to Chapter 11.
5 The basic insight into the offset coefficient was first developed by Kouri–Porter.
6 See V. Argy and P. Kouri (1974).
7 This is the approach in V. Argy and P. Kouri (1974).
8 V. Argy and Z. Hodjera (1973); P. Kenen (1976); C. Stem, J. Makin and D. Logue (eds) (1976); R. G. Di Calogero (1977); W. G. Minot (1974); M. Fase (1976).
9 For evidence on the synchronisation of business cycles see D. Ripley (1978). The evidence available suggests that the synchronisation of business cycles, if anything, would have increased in the second half of the 1960s and into the early 1970s.
10 For some evidence relating to this see Chapter 24.
11 See R. G. Di Calogero (1977) for a test along these lines for the more recent period.
12 See M. E. Kreinin and L. H. Officer (1978).
13 See C. Stem, J. Makin and D. Logue (eds) (1976); M. Fase (1976); R. G. Di Calogero (1977).
14 See Chapter 19.
15 See M. E. Kreinin and L. H. Officer (1978), pp. 52–9 for some discussion of this.
16 See M. E. Kreinin and L. H. Officer (1978), pp. 57–9. See also P. J. K. Kouri and M. Porter (1974); M. J. M. Neumann (1978); Z. Hodjera (1976).
17 For example, Euro-currency markets are more closely integrated than domestic markets.
18 An important implication of all this is that even in a fixed rate world perfect financial integration need not imply complete loss of control over the volume of money. See also Chapter 19.
19 M. E. Kreinin and L. H. Officer (1978), p. 71.
20 V. E. Argy and P. J. K. Kouri (1974); R. J. Herring and R. C. Marston (1977); J. Artus (1976); W. Branson, H. Halttunen and P. Masson (1977). See also M. E. Kreinin and L. H. Officer (1978), pp. 59–60.
21 M. E. Kreinin and L. H. Officer (1978), pp. 59–60.
22 It should be pointed out, however, that so long as sterilisation is not complete (is less than 1), the longer-run implications are very similar to the case where sterilisation is zero.
23 R. Dornbusch and P. Krugman (1976); OECD (1973).
24 I. B. Kravis and R. E. Lipsey (1971). See also I. B. Kravis and R. E. Lipsey (1978).
25 P. Isard (1977).
26 I. B. Kravis and R. E. Lipsey (1978).
27 See: G. Fromm and L. R. Klein (1973); J. F. Helliwell (1971); J. Laury, G. Lewis and P. Ormerod (1978); J. Helliwell, T. Maxwell, H. Waslander (1979); P. Jonson, E. Moses and C. Wymer (1977); C. Fitzgerald and C. Higgins (1977).

Part Three

Global Inflation and Unemployment

Chapter 15

Theories of Global Inflation – the 1970s

Introduction

The global acceleration in inflation in the early 1970s sparked a heated controversy over its fundamental causes.[1] The controversy will be reviewed in this chapter. At the same time, an attempt will be made to indicate the mechanisms by which external influences impinge on domestic inflation. Chapters 16 and 17 then examine the empirical evidence bearing on some of these controversies.

Table 15.1 summarises some of the facts on inflation. It shows the trends in the rate of inflation from 1966 to 1977 for the world as well as for select industrial countries. Two facts stand out from the table. First, the noticeable acceleration in the rate of inflation in these countries some time in the late 1960s or early 1970s. For example, in Canada, France, the UK and the USA the acceleration came as early as 1968/69; by contrast, in Australia, Germany, Italy and Japan the acceleration came a year or two later in 1970/71. Second, the sharp jump in the rate of inflation in all of the countries in 1973/74. In trying, then, to account for the inflationary experience of the industrial countries in the first half of the 1970s, we need to make a distinction between an early phase in the late 1960s and early 1970s and a later phase in 1973/74.

The USA as the Source of the Global Inflation of the Early 1970s

One school traces the origins of the inflationary experience of the 1970s to US policies in the late 1960s and early 1970s. According to this view US policies contributed in two distinct ways to world inflation. First, as a result of the Vietnam War and the social programmes of the Johnson years, fiscal policy became expansionary, and this fiscal expansion was, in the late 1960s, financed by monetary growth. This led to an acceleration in inflation which was then transmitted to the rest of the world. Second, the USA, beginning in 1970/71, also followed (as we saw) an expansionary monetary policy to counteract the recession at the time. This led to a sharp fall in domestic (and Euro-dollar) interest rates. As a consequence, the rest of the industrial world experienced large inflows of capital inflating their own volume of money and laying the foundations for their accelerating inflation. We have then a transmission, first, predominantly through increased prices and associated current account surpluses in the rest of the world and, second, through lower interest rates and large capital account surpluses outside the USA.

The Sociological Explanation

Another school traces the origins of the inflation of the early 1970s predominantly to domestic (home-grown) factors, which happened to be common to many of the industrial countries. The idea underlying all these explanations is that a number of sociological–political–cultural factors combined to generate persistent wage pressures in several countries in the late 1960s and early 1970s. These pressures were then accommodated by monetary growth.

Two particular (not entirely unrelated) themes appear to dominate this sociological literature. One theme asserts that the growth of the public sector, common to the industrial world, exerted major cost-push and/or demand-pull pressures on inflation. This particular theme is taken up and examined in Chapter 16.

A second theme is the view that wage earners exert pressures for increased wages on the strength not only of market forces or of recent price developments but also of an 'aspirations gap'.[2] This 'aspirations gap' is defined as the difference between a target and the actual rate of growth of real disposable incomes. In turn, the target growth of real disposable incomes for a relevant group may be founded on past experience, on real living standards in other countries or on new aspirations. The theory would predict, for example, that the rate of growth of nominal wage demands in a particular country will accelerate if:

(1) The rate of growth of productivity, and hence real income, slows down.
(2) The burden of taxes on households increases without perceived matching benefits flowing from the public sector.
(3) The share of wages in factor incomes (or the share of certain skilled workers – salary earners) falls.
(4) The country's relative standard of living deteriorates and/or there is increased awareness of inter-country living standards, and/or there is a large wage advance in neighbouring countries.

Table 15.1 Rates of inflation (consumer) select industrial countries and percentage change in world commodity price index

Country	*1966*	*1967*	*1968*	*1969*	*1970*	*1971*	*1972*	*1973*	*1974*	*1975*	*1976*	*1977*
Australia	3.1	3.1	2.7	3.0	3.9	6.0	5.9	9.4	15.1	15.2	13.5	12.3
Canada	3.8	3.6	4.1	4.5	3.4	2.8	4.8	7.6	10.9	10.8	7.6	8.0
France	2.6	2.8	4.5	6.1	5.9	5.4	6.0	7.4	13.6	11.8	9.2	9.5
Germany	3.6	1.7	1.6	1.9	3.4	5.2	5.5	7.0	7.0	5.9	4.6	3.9
Italy	2.4	3.8	1.3	2.7	5.0	4.8	5.7	10.8	19.1	17.2	16.7	17.0
Japan	4.9	4.1	5.6	5.6	7.3	6.3	4.8	11.7	22.7	12.2	9.3	8.1
United Kingdom	3.9	2.5	4.7	5.5	6.4	9.5	7.1	9.2	15.9	24.2	16.6	15.8
United States	3.0	2.8	4.2	5.4	5.9	4.3	3.3	6.2	11.0	9.2	5.7	6.5
World	5.1	4.3	5.0	5.2	6.0	5.9	5.8	9.4	15.0	13.3	11.0	11.3
Commodity prices (% change)[a]	0.1	−3.6	−0.5	7.7	6.3	1.2	12.1	50.0	67.8	− 9.0	5.4	10.3

Sources: International Monetary Fund, *International Financial Statistics. Monthly Report of the Deutsche Bundesbank* (Commodity Prices).

[a]Food and industrial raw materials – dollar basis.

(5) There is an upward revision of aspirations or expectations.

Jackson–Turner–Wilkinson[3] have emphasised the role of (2) particularly in the context of the UK.[4] Numerous other British economists have also placed considerable emphasis on (5). The upward revision of aspirations has been variously traced to combinations of a 'new climate of permissiveness', a 'full employment guarantee', the New Left influence, more generous unemployment benefits, less employer resistance due to higher capital intensity, social tensions created by the escalation of the Vietnam War, changes in trade union leadership favouring the younger and more militant.[5] Finally, Panic and Baxter[6] emphasise (4) arguing that with the world increasingly integrated and with the spread of multinationals, the competitive ethos at the international level produces an 'aspirations gap' leading to inflationary pressures.

The Commodity Price Shocks of 1973 and 1974

There is widespread agreement that the big increase in commodity prices that occurred in 1973 and 1974 exerted a significant cost-push effect on prices.

The reasons for the substantial increase in non-oil commodity prices (including food) in 1973 were complex. They include the coincidence of very high levels of activity in all the industrial countries, speculative demands (in part related to the international monetary crisis and the collapse of the fixed rate regime) and supply shortfalls in several commodity groups.[7] Then, beginning late 1973, following the Yom Kippur War in the Middle East, OPEC quadrupled its oil price, sending shock waves throughout the oil-consuming economies.

Imported Inflation in the Neo-Keynesian Model

The complete model of aggregate demand and aggregate supply spelt out in Chapter 11 will now be used to illustrate how, in an adjustable peg regime, inflation can be imported into a country from overseas. At the same time, our model allows us to identify domestic, as distinct from external, sources of inflation.

The basic model, it will be recalled, was composed of four markets: a goods market, a money market, a foreign exchange market and a labour market. Given the aims of this section, the model now needs to be extended in a number of ways. First, we allow for the use of exchange controls or various devices to control the movement of capital into and out of the country.[8] Second, we allow for a 'wage shock', in the sense that there is an increase in wage pressures at any given level of prices and real demand.[9] Third, and most important, we allow the monetary and fiscal authorities to vary the macro-instruments at their disposal to counteract disturbances originating overseas.[10]

The model allows us to identify three ways in which foreign conditions may influence domestic prices; first, through changes in foreign prices; second, through changes in foreign interest rates; third, through changes in real foreign demand. The extended model also identifies several domestic sources of inflation. These are the contribution of domestic monetary policy (the change in the domestic assets of the central bank) to the volume of money, discretionary fiscal policy, the change in the exchange rate, the capital flow regulations and the wage shock component. Except for the last, which originates in the private sector, all the other domestic sources are effectively policy instruments, which, of course, may be directed at counteracting external influences.

Since our major concern is with the external origins of inflation we focus now on the ways in which our three external sources interact on the domestic economy. We develop these in two steps. Initially, we assume that policy is neutral; this means, assuming the exchange rate is fixed, there is no sterilisation (the domestic assets of the central bank are held fixed) and no attempt is made to counteract external influences. Subsequently, we try to allow for counteracting macro-policy.

Consider, first, the effects of an increase in foreign prices. This will have four important impacts on the domestic economy. First, there will be substitution effects. If the Marshall–Lerner condition held, the substitution effects, in themselves, will lead to an excess demand for domestic goods. Second, the assumed improvement in the trade balance will lead to some increase in international reserves which, in turn, will increase the volume of money. Third, because we allow wages to adjust (fully) to changes in the overall price level, a change in foreign prices also leads to a wage–price spiral in the economy. Fourth, the combined effects of price changes, changes in real demand and in the current account will lead to a change in the interest rate and, in turn, in capital movements.

Full adjustment will take time. In the model, in long-run equilibrium, output and the interest rate will be unchanged while domestic prices will have increased in the same proportion as foreign prices. At the same time, the balance of payments will be restored to equilibrium, while monetary growth, coming from the improvement in reserves, will accommodate the increase in prices. This result is shown graphically in Figure 15.1. The increase in foreign prices shifts the aggregate supply schedule to the left and the aggregate demand schedule to the right (assuming substitution effects are non-perverse).

This demonstrates that with a passive government policy an increase in foreign prices will, ultimately, be fully imported. The result is consistent with equilibrium in our four markets. With domestic prices increasing in the same proportion as foreign prices, the labour market can only be in equilibrium if output did not change. Also with output, the interest rate and relative prices unchanged, the real demand for goods cannot change, so the goods market is in equilibrium. The money market will also be in equilibrium because the proportionate increase in prices will be accommodated by a proportionate increase in the volume of money leaving the interest rate unchanged. Finally, with relative prices, the interest rate and output all unchanged, the foreign exchange market will return to equilibrium.

No other outcome is consistent with equilibrium in all markets. To illustrate, suppose domestic prices increased less than proportionately. Then output must fall to equilibrate the labour market; the reason is that in this case the real wage rate to employers must have risen, forcing some reduction in production. However, with output down, the competitive position improved and the interest rate up, the foreign exchange market cannot be in equilibrium. So the surplus in the balance of payments will increase the volume of money, forcing up domestic prices and output and forcing down interest rates.

Figure 15.1 *The effects of an increase in foreign prices on domestic inflation*

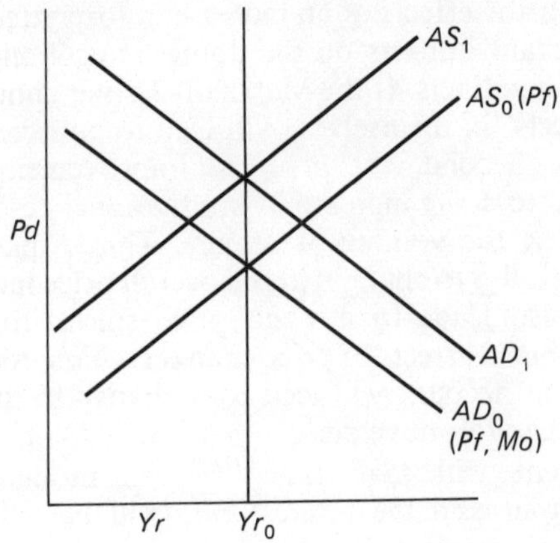

Now consider the effects of a reduction in foreign interest rates. There will be an inflow of capital which, by assumption, is allowed to increase the volume of money. Again, graphically, the aggregate demand schedule shifts to the right, increasing both output and domestic prices. Now with foreign prices and the exchange rate fixed, the real wage rate to suppliers of labour can remain unchanged, while, at the same time, the real wage rate to employers will fall, allowing some inducement to increase output. In equilibrium, too, the surplus in the capital account will be exactly offset by the deficit in the current account associated with the increase in prices and output.

Finally, consider the effects of an increase in real foreign demand. Domestic prices will be affected in two ways. First, there is a direct increase in the real demand for domestic goods. Second, the associated surplus in the balance of payments will lead to an inflow of money from overseas. Equilibrium will be restored to the balance of payments, with the increase in output and prices serving to offset the increase in foreign demand.[11] Graphically, this result is represented by a shift to the right in the aggregate demand schedule.

In all three instances, then, changes in overseas conditions were transmitted domestically in the form of an increase in domestic inflation. This treatment of imported inflation differs from the conventional treatment in the literature, which recognises three principal ways in which a country may import inflation from the rest of the world in a fixed rate regime. These are through (1) increases in the prices of internationally traded goods, (2) increases in foreign demand, and (3) the monetary effects of surpluses in the balance of payments.[12] Our model explicitly allows for the first two but its treatment of the third is distinctive. A surplus, per se, in the balance of payments which is not, say, sterilised does not necessarily indicate imported inflation; it may, for example, be the result of changes in domestic impulses. Moreover, any surpluses associated with changes in the prices of internationally traded goods or in foreign demand are explicitly accommodated in the model and do not represent an independent source of inflation. We do, however, recognise a third independent source of imported inflation from changes in foreign interest rates.

So far we have assumed that governments are passive, allowing external influences to make their full impact on the domestic economy. In reality, of course, the monetary and fiscal authorities may try to counteract the external disturbances to the domestic economy. The effects of an increase in foreign prices may be neutralised by a revaluation; the effects of a drop in the foreign interest rate may be offset by a combination of sterilisation policies and changes in capital controls or, again, the effects of an increase in real foreign demand may be offset by a deflationary fiscal policy combined with sterilisation operations (to mop up the increase in the cash base associated with the increase in reserves).[13]

The important methodological point emerges that if we want to know the extent to which inflation was, in fact, imported into a particular economy we need to know not only how the external influences behaved but also how policy responded to these disturbances. In other words, it is not sufficient to know that external influences are potentially inflationary; it is also important to know the degree to which these influences were counteracted by domestic policy.

One further comment about the complete model is in order. The complete model serves to demonstrate how complicated the relationship is between monetary growth and inflation. For example, in the model, foreign prices will directly affect the domestic price level, improve reserves and lead to accommodating increases in the volume of money; or a wage 'shock' may lead to unemployment which the monetary authorities may try to counteract by increasing the volume of money. In both these instances, inflation accelerated first and was followed by an acceleration in monetary growth.

Imported Inflation in the Two-sector Monetarist Model

We now turn to the two-sector monetarist model of Chapter 13 and use it to show how foreign inflation is imported in models of this kind.[14]

Consider, first, the case where only real adjustment takes place and there are no capital flows. A rise in foreign prices will raise the price of traded goods proportionately, while initially the price of non-traded goods will be unchanged. Production of traded goods will now be more profitable so resources will move away from non-traded goods and towards the production of traded goods. Now, however, with the price of non-traded goods relatively more attractive consumption will switch towards non-traded goods.

With the overall price level rising and initially the money supply fixed, real money balances will fall, the interest rate will rise and real private expenditure on both traded and non-traded goods will fall. Assuming that the substitution effect is dominant, there will be an excess demand for non-traded goods, which will now raise the price of non-traded goods.[15] At the same time, the increase in production of traded goods combined with the unambiguous fall in the demand for traded goods will generate an excess supply of traded goods, which leads to an improvement in the current account. This increases the money supply, relieving, in part, the monetary shortage. With the interest rate now falling, demand for both traded and non-traded goods will rise. So long as the interest rate is above its initial level the rise in the price of traded goods must exceed the rise in the price of non-traded goods and so the current account must continue to be in surplus. Full equilibrium is reached when the original interest rate is restored, the price of non-traded goods increases in the same proportion as the price of traded goods and the economy reverts back to its original point of production (on its transformation schedule).

Graphically, the solution is shown in Figure 15.2 where A represents the starting position. A rise in foreign prices now shifts the *NT* and *TB* schedules to the right and the *LM* schedule to the left. Initially, the economy is placed at B where there is a current account surplus. This leads to an increase in the volume of money shifting the *LM* schedule to the right until full equilibrium is reached at C where domestic prices and the volume of money have increased in the same proportion as foreign prices, leaving the domestic interest rate unchanged.

This result is consistent with equilibrium in all three markets. With the original price ratio and the interest rate restored the markets for traded and non-traded goods are in equilibrium. Also the money market is in equilibrium with the volume of money accommodating the increase in domestic prices.

Figure 15.2 *The effects of foreign inflation on domestic prices in the two-sector monetarist model*

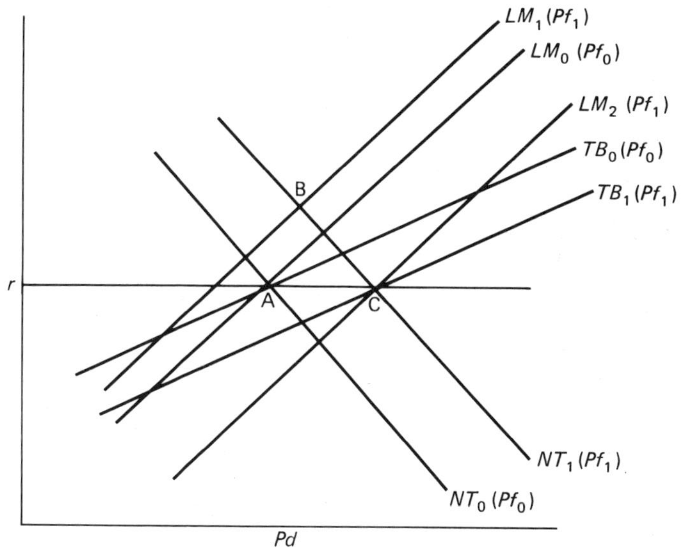

To appreciate this suppose that, in fact, domestic prices had not risen in the same proportion and the interest rate was now higher than initially. There would then be an excess supply of traded goods and an excess demand for non-traded goods. The associated surplus would then draw more money into the economy forcing the domestic price level up and the interest rate down.

Finally, consider the case where there is perfect financial integration. The initial higher interest rate will induce an inflow of capital which will add to the volume of money. At the same time, the excess demand for non-traded goods will force up the price of non-traded goods, create an excess demand for money and attract a further inflow of capital. This continues until the original price ratio is restored. The solution is the same as the previous one, except that the increase in the volume of money will come from the inflow of capital and not from the current account surplus. This also means that the adjustment is much quicker, without necessitating a shift in resources.

The result – that inflation is fully imported – is the same result we reached in the neo-Keynesian model, despite the fact that the mechanism of adjustment is quite different in the two cases. This is a reassuring result, allowing us to assert with some confidence that in a fixed rate world and no sterilisation, a rise in foreign prices will lead to a proportionate rise in domestic prices, leaving output unchanged. It is also worth noting here that exactly the same analysis applies to an exogenous devaluation, which, for the conditions assumed, would lead to a proportionate change in domestic prices, with output unchanged.

Annex

Notation

Pd = domestic price level
Pf = foreign prices denominated in foreign currency
rf = foreign interest rate
Yf = foreign real GNP
Yr = real GNP

The solutions for prices and output, to the neo-Keynesian model of Chapter 11, for the three exogenous changes (in *Pf, rf* and *Yf*) are:

$$\Delta Pd = \Delta Pf - \frac{\alpha_3\alpha_{12}}{k}\Delta rf + \frac{\alpha_{20}(\alpha_3 + \alpha_{12})}{k}\Delta Yf \qquad (15A.1)$$

$$\Delta Yr = -\frac{\alpha_3\alpha_{12}\alpha_{15}(1-\alpha_{14})}{k}\Delta rf + \frac{\alpha_{20}\alpha_{15}(1-\alpha_{14})(\alpha_{12}+\alpha_3)}{k}\Delta Yf \qquad (15A.2)$$

where

$$k = \alpha_{15}(1-\alpha_{14})[\alpha_3\alpha_9 + \alpha_{12}(1-\alpha_1+\alpha_9)] + ML(\alpha_{12}+\alpha_3)$$
$$ML = X(edx + edm - 1)$$

This confirms the argument in the text that without sterilisation an increase in foreign prices (*Pf*) will have no effect on output and will increase domestic prices proportionately. At the same time, a decrease in foreign interest rates (*rf*) or a rise in foreign output (*Yf*) will raise both domestic prices and output.

It can also easily be shown that an increase in foreign prices will leave the interest rate unchanged, that a fall in the foreign interest rate will lower domestic interest rates and, finally, that an increase in foreign output will actually lead to a fall in the domestic interest rate.

In the monetarist model (with and without capital movements) an increase in foreign prices will lead to a proportionate increase in domestic prices and in the volume of money, leaving the domestic interest rate unchanged.

Notes for Chapter 15

1 L. Krause and W. Salant (eds) (1977); J. M. Parkin and G. Zis (eds) (1976); OECD (1973).
2 See J. Baxter (1973).
3 D. Jackson, H. Turner and F. Wilkinson (1975).
4 See Chapter 16.
5 See the roundtable discussion (by F. Machlup, S. Marris, A. Lindbeck and H. Johnson) in E. Claasen and P. Salin (eds) (1972).
6 M. Panic (1978), Chapter 6; J. Baxter (1973).
7 Notably here the bad harvests in the Soviet Union and the collapse of the Peruvian anchovy catch. The use of price controls in the early 1970s in several countries also contributed to the shortfalls.
8 Technically, this is allowed for by a disturbance term in the capital flow equation.
9 This could be accommodated in the model by allowing a disturbance term in the aggregate supply equation.
10 Again, this is easily accommodated by postulating 'reaction functions' for the monetary and fiscal authorities.
11 In this case, too, the domestic interest rate will fall in equilibrium. This will also serve to offset the effects of the increase in foreign output on the balance of payments. See the Annex.
12 See, for example, OECD (1973); W. S. Salant (1977), pp. 179–93. Panel discussion by F. Machlup, Steven Marris, A. Lindbeck and H. Johnson, in E. Claasen and P. Salin (eds) (1972).
13 For a further discussion of how macro-instruments might be directed at counter-acting particular types of disturbances see Chapter 32.
14 This is what M.v. Whitman calls 'global monetarism'. See M.v. Whitman (1975); see also A. K. Swoboda (1977).
15 In theory, the reduction in expenditure may more than offset the substitution effect, forcing down the price of non-traded goods. This case will not be considered further.

Chapter 16

Public Sector Growth and Inflation – 1965 to 1975

Introduction

The view that public sector growth is inflationary is widely held. As early as 1945 Colin Clark had argued, in a controversial paper, that inflationary pressures would be created when the government's share of national income would exceed 25 per cent.[1] More recently Clark, who continues to be a leading protagonist of this view, has said 'the basic cause of inflation is excessive government expenditure and the excessive taxation which goes with it'.[2] Milton Friedman[3] takes a similar line when he argues:

> The more fundamental source of inflation in all our countries and of our economic difficulties has been the change in philosophy that occurred some time in the 1930s and earlier away from the belief in an individualistic society and toward a belief in the welfare state. The basic source of our difficulties is really the movement toward a welfare state because it is that movement toward a welfare state that had increasingly led us to expand our scope of government. And as government has expanded its scope, it has become increasingly difficult to finance the activities of governments by direct taxes and therefore has made the implicit hidden tax of inflation an ever more attractive strategy.

This is also the view of Jackson–Turner–Wilkinson:[4]

> The fact that this (inflationary) disturbance started in the industrial countries . . . appears to confirm the importance we attach to the fundamental change in the background conditions of the preceding era (of moderate inflation) which was brought about in the late 1960s by the great increase in direct taxation on wage earners.

Bacon–Eltis,[5] following a route very similar to Jackson–Turner–Wilkinson, assert:

> The British people voted for higher social spending and then set off rapid wage inflation when they realised to their surprise that they were expected to pay for it . . . If workers are frustrated by rising taxation either inflation will accelerate (if the money supply is allowed to expand) or unemployment will rise (if the money supply is controlled) . . . Governments will be faced with the choice of either more inflation than in the past or more unemployment or, as a third alternative, tougher incomes policies with stronger sanctions.

Finally, the link between public sector growth and inflation is the dominant theme in the very recent book by Buchanan–Wagner[6] who argue:

> Budget deficits, inflation and an accelerating growth in the relative size of government – these have become characteristic features of the American political economy in the post-Keynesian era . . . We do suggest that it is reasonable to describe inflation as one consequence of budget deficits and hence indirectly as a consequence of the Keynesian conversion.

These quotations suggest that there are basically two views about how public sector growth can generate inflation. One view, represented by the British economists (notably Bacon–Eltis and Jackson–Turner–Wilkinson), emphasises a tax (cost) push element in the inflationary process (with monetary accommodation following) while a second view, represented by American economists (notably Friedman and Buchanan), emphasises the effects of public sector growth on real demand, deficits and monetary growth.

The Growth of the Public Sector

The salient facts on recent public sector growth for select industrial countries are presented in Table 16.1. It shows that the weight of public expenditure in GDP was larger in the first half of the 1970s than in the second half of the 1960s in each of the eight countries. In four of the eight countries, the growth of the government sector accelerated very substantially in the years 1974/75. For example, whereas the mean growth in the public sector in 1970–73 was some 1.9 percentage points for the eight countries, the mean growth in 1974/75 was about 4.4 percentage points, about twice the earlier acceleration. This acceleration in growth in the later period was particularly sharp in Australia, Germany and the UK.

Public Sector Growth, Deficits and Money Creation

One way to test the thesis that public sector growth is inflationary is to look to see if there is a close association for each country between:

Table 16.1 Total public expenditure as percentage of GDP

Country	*1965–69* *(1)*	*1970–73* *(2)*	*1974–75* *(3)*	*(2)–(1)* *(4)*	*(3)–(2)* *(5)*
Australia	26.3	26.9	31.8	0.6	4.9
	(17.9)	(18.3)	(22.1)		
Canada	31.6	36.3	39.3	4.7	3.0
France	37.3	38.1	41.4	0.8	3.3
Germany	36.0	37.3	43.6	1.3	6.3
Italy	35.6	38.8	42.6	3.2	3.8
Japan	19.6	21.0	25.6	1.4	4.6
United Kingdom	37.1	38.5	45.2	1.4	6.7
United States	30.7	32.9	35.2	2.2	2.3

Source: OECD (1976a).
General Government current disbursements plus investment.
(Brackets for Australia represent Central Government).

(1) the relative size of the public sector and the relative size of the deficit; and (2) the relative size of the deficit and monetary growth.

The relationship between the relative size of the public sector and the relative size of the deficit can be seen by comparing Table 16.2 with Table 16.1. Table 16.2 shows the mean public sector deficit for the same three periods for each of the eight countries. In Italy, Canada and the USA, the deficit rose in line with the growth of the public sector. On the other hand, despite public sector growth in the early 1970s in Australia, France, Germany, Japan and the UK the relative size of the deficit actually fell. All the countries experienced a large increase in the relative size of their public sector deficits in 1974/75, some of which could be explained by the additional fiscal stimulus but most of which would be explained by the sharp decline in economic activity in those years.

Table 16.3 examines the evidence for the view that there is some association between the size of the deficit and monetary expansion.[7] Two tests are applied. A first test involves looking at the association between the size of the deficit as a percentage of GNP/GDP and the contribution to monetary growth by the government's borrowing from and/or running down its deposits with the central bank. The table shows the correlation coefficient between these two series (*DEF, CBF*). The correlation coefficient is positive and significant at the 5 per cent level only in Italy; there is, however, a positive relationship in

Table 16.2 Public sector net deficits (+) as a percentage of GDP/GNP – 1965 to 1975

Country	*1965–69*	*1970–73*	*1974–75*
Australia	1.7	0.7	2.5
Canada	−0.9	−0.5	0.8
France	0	−0.7	0.8
Germany	0.8	−0.5	3.7
Italy	2.7	5.4	8.2
Japan	−1.3	−1.8	2.1
United Kingdom	1.2	0.4	4.6
United States	0.7	1.0	2.5

Sources: For all countries except Australia:
OECD, General Government net lending as per cent of GDP/GNP – Table 1 (1976b).
For Australia: (Central Government) *Budget Papers,* financial year overall deficit as per cent of GDP.

Germany and the UK. In the other four countries the relationship is weak.

A second test looks at the association between the deficit (as defined) and the actual growth in base money (*H*). Any association between deficits and monetary growth on this test requires not only that deficits be financed by central banks but also that this source of monetary growth be dominant. Again the correlation is significant and positive only for Italy. In Germany the association now breaks down altogether while in the UK it is weaker.

A quite different way to proceed is to estimate a reaction function for the monetary authorities (in other words, explain by the use of econometrics the behaviour of the monetary authorities). This reaction function would have the budget deficit as one explanatory variable. This is the approach, for example, in Niskanen,[8] Gordon[9] and Willett–Lancy.[10] Niskanen assumes that the Federal Reserve System in the USA reduces the money supply when real economic growth or inflation accelerates and increases the money supply when the federal deficit increases. His conclusion is that when explicit account (by use of a dummy) is taken of the large shift in monetary policy in the last decade there is virtually no significant effect of the federal deficit on money. Gordon estimates a monetary reaction function for eight countries (Canada, France, Italy, Japan, Germany, Sweden, USA and the UK) using the following variables: wage rates, capacity utilisation, prices of traded goods, the fiscal deficit, international reserves and political dummies. Of the eight countries, the fiscal deficit is positive and significant only in Japan. Willett–Lancy estimate equations for monetary growth in the UK and Italy for the years 1956–76 using wage growth, the change in foreign reserves, the central government deficit and the difference between the growth of

Table 16.3 Correlations of deficits (*DEF*), central bank financing (*CBF*) and monetary (base money) growth (*H*)

Country	*DEF, CBF*	*DEF, H*
Australia	−0.24	−0.25
Canada	0.32	0.45
France	0.25	−0.64[a]
Germany	0.62	−0.41
Italy	0.75[a]	0.86[a]
United Kingdom	0.56	0.39
United States	0.18	0.31

Sources: DEF For all countries except Australia: General Government OECD (1976b). For Australia: *Budget Papers*, overall deficit, as percentage of GDP, of Central Government.

CBF International Monetary Fund, *International Financial Statistics*.
Increase in central bank claims on government adjusted (where available) for changes in government deposits in Central Bank – divided by base money at start of period. This represents the percentage change in base money for each country attributable to Central Bank 'financing' of the government.
For Australia: June to June change in claims on government – divided by base money at start of period.

H Percentage change in base money over relevant period.

[a]Significant at the 5% level.

import and consumer prices (to capture the excess import price pressure). The results are indecisive; when all four variables are used the deficit is not significant; however, when the wage variable is dropped the deficit is significant for both countries, suggesting collinearity between these two variables.

Tax-push Inflation – the Evidence

Apart from the effects on real demand, public sector growth may contribute to inflation by exerting a tax-push effect on prices.

Table 16.4 shows the changes in the overall burden of taxation in the sample of countries as well as the changes in the burden of particular taxes. Certain features of the table are quite striking. First, as expected, in all countries the overall tax burden increased between the mid-1960s and the mid-1970s. Second, the combined burden of taxes on enterprises (including company taxes, taxes on goods and services and social security charges), showed very little change for nearly all the countries over the period. Third, there was a significant increase in the burden of taxes on households (including social security) in all the countries. In nearly all the countries, too, this increased burden accounted very largely for the increased overall tax burden. The increase in expenditure by governments was, therefore, predominantly financed by the increase in taxes on households.

Table 16.4 Tax burdens (general government) as percentage of GDP

Country	Overall			Social Security[a]			Personal			Company			Goods and Services		
	1965–69	*1970–73*	*1974–75*	*1965–69*	*1970–73*	*1974–75*	*1965–69*	*1970–73*	*1974–75*	*1965–69*	*1970–73*	*1974–75*	*1965–69*	*1970–73*	*1974–75*
Australia	24.9	26.2	29.4	—	—	—	8.9	10.1	13.0	3.8	4.1	3.9	7.2	7.0	7.4
Canada	28.8	31.6	33.6	2.4	2.9	3.2	7.4	10.6	11.2	3.9	3.6	4.6	9.2	9.1	9.2
France	35.3	35.3	36.4	12.5 (2.4)	13.2 (2.7)	14.4 (3.1)	3.9	4.0	4.4	1.7	2.1	2.5	13.2	13.0	12.3
Germany	32.4	34.2	36.1	8.9 (3.9)	10.5 (4.7)	11.8 (5.2)	8.5	9.7	11.0	2.3	1.7	1.7	9.8	9.6	8.9
Italy	30.0	30.3	31.4	10.5	11.8	13.7	3.4	3.6	5.0	2.1	2.1	1.9	10.9	10.1	9.5
Japan	18.2	20.2	21.2	3.5 (1.3)	3.9 (1.5)	4.9 (1.8)	3.9	5.0	5.2	3.4	4.0	4.3	4.5	4.0	3.2
United Kingdom	33.8	35.2	36.4	5.1 (2.4)	5.6 (2.6)	6.6 (2.8)	10.3	11.3	13.4	2.3	2.8	2.5	9.5	9.2	8.8
United States	27.8	29.6	30.3	4.9 (2.0)	6.1 (2.5)	7.2 (2.9)	9.0	10.0	10.1	4.3	3.4	3.3	4.9	5.1	4.9

Source: OECD (1978e).

[a] Figures in parentheses represent employees' social security contribution as a percentage of GDP (where available).

What is the implication of this development for inflation? There is now growing empirical support for the view that higher tax rates on income are, in some countries, being shifted forward in the form of higher nominal wages.[11] In one of the most recent of these studies the OECD[12] estimates equations for price and wage determination for a number of member countries. Income tax rates are explicitly allowed in the wage determination process. They conclude (p. 52) that:

> Forward tax shifting of personal income taxes is strongly supported by the results, suggesting that net-of-tax wage bargaining has become a real phenomenon in most OECD countries. The degree of tax shifting varies considerably however. The regression results obtained are consistent with more or less full net-of-tax bargaining in Belgium, Germany, the UK, Sweden and Finland. In Denmark and Canada the phenomenon may be more moderate with approximately two-thirds of taxes shifted, while the US and the Netherlands are at the lower end of the scale with income tax shifting estimated to be about one-third.

Using a more refined model of the wage bargaining process, where now the response of wage demands to taxation depends on whether real income aspirations are met, they find that:

> In the Scandinavian countries as well as in Australia, Belgium and in the UK there is a significant tendency for nominal wage demands to be raised where necessary to 'catch-up' any past shortfall in real after-tax wages compared with their normally expected increase.

As it happens this is also fairly consistent with results obtained from the other model.

Peacock–Ricketts[13] attempt some cross section tests of the relationship between relative tax (or expenditure) burdens and relative rates of inflation for a number of OECD countries for the years 1965–72. They find no evidence of any relationship between the average tax (or expenditure) burden and the average rate of inflation over that period for twenty OECD countries. This is so even when relative income and the rate of growth of GDP per head in those years were included as additional variables. However, when the change in the tax (or expenditure) burden between 1965 and 1972 is used (together with relative income and growth in real standards) the explanatory power improves somewhat,[14] particularly for the change in direct taxes. These authors are rightly cautious and modest in their claims for tests of this kind. There are many complex influences accounting for differences in the rate of inflation across countries and it is most difficult to isolate the role of relative tax burdens; moreover, the problem of reverse causation running from inflation to tax burdens is difficult to overcome.

Conclusions

The tentative conclusions to be drawn from our analysis are the following. With the exception of Italy, public sector growth in general does not appear to have contributed in any significant way to real demand in the economy by accelerating monetary growth through larger deficits.

On the other hand, the increased burden of income taxes, and the increased awareness of these taxes combined with the lack of perception of the benefits derived from the additional expenditures must have contributed in some degree, especially in the first half of the 1970s, to the inflationary spiral in the industrial countries. This would have been particularly striking in Australia, Canada, Germany and the UK and most in evidence in 1974/75 when the burden rose most sharply in Australia, Germany, Italy and the UK. Thus Colin Clark's view that there are limits to taxable capacity appears now to be vindicated albeit at somewhat higher levels than he had himself anticipated; moreover, these taxable limits may well be different in the different countries.

Notes for Chapter 16

1 C. Clark (1945). Clark argued that the wage and price inflation induced by the bigger tax burden would itself tend to restore the original government's share.
2 C. Clark (1976).
3 Quoted in J. W. Nevile (1976).
4 D. Jackson, H. Turner and F. Wilkinson (1975), p. xi.
5 R. Bacon and W. Eltis (1976). The views of Bacon and Eltis are developed in several publications. For their most recent presentation and also a critical evaluation of their work see C. Hadjimatheou and A. Skouras (1979); and R. Bacon and W. Eltis (1979).
6 J. Buchanan and R. Wagner (1977), p. 56. See also K. Brunner (ed.) (1978), pp. 569–81.
7 See also on this OECD (1977b), Chapter 2.
8 W. Niskanen (1978).
9 R. Gordon (1977).
10 T. Willett and L. Lancy (1978).
11 OECD (1978d), pp. 51–5 and Annex B; V. Argy and J. Salop (1979). See also the literature cited in these two references.
12 OECD (1978d).
13 A. Peacock and M. Ricketts (1978).
14 Similar results are obtained by D. Smith (1975).

Chapter 17

Global Inflation – the Evidence

The US Contribution to Global Inflation (1960–1973)

As indicated in Chapter 15, the USA can transmit inflation in three ways: first, by higher export prices for its products sold overseas; second, by lowering its own interest rates and inducing inflows of capital into the rest of the world; third, by increasing its own level of

Table 17.1 The US contribution to world inflation – 1960 to 1973 summary

	1960–64	*1965–66*	*1967–68*	*1969–72*
1. $\dot{P}x$	+0.6	+3.1	+1.6	+3.8
	1960–64	*1965–68*	*1969–70*	*1971–72*
2. r_{US}	3.0	4.8	6.5	4.2
	(1.7)	(1.9)	(0.9)	(0.3)
3. r_{eu}	4.0	5.7	9.2	6.0
	1960–64	*1965–68*	*1969–71*	*1972–73*
4. $\dot{M}_{US}$	3.8	14.1	5.7	9.9
5. $\dot{Y}r_{US}$	4.0	4.8	1.9	5.6
	1960–64		*1965–68*	*1969–73*
6. $\frac{M}{Y}$	4.3		4.9	5.9

Source: IMF, *International Financial Statistics.*

$\dot{P}x$ = percentage increase in US export prices

r_{US} = US Treasury Bill rate (brackets show real interest rates – defined simply as the nominal less the rate of inflation)

r_{eu} = Euro-dollar rate in London

$\dot{M}_{US}$ = percentage increase in volume of US imports

$\dot{Y}r_{US}$ = percentage increase in real US gross national product

$\frac{M}{Y}$ = ratio (percentage) of imports to gross national product (US)

Numbers in parentheses in line 2 represent real interest rates.

activity and/or through structural shifts in its own demand for the rest of the world's exports.

Table 17.1 summarises the evidence bearing on these three transmission mechanisms. US export prices rose rapidly in 1965/66, then slowed down in the subsequent two years but rose again sharply in the years 1969–72. US short-term interest rates rose in the years 1965–68 but there was a sharp upsurge in 1969/70 followed by an even sharper decline. These fluctuations were magnified in the Euro-dollar market. Line 2 shows, however, that real interest rates (in brackets) actually continued to fall after 1968.[1] Lines 4 and 5 show the percentage increase in the volume of imports and real GNP in the USA. In 1965–68 the volume of imports rose very rapidly, then fell sharply but rose again in 1972/73. The major discrepancy with real output growth occurs in 1965–68 when imports rose very much more sharply than real GNP.[2]

To summarise, the impulses are conflicting in particular phases. For example, in 1969/70 the USA was directly transmitting inflation through its higher export prices but, at the same time, transmitting deflation through its relatively high interest rates and, additionally, through its lower rate of growth in real demand. In 1971/72, however, the impulses became predominantly inflationary. Export prices continued to rise fairly rapidly but now interest rates collapsed and real demand had begun to accelerate. In trying, therefore, to understand the phenomenon of world inflation, and particularly the US contribution, these years assume considerable importance.

The Sociological Explanation

How much of the wage–price pressures in the late 1960s and early 1970s can be accounted for by sociological influences?

There now exists an extensive econometric literature designed to test the hypothesis that non-economic forces (additional to or in lieu of traditional economic influences) are significant or dominant in the determination of wages and prices. These econometric studies use various devices to represent these sociological forces. For example, some use dummies to capture periods which are supposed to be characterised by an eruption in wage demands; others again use strike variables or levels of, or changes in, unionisation as manifestations of militancy-frustration.

Typical of the multi-country studies are those by Perry, Ward–Zis, Gordon and Laidler.[3] Perry and Gordon both experiment with dummies for the wage explosions, while Ward–Zis and Laidler use strike and unionisation variables. Perry and Gordon both agree that dummies in France (1968), the UK (1970) and Italy (1970) add significantly to the explanatory power of the wage equations.[4] There is also some (but less) support for dummies in Germany (1970) and Japan (1968 and/or 1970). There is, however, less agreement on the role of the strike and unionisation variables. The studies are too diverse and too inconclusive to summarise, but there is (some) fairly firm evidence of a significant strike variable for Italy.

Both Laidler and Gordon agree that there is less evidence to support the sociological view of price as distinct from wage inflation. Laidler finds the strike variable even weaker in a price equation. Gordon evaluates the role of the dummy in a price equation and the extent to which wage changes are subsequently accommodated by changes in the volume of money. His conclusions (for his eight countries) are worth quoting in full:

> About one-third of the 1967–70 acceleration in wage growth in the seven (the UK, Canada, Germany, Italy, France, Japan and Sweden) is attributable to the contribution of the dummy variables in the wage equation for the seven . . . The portion of the wage acceleration contributed by the wage-push dummy variables in the seven did not feed through into price change. For the seven the dummy contribution had essentially a zero sign in the price equation and in all countries other than the UK its coefficient was insignificantly different from zero. There is no sign of the passive accommodation of wage change by monetary authorities required if an inflation initiated by wage push is to continue. It is fitting that the wage push hypothesis comes closest to fulfilling its macroeconomic requirements in the UK where it has received such widespread attention.[5]

To conclude, then, there appears to be sufficient evidence to support the view that some exogenous forces were probably, in part at least, responsible for the upsurge in wage inflation in the late 1960s and early 1970s in several industrial countries. However, there is conflicting evidence on the issue of the extent to which this manifested itself in an acceleration in inflation.

It is one thing, however, to establish that there may have been some sociological influences at work; it is another to explain what these sociological influences actually were. Nordhaus attempts a direct test of the aspirations gap hypothesis by extending the expectations-augmented Phillips curve to allow, alternatively, for either the rate of growth of real consumption or the gap between the expected growth of consumption (proxied by past values) and the actual growth of consumption.[6] The 'aspirations gap' does not add to the explanatory power in any of the equations for the seven industrial countries in his study. Panic,[7] on the other hand, finds that within the OECD there is

Table 17.2 Indicators of 'aspirations gap'

Country	(1) Possible Year(s) of Wage[a] Explosion	(2) Real private final consumption expenditure per capita % change				(3) Compensation of employees as % of domestic factor incomes				(4) Ratio % change private consumption expenditure per capita to OECD				(5) Private consumption per capita ratio to OECD			
		1962–65	*1966–67*	*1968–69*	*1970–73*	*1962–65*	*1966–67*	*1968–69*	*1970–73*	*1962–65*	*1966–67*	*1968–69*	*1970–73*	*1962–65*	*1966–67*	*1968–69*	*1970–73*
Australia	1970–71																
	1974	3.3	2.5	3.9	2.8	62.7	64.5	64.1	66.3	0.81	0.74	0.98	0.74	1.0	0.97	0.96	0.94
Canada	—	3.5	3.1	3.2	4.8	68.1	70.3	71.5	72.5	0.86	0.94	0.80	1.3	1.3	1.3	1.3	1.3
France	1968	4.7	4.1	4.2	4.8	61.5	61.7	62.9	64.4	1.1	1.2	1.1	1.3	0.93	0.94	0.94	0.97
Germany	1969–70	4.0	1.4	5.6	4.0	64.4	66.0	65.2	69.2	1.0	0.41	1.4	1.1	0.92	0.90	0.90	0.94
Italy	1969–70																
	1973	4.5	6.4	4.8	4.2	56.8	56.8	57.0	62.2	1.1	1.9	1.2	1.1	0.57	0.58	0.60	0.61
Japan	1968–70	8.1	8.2	8.3	6.6	53.8	54.7	53.1	57.0	2.0	2.4	2.1	1.7	0.43	0.48	0.53	0.58
UK	1969–70																
	1973–74	2.1	1.3	1.2	3.7	75.2	76.3	75.6	77.1	0.51	0.38	0.30	0.97	0.87	0.83	0.78	0.77

Source: OECD (1976a), main aggregate.
[a]Derived from a study of the literature on global inflation.

a tendency for the country with the lower average level of real income to have a higher rate of inflation.

Table 17.2 is intended to provide some (suggestive) indicators of the aspirations gap for some select countries. This 'aspirations gap' might be invoked to 'explain' a wage explosion in an individual country or, more generally, the increased inflationary pressures of the early 1970s.

Column (1) shows the year(s) when a wage explosion may have taken place in each of the countries. The columns under (2) show the percentage change in real private final consumption expenditure per capita for different periods. This measure is intended to capture changes in real consumption per capita due to changes in real disposable incomes from whatever source. Columns (3) show the shares of employee compensation in domestic factor incomes over the same periods. Columns (4) show the ratio of the percentage change in real consumption per capita to the percentage change in consumption per capita for the OECD as a whole. Finally, columns (5) show the ratio of real private consumption expenditure per capita in each country to the OECD average (a measure of relative as well as changing relative living standards).[8]

Easily the most important conclusion to be derived from Table 17.2 is the degree to which the UK appears to conform to the 'aspirations gap' or 'frustration' hypothesis as a possible source of inflation. This appears to lend particular credence to the emphasis that British economists have placed on this aspect of inflation. In the UK the percentage increase in real consumption per capita clearly slowed down by the second half of the 1960s. At the same time, the gains in real consumption per capita were clearly considerably less than the OECD average, while her real living standard was not only below average but fell progressively even further behind the OECD average. Finally, the share of employee compensation had actually fallen marginally towards the end of the 1960s. None of this, of course, is to say that the UK wage explosion in 1970 was necessarily due (even partly) to 'frustration', but the data does suggest that it could have played some part.

On the other hand, it is harder to find support for the hypothesis for any of the other countries that had wage explosions. It is true, for example, that the percentage increase in real consumption per capita had slowed down in Italy by the late 1960s, but it was still high and better than the OECD average. Nor had the share of employee compensation fallen and, although real living standards were below average, her relative position was improving.

If the 'aspirations gap' hypothesis, at least as we have represented it, is difficult to accept as an explanation for the wage explosions, it appears to be even less acceptable as an explanation of the inflationary experience of the early 1970s. For most of the countries, real consumption per capita grew about as rapidly (and in some cases more rapidly) in the early 1970s as (than) in the second half of the 1960s. Moreover, in all of the countries, the share of employee compensation rose fairly sharply in the early 1970s.

Although an important element, the 'aspirations gap' hypothesis is not the only theme in sociological explanations of inflation. For example, in both France and Italy the wage explosions were associated with social, cultural and political tensions. In those countries these tensions were clearly far more important in accounting for the wage explosions than any aspirations gap.

In the UK, in 1969/70, there were the lagged effects of the devaluation of 1967, the threatened Industrial Relations Bill and the collapse of the incomes policy, while in Australia, in 1974, there was the decision to grant equal pay to women, the growth in the tax burden and the possible encouragement to larger wage claims by the new Labour Government.

Domestic and External Sources of Inflation – the Model Applied to Four Countries (1970–1973)

The neo-Keynesian model discussed in Chapter 15 will now be applied to four countries: Australia, Germany, Italy and the UK. It will be recalled that our model identified three external sources of inflation (changes in foreign prices, in foreign real demand and in the foreign interest rate) and five domestic sources (the contribution to the volume of money from the change in the domestic assets of the central bank, changes in discretionary fiscal policy, the exchange rate, capital controls and, finally, a wage shock). These external, as well as the domestic, sources of inflation,[9] in percentage change form, are all shown for these four countries for the years 1967–73 in Tables 17.3 to 17.6.

As in the theoretical discussion we can apply the analysis in two stages. First, we ask how the three external influences behaved in the critical years of the early 1970s. Second, we ask to what degree these external influences may have actually influenced domestic inflation.

The external influences are shown in columns (2) to (4) for the four countries.[10] The results are quite striking. First, in each case, the foreign price (in US dollar terms) started accelerating around 1970/71.[11] Second, as we have seen previously, the Euro-dollar interest rate fell sharply between 1970 and 1972. Third, real foreign demand also accelerated in 1972/73. Nineteen seventy-two, therefore, was a year when all external influences seemed to be pushing strongly in the one direction.

To what extent, however, were these external influences actually

Table 17.3 Australia – domestic and external impulses – 1967 to 1973

Year		External impulses				Domestic impulses							
	$\dot{P}$ (1)	$\dot{P}m$ (2)	$\dot{P}x$ (2a)	$\dot{Y}f$ (3)	R_{eu} (4)	$\frac{\Delta D}{H_{-1}}$ (5)	FP (6)	$\dot{E}$ (7)	A (8)	$\frac{B}{H_{-1}}$ (9)	$\dot{M}o_1$ (10)	$\dot{M}o_2$ (11)	U (12a)
1967	3.1	0.4	– 5.6	5.6	5.5	13.3	3.1	0		– 5.4	6.8	8.1	1.6
1968	2.7	– 1.5	– 1.0	13.0	6.4	7.0	2.9	0		2.4	7.1	8.0	1.6
1969	3.0	3.1	2.0	12.7	9.8	10.1	2.3	0		– 0.5	8.2	9.0	1.6
1970	3.9	3.5	– 3.1	8.6	8.5	– 14.5	2.5	0	?	13.9	6.0	6.4	1.4
1971	6.0	7.4	2.0	6.6	6.6	– 27.7	3.0	– 2.0	?	46.1	4.9	7.0	1.6
1972	5.9	9.3	20.6	11.6	5.5	– 43.0	2.9	– 4.7		62.9	11.2	13.1	2.2
1973	9.4	19.3	52.8	14.3	9.2	46.5	4.9	– 16.0		– 22.0	22.5	23.3	1.9

Notation: See page 190.

Table 17.4 Germany – domestic and external impulses – 1967 to 1973

Year		External impulses				Domestic impulses							
	$\dot{P}$ (1)	$\dot{P}m$ (2)	$\dot{P}x$ (2a)	$\dot{Y}f$ (3)	R_{eu} (4)	$\frac{\Delta D}{H_{-1}}$ (5)	FP (6)	$\dot{E}$ (7)	A (8)	$\frac{B}{H_{-1}}$ (9)	$\dot{M}o_1$ (10)	$\dot{M}o_2$ (11)	OG (12)
1967	1.7	– 1.0	1.2	6.4	5.5	– 3.1	0.4	0		– 0.2	3.2	11.5	– 10.0
1968	1.6	– 2.0	– 0.1	15.1	6.4	– 7.0	0.9	0		13.9	8.1	15.1	– 4.8
1969	1.9	3.3	2.6	14.5	9.8	22.3	0.3	– 2.0		– 19.0	9.9	16.0	1.6
1970	3.4	7.7	5.4	10.0	8.5	– 17.7	1.8	– 7.0	?	39.2	6.5	9.5	2.3
1971	5.2	3.8	5.4	4.5	6.6	– 9.2	1.1	– 4.5		24.2	12.3	13.9	– 0.8
1972	5.5	6.7	9.0	10.8	5.5	6.2	0.9	– 8.4		20.1	13.6	15.2	– 2.8
1973	7.0	26.9	18.4	16.2	9.2	– 19.4	0.5	– 16.2		26.8	5.6	13.2	– 1.0

[illegible] – domestic and external impulses – 1967 to 1973

Year		External impulses			Domestic impulses							
	$\dot{P}$ (1)	$\dot{P}m$ (2)	$\dot{P}x$ (2a)	$\dot{Y}f$ (3)	R_{eu} (4)	$\frac{\Delta D}{H_{-1}}$ (5)	FP (6)	$\dot{E}$ (7)	A (8)	$\frac{B}{H_{-1}}$ (9)	$\dot{M}o_1$ (10)	$\dot{M}o_2$ (11)	OG (12)
1967	3.8	1.1	0.8	4.8	5.5	7.3	0.11	0		5.0	13.6	13.9	−2.7
1968	1.3	0.4	−0.5	18.6	6.4	9.1	1.05	0		−1.1	13.4	12.9	0
1969	2.7	0.8	3.0	14.9	9.8	16.9	0.77	0		−3.8	14.9	12.6	0.4
1970	5.0	3.3	6.4	9.8	8.5	9.2	0.32	0	?	3.2	21.7	12.7	2.2
1971	4.8	6.4	5.5	8.4	6.6	11.6	1.07	−1.4		5.4	23.0	15.4	−3.3
1972	5.7	9.3	8.9	11.5	5.5	17.4	1.44	−5.7		−3.4	18.6	17.9	−4.7
1973	10.8	28.2	21.0	14.1	9.2	17.4	1.18	0	?	−0.3	20.4	20.1	−0.4

Notation: See page 190.

Table 17.6 United Kingdom – domestic and external impulses – 1967 to 1973

Year		External impulses			Domestic impulses							
	$\dot{P}$ (1)	$\dot{P}m$ (2)	$\dot{P}x$ (2a)	$\dot{Y}f$ (3)	R_{eu} (4)	$\frac{\Delta D}{H_{-1}}$ (5)	FP (6)	$\dot{E}$ (7)	A (8)	$\frac{B}{H_{-1}}$ (9)	$\dot{M}o_1$ (10)	$\dot{M}o_2$ (11)	OG (12)
1967	2.5	0	1.6	5.0	5.5	25.0	1.71	1.7		−20.3	3.8	5.4	−4.5
1968	4.7	−2.9	1.3	14.9	6.4	37.3	−0.07	14.8		−33.4	4.6	8.8	−1.4
1969	5.5	3.0	3.9	12.9	9.8	−12.3	−1.48	0		14.3	−0.5	3.8	−0.9
1970	6.4	4.7	6.0	9.2	8.5	−26.8	0.26	0	?	38.4	7.0	5.8	−3.3
1971	9.5	6.4	5.1	5.6	6.6	−74.5	1.28	−2.0		69.4	13.3	12.7	−6.1
1972	7.1	6.7	8.5	9.1	5.5	48.8	2.54	−2.2		−27.6	16.8	22.9	−5.8
1973	9.2	24.2	17.9	16.1	9.2	24.9	1.68	2.0	?	6.6	10.1	25.5	0.4

Notation: See page 190.

Tables 17.3 to 17.6 – Notation and Sources

(1) $\dot{P}$ = percentage change in consumer prices

(2) $\dot{P}m$ = percentage change in the price of imports – in US dollar terms

(2a) $\dot{P}x$ = for Australia: percentage change in the price of exports – in US dollar terms
for Germany, Italy and the UK: weighted percentage change in the price of manufactured exports (in US dollars) by competitors (from *OECD Economic Outlook – Occasional Studies*, July 1978, calculated from Tables 5 and 13, pp. 47 and 51)

(3) $\dot{Y}f$ = percentage change in foreign demand
weighted percentage change in volume of imports by rest of world (IMF calculations) – except Australia
for Australia: percentage change in volume of imports – all industrial countries

(4) R_{eu} = Euro-dollar – 3-month rate

(5) $\frac{\Delta D}{H_{-1}}$ = change in domestic assets of central bank as a percentage of base money – end of previous year (the change in domestic assets was calculated as a residual from the change in base money less the change in net foreign assets)

(6) FP = measure of discretionary effect of fiscal policy on GNP (OECD measure) – except Australia (from *OECD Economic Outlook – Occasional Studies*, July 1978)
for Australia: measure of discretionary fiscal policy calculated by J. Nevile (1975) and J. Nevile (1977)

(7) $\dot{E}$ = percentage change in the exchange rate (units of domestic currency per US dollar)

(8) A = possible wage shock

(9) $\frac{B}{H_{-1}}$ = change in net foreign assets as percentage of base money – end of previous year (that is, contribution of change in net foreign assets to percentage change in base money)

(10) $\dot{M}o_1$ = percentage change in narrow money

(11) $\dot{M}o_2$ = percentage change in broad money

(12) OG = output gap calculated as actual less potential output as percentage of potential output
Source: J. Artus (1977)

(12a) U = unemployment rate
for Australia – national sources

(Except where specifically noted all data are taken from the International Monetary Fund, *International Financial Statistics.*)

offset or allowed to influence the domestic inflation? This is an extremely difficult question to answer. Ideally, we would need to know how inflation would have behaved in the early 1970s if the trends in the external influences (say, in the mid-late 1960s) had, in fact, been maintained. This could only be undertaken if we had good econometric estimates of the equations underlying the model, including the policy reaction functions. Since we do not have this information in the detail required, we have to fall back on judgements about the possible contributions of the external influences.

The cases of Australia, Germany and the UK can be taken together because they have several features in common. In all three cases, there was something of a wage eruption in 1970 and/or in 1971; whereas, however, this eruption was relatively mild in Australia and Germany, it was severe in the UK. In all three cases, too, the relatively higher domestic interest rates attracted massive capital inflows into the economies. The buildup in reserves in all three cases led to expectations of a revaluation, accelerating further the inflows of capital. In Australia, the big increase in export prices transformed the current account by 1972/73 from a deficit into a substantial surplus. The contribution of the balance of payments to base money growth B/H_{-1}, shown in the tables, was very substantial in all three countries. Domestic monetary policy $\Delta D/H_{-1}$ was deflationary and was directed at counteracting the effects of the massive capital inflows on the domestic base money. In addition, all three countries took measures to restrict the inflows of capital; in Australia's case these measures came late (in September 1972) well after the inflows had already made their impact. In Germany and Australia, the revaluations in 1970–73 served to offset the effects of the acceleration in import prices; in Australia's case, however, the revaluations were not nearly enough to offset the huge increase in export prices. In the UK, there was only a very small net revaluation over the four years, nowhere near sufficient to offset the acceleration in import prices.

In Australia and Germany the issues are relatively clear. The initial wage shock of 1970/71 may have exerted some cost-push effect on the domestic price level but the subsequent acceleration in monetary growth could hardly be explained away as an attempt to accommodate the eruption in wages. A much more plausible argument would be that the attempt to sterilise the inflows combined (in Germany's case) with the restrictions on the inflows of capital did not succeed in moderating the growth in the volume of money, which was, in any event, excessive relative to the wage eruption. It does appear, therefore, that in these two countries the external contribution was probably dominant.[12]

By contrast, the case of the UK is more ambiguous. It could be contended that the UK did not lose control over the volume of money and that the accelerated monetary growth in 1971 and 1972 was necessary to accommodate the wage explosion and prevent the emergence of additional unemployment.[13]

Italy has some parallels but also some significant differences with the other three countries. Italy in 1970 had a severe wage shock comparable to the UK. At the same time, revaluations between 1970 and 1972 almost exactly offset the acceleration in import prices. On the other hand, despite the drop in Euro-rates, the continued social and political unrest led to large capital outflows in the years 1970–72. At the same time, the acceleration in monetary growth in 1970–73 came from domestic not external sources and was directed at counteracting the slack in the domestic economy, which was itself not unrelated to the wage explosion[14] (see last column of Table 17.5). It was, in fact, the big increase in the budget deficit in those years which contributed to the monetary growth.

By way of summary, then, we have, at one extreme, Australia and Germany where the monetary acceleration was externally induced. By contrast, we have, at the other extreme, Italy where its own monetary acceleration was home grown. In the case of the UK, there remains some dispute about how much of the monetary acceleration was essentially home grown and how much externally induced.

The Inflationary Upsurge of 1973–1975

Two factors account for the inflationary upsurge in 1973–75. The first is the lagged effects of the excess monetary growth in the early 1970s (see Table 17.7). The second is the big increase in commodity prices that occurred in 1973 and 1974 (see the last column of Table 15.1).

To test these contentions in a broader context, an attempt was made to determine how much of the differences across countries in the rate of change in the consumer price index ($\dot{P}$) for the years 1972–76 could be accounted for in terms of differences in the excess of money growth over the growth in real output ($\dot{Mo} - \dot{Yr}$) over the years 1971–75 and, as well, in terms of differences in the percentage change in import prices ($\dot{Pm}$) in domestic currency terms, again over the years 1971–75. The results, for twenty-four developed countries (excluding Malta, Luxembourg and Yugoslavia), were:

$$\dot{P} = \underset{(0.84)}{1.39} + \underset{(2.7)}{0.56}\,(\dot{Mo}_1 - \dot{Yr}) + \underset{(2.3)}{0.32}\,\dot{Pm} \qquad R^{-2} = 0.71$$

$$\dot{P} = \underset{(-0.17)}{-0.47} + \underset{(1.7)}{0.52}\,(\dot{Mo}_2 - \dot{Yr}) + \underset{(2.2)}{0.38}\,\dot{Pm} \qquad R^{-2} = 0.65$$

(t ratios shown in parentheses)

These results confirm the importance of both excess monetary growth

Table 17.7 Inflation and excess monetary growth – select countries

	Rate of inflation			*Rate of growth of money ($\dot{M}o_1$) per unit of output*[a]			*Rate of growth of money ($\dot{M}o_2$) per unit of output*[a]		
	1967–70	*1971–74*	*1975–77*	*1966–69*	*1970–73*	*1974–76*	*1966–69*	*1970–73*	*1974–76*
World	5.1	8.0	12.2	8.6	11.8	12.8	—	—	—
Australia	3.2	9.1	13.7	0.8	6.0	7.7	2.6	7.3	11.9
Canada	3.8	6.5	8.7	1.4	1.5	3.0	5.2	7.8	14.7
France	4.8	8.1	10.1	1.5	4.0	10.0	6.1	8.9	13.6
Germany	2.1	6.2	4.8	2.3	5.0	8.8	8.3	7.3	8.2
Italy	3.2	10.1	16.9	7.9	16.7	13.0	7.6	12.3	19.1
Japan	5.7	11.4	9.8	3.7	13.9	10.1	3.9	12.0	11.1
UK	4.8	10.4	18.9	0.4	8.0	11.0	3.8	12.4	11.8
USA	4.6	6.2	7.2	1.4	2.7	3.3	3.3	7.4	6.9

Source: International Monetary Fund.
[a]($\dot{M}o_1$) Narrow money. ($\dot{M}o_2$) Broad money. Lagged one period relative to the rate of inflation.

and the increase in import prices in explaining a good deal of the inter-country difference in the inflationary experience.

Notes for Chapter 17

1 As far as capital flows are concerned, real interest rates are more relevant only if changes in the rate of inflation are associated with changes in expectations about the strength of the US dollar. In other words, if US interest rates and the US rate of inflation rise by two percentage points and the USA is expected to devalue by 2 per cent relative to the rest of the world, the higher nominal interest rate will not induce an inflow of capital into the USA. In the years 1968–72 capital flows were dominated by the movements in the nominal interest rate in the USA.

2 Some of this can be attributed to the loss in competitive position but, in addition, there were structural shifts, including an increase in the openness of the US economy (see line 6).

3 G. Perry (1975); R. Ward and G. Zis (1974); R. Gordon (1977); D. Laidler (1976b).

4 See E. Spitaeller (1976). This study includes the UK and France and confirms the findings of the other studies. See also F. Modigliani and E. Tarantelli (1977). They also find that trade union activity exerts an independent influence on the growth of wages.

5 For a contrary view for Italy see T. Willett and L. Lancy (1978).

6 W. Nordhaus (1972). See also OECD (1978d).

7 M. Panic (1978).

8 The table is deficient in that it does not, of course, pick up exogenous changes in aspirations (as suggested in Chapter 15). Another useful indicator might be changes in real after-tax incomes excluding transfers. For example, if taxes and transfers both increase, leaving disposable incomes unchanged, there might yet be wage pressures from those groups whose real incomes fell.

9 Excluding capital controls. These are briefly discussed in the text but also in Chapter 6.

10 For Australia a change in real foreign demand tends to manifest itself in a change in the export prices that she receives in foreign markets. For this reason the percentage change in the price of exports, expressed in US dollars, is also shown as an alternative external source of inflation. An increase in export prices will increase the incomes of the exporters, who, in turn, will spend more and transmit the inflationary impulse to the economy as a whole.

11 The foreign price is represented by the percentage change in import prices in US dollars for all four countries. For Germany, Italy and the UK world prices are also represented by the weighted percentage change (in US dollars) in the price of competitors' manufactured exports.

12 For Germany see O. Emminger (1977). Emminger (p. 29) concedes that 'owing to persistent inflows from abroad, German monetary policy had been forced to accept adjustment through inflation'.
For Australia see V. Argy and J. Carmichael (1976). P. Jonson (1973); M. Porter (1974).

13 For two different points of view about the UK experience see: J. Williamson and G. Wood (1976); D. Laidler (1976a).

14 For the Italian case see T. Willett and L. Lancy (1978). They find that for Italy (and the UK) the growth in wages is significant in accounting for monetary growth.

Chapter 18

The Downturn (1974–1975) and the Conservative Reaction (1976–1978)

Introduction

Table 18.1 shows that, beginning some time in 1974, the industrial countries experienced a sharp falling off in economic activity. In all countries this manifested itself in a dramatic decline in their rate of growth of real GNP. In most countries, too, this was also reflected, with something of a lag, in an increase in their unemployment rates, which reached levels unprecedented since the war. Those countries that did not experience a big increase in unemployment during 1974/75 (in Table 18.1 – Japan and Italy) were principally those with legal or institutional constraints on the dismissal of workers.

As with the acceleration in inflation, the collapse in economic activity was a global phenomenon. Again, the explanation has to be sought either in terms of common influences originating domestically or in terms of external influences to which they were all similarly exposed (or, of course, in terms of a combination of the two influences). These influences, as it happens, are not too difficult to identify. First, the nations of the industrial world experienced, during 1972/73, a rapid and synchronised acceleration in their economic activity and it is almost certain that, independently of any new developments, there would have been some slowing down in activity during 1974. Second, the oil price shock, to which the oil-consuming world was exposed at the end of 1973, would, by itself, have had significant repercussions on domestic activity. Third, the industrial countries, in general, responded to the 1973 boom, the upsurge in inflation in 1974 and the large current account deficits by implementing similar restrictive macro-policies, notably on the monetary front. Fourth, once the downturn had got under way, the coincidental declines in economic activity would have been transmitted across countries, aggravating the situation further.

This chapter will substantiate most of these points in more detail.

Table 18.1 Rates of unemployment and percentage change in real GNP – select countries 1970 to 1975

	Rates of unemployment (% change in real GNP)			
Country	*Mean 1970–73*	*1973*	*1974*	*1975*
Australia	1.8	1.9	2.3	4.4
	(5.0)	(6.1)	(2.4)	(1.9)
Canada	6.1	5.6	5.4	7.1
	(5.7)	(7.5)	(3.5)	(1.2)
France	2.1	2.1	2.3	4.0
	(5.6)	(5.4)	(2.6)	(−0.1)
Germany	0.9	1.3	2.7	4.9
	(4.4)	(4.9)	(0.5)	(−2.6)
Italy	3.3	3.5	2.9	3.3
	(4.2)	(6.9)	(3.9)	(−3.5)
Japan	1.3	1.3	1.4	1.9
	(9.2)	(9.8)	(−1.0)	(2.4)
United Kingdom	2.8	2.6	2.5	3.9
	(3.6)	(6.6)	(−0.6)	(−1.6)
United States	5.4	4.9	5.6	8.5
	(3.5)	(5.4)	(−1.3)	(−1.0)

Source: OECD Economic Outlook.

The Effect of an Oil Price Shock on Activity – Theoretical Analysis

Before examining in detail the various factors that contributed to the decline in economic activity, we evaluate, first, the effects of an oil price shock to a single economy, holding constant, initially, the coincidental repercussions on the rest of the world and domestic monetary, exchange rate and fiscal policies.[1]

There are five primary effects on economic activity: first, a direct real demand effect; second, a direct real money balance effect; third, a cost of input effect; fourth, a wage-adjustment effect; fifth, a terms of trade effect.

The demand for oil being price inelastic, an increase in the price of oil will result in an increase in oil payments overseas. Assuming, as a first approximation, that aggregate money expenditure is fixed, the increased commitment to spend overseas must represent a diversion away from expenditure on domestic goods. At the same time, counteracting this, there might be some offsetting increase in the country's exports to the OPEC countries. The net reduction in domestic expenditure is, then, a measure of the initial direct real demand effect.

An increase in oil prices also has a direct effect on the price of final products (the consumer price index). Given the volume of money, this reduces real money balances, raises interest rates and reduces real domestic demand.

Again, oil is an important input in domestic production. A rise in the price of oil, given domestic wages, means that the price of domestically produced goods must rise to compensate for the increased costs, if producers are to maintain their level of production. The consumer price index will then be affected directly and, through the cost of input effect, indirectly by the increase in the price of oil. At this point, wages may adjust partially or fully to the increase in the general price level. This will have further repercussions on real money balances, the price of domestically produced goods and, in turn, on real demand.

Finally, the terms of trade effect represents the effects on domestic expenditure consequent on the decline in the community's real income.[2] If it is assumed that some proportion (say, 20 per cent) of this decline in real income is reflected in reduced savings, this is tantamount to saying that nominal expenditure will now increase in some degree (in our example by about 20 per cent of the real income effect). This would partially offset the other deflationary effects of the oil price shock.

Macro-policy may relieve or aggravate the effects on economic activity, depending on the relative priorities attached to inflation and unemployment. Moreover, overseas conditions will be simultaneously affected in similar ways and these changes will have further important repercussions on the domestic economy.

A Framework for the Analysis of the Downturn

The aggregate demand component of our neo-Keynesian model will now be used to analyse the downturn. It is possible to derive (see Annex), as a reduced-form solution to the aggregate demand sector, an equation which asserts that the percentage change in real output can be explained by (1) the percentage change in real money balances, (2) the percentage change in foreign output, (3) a measure of discretionary fiscal policy, (4) a measure of the economy's percentage change in its competitive position for non-oil goods and (5) the increase in expenditure on oil imports, as a proportion of GNP (our direct real demand effect). These five component influences on real GNP are shown in Table 18.2 in columns (3) to (7).

The table suggests that a principal factor in the collapse of economic activity was the sharp decline in the rate of growth in real

Table 18.2 Principal influences on output 1973 to 1975

Country	(1) $\dot{M}o$			(2) $\dot{P}$			(3) $\dot{M}o - \dot{P}$			(4) Discretionary Fiscal Policy			(5) Net Direct Demand Effect (oil shock)	(6) % Δ in Real Foreign Demand Weighted (Adj.)			(7) % Δ in Real Exchange Rate[a]		
	1973	*1974*	*1975*	*1973*	*1974*	*1975*	*1973*	*1974*	*1975*	*1973*	*1974*	*1975*	*1974*	*1973*	*1974*	*1975*	*1973*	*1974*	*1975*
Australia	22.5	3.4	13.7	9.4	15.1	15.2	13.1	−11.7	−1.5	4.9	4.2	9.1	—	18.0	7.0	−8.6	NA	NA	NA
	(23.3)	(13.0)	(17.2)				(13.9)	(−2.1)	(2.0)					(2.9)	(1.1)	(−1.4)			
Canada	11.9	5.4	7.8	7.6	10.9	10.8	4.3	−5.5	−3.0	1.29	1.51	1.91	—	6.7	0.3	−3.5	+2.0	−0.1	+5.0
	(15.2)	(24.7)	(13.9)				(7.6)	(13.8)	(3.1)					(1.7)	(0.1)	(−0.9)			
France	10.0	11.8	10.8	7.4	13.6	11.8	2.6	−1.8	−1.0	0.96	2.59	0.27	−2.1	15.1	10.6	0.6	−2.3	+5.0	−7.6
	(14.6)	(17.9)	(14.1)				(7.2)	(4.3)	(2.3)					(3.3)	(2.3)	(0.1)			
Germany	5.6	5.9	14.1	7.0	7.0	5.9	−1.4	−1.1	8.2	0.48	1.44	1.37	−1.4	16.2	8.6	0.1	−6.8	−0.1	+5.2
	(13.2)	(9.6)	(11.7)				(6.2)	(2.6)	(5.8)					(4.9)	(2.6)	(0.0)			
Italy	20.4	15.9	9.2	10.8	19.1	17.2	9.6	−3.2	−8.0	1.18	0.66	1.22	−2.8	14.1	7.8	3.7	+6.0	+2.7	−6.1
	(20.1)	(20.7)	(20.2)				(9.3)	(1.6)	(3.0)					(3.4)	(1.9)	(0.9)			
Japan	26.4	13.3	10.3	11.7	22.7	12.2	14.7	−9.4	−1.9	0.73	0.74	1.88	−2.4	12.1	10.5	1.7	−8.7	−0.2	−5.8
	(23.0)	(12.9)	(12.7)				(11.3)	(−9.8)	(0.5)					(1.6)	(1.4)	(0.2)			
United Kingdom	10.1	3.5	15.0	9.2	15.9	24.2	0.9	−12.4	−9.2	1.68	1.13	−0.38	−2.6	16.1	11.2	1.9	+7.1	−2.8	−2.1
	(10.0)	(3.5)	(18.9)				(0.8)	(−12.4)	(−5.3)					(4.5)	(3.1)	(0.5)			
United States	7.2	4.3	4.4	6.2	11.0	9.2	1.0	−6.7	−4.8	0.49	−0.02	1.23	−1.0	20.1	10.2	0.2	+8.4	+2.0	+3.6
	(12.4)	(10.2)	(7.1)				(6.2)	(−0.8)	(−2.1)					(1.4)	(0.7)	(0.0)			

Sources: See p. 199.
[a] + = improvement in competitiveness; − = decline in competitiveness; NA = not available.

Sources – Table 18.2

Columns (1)–(3)

Percentage Change in Real Money Balances ($\dot{Mo} - \dot{P}$)(column 3)

Percentage change in $\dot{Mo}$ (column 1) less percentage change in consumer prices (column 2)

Numbers in parentheses in column 1 represent broad money (money plus quasi-money)

From International Monetary Fund, *International Financial Statistics.*

Column (4)

Discretionary Fiscal Policy

For all countries other than Australia: OECD (1978a) (Table 1 – Discretionary Effects).

For Australia: J. Nevile (1975, 1977).

Column (5)

Net Direct Demand Effect (Oil Price Shock)

Increase in oil payments in 1974 less increase in exports to OPEC countries as percentage of GNP.

From *OECD Economic Outlook.*

Column (6)

Percentage Change in Real Foreign Demand Weighted (Adjusted)

For all countries other than Australia: trade weighted percentage increase in volume of imports in the rest of the world (IMF calculations – unpublished).

For Australia: trade weighted percentage increases in volume of imports of Japan, USA, New Zealand and the UK

Numbers in parentheses represent trade weighted percentage increase in volume of imports multiplied by share of exports in GNP

Column (7)

Percentage Change in Real Exchange Rate

The measure used is the relative unit current cost in a common currency.

See OECD (1978b), Table 3.

money balances (that is, the rate of growth of money less the rate of inflation). There are two reasons to account for this. On the one hand, there was some slowing down in monetary growth by 1974 in most of the countries to counteract the inflation. This slowing down was particularly severe in Australia, Japan and the UK. On the other hand, as we saw, there were the lagged effects on inflation of earlier monetary growth and, in addition, supply factors acting directly on the price level. For most industrial countries there was the oil price shock; for Australia there was the indirect effect of the oil price shock (showing up in world import prices) and some effect of its own wage explosion in 1974. The combination of a reduction in nominal monetary growth, as well as an acceleration in inflation, produced a very sharp real monetary squeeze.

The oil price shock also had a significant direct deflationary effect on real demand in all countries except Australia and Canada (see column 5), while real foreign demand had fallen very sharply in all countries by 1975 (see column 6), contributing further to the collapse in activity.

By contrast, there is little evidence to suggest, for most countries, that tightening fiscal policies contributed to the downturn. Only in the UK is this clearly in evidence. In Italy and the USA fiscal restriction may have made a marginal contribution to the fall in economic activity in those years. On the other hand, in Australia, Canada, France, Germany and Japan the downturn in 1974/75 was actually associated with more expansionary fiscal policies.

Finally, the effect of the percentage change in the real exchange rate, as expected, varies across the countries (see column 7). Only in the UK is there evidence of a sustained (possible) deflationary effect during 1974/75 attributable to a decline in the competitive position.[3]

The Emergence of the Real Wage Gap

Consider, again, the case of a country exposed to an oil price shock. Recalling what we said earlier about the wage adjustment effect, several possibilities emerge. First, an incomes policy may succeed in minimising the wage adjustment and securing a reduction in real wages. Second, wages may adjust substantially but monetary policy is permissive. In this case, unemployment may be avoided, at least initially, but at the cost of a wage–price spiral and substantially more inflation. Third, wages adjust but now monetary policy is not accommodating. In this case, the increase in wages cannot be passed on in higher prices, real wages (that is, wages deflated by the price of domestically produced goods) will rise above the growth of productivity, the real demand for labour will fall and unemployment will grow. This situation, where real wages are allowed to rise faster than productivity, has been called by the OECD 'the real wage gap'.[4]

Unemployment of this kind needs to be carefully distinguished from unemployment due to a deficiency in aggregate demand (for example, from a shift to the left in the aggregate demand schedule).[5] In the latter case, expansionary policies can serve to correct the deficiency. By contrast, expansionary policies in the face of unemployment created by excessive real wages may well lead to a vicious and unstable wage–price spiral.

Many countries experienced a real wage gap during 1974/75. In most cases, it was related to the oil price shock; in some, however (for example, Australia), it was related to an exogenous wage push. The OECD has calculated this real wage gap for its member countries and the results are shown in Table 18.3.

Table 18.3 Real wage gap[a] (Index 1972=100)

Country	*1973*	*1974*	*1975*	*1976*	*1977*	*1978*
United States	98.4	98.9	97.8	96.9	96.9	98.5
Japan	104.3	108.8	112.0	109.2	109.3	106.3
Germany	100.7	103.7	102.2	98.5	98.9	97.7
France	101.5	104.6	106.8	104.4	105.3	104.4
United Kingdom	100.7	107.9	112.6	107.3	103.4	103.2
Canada	98.2	99.7	104.3	105.8	107.0	105.1
Italy	102.4	102.8	106.7	105.4	106.5	104.9
Australia	104.0	112.6	110.2	110.0	111.2	108.9
Austria	99.7	100.5	104.3	101.2	100.4	103.9
Belgium	101.2	104.3	113.0	110.1	112.0	113.3
Denmark	104.9	104.9	108.4	105.4	99.2	93.9
Finland	99.6	102.5	103.7	104.0	95.4	90.9
Ireland	101.2	110.7	115.2	113.0	112.8	117.0
Netherlands	98.1	101.4	103.2	99.4	97.6	99.1
Norway	99.4	100.2	105.3	105.6	108.5	106.9
Spain	100.3	101.5	100.4	101.8	101.3	99.8
Sweden	97.0	96.3	97.7	99.6	104.3	100.8

Source: OECD Economic Outlook (July 1979), p. 143.

[a]Difference between real wages and salaries per head of dependent employment and terms of trade adjusted real GDP per head of total employment.

The table reveals that, of the seven major industrial countries, plus Australia, the real wage gap was particularly large in Japan, the UK and Australia. It was also substantial in France, Italy and Canada. By contrast, in Germany it was moderate while the USA experienced a reverse real wage gap. This absence of a real wage gap in the USA may, possibly, help to explain the fact that of the eight countries, the

USA was the most successful in bringing down the rate of unemployment over the years 1976–78.

The Conservative Reaction (1976–1978) and the Triumph of Monetarism

Despite the persistence of unemployment levels and unused capacity, which were high by historical standards (see Tables 18.1 and 18.4), inflation rates in most industrial countries remained relatively high in the years 1976–78, although these had come down from the heights of 1974/75. How did governments respond to the economic conditions with which they were faced? (See, also, Chapter 29.)

Table 18.4 compares the discretionary fiscal stance in the years

Table 18.4 Trends – select industrial countries

Country	*Rates of unemployment (percentage change in real GNP)*			*Discretionary fiscal policy*[a]			
	1976	*1977*	*1978*	*Mean 1970–73*	*1976*	*1977*	*1978*
Australia	4.4 (3.4)	5.6 (1.7)	6.3 (2.7)	3.3	6.8	3.6	3.5
Canada	7.1 (5.8)	8.1 (2.7)	8.4 (3.4)	1.47	1.23	0.76	1.04
France	4.2 (4.6)	4.8 (3.0)	5.3 (3.3)	0.98	0.96	1.10	1.14
Germany	4.7 (5.6)	4.6 (2.6)	4.4 (3.4)	1.06	0.31	−0.11	1.03
Italy[b]	6.7 (5.6)	7.2 (2.0)	7.2 (2.6)	1.00	−1.80	0.60	−0.28
Japan	2.0 (6.0)	2.0 (5.4)	2.2 (5.6)	1.20	0.88	0.89	1.41
United States	7.7 (5.5)	7.1 (4.9)	6.0 (4.0)	0.54	−0.12	0.54	0.91
United Kingdom	5.4 (3.6)	5.7 (2.0)	5.6 (3.2)	1.44	0.74	−1.28	0.56

Sources: Discretionary Fiscal Policy.
For all countries other than Australia: *OECD Economic Outlook* (July 1978), Table 13.
For Australia: J. Nevile (1975) and J. Nevile (1977) (communicated privately).

[a]The figures for 1976–78 are not exactly comparable to the earlier figures or those in Table 18.2. Compare, for example, the July 1978 OECD Economic Outlook with the Budget Indicators in the July 1978 OECD Occasional Studies.

[b]Survey coverage changed so the unemployment rates are not comparable to Table 18.1.

1976–78 with the mean of the years 1970–73. What is most striking about the table is the evidence it presents of fiscal conservatism. In all the countries unemployment rates were significantly higher during 1976–78 than in the earlier period (1970–73) (see Table 18.1), yet the fiscal stimulus in the later period was either roughly the same as in the earlier years (as in Australia, France, Japan and the USA) or significantly more deflationary (as in Canada, Germany, Italy and the UK).

On the monetary front the most important development was the growing acceptance by monetary authorities of the view that they should announce monetary targets in advance.[6] Germany (in 1974) and the USA (in 1975) had taken the lead in this respect and they were subsequently followed by all the major industrial countries.

Despite the apparent unanimity in the switch there are (to 1979) differences among the countries in the ways in which monetary targeting was implemented. Some (Canada and Switzerland) focus on narrow money, while the USA announces targets in three definitions of money (*M*1, *M*2 and *M*3). Germany has a central bank money target, while Italy has a domestic credit target. Some prefer a band while others prefer a fixed target. A fixed target is used in Switzerland and, until 1978, was used by Germany. Bands are used in Canada, the USA, Australia, the UK and, now, Germany.[7]

Why did most industrial countries switch to monetary targeting? First, there was the determination to avoid a repetition of the years 1970–72 when monetary growth exploded in the industrial countries. Second, there was the disappointing performance of discretionary monetary management, with the growing conviction that steadier monetary growth might improve an economy's performance.[8] In this context, too, monetary targets become a means of avoiding overreaction to changing circumstances. At the same time, there was disillusionment with the use of interest rates as targets for monetary management.[9]

Third, in some countries (for example, the UK), monetary targeting was seen as an alternative to the discipline provided by fixed exchange rates or as an alternative to an incomes policy. Fourth, with large and growing public sector deficits monetary targeting was viewed as a means of constraining the potential for monetary creation. Fifth, the announcement of monetary targets was seen as a way of influencing expectations about inflation. A gradual deceleration in monetary growth, under these conditions, might bring down the rate of inflation with minimal real effects on the economy. Sixth, the announcement of monetary targets is also seen as a means of limiting the political element in economic policy-making. Seventh, there is the element of contagion, the spread of fashions and, in some cases, pressures from other countries or international organisations to conform. Finally, there were theoretical developments supporting a constant growth rate

Table 18.5 Projected monetary stance – select industrial countries

Country	Targeted monetary growth				Projected rate of inflation				Implied targeted real monetary growth			
	1976	*1977*	*1978*	*1979*	*1976*	*1977*	*1978*	*1979*	*1976*	*1977*	*1978*	*1979*
Australia[a] (*M*3)	10–12	8–10	6–8	10.0	13.0	12.0	8.0	10.0	−3.0 −1.0	−4.0 −2.0	−2.0 0.0	 0.0
Canada[b] (*M*1)	8–12	7–11	6–10	—	9.0	6.9	6.1	—	−1.0 +3.0	+0.1 +4.1	−0.1 +3.9	—
France (*M*2)	—	12.5	12.0	11.0	—	8.0	7.6	10.0	—	+4.5	+4.4	+1.0
Germany[c]	8.0	8.0	8.0	6–9	5	4	3.5	3.8	+3	+4	+4.5	+2.5 +5.2
United Kingdom[d] (*M*3)	9–13	9–13	8–12	—	12.6	13.5	8.3	—	−3.6 +0.4	−4.5 −0.5	−0.3 +3.7	—
United States (*M*2)	7.5– 10.5	7.0– 10.0	6.5– 9.0	5.0– 8.0	6.2	5.5	6.0	8.8	+1.3 +4.3	+1.5 +4.5	+0.5 +3.0	−3.8 −0.8

Source: OECD (1979a).
[a]Twelve months beginning July 1.
[b]Twelve months beginning March 1976, June 1977 and June 1978.
[c]Central Bank Money.
[d]Twelve months beginning April.

rule. This attack on discretionary monetary policy came from monetarists who argued that, in a world of rational expectations, systematic monetary policy (in the sense that policy responds predictably to trends in economic activity) could have no effect on real output.[10]

Is there evidence of a conservative stance in the application of monetary targeting? Perhaps the simplest way to test this is to relate the targeted rate of growth in the volume of money to the projected rate of inflation over roughly the same period. This gives some indication of intention in respect of the planned rate of growth in real money balances. Table 18.5 presents this evidence.

To be able to judge whether a given projected rate of growth of real money balances is modest or expansive one also needs to be armed with some projected percentage change in velocity. Strictly the sum of the projected growth in real money balances and the projected growth in velocity would give some indication of the 'room' allowed for real output growth in the economy. As it happens, velocity has been very unstable in recent years, making it, in fact, very difficult to project on the basis of recent experience. The German experience is particularly revealing here. Between 1975 and 1978 there were projections of the percentage change in velocity. In three of these years (1975, 1977 and 1978) the errors were between 3.5 and 4.5 percentage points.[11]

The wide bands in most countries allow a large range in variation in the projected growth in real money balances. In some countries, notably Australia and the UK, the projected real rates of growth appear very modest, while in nearly all countries these projected real growth rates were on the conservative side in the light of the substantial excess capacity of those years. For example, if we assume that output must grow by something like 3–4 per cent to absorb productivity growth and growth in the labour force, this would leave little room for any significant reduction in unemployment. In all countries, too, the projected growth in real money balances was well below that achieved in 1970–73. These conclusions are also consistent with the OECD review of monetary targeting and monetary trends since 1975 in member countries.[12] They refer to monetary growth since 1974/75 as 'comparatively moderate' reflecting a 'strategy of cautious monetary restraint'.

Annex – Derivation of Basic Equation from Neo-Keynesian Model of Chapter 11

Notation

Ar = real absorption

E = exchange rate (units of domestic currency per unit of foreign currency)

edm = elasticity of demand for imports
edmp = elasticity of demand for oil imports
edx = elasticity of demand for exports
Gr = real government expenditure
Mn = volume of 'other imports'
Mo = money supply
Mp = original volume of oil imports
P = overall price level
Pd = domestic price level
Pfn = price of 'other imports'
Pfp = price of oil imports
X = volume of exports
Yf = foreign real GNP
Yr = real GNP

A dot over symbol represents percentage change.

We now represent GNP and its components as:

$$Yr.Pd = Ar.Pd + X.Pd - Mp.Pfp.E - Mn.Pfn.E \qquad (18A.1)$$

$$Mp = -\alpha_{30} Pfp.E + \alpha_{31} Yr \qquad (18A.2)$$

Differentiating and converting a slope into an elasticity we have:

$$\Delta Mp = -Mp.edmp\Delta(Pfp.E) + \alpha_{31}\Delta Yr \qquad (18A.3)$$

If all other equations of the model are retained,[13] and if we convert all variables in rate of change form we can derive the following expression:[14]

$$\dot{Yr} = \frac{\alpha_3}{k}\left(\frac{Mo}{Yr}\right)(\dot{Mo} - \dot{P}) + \left(\frac{X}{Yr}\cdot\frac{\alpha_6}{k}\right)\dot{Yf} + \left(\frac{Gr}{Yr}\right)\frac{\alpha_6}{k}\dot{Gr}$$

$$-\left(\frac{X}{Yr}\right)\alpha_6\left(\frac{edx + edm - 1}{k}\right)(\dot{Pd} - \dot{Pfn} - \dot{E})$$

$$-\frac{\alpha_6}{k}\left(\frac{Mp}{Yr}\right)(1 - edmp)(\dot{Pfp} + \dot{E}) \qquad (18A.4)$$

where $k = \alpha_6(1 - \alpha_1 + \alpha_{31} + \alpha_9) + \alpha_3\alpha_4$.

In this reduced form equation the percentage change in real output ($\dot{Yr}$) is explained by (1) the percentage change in real money balances ($\dot{Mo} - \dot{P}$), (2) the percentage change in real foreign output ($\dot{Yf}$), (3) a measure of the contribution of discretionary fiscal policy to the change in real output (approximated by $\dot{G}r$), (4) the percentage change in the real exchange rate for non-oil goods ($\dot{P}d - \dot{P}fn - \dot{E}$) and (5) the oil price shock ($\dot{P}fp$), which would have a negative effect provided, as expected, $edmp<1$.

Notes for Chapter 18

1 A general reference on this is E. Fried and C. Schultze (eds) (1975).
2 One measure of this reduction in real income is the volume of oil imports, after the price shock, multiplied by the increase in the price of oil.
3 A crude measure of the terms of trade effect would be the increase in import payments as a proportion of GNP multiplied by an assumed savings ratio. If we take the savings ratio as 0.2 the fall in the terms of trade would have provided a small stimulus to GNP of the order of 0.2 per cent to 0.7 per cent of GNP for the countries.
4 *OECD Economic Outlook* (December 1978) and (July 1979).
5 See G. Maynard (1978).
6 OECD (1979a). The switch to monetary targeting, in principle, was a victory for monetarist thinking. At the same time, practice has not entirely conformed to monetarism. Not only have money growth rates diverged from targets on many occasions but they have also fluctuated more widely than monetarists themselves would have liked. See, for example, M. Friedman (1979a), p. 35.
7 A band is supposed to have two advantages: one is that it allows for the fact that the volume of money cannot be tightly controlled, another is that it gives central banks a little more flexibility. On the other hand, if bands are too wide they may generate too much uncertainty in the public mind.
8 For an evaluation of this argument and some empirical evidence bearing on it see V. Argy (1979).
9 The traditional argument favouring the use of a money, in preference to an interest rate, target is that real disturbances (which shift the *IS* schedule) are more important than demand for money disturbances (shifts in the *LM* schedule). In these conditions, a money target will serve as a more effective stabiliser than an interest rate target. See W. Poole (1970).
10 See R. J. Gordon (1978). See also Chapter 29.
11 See OECD (1979a), p. 41.
12 Ibid, pp. 63–4.
13 Remembering that our original *M* is now *Mn*. Also we now use the original money demand equation to allow for a direct real balance effect.
14 This assumes that $Ar = Yr$ and $Mn = X$. This, of course, is only a convenient approximation.

Part Four

Managed Floats – 1973 to 1978

Chapter 19

The Forward Market – Analysis and Evidence

Introduction

A forward exchange rate is a rate quoted for a currency transaction to be undertaken some time in the future. For example, a three-month forward rate for the mark–dollar exchange rate is the going rate at which operators in foreign exchange markets may buy or sell marks against the US dollar.

Forward rates play a most important role in trade, in speculation and in capital movements; an understanding therefore of how they are determined is essential to an integrated study of international monetary theory and policy.[1]

This chapter will examine, in some detail, the fundamental determinants of the forward rate under flexible exchange rates.

Notation used in this chapter

E = spot rate (expressed as units of the domestic currency per unit of the foreign currency)

Ee = expected exchange rate

F = 3-month forward rate (defined as in E)

$FD = \frac{(F-E)}{E}$ = forward discount on domestic currency (positive)

r = 3-month (home) interest rate

rf = comparable 3-month (foreign) interest rate

D_{AS} = net demand for spot US dollars by arbitrageurs

S_{AF} = net supply of forward US dollars by arbitrageurs

D_{SF} = net demand for forward US dollars by speculators

S_{TS} = net supply of spot US dollars by traders and long-term capital flows

The Determination of the Forward Rate under Flexible Exchange Rates

We identify three participants in the foreign exchange market: the pure arbitrageurs, the pure speculators and the trader–hedgers. The behaviour of each of these will first be described and it will then be shown how they interact in the market to shape the movements in the spot and forward rates.

The Pure Arbitrageur

The pure arbitrageur, by definition, will seek the highest net rate of return from the use of available funds without assuming any exchange risk. Assume he has x units of domestic currency to dispose of. At any point of time he is faced with given domestic and foreign interest rates and given spot and forward rates. He has the option of investing overseas without exchange risk or domestically. If he invests overseas x/E represents the foreign currency value of his investment, which, after three months, will be worth $(x/E)(1+rf)$ in foreign currency or (after conversion at the existing forward rate) $(x/E)(1+rf).F$ in domestic currency. If, on the other hand, he invests domestically the value of the investment after three months would be $x(1+r)$.

Therefore, in the foreign exchange market, the pure arbitrageur will buy the foreign currency (assumed henceforth to be the US dollar) spot and sell the foreign currency forward if:

$$\frac{F}{E}\cdot x(1+rf)>x(1+r)$$

or, substituting $FD+1$ for F/E and disregarding the (small) term $FD.rf$, if:

$$rf-r+FD>0$$

where $rf-r$ is the uncovered interest differential and the expression on the left-hand side is the covered interest differential, which is simply the interest rate differential adjusted for the forward discount on the domestic currency.

More formally, we have, in the spot market:

$$D_{AS}=a(rf-r+FD) \qquad (19.1)$$

and in the forward market (disregarding the, small, interest accrual on the transaction):

$$S_{AF}=a(rf-r+FD) \qquad (19.2)$$

How responsive will arbitrageurs be to changes in the covered differential, or, in other words, how large is the coefficient *a*?

The interest rate parity theory, in its crudest form, assumes that flows of funds will take place until the returns from foreign and domestic investment are equalised. In this special case the covered interest differential is reduced to zero and *a* then approaches infinity. However, many factors may constrain the unlimited movement of funds by arbitrageurs. Briefly, these include: the costs of transaction, exchange controls, insufficient funds or rising costs of obtaining funds, portfolio diversification, potential difficulties in repatriating funds, rising opportunity costs in terms of inconvenience or illiquidity.[2]

The arbitrageur's function is represented graphically in Figure 19.1.[3] The spot function represents Equation (19.1) while the forward function represents Equation (19.2). It is assumed that *a* is not infinitely elastic. (If *a* were infinitely elastic the schedule would be horizontal.) The spot function assumes that *rf, r* and *F* are given. From Equation (19.1) it is seen that as *E* increases the demand for US dollars will drop because the forward discount (premium) on the domestic currency is reduced (increased). The forward function assumes that *rf, r* and *E* are given. From Equation (19.2) it is seen that as *F* increases the forward supply of US dollars increases (that is, US dollars will be sold forward).

Figure 19.1 *The Arbitrage function – the spot and forward markets*

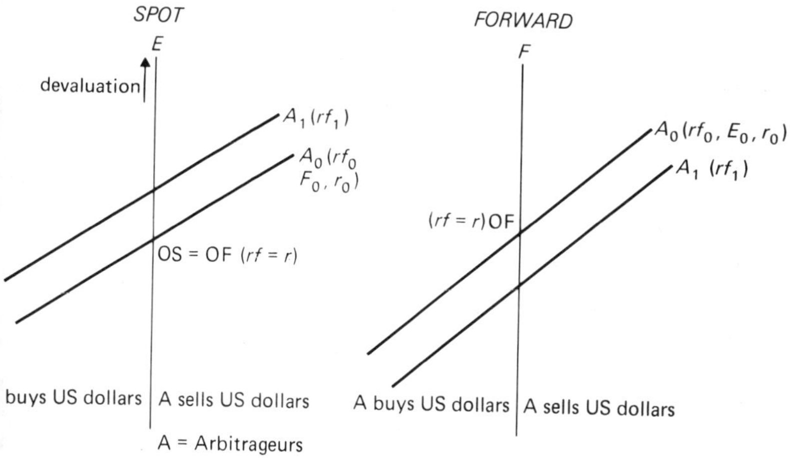

Points OS and OF represent the interest rate parity case where there is no net demand for US dollars spot or forward and, for convenience, the two interest rates as well as the spot–forward rates are assumed to be equal. A rise in the foreign interest rate will shift the spot function to the left and the forward function to the right, inducing a spot purchase of US dollars and an equivalent forward sale of US dollars.

The Pure Speculator

A speculator assumes an exchange risk with the objective of making a profit. He can speculate through the spot market or through the forward market. The former is called arbitrage speculation and the latter pure speculation. In the first case, the speculator moves funds across countries without forward cover with the expectation of gaining from a change in the exchange rate; in the second case, the speculator will buy or sell US dollars in the forward market with the expectation of gaining from the difference between the current forward rate and the spot rate expected in three months. In contrast to pure speculation, arbitrage speculation involves a spot movement of funds (and hence of reserves) and requires command over financial resources.

Assuming a perfect capital market, what determines the choice between the two forms of speculation? Again suppose that x units are initially available to be invested and that there is speculation against the domestic currency. The arbitrage speculator will buy US dollars spot and sell these in three months at the expected spot rate. The expected value in domestic currency from this speculation is then:

$$\frac{x}{E}(1+rf)\cdot Ee$$

By contrast, the pure speculator will buy US dollars forward and sell these in three months at the spot rate expected. The expected value in domestic currency from this speculation[4] is:

$$\frac{x(1+r)}{F}\cdot Ee$$

Spot speculation is therefore more profitable if:

$$\frac{x}{E}(1+rf)\cdot Ee > \frac{x(1+r)}{F}\cdot Ee$$

$$\frac{F}{E}(1+rf) \text{ or } > (1+r)$$

which turns out to be the same as the interest arbitrage condition.

In other words, if the net covered differential is positive it is more profitable to speculate on the spot than on the forward market. In this case, one may visualise the speculator, first, acting as a pure arbitrageur (that is, buying US dollars spot and selling them forward); since the covered differential is positive this in itself will yield a net gain. At the same time, he expects the spot rate to be above[5] the present forward rate. He will, therefore, gain further by buying US dollars forward. This amounts to saying that arbitrage speculation is equivalent to covered arbitrage (which we have already accommodated) plus the purchase of US dollars forward (pure speculation). For this reason it is possible, methodologically, to focus only on the role of the pure speculator in the forward market, disregarding the arbitrage speculator.

Formally, now, we may represent the pure speculators as follows:

$$D_{SF} = b(Ee - F) \tag{19.3}$$

This asserts that the net demand for US dollars forward is a function of the difference between the expected spot rate and the forward rate. For example, if the expected spot rate is greater than the current forward rate, speculators will buy US dollars forward. Here b is the sensitivity of the speculators' function. This speculators' function (assumed to be imperfectly elastic) is represented in Figure 19.2. The function assumes given expectations. OF represents the point at which the forward rate equals the expected spot rate. As the forward rate increases above that there will be an incentive to sell US dollars forward. If expectations change, for example, if the spot rate is expected to rise (devalue), the function will shift to the right (S_1).

Figure 19.2 *The pure speculators' function in the forward market*

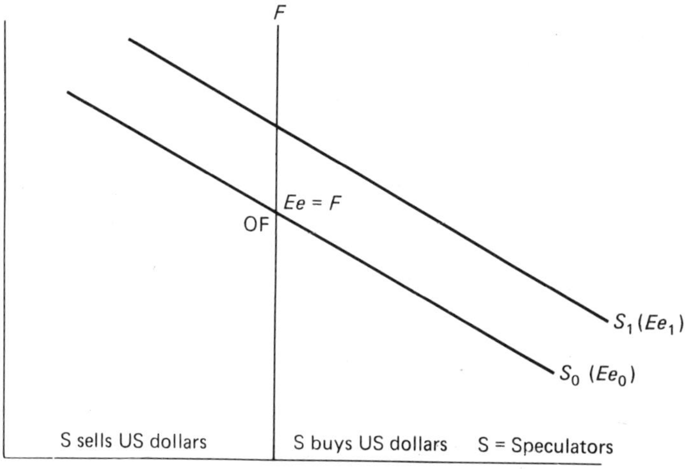

What determines the degree of response of speculators to a difference between the forward rate and the expected spot rate? Briefly, it will depend on the degree of certainty with which expectations are held and the degree of diversity in opinion among speculators. If Ee was held with certainty and expectations were uniform b would approach infinity (in other words, the forward rate would always equal the firmly held expected spot rate).

Trader–Hedgers

We now need to introduce our third participants, the trader–hedgers into the analysis. In what follows we assume, for simplicity, that all contracts are written in foreign currency (US dollars) and focus primarily on the importer, although a similar analysis is applicable to the exporter.

Traders receive and make payments in foreign currency in the normal course of their business. Traders may be hedgers (risk avoiders) or speculators (that is, they assume some exchange risk). In turn, it is possible to hedge in the spot market or in the forward market. Consider, first, the case of spot hedging. The importer has to make a payment x in US dollars currently or $x(1+rf)$ in three months. The cost of spot payment is, therefore, Ex.[6] On the other hand, the importer can buy $x(1+rf)$ US dollars in the forward market. The cost will be $Fx(1+rf)$ in domestic currency. The present value of this future commitment is

$$\frac{Fx(1+rf)}{(1+r)}$$

So hedging will be undertaken in the spot market if:

$$\frac{Fx(1+rf)}{1+r} > Ex$$

or

$$\frac{F}{E}(1+rf) > 1+r$$

which again is the interest arbitrage condition. The choice, therefore, between spot and forward hedging depends on the covered interest differential. It should be noted that spot hedging requires immediate funds and involves a spot outpayment while forward hedging does not require immediate funds and involves an outpayment in the future.

Traders can also be speculators. In other words, they may assume an exchange risk by not covering. For example, if an importer expects the future spot rate to drop below the current forward rate he will – other things being equal – hold off covering in the expectation that the US dollars he requires will cost less in domestic currency.

Exporters can also hedge either by selling their expected US dollar earnings in the forward market or by borrowing US dollars currently (to invest domestically) (that is, create a liability in US dollars to match the asset). Finally, the exporter can also speculate (for example, by not selling his US dollars forward if he expects a devaluation of the domestic currency).

Traders will now formally be incorporated in the model as follows. One useful and convenient way to proceed is to assume that all trade transactions are hedged through the spot market (for example, if payment is made by importers when due through the spot market and exporters are paid when due and convert their US dollar proceeds through the spot market). Of course, this is not what really happens but it will be shown that the other possible alternatives are already accommodated within our framework.

Suppose importers, in fact, hedged forward. This operation can be viewed as combining spot hedging with pure arbitrage (which is already allowed for). For example, if importers buy US dollars in the spot market to effect payment to overseas suppliers but conditions are more favourable to forward hedging (for instance, because, other things being equal, the domestic interest rate is relatively high), then we can visualise a further transaction which entails the selling of the US dollars spot (so liquidating the original transaction) and the buying of US dollars forward (the equivalent of a pure arbitrage transaction). The net result is the equivalent of forward hedging. Again, if importers in fact do not hedge, and speculate on a revaluation (which would reduce the ultimate cost in domestic currency), we can view this outcome as combining spot hedging with pure arbitrage and, additionally, pure speculation (the sale of US dollars forward, which now liquidates the forward position as well).

Recognition that traders also engage in both speculation and arbitrage has the most important implication that the pure arbitrage and speculators' functions will tend to be somewhat more elastic (responsive) than in the absence of traders.

Formally, we now incorporate traders in the model along the lines indicated above. The volume of transactions coming forward for payment in the spot market is determined by the spot rate itself, as well as of course by other influences (for example, relative output, prices, etc.). Also there will be some exogenous long-term capital transactions in the spot market. If S_{TS} denotes the net supply of US dollars by traders and long-term capital flows then:

$$S_{TS} = cE + TA \qquad (19.4)$$

where TA is the exogenous component. We assume that a devaluation (revaluation) increases the net supply of US dollars. This function is represented in Figure 19.3 in the spot market by the T schedule.

The Dynamics

Before we present the full model and put it to work, one difficulty needs to be faced. Our analysis has focused on a single point in time (involving transactions with a duration of three months). One might ask at this point what happens in the subsequent period, three months later, when forward transactions have to be unwound. Are there implications for spot transactions then?

Since our traders are assumed to function only in the spot market, we may focus only on the pure arbitrageurs and pure speculators. Suppose arbitrageurs (in response to a rise in foreign interest rates) buy US dollars spot and sell them forward to the pure speculators. At the termination of the contract the arbitrageur will transfer ownership of a US dollar deposit in a US bank to the speculator. In return the speculator will transfer ownership of a deposit in domestic currency in a domestic bank to the arbitrageur. In other words, there will be a swap of foreign and domestic deposits between these participants. At this point there is no spot transaction. However, the speculator will (presumably) now unwind his position, selling his US dollar position acquired from the arbitrageur for domestic currency and this does create a spot transaction. The conclusion here is that the pure speculators' transactions in one period have a counterpart in a reverse spot operation in the subsequent period (three months hence, in our analysis). These points will not be pursued but they would somewhat complicate the analysis, if, for example, it were extended into subsequent periods.

The Full Model

Spot

$$D_{AS} = a(rf - r + \frac{F-E}{E}) \tag{19.1}$$

$$S_{TS} = cE + TA \tag{19.4}$$

Forward

$$S_{AF} = a(rf - r + \frac{F-E}{E}) \tag{19.2}$$

$$D_{SF} = b(Ee - F) \tag{19.3}$$

The full model is summarised above where Equations (19.1) and (19.4) represent the demand and supply of spot US dollars, respectively, while Equations (19.2) and (19.3) represent the supply and demand for US dollars forward, respectively.

Figure 19.3 *Effects of a rise in the foreign interest rate*

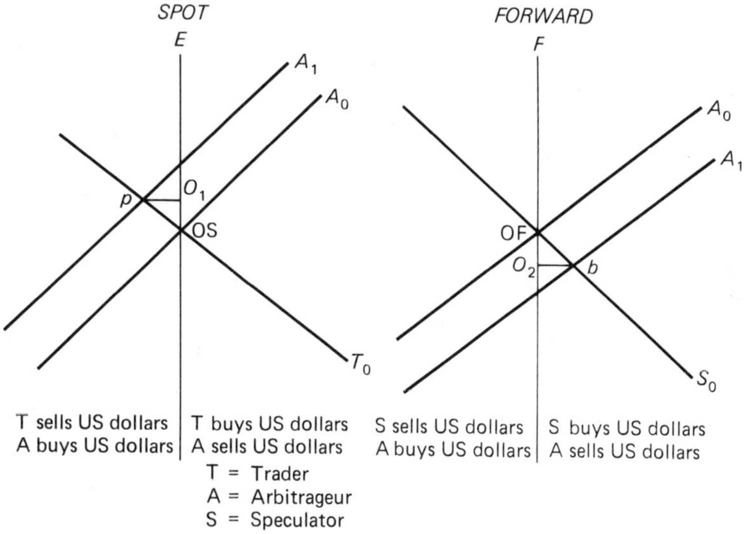

In equilibrium in the two markets we have:

$$D_{AS} = S_{TS} \tag{19.5}$$

and

$$S_{AF} = D_{SF} \tag{19.6}$$

In other words, the demand for spot dollars is equated to the supply and the demand for forward dollars is equated to the supply.

The graphical representation of the full model, now taking account of arbitrageurs, speculators and traders, is shown in Figure 19.3. Initial equilibrium is assumed to satisfy the interest arbitrage condition, with OF = OS and $r = rf$.

The model can be solved for the spot and forward exchange rates in response to changes in the exogenous variables. The solutions are:[7]

$$\Delta E = \frac{ab}{ac+bc+ab}(\Delta rf - \Delta r) + \frac{ab}{ac+bc+ab}\Delta Ee$$

$$-\frac{a+b}{ac+bc+ab}\Delta TA \tag{19.7}$$

$$\Delta F = -\frac{ac}{ac+bc+ab}(\Delta rf - \Delta r) + \frac{b(a+c)}{ac+bc+ab}\Delta Ee - \frac{a}{ac+bc+ab}\Delta TA \qquad (19.8)$$

We can also solve for the change in the forward discount, which is $\Delta F - \Delta E$:

$$\Delta F - \Delta E = -\frac{a(b+c)}{ac+bc+ab}(\Delta rf - \Delta r) + \frac{bc}{ac+bc+ab}\Delta Ee + \frac{b}{ac+bc+ab}\Delta TA \qquad (19.9)$$

Finally, the solution for the demand for (supply of) arbitrage funds is:

$$\Delta D_{AS} = \frac{abc}{ac+bc+ab}(\Delta rf - \Delta r) + \frac{abc}{ac+bc+ab}\Delta Ee + \frac{ab}{ac+bc+ab}\Delta TA \qquad (19.10)$$

The Effects of an Increase in the Foreign Interest Rate

A rise in the foreign interest rate will normally raise (devalue) the spot rate (Equation 19.7), lower (revalue) the forward rate (Equation 19.8), lower the forward discount (Equation 19.9) and generate some net capital outflow (Equation 19.10). Dollars will be bought spot from traders (because the devaluation will improve the trade balance and hence induce an increased supply of US dollars) while dollars will be sold forward to speculators (who will be induced by the lower forward rate to buy more US dollars). This solution is shown in Figure 19.3. Since the spot (forward) arbitrage schedule assumes the forward (spot) exchange rate is given there will be a succession of (progressively smaller) shifts in the arbitrage schedules until equilibrium is finally established. The successive shifts are not shown on the chart. The outflow is O_1p which is equal to O_2b.

It is clear that the net outcome will depend very much on the slopes of the various functions. Two special cases are worth considering. The first is the case where the arbitrage schedule is infinitely elastic (interest parity holds, $a \rightarrow \infty$). The coefficient for the spot rate is now

$b/(b+c)$, for the forward rate $c/(b+c)$ and for the forward discount 1. The spot rate will rise, the forward rate will drop and the forward discount will fall by the amount of change in the foreign rate (ensuring a covered differential of zero).

In what proportions will the spot and forward rates change? This clearly depends on the slopes of the spot-trader functions and the speculator functions. If $c=0$ (there is no response from spot traders),[8] then the spot rate will rise to the full extent of the rise in the foreign rate while the forward rate will remain unchanged. The full brunt of the change in the forward discount will be borne by the spot rate (see Equations 19.7–19.9). Equation (19.10) also shows that in this case the net outflows of capital will also be zero. If $b=0$ (there is no response in the forward market from speculators) then the spot rate will remain unchanged and the forward rate will now bear the full brunt of the change in the forward discount. Again the net outflows will be zero.

The second special case is the one where the speculators' schedule is perfectly elastic ($b \to \infty$). This is the case where expectations are firmly held and uniform. This special case deserves particular emphasis as now the forward rate is determined only by speculators. As should be evident from the previous discussion a rise in the foreign rate will only affect the spot rate.

The Effects of an Exogenous Change in Expectations (an Expected Devaluation)

A rise in *Ee* will increase both the spot and the forward exchange rates and increase (lower) the forward discount (premium). At the same time there will be an outflow of capital (Equation 19.10). Speculators will sell the domestic currency forward, tending to push the forward rate up. The increased forward discount will induce arbitrageurs to buy US dollars spot and sell them forward. In the partial equilibrium envisaged in this model, arbitrageurs would be buying dollars spot from the traders and selling them forward to the speculators. This outcome is shown in Figure 19.4 where *ab* and *cd* represent the spot and forward transactions, respectively.

If the arbitrage function is infinitely elastic the spot and forward rates will both rise by $b/(b+c)$ leaving the forward discount unchanged. The reason is simply that the forward discount is completely constrained by the assumed fixed interest differential. By contrast, if the speculators' schedule is infinitely elastic the forward rate will rise by the expected devaluation (the coefficient of ΔEe in Equation (19.8) is 1).

The Forward Rate as a Proxy for the Expected Spot Rate

An important issue, surrounding which there is considerable

Figure 19.4 *Effects of an exogenous change in expectations (devaluation)*

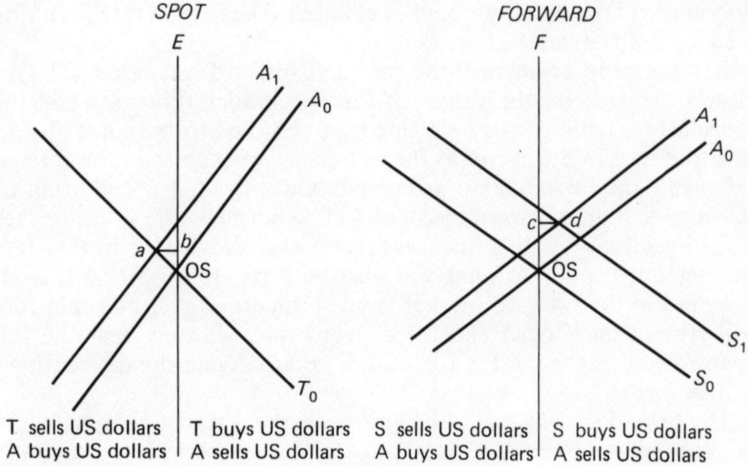

confusion, is the question of the extent to which the forward rate can be taken to represent the expected (most probable) spot rate.

We have seen that so long as there is some uncertainty about the expected spot rate fluctuations in the interest differential (or in trade/capital flows) may lead to fluctuations in the forward rate around this (most probable) forecast. Moreover, changes in expectations need not change the forward rate by the same amount. In these circumstances, then, the forward rate will not represent the best forecast rate. The forward rate will, however, remain a good approximation of the best forecast rate if it is dominated by fluctuations in the expected spot rate. (See Equation 19.8).

To the extent that there are transaction costs it is also clear that there may be some deviation between the prevailing forward rate and the expected spot rate. Again, insofar as there are restrictions on the use of the forward market the forward rate may be prevented from reflecting expectations. Finally, if speculation is monopolistic, the speculator will take account of his own operations on the forward rate and maximise profits at a forward rate which diverges from the expected spot rate, even if expectations were, in fact, held with certainty.

To summarise, then, and taking everything into account, the forward rate will exactly reflect exchange rate expectations if four conditions are met. First, there are no transaction costs. Second, there is no uncertainty about future exchange rates. Third, there are no significant restrictions on the use of the forward market. Fourth, speculation is competitive.

The third and fourth conditions are probably satisfied for the major currencies. This means that the forward rate will normally differ from the expected spot rate by a (small) band reflecting transaction costs and, as well, by an (unknown) band reflecting uncertainty (the risk premium). We have, however, argued that if the movement in the forward rate is dominated by changes in expectations, the forward rate will not be a bad approximation of the best expected spot rate.

Empirical Studies

The Interest Parity Theory

Several types of tests of the interest parity theory may be undertaken. One test involves computing a covered interest differential for two currencies; conformity with the theory then requires that the differential be constrained within a margin that allows for the costs of transacting in currencies and securities. A study of this kind was carried out for various periods and currencies by Frenkel and Levich.[9] They made careful computations of these transaction costs,[10] and then calculated the percentage of the total observations (weekly) that were within the band represented by these transaction costs. They found that in the periods 1962–67 (with fixed rates) and 1973–75 (with flexible rates) a very high proportion of the observations (ranging from 82 per cent to 100 per cent) were within the band but for the turbulent period of 1968/69 a much lower proportion (ranging from 30 per cent to 67 per cent) were within the band. These results were further reinforced when Frenkel and Levich recalculated the profit opportunities after allowing for an information and action lag. While significant profits remained in the turbulent period, these were reduced substantially for the other two periods.

A second test involves regressing the forward discount against the interest differential as in:

$$FD = a_1 + a_2(rf - r) \qquad (19.11)$$

The theory would then be confirmed if $a_1 = 0$ and $a_2 = -1$.

Spraos[11] carefully reviewed a large number of studies that carried out regressions like Equation (19.11). Unfortunately, no clear conclusion emerged, with some studies conforming, others not. For the most recent period we obtained the following result for the mark and sterling:[12]

$$FD = \underset{(-1.3)}{-0.12} \; \underset{(27.6)}{-0.97}\,(rf - r) \qquad \bar{R}^2 = 0.93 \; DW = 1.2$$

(mark–dollar January 1974 to August 1978)

(19.12)

$$FD = +0.3 \quad -1.1\,(rf - r) \qquad \bar{R}^2 = 0.57 \; DW = 1.3 \qquad (19.13)$$
$$\quad (-0.6) \quad (9.4)$$

(sterling–dollar January 1973 to August 1978)

(*t* ratios are shown in parentheses)

It would appear, therefore, that for both Germany and the UK the conditions required for the interest parity theory hold.[13]

By way of summary, the evidence presented here and in the literature suggests that interest parity holds well for external Euro-currency markets; it also appears to hold for some internal credit markets (notably the dollar–mark, the sterling–mark and the Canadian–US dollar), but particularly during relatively 'quieter' periods.

The Forward Rate as a Predictor of the Spot Rate

Assuming the forward rate reflects the expected spot rate, (an assumption which we have already questioned), a good deal of work has been carried out aimed at determining how good a predictor the forward rate is of the future spot rate. Typical of these exercises are those by Aliber[14] and the IMF.[15] Aliber calculates mean absolute percentage differences between forward rates and the spot exchange rate actually observed at the time the forward contract matures. Not surprisingly he finds that, in general, forward rates are substantially poorer predictors during the flexible rate period (March 1973 to November 1974) than during the fixed rate period (December 1967 to July 1969). Similar calculations are reported by the IMF for the period 1973–77. They find that, for the earlier period at any rate, the error is significantly less for Canada than for other currencies. More important is the finding that, in general, the errors have tended to be reduced since 1973. This, they conclude, may be in part because participants have become better at predicting under flexible exchange rates and in part because conditions may have become somewhat more stable, thus facilitating prediction.

There has also been a considerable research effort aimed at determining how efficient forward markets are.[16] Markets are designated as efficient if they make use of all available information in the formation of expectations. One way to proceed in testing for efficiency is to estimate some variant of a regression of the form:

$$S_{t+n} = a + bF_{t,n} \qquad (19.14)$$

where n is the maturity of the forward contract. The conditions required for market efficiency are that $a = 0$, $b = 1$ and that residuals from the equation be not serially correlated. If these conditions do not hold and the forward rate is a biased predictor of the future spot rate then this bias, it is contended, could have been exploited by the alert investor and, in this sense, markets would not have been efficient. Studies reviewed by Levich tend to confirm that forward markets have, in fact, been efficient as defined above. A more stringent test of efficient markets, however, by Tryon,[17] using now the first difference in the spot rate on the left and the difference between the corresponding forward rate and the spot rate on the right, finds against the efficient markets hypothesis for four out of six currencies.

An alternative way to proceed is to compare the forecasting performance of the forward rate against other forecasting models. What forecasting models can be used to predict exchange rates as alternatives to the forward rate? At the simplest level one can use all information contained in past exchange rates as predictors. An alternative is to predict exchange rates on the strength of some very simple underlying model such as purchasing power parity (PPP). Or, again, these two 'models' could be combined as predictors. Still, again, a more sophisticated structural model could be used as a basis for prediction (drawing, for example, on an Equation such as (19.7) above). Finally, one might compare the forward rate as a predictor with professional forecasts in the market place, without knowing anything about the underlying model(s) used by the professional forecasters.

Empirical work in this area to date has been inconclusive.[18] There is some empirical work that finds that the lagged spot rate can perform marginally better than the forward rate. By contrast, predictions based on purchasing power parity are significantly inferior to predictions based on the forward rate. Finally, an interesting study by Levich[19] compares the predictions of advisory services, however these are derived, with the predictions represented by the forward rate. His conclusion is that most advisory service forecasts are not as accurate as the forward rate.

It is convenient, when considering this test to distinguish two possibilities. The first case is the one where the forecasting model performs better than the forward rate. This is consistent with the hypothesis that the forward rate is not reflecting (best) expectations, as discussed previously, or again with the hypothesis that forward markets are not efficient. It is not, in fact, possible to discriminate between these two hypotheses.

The second case is the one where the forward rate outperforms other forecasting models. This outcome is consistent with efficient markets but is not conclusive evidence of efficiency. For example, it is possible that one has not exhausted potential forecasting models and that there are some alternative models which could have outperformed the forward rate.

The conclusion to be drawn here is that there is a greater presumption that forward markets are efficient if the forward rate outperforms other forecasting models, than if these forecasting models outperform the forward rate.

Notes for Chapter 19

1 See, on this: S. C. Tsiang (1959); E. Sohmen (1966).
2 For a detailed review of these factors see T. Willett and L. Officer (1970).
3 This follows the presentation in P. Clark and H. Grubel (1972).
4 Note that this allows for the fact that the x funds are 'available' over three months for investment and therefore will cumulate to $x(1+r)$.
5 The reader is reminded that a higher exchange rate means a devaluation.
6 It makes no difference, of course, whether we assume that the trader does not make the payment immediately overseas but invests overseas for the three months and then pays $x(1+rf)$.
7 Initial values of E and F are set equal to 1.
8 This case is far from being unrealistic since one would normally expect a lag in the adjustment of the trade balance to the exchange rate. See Chapter 21.
9 J. Frenkel and R. Levich (1977).
10 These costs varied for different periods. They ranged from a low of about 0.22 to a high (for the most recent period) of about 1.15. These represent minimum differentials before it becomes profitable to shift funds. For a review of earlier estimates see T. Willett and L. Officer (1970), p. 251.
11 J. Spraos (1972).
12 For Equation (19.12) the three-month Euro-dollar rate and the German three-month interest deposit rate were used. The interest rates in Equation (19.13) are the two Treasury Bills. This was the equation that performed best.
13 A third type of test is a refinement on the second test, to allow for influences other than the interest differential on the forward rate (as in our own model presented above). See: H. Stoll (1968); J. Kesselman (1971); R. D. Haas (1974); B. McCallum (1977a).
14 R. Aliber (1976).
15 IMF *Annual Report* (1977), pp. 27–8.
16 See J. Frenkel (1978); R. M. Levich (1979a).
17 R. Tryon (1979).
18 For a review of other work here see: R. Levich (1979a); M. Mussa (1979); W. B. Cornell (1977); V. Argy and K. W. Clements (1980).
19 R. Levich (1979b).

Chapter 20

Exchange Rate Behaviour – Theoretical Analysis

Introduction

With exchange rates since early 1973 largely determined by market forces, it is important now to be able to identify the principal influences underlying exchange rate movements. With this general aim in mind, this chapter examines four approaches to the analysis of exchange rate behaviour.[1] The first, and oldest, is the Purchasing Power Parity theory (PPP). The second draws on the neo-Keynesian model of Chapter 11. The third is monetarist inspired. The fourth, and most recent, focuses on the role of wealth and portfolio balance.

Notation used in this chapter

subscript A = country A
subscript B = country B
Ar = real absorption
B = balance of payments
CA = current account of the balance of payments
DB = domestic bonds
E = exchange rate (units of domestic currency per unit of foreign currency)
Ee = expected exchange rate
FC = value of foreign assets in foreign currency held by residents
Gr = real government expenditure
K = net capital flows
Mo = money supply
P = overall price level
Pf = foreign prices denominated in foreign currency
PN = price of non-traded goods
PT = price of traded goods
r = domestic interest rate
rf = foreign interest rate

We = domestic wealth
Yf = foreign real GNP
Yr = real GNP

A dot over symbol represents percentage change.

Relative Purchasing Power Parity Theory

The relative Purchasing Power Parity theory (PPP) asserts that exchange rates will move over time in line with changes in relative purchasing power.[2] For example, the bilateral version of the theory asserts that the percentage change in the exchange rate, from a base year to a terminal year, for any two currencies (say, the German mark and the US dollar) would be determined by the relative rate of inflation in the two countries.

The theory's principal difficulties and limitations may be easily summarised. First, there is a problem in the selection of a base year for the exercise. One assumption implicit in any test of PPP is that the exchange rate is in equilibrium in the base year, which of course may not hold.

Second, there is the important question of the appropriate choice of price index on which to base the calculations. The choice here, which embraces export prices, wholesale prices, unit labout costs, implicit GNP deflators and the cost of living, depends on the underlying theory.

In Keynesian analysis the emphasis is on the price of tradables (that is, on those goods that enter competitively in trade). Keynesians, as we have seen, tend to start with the assumption that prices of domestically produced goods, including tradables, are largely determined by domestic unit labour costs (adjusted for the prices of imported inputs). Over the longer run, if the increase in the price of tradables departs significantly from the increase in comparable overseas prices, the change in the competitive position will bring into play corrective forces that will result in a change in the exchange rate. In selecting a price index, therefore, Keynesians tend to apply two criteria – first, the extent to which it focuses on tradables and second, the statistical reliability of the series. How do these criteria apply to the available price series?[3] Export prices concentrate on goods that are actually traded while wholesale prices cover goods that are traded as well as tradable. Export prices tend to be statistically unsatisfactory as they are calculated as average values rather than proper unit prices. On the other hand, there are international differences in the scope and weighting of wholesale prices. Moreover, in the case of both indices there arises the difficulty that to the extent that foreign competition has some direct influence on the price of traded and tradable goods, these prices might not reflect domestic costs. From this standpoint unit labour costs in manufacturing have the important advantage that they are a more direct measure of the competitive positions. However, reliable data on comparable costs, taking account of all labour charges, is difficult to compile. Consumer prices are more comparable across countries but they are unsatisfactory for other reasons. They include non-tradables, exclude some tradables (for example, investment goods) and are open to the productivity bias. For example, countries that have a large share of non-tradables in GNP or where the productivity advantage in tradables is relatively high will experience, other things being equal, a relatively high rate of increase in overall prices which will make their currencies appear overvalued[4] (see Annex 1). The GDP deflator is also comparable across countries but open to objections similar in quality to those levelled at the consumer price index, although in lesser degree.

Monetarists, we have seen, start with the presumption that the 'law of one price' holds for all tradable goods. Therefore, their rate of growth across countries, measured in a common currency, must, by definition, be the same. It follows that both export and wholesale prices, comprising as they do traded and tradable goods, are useless for purposes of testing PPP. A much more broadly-based index that includes non-tradables is, therefore, required. Since inflation in each country is determined by the relative excess of nominal money balances over the demand for money the appropriate price index according to monetarists is the deflator for money balances (see later discussion); there is, however, no index that exactly corresponds to this deflator. It follows therefore that none of the available price indices is by itself satisfactory.[5]

Third, and most important, changes in relative real income growth, longer-run structural changes in demand, oil price shocks, changes in the degree of protection and in capital flows may all offset the effects of differences in competitive positions, making relative PPP inappropriate.

Finally, there is the problem of causation. It is contended that causation might run not just from relative inflation to exchange rates but also from exchange rates to relative inflation. This question is taken up in various forms later in the chapter and also in subsequent chapters, so we need not pursue it in any detail here. It suffices to say that there are several realistic ways in which exchange rate changes may precede in time changes in relative prices. To take two examples: if there is a monetary expansion in one country and asset markets adjust first, the devaluation may precede the subsequent adjustment in prices. Indeed, as we show later, the subsequent increase in prices may actually be associated with some strengthening of the currency.

Or, again, suppose that we have a structural change that involves, say, either a reduction in the rate of inflow of capital or a reduction in the demand for a country's exports. The currency will have to devalue. If the real wage rate is fixed and there is domestic monetary accommodation, the devaluation will simply raise domestic prices in the same proportion without ultimately correcting the structural imbalance. In this instance it is the devaluation that will have triggered the price change rather than the reverse (see Chapter 25).

Notwithstanding these difficulties PPP continues to have considerable appeal, especially for longer-term analysis, and indeed has experienced a revival in recent years, partly because exchange rates have become more flexible, and partly because it is thought that PPP might provide a possible basis for intervention under managed floats (see Chapter 26).

Neo-Keynesian Analysis

The Basic Framework

Whatever the merits of PPP as a longer-run explanation of exchange rate movements it clearly cannot explain short-run movements in the exchange rate. This section draws on our neo-Keynesian model to provide the insights into the short-term as well as the long-term behaviour of exchange rates.

The first step is to adapt the model to provide the basic analytical framework that will define the driving forces underlying exchange rate behaviour. The only extension required to the model is to accommodate the important role of exchange rate expectations. We do this very simply by allowing for exchange rate expectations in the capital flow equation which now becomes:

$$K = \alpha_{12}\left[r - rf - \left(\frac{Ee - E}{E}\right)\right] \tag{20.1}$$

where *Ee* is the expected exchange rate assumed, for simplicity, to be equal to the forward rate. Taking expectations into account, the model then has a solution that takes the following form:

$$E = E(Mo, Gr, Yf, rf, Pf, Ee, AE) \tag{20.2}$$

where *AE* stands for 'other influences' on exchange rates.

This framework allows us to identify three major forces driving exchange rate behaviour: first, and most important, the fundamental forces identified by the model – these are the volume of money (*Mo*), government expenditure (*Gr*) (or more generally fiscal policy), output in the rest of the world (*Yf*), the interest rate in the rest of the world (*rf*) and prices in the rest of the world (*Pf*); second, the way in which exchange rate expectations (*Ee*) are formed; third, the dynamics of exchange rate adjustment to these fundamental (and other) forces.

In evaluating the dynamics of adjustment it is also helpful to make a distinction between three different time horizons, corresponding, in effect, to different phases of adjustment. A first phase is the asset adjustment phase, when only financial markets adjust. This would encompass a period of perhaps a few weeks, following a monetary change, before real markets have had time to adjust. A second phase corresponds to the phase when output is adjusting, and before there is any substantial impact on prices and labour markets. This, as we saw, encompasses a period of, say, a year to perhaps a year and a half following a real or monetary disturbance. A third phase is the one within which prices and labour markets have fully adjusted. In the context of our own model, it represents the situation where the original real wage rate is actually restored.

The Formation of Exchange Rate Expectations

Before we apply this framework we need some explanation of exchange rate expectations. There are many different ways, in principle, to explain exchange rate expectations. We limit ourselves to three types of explanations. These are adaptive, extrapolative and rational.[6]

Adaptive exchange rate expectations assume that expectations are formed on the basis of past values of exchange rates, with geometrically declining weights the more distant the exchange rate.[7]

Extrapolative exchange rate expectations assume that the future exchange rate is determined by the current exchange rate adjusted for the actual change in the exchange rate. Formally:

$$Ee = E + m(E - E_{-1}) \tag{20.3}$$

This formulation has the advantage that it can accommodate a variety of possible expectations. Consider three possibilities: $m = 0$, $m > 0 \leq 1$, $m < 0 \geq -1$. If $m = 0$ the expected exchange rate is equal to the current exchange rate. If m is positive then this implies that when the exchange rate is rising there is an expectation of a further rise. For example, if $m = 1$ the whole of the increase is projected into the future. On the other hand, when m is negative an increase in the exchange rate will generate expectations that the future exchange rate will fall. For example, if $m = -1$ the expected exchange rate is equal to the past exchange rate, so any current change is totally discounted. With $m = 0$ exchange rate expectations are neutral, with $m > 0$ expectations are elastic, while with $m < 0$ expectations are inelastic.[8]

Still another approach is based on quasi-rational expectations. For example, expectations may be based, in part at least, on PPP considerations.[9] Alternatively, the expected exchange rate may be based on the exploitation of all the evidence contained in current and past movements in the exchange rate.[10]

Finally, fully rational expectations assume that expectations are based on the expected values of the very same variables that, it is contended, determine the exchange rate.[11] In other words, expectations draw on the best available information about the way in which the economy works.

One difficulty in assuming fully rational expectations is the following. Suppose that the question of what determines the exchange rate is highly contentious in the sense that there is no agreement on which key variables determine the exchange rate. It is not clear how rational expectations would be formed in this case. To construct a particular theoretical framework and then to assume that the same theoretical framework forms the basis of expectations would seem, on the face of it, to be somewhat inappropriate.

Nevertheless, and despite these reservations, there is something intuitively appealing in the notion that a hypothesis that is held to explain exchange rates might well also be the basis for the formation of expectations.

To illustrate the way in which fully rational expectations are formed consider a relatively simple model of exchange rate determination:

$$Et = \alpha_1 Vt + \alpha_3 Vt_{-1} + \alpha_2 Eet \tag{20.4}$$

This says that the exchange rate is explained by the current and previous values of a number of independent variables summarised in V (for example, as in Equation (20.2) above) and also by the exchange rate expected for the period t_{+1} in period t.

If expectations are rationally formed, then:

$$Eet = \alpha_1 Vet + \alpha_3 Vet_{-1} + \alpha_2 Eet_{+1} \tag{20.5}$$

The exchange rate expected in the subsequent period will thus be determined by the values of the independent variables expected in the subsequent period (*Vet*), the independent variables expected for the current period (which may in fact be known) and the exchange rate expected two periods hence (since that will also influence the rate expected in the next period).

A quite different way again to proceed in trying to arrive at exchange rate expectations is to draw on 'outside' information about exchange rate expectations, without trying to explain how these expectations are actually formed. For example, there may be indications from regular surveys about exchange rate expectations, or some proxy for exchange rate expectations (such as the forward rate) might be used.

Where does all this leave us? Unfortunately, no one approach has a decided advantage over the others. To some degree, expectations will be formed on the basis of expected movements in the variables thought to influence exchange rates, including new political/social developments. At the same time, some weight will presumably also be given to recent trends in exchange rates: whether expectations will be elastic or inelastic will depend on the particular environment at the time expectations are formed.

Illustrative Sources of Exchange Rate Instability in a Neo-Keynesian Framework

We now attempt to apply the general framework to an analysis of the effects on exchange rates, over different time horizons, of three types of disturbances: a change in foreign output, a change in foreign prices and a domestic monetary disturbance.

In dealing with the first two disturbances we assume that the interest rate is fixed by the monetary authorities over the relevant time horizon. The assumption allows us to disregard the effects on capital flows of interest rate differences as such, focusing only on capital flows induced by exchange rate expectations.

Consider, to begin, the longer-run effects of a sustained increase in foreign output.[12] The initial current account surplus will, at first, lead to a revaluation that will restore equilibrium to the balance of payments. In due course, however, with wages fully adjusting and monetary accommodation, the effects of the revaluation will be fully offset by a reduction in domestic prices. This will necessitate a further revaluation which again, in turn, will be neutralised by a reduction in domestic prices. Eventually, all other things being equal, the economy settles down with a lower rate of inflation and an equivalent rate of appreciation of the currency. The severity of this wage–price–revaluation spiral (that is, the rate of price change and revaluation required) depends on the speed of adjustment of labour markets (see Chapter 25). In essence, we have here an unstable exchange rate, in an upward direction, because under the conditions assumed (fixed interest rates and an attempt to restore real wages) the exchange rate cannot be counted on to correct a sustained disequilibrium to the current account.

In the shorter term (our second time phase) the analysis is much more complicated. We focus here on the roles of import and export demand elasticities and expectations in generating potential exchange rate instability.

Suppose, initially, that the Marshall–Lerner condition holds but that there are lags, extending over two periods, in the adjustment of the current account to a change in the exchange rate. At the same time, we want to evaluate outcomes, first, for neutral exchange rate expectations and, second, for fully rational exchange rate expectations, as defined earlier.

An Annex demonstrates that the short-run solution for the exchange rate to our neo-Keynesian model with neutral exchange rate expectations is:

$$\Delta E = -\frac{\alpha_{20}}{ML_1}\Delta Yf - \frac{ML_2}{ML_1}\Delta E_{-1} \qquad (20.6)$$

The solution for the exchange rate after full adjustment, within this phase (so that $\Delta E = \Delta E_{-1}$), is:

$$\Delta E = -\frac{\alpha_{20}}{ML_1 + ML_2}\Delta Yf \qquad (20.7)$$

where ML_1 is the first period effect and ML_2 the second period effect of an exchange rate change on the current account.

Three features of these results are worth emphasising. First, assuming full adjustment is attained, the exchange rate overshoots, in the sense that the initial revaluation is larger than the revaluation required after full adjustment. This is indicated by the fact that

$$\frac{\alpha_{20}}{ML_1} > \frac{\alpha_{20}}{ML_1 + ML_2}$$

Second, Equation (20.6) is a first order difference equation with a negative coefficient for the lagged dependent variable. Provided $ML_2/ML_1 < 1$ this will lead to damped fluctuations in the exchange rate. Third, if $ML_2/ML_1 > 1$ the currency may, in principle at any rate, become unstable in the sense that the amplitude of the fluctuations in the exchange rate will increase over time.

What is the economic meaning of these results? In period 1 the increase in foreign output will improve the current account and this will lead to a revaluation. Because, however, there are lags in the adjustment of the current account to a change in the exchange rate, the initial effect of the revaluation is weaker than the longer-term effect; hence, the exchange rate will have to revalue substantially initially to secure equilibrium to the current account. The complications surface in the next period. The initial revaluation will continue to cause the current account balance in period 2 to deteriorate, so now a devaluation (some reversal) is required to restore equilibrium to the current account. In period 3 the second period devaluation will continue to improve the current account, now requiring a revaluation to restore equilibrium. This explains the cyclical mechanism at work.

How can instability be generated? Suppose $ML_2 > ML_1$. Then, in our example, in period 2 the deficit in the current account balance requiring to be offset by a devaluation is larger than the initial current account surplus flowing from the increase in foreign output, so the devaluation in period 2 will need to be larger than the period 1 revaluation. At the same time, in period 3 the revaluation will now need to be still larger than the period 2 devaluation. The adjustment then, in this case, is inherently unstable.

The overshoot and the potential instability are all removed, it would seem, by rationally-based expectations. Speculators in period 1 anticipating a devaluation will buy the foreign currency and so weaken the initial revaluation. More precisely, if speculators have firmly held expectations about the exchange rate after full adjustment, as defined here, they will operate in the foreign exchange market in a way that will ensure that the current spot rate is the same as the forward rate (in the period of full adjustment).

The case where the Marshall–Lerner condition is initially perverse (there are J curve effects) is also interesting. With neutral expectations the exchange rate will, in principle, explode. The initial revaluation will only increase the current account surplus, leading to a larger revaluation, a still larger surplus, and so on. It is evident that the exchange rate can only be stabilised if speculators anticipated some reversal and entered the market to buy the foreign currency.

In the long run an increase in foreign prices will be exactly offset by a revaluation of the currency; in the shorter term, however, there are interesting differences from the previous case. Substitution effects will lead to an improvement in the current account and this in turn will strengthen the domestic currency. However, in this case, even with neutral expectations and lags in the effects of exchange rate changes there will be no overshoot, the reason being that the same lags in adjustment will apply to foreign price changes. Initially there will be only a small improvement in the current account so that even though the effects of exchange rate changes are weak, this is exactly offset by the fact that the need for adjustment is also diminished. In the subsequent period the continued deterioration in the current account due to the earlier revaluation is exactly matched by the continued improvement due to the earlier foreign price changes, so no further adjustment in the exchange rate is required.

Finally, we turn to the case of a sustained expansion in the volume of money and focus only on its distinctive features. First, in the long run, it leads to a proportionate increase in the domestic price level, as well as a proportionate devaluation of the currency. At the same time, output and the interest rate will return to their original levels. These outcomes are consistent with equilibrium in all markets. With the real exchange rate (exchange rates adjusted for relative prices) restored, output in the labour market cannot change. With the interest rate and output unchanged and with prices increasing in the same proportion the money market will also be in equilibrium. Finally, with the real exchange rate and the interest rate both restored, the foreign exchange and the goods markets must also be in equilibrium. It is in this context in particular that PPP comes into its own as a 'long-run' theory of exchange rate determination.

Second, a monetary change now allows us to deal with our first asset adjustment phase, before real markets have adjusted. Suppose that capital is perfectly mobile and that there is a rationally based expectation that in the longer run prices will rise and the exchange rate will devalue in the same proportion. This virtually fixes the expected future exchange rate. Now the expansion in the volume of money will lower interest rates. With the interest rate differential favouring the rest of the world the exchange rate must then devalue by more than its expected longer-run devaluation if the interest rate differential is to approximate the expected revaluation of the currency. In other words, given the interest rate differential and the expected future exchange rate, the spot rate must be weaker than the future rate if the incentive to move capital out of the country provided by the interest rate differential is to be offset.

In due course, however, real markets will adjust and prices and interest rates will gradually move upwards. As prices and interest rates adjust the exchange rate will move back towards its longer-term equilibrium point. It is interesting to note that, in this kind of model, increasing output and domestic prices are now associated with a gradual strengthening of the exchange rate.[13]

Exchange rates may be unstable for other reasons (as represented by *AE* in Equation (20.2)). Political developments or policy announcements may influence expectations and lead to sharp changes in exchange rates. Shocks in the form of a change in the oil price will have different effects on a country's balance of payments and hence on relative exchange rates. Also it is easy to see how long lags or perverse effects associated with exchange rate changes can destabilise exchange rates: suppose a country has a large current account deficit that has to be corrected by an exchange rate change. Speculators, observing that exchange rate changes are not having the desired effects, may well become impatient and over-react.

Also, intervention may destabilise exchange rates. For example, if the exchange rate is maintained in the face of longer-run trends, then when intervention is finally abandoned the currency may become particularly unstable during the initial period of readjustment.

Finally, in a reserve currency world any shifts out of reserve currencies will lead to some weakening of those currencies vis-à-vis the rest of the world.

To sum up the argument, then, we can conclude that instability in the underlying economic variables is a principal cause of instability in the behaviour of exchange rates in the short term. Given the behaviour of the underlying macro-variables we have also argued that, all other things being equal, exchange rate instability will be greater the longer the lags and the more perverse the initial effects associated with exchange rate changes. Also, to the extent that asset (financial) markets adjust more quickly than real markets monetary instability may lead to an over-reaction in exchange markets. Finally, some of the inherent instability in exchange rates may be attenuated to the extent that exchange rate expectations are stabilising.

Monetarist Analysis

The key idea in monetarist analysis is that the exchange rate between any two currencies is essentially an asset price that is determined by the relative supplies of money, and also by the relative demands for money. The emphasis is thus on asset adjustment rather than flow variables.

The principal assumptions in the monetarist analysis are that output is exogenous, that PPP holds continuously for traded goods, that there is perfect financial integration and, finally, that exchange rate expectations are rationally based.

We now present a relatively simple model, embodying all of these assumptions, which is very much in the spirit of monetarist thinking.[14]

Suppose we want to explain a bilateral exchange rate (say, the US dollar–mark rate) which involves two currencies and two economies (A and B). A first step is to define a demand for money equation for each of the two economies. Using Cagan's[15] well-known formulation we have:

$$\dot{Mo}_{A} = \dot{P}_{A} + \alpha_1 \dot{Yr}_{A} - \alpha_2 \Delta r_{A} \qquad (20.8)$$

where $\dot{Mo}_{A}$, $\dot{P}_{A}$ and $\dot{Yr}_{A}$ are, respectively, rates of change in the volume of money, prices and output. Here r_A is the interest rate in A. This typical demand for money equation asserts that the percentage change in the demand for money (assumed to be equal to supply) is a function of the percentage change in prices, in output and the change in the interest rate.

Monetarists tend to simplify by assuming that the money demand equations are the same for the two relevant economies. So for B we have:

$$\dot{Mo}_B = \dot{P}_B + \alpha_1 \dot{Yr}_B - \alpha_2 \Delta r_B \tag{20.9}$$

The second step is to allow for the assumption that the interest rate differential reflects exchange rate expectations. For changes in interest rates this assumption can be approximated by:

$$\Delta r_A - \Delta r_B = \left(\frac{Ee - Ee_{-1}}{Ee_{-1}}\right) - \left(\frac{E - E_{-1}}{E_{-1}}\right) = \dot{Ee} - \dot{E} \tag{20.10}$$

where *Ee* and *E* are, respectively, the expected and actual exchange rate.[16]

The third step is to allow for PPP in traded goods:

$$\dot{PT}_A - \dot{PT}_B = \dot{E} \tag{20.11}$$

where $\dot{PT}_A$ and $\dot{PT}_B$ represent the percentage change in the price of traded goods in A and B, respectively.

The money demand deflator (*P*) is composed of traded as well as non-traded prices (*PN*). We can then write:

$$\dot{P}_A = \alpha_{14} \dot{PN}_A + (1 - \alpha_{14}) \dot{PT}_A \tag{20.12}$$

where α_{14} and $(1 - \alpha_{14})$ represent, respectively, the relative weights attaching to non-traded as well as traded goods.

Again we simplify by assuming that these weights are the same in the two countries,[17] so:

$$\dot{P}_B = \alpha_{14} \dot{PN}_B + (1 - \alpha_{14}) \dot{PT}_B \tag{20.13}$$

The fourth step is to explain the formation of non-traded prices. Our own treatment is to assume that they adjust with a distributed lag to the price of traded goods. In other words, we assume that, following a disturbance, exchange markets adjust first, leading to a change in the price of traded goods and this, in turn, through substitution effects, forces corresponding changes in the prices of non-traded goods. We have then:

$$\dot{PN}_A = \alpha_{20} \dot{PT}_A + (1 - \alpha_{20}) \dot{PN}_{A-1} \tag{20.14}$$

and

$$\dot{PN}_B = \alpha_{20} \dot{PT}_B + (1 - \alpha_{20}) \dot{PN}_{B-1} \tag{20.15}$$

where α_{20} is the speed with which non-traded prices adjust to traded prices, so that as α_{20} approaches unity the speed of adjustment increases.

Finally, without representing this formally, we have the assumption of rational expectations which simply asserts that the complete model as presented above is 'known' to operators in the market and forms the basis for their expectations about future exchange rates.

Since we are interested in how exchange rates are determined this model can be solved for the exchange rate. After subtracting Equation (20.9) from Equation (20.8) and making the appropriate substitutions we have:

$$\dot{E} = \frac{1}{k}(\dot{Mo}_{A} - \dot{Mo}_{B}) - \frac{(1-\alpha_{20})\alpha_{14}}{k}(\dot{PN}_{A} - \dot{PN}_{B-1}) + \frac{\alpha_2}{k}\dot{Ee} - \frac{\alpha_1}{k}(\dot{Yr}_{A} - \dot{Yr}_{B}) \qquad (20.16)$$

where $k = \alpha_2 + \alpha_{14}\alpha_{20} + (1 - \alpha_{14})$.

Equation (20.16) asserts that the percentage change in the exchange rate is determined by the difference in monetary growth in the two countries, the difference in the rate of inflation for non-traded goods in the previous period, the percentage change in the expected exchange rate and the relative output growth in the two economies. The driving forces moving the exchange rate in this framework are in effect the relative monetary growth and the relative output growth. To understand then how this model works we need to focus on how changes in these key variables affect the exchange rate, drawing essentially on the monetarist model we presented in Chapter 13.[18]

Consider, first, the long-run solution to the model:

$$\dot{E} = (\dot{Mo}_{A} - \dot{Mo}_{B}) - \alpha_1(\dot{Yr}_{A} - \dot{Yr}_{B}) \qquad (20.17)$$

According to this solution an acceleration in monetary growth in A results in an equal proportionate devaluation while an acceleration in output growth in A results in a revaluation, the coefficient associated with output being the output elasticity of the demand for money (which could, of course, also be 1).

Now consider the rationale for these results. The immediate effect of an increase in the volume of money (a once-and-for-all change in monetary growth) is to lower A's interest rate. At the same time, there will be a rationally based expectation that the exchange rate will 'ultimately' devalue in the same proportion. So long as A's interest rate remains below B's interest rate the actual devaluation must exceed the expected devaluation. (In other words, there must be an expected revaluation – see Equation (20.10).) Initially, then, to equilibrate asset markets there must be a devaluation. But the devaluation will lead to a proportionate increase in the price of traded goods (see Equation 20.11), increasing the demand for money and hence the domestic interest rate. All of this, it needs to be emphasised, happens very quickly and simultaneously.

At this point, however, the price of non-traded goods has fallen behind the price of traded goods. There will, therefore, be substitution effects – in consumption favouring non-traded goods and in production favouring traded goods. With perfect financial integration a realistic scenario is that the switch in consumption to non-traded goods will raise the price of non-traded goods, increase the demand for money, raise the interest rate further and force a revaluation of the currency, reversing some of the original devaluation. Our Equations (20.12) and (20.13) embody this adjustment mechanism whereby non-traded prices now gradually adjust to traded prices. With time the increase in the price of traded goods will be partially reversed while the price of non-traded goods will have increased at the same rate as the price of traded goods.

An increase in output will increase the demand for money, leading to a revaluation. The associated higher domestic interest rate implies an expectation now of a devaluation. This eventuates because the lower price of traded goods will again lead to substitution effects, forcing a devaluation and reversing some of the original drop in the price of traded goods. In the end the price of traded and non-traded goods will have fallen to the same degree and the original interest rate will be restored.

These dynamic results are demonstrated more formally in the solution shown in Equation (20.16). For example, if $\dot{Mo}_A = \dot{E}e$ (the rational expectations case), the short-term devaluation is $(1+\alpha_2)/k > 1$, so there is an overshoot.[19] At the same time, the short-term effect of an increase in output (with $\dot{E}e = -\alpha_1 \dot{Yr}_A$ – the long-term effect) is $\alpha_1(1+\alpha_2)/k > \alpha_1$. The overshoot, it must be emphasised, originates in the fact that in this model, non-traded prices adjust with a lag. If there were no lag, so that $\alpha_{20} = 1$, the solution would be:

$$\dot{E} = \frac{1}{1+\alpha_2}(\dot{Mo}_A - \dot{Mo}_B) + \frac{\alpha_2}{1+\alpha_2}\dot{E}e - \frac{\alpha_1}{1+\alpha_2}(\dot{Yr}_A - \dot{Yr}_B) \quad (20.18)$$

which is frequently the form in which monetarists explain the short-term behaviour of exchange rates.

It is worth noting here that this chapter so far has identified several ways in which exchange rates might overshoot. An interesting distinction exists between an overshoot that is consistent with rational expectations (as in the monetary overshoot in this section) and an overshoot that surfaces because expectations are not rationally based (as in an earlier illustration).

Portfolio Balance Analysis

Thus far we have looked at Keynesian and monetarist approaches to exchange rate determination. There is now also a newer, distinctive, approach[20] that focuses on the role of wealth and portfolio balance in exchange rate determination. The approach is interesting and provides some useful insights, neglected by the other approaches.

The approach, in its simplest and purest form,[21] can be summarised in three equations.[22] These are:

$$\frac{Mo}{We} = -\alpha_1 r - \alpha_2 rf \tag{20.19}$$

$$\frac{DB}{We} = \alpha_3 r - \alpha_4 rf \tag{20.20}$$

$$We = Mo + E.FC + DB \tag{20.21}$$

Equation (20.19) asserts that the proportion of financial wealth residents desire to hold in the form of money is a negative function of domestic and foreign interest rates. Equation (20.20) says that the proportion of wealth held in bonds is a positive function of the domestic interest rate and a negative function of the foreign interest rate. Equation (20.21), which is an identity, defines wealth as composed of the volume of money, foreign assets (in domestic currency) and domestic bonds. Implicit in this equation is a (residual) equation which explains the share of wealth absorbed in foreign assets as a negative function of the domestic interest rate and a positive function of the foreign interest rate. The three equations jointly determine *E, We* and *r*, with *DB, FC, Mo* and *rf* exogenous to the system.

If we substitute Equation (20.21) into Equation (20.19) and again into Equation (20.20) we obtain functions that define, respectively, monetary and bond market equilibrium. Monetary equilibrium is represented by:

$$\Delta r = -\frac{\alpha_2}{\alpha_1}\Delta rf - \left(\frac{We - Mo}{\alpha_1 We^2}\right)\Delta Mo + \frac{Mo}{\alpha_1 We^2}\Delta FC + \frac{FC.Mo}{\alpha_1 We^2}\Delta E + \frac{Mo}{\alpha_1 We^2}\Delta DB \tag{20.22}$$

The relationship between the interest rate and the exchange rate, holding *rf, Mo* and *FC* constant, is shown as *LM* in Figure 20.1. It is positively sloped because if the domestic interest rate increased, given the exogenous variables, the proportion of wealth held as money must fall and this requires a devaluation that will increase the domestic currency value of foreign asset holdings.

Figure 20.1 *Bond and money market equilibrium in the portfolio balance approach*

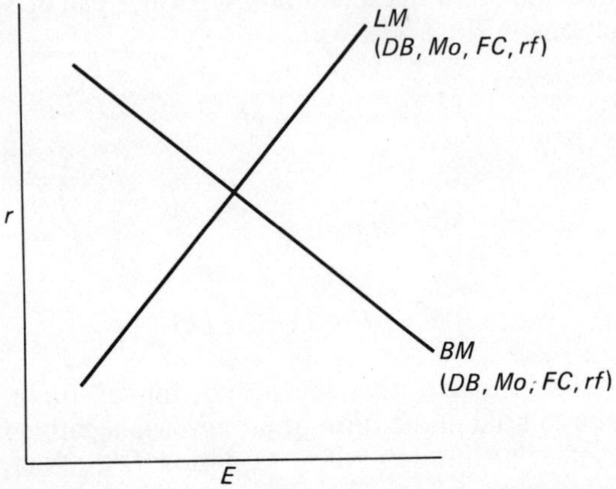

At the same time, bond market equilibrium is defined by:

$$\Delta r = \left(\frac{We - DB}{\alpha_3 We^2}\right)\Delta DB - \left(\frac{DB}{\alpha_3 We^2}\right)\Delta Mo - \left(\frac{DB}{\alpha_3 We^2}\right)\Delta FC - \left(\frac{DB.FC}{\alpha_3 We^2}\right)\Delta E + \left(\frac{\alpha_4}{\alpha_3}\right)\Delta rf \quad (20.23)$$

The relationship between the interest rate and the exchange rate that will equilibrate the bond market, holding the other variables fixed, is shown as *BM* in Figure 20.1. The schedule is negatively sloped because, if the interest rate increased, the proportion of wealth held in the form of bonds would rise and this would require a revaluation to lower the valuation of foreign assets.

These two functions together enable us to solve for the interest rate and the exchange rate, given disturbances to the system coming from changes in *DB, Mo, FC* and *rf*. The direction of change in *E* and *r* for each exogenous change is provided in Table 20.1.

Consider an increase in the volume of money. The *LM* schedule will shift to the right while the *BM* schedule will shift to the left. The end result is a fall in the domestic interest rate and a devaluation (see the mathematical solutions in Table 20.1). What does this actually mean?

Table 20.1 Portfolio balance approach effects of disturbances on E^a and r

Disturbance	Direction of change in E	Direction of change in r
DB	?	+
Mo	+	–
FC	–	0
rf	+	?

[a]An increase in E means a devaluation.

Mathematical solutions

$$\Delta E = \left(\frac{We - DB}{\alpha_3 We^2} - \frac{Mo}{\alpha_1 We^2}\right)\frac{\Delta DB}{k_1} - \left(\frac{DB}{\alpha_3 We^2} - \frac{We - Mo}{\alpha_1 We^2}\right)\frac{\Delta Mo}{k_1}$$

$$+ \left(\frac{\alpha_4}{\alpha_3} + \frac{\alpha_2}{\alpha_1}\right)\frac{\Delta rf}{k_1} - \left(\frac{DB}{\alpha_3 We^2} + \frac{Mo}{\alpha_1 We^2}\right)\frac{\Delta FC}{k_1}$$

$$\Delta r = \left(\frac{\alpha_4 We^2}{DB.FC} - \frac{\alpha_2 We^2}{FC.Mo}\right)\frac{\Delta rf}{k_2} + \left(\frac{We - DB}{DB.FC} + \frac{1}{FC}\right)\frac{\Delta DB}{k_2}$$

$$- \left(\frac{We - Mo}{FC.Mo} + \frac{1}{FC}\right)\frac{\Delta Mo}{k_2}$$

where $k_1 = \frac{FC.Mo}{\alpha_1 We^2} + \frac{DB.FC}{\alpha_3 We^2}$

$k_2 = \frac{\alpha_1 We^2}{FC.Mo} + \frac{\alpha_3 We^2}{DB.FC}$

Also $\alpha_3 > \alpha_1$ given the assumptions made about substitution and the wealth constraint.

The excess supply of money leads to an excess demand for domestic bonds and for foreign bonds. The domestic interest rate falls and the currency devalues raising the valuation of foreign assets. These outcomes are consistent with equilibrium in the money, bond and (implicitly) foreign asset markets. Now the money–wealth ratio will rise and the bond–wealth ratio fall while the foreign asset–wealth ratio rises. (Whether the currency devalues initially proportionately as much, more or less than the change in money is in fact ambiguous in this particular model.)

A rise in the foreign interest rate will shift the *LM* and the *BM* schedules to the right. This leads to an excess supply of money and domestic bonds and an excess demand for foreign assets. Equilibrium is achieved by a devaluation but the effect on the domestic interest rate is ambiguous.

An increase in the domestic supply of bonds (say, as a result of a budget deficit) will shift the *LM* schedule to the left and the *BM* schedule to the right. This leads to an excess supply of domestic bonds and an excess demand for money and foreign assets. Equilibrium requires a rise in the domestic interest rate but the effect on the exchange rate is now ambiguous.

Finally, a change in foreign asset holdings (say, as a result of a current account surplus) shifts the *LM* and *BM* schedules to the left. This leads to an excess demand for domestic bonds and money, which leaves the domestic interest rate unchanged but strengthens the domestic currency.[23]

Several features of this approach are worth emphasising. First, the driving forces in this framework are the change in the current account (the change in net foreign assets), the change in the net holdings of domestic bonds (for instance, from a budget deficit), the change in the volume of money and the change in the foreign interest rate. The current account variable captures the several influences acting on it (for example, relative inflation, relative output)[24] while the domestic bond variable captures one aspect of fiscal policy. Second, this approach tends to assume imperfect substitution between domestic and foreign assets. Third, the approach, in its purest form, disregards exchange rate expectations but it is not difficult to incorporate expectations within the framework.[25] The distinctive element in the approach is that it provides a mechanism by which asset markets adjust instantaneously without having to invoke expectations. At the same time, it does not neglect the longer-term influences acting on the exchange rate.

At the methodological level, it would be possible to incorporate some at least of the features of the portfolio balance approach into our neo-Keynesian model of aggregate demand and aggregate supply. Our first asset market phase would then allow for wealth-valuation effects as well as the effects of exchange rate expectations. Our second phase would allow for adjustments to real output, while our last phase would require not only that the real wage rate be restored but also that portfolio balance hold and that aggregate demand fully adjust to changes in the stocks of financial assets.

Annex 1

Notation

$\dot{P}_A$ = overall rate of inflation in A
$\dot{P}_B$ = overall rate of inflation in B
$\dot{PN}_A$ = rate of increase in non-traded prices in A
$\dot{PT}_A$ = rate of increase in traded prices in A
$\dot{QN}_A$ = rate of growth of productivity in the non-traded sector in A
$\dot{QT}_A$ = rate of growth of productivity in the traded sector in A

$\dot{WN}_A$ = growth of wages in the non-traded sector in A
$\dot{WT}_A$ = growth of wages in the traded sector in A

$$\dot{P}_A = b_1\dot{PT}_A + (1-b_1)\dot{PN}_A \qquad (20A.1)$$

$$\dot{WN}_A = \dot{WT}_A \qquad (20A.2)$$

$$\dot{PT}_A = \dot{WT}_A - \dot{QT}_A \qquad (20A.3)$$

$$\dot{WT}_A = \dot{QT}_A \qquad (20A.4)$$

$$\dot{PN}_A = \dot{WN}_A - \dot{QN}_A \qquad (20A.5)$$

These equations are largely self-explanatory. Equation (20A.2) reflects the assumption that the growth of wages is uniform across the two sectors, while Equation (20A.4) is a simplification that assumes that the growth of wages in the key (traded goods) sector is equal to the growth of productivity in that sector. In each sector the rate of increase in prices reflects the increase in unit labour costs, while the increase in the overall price level is a weighted average of the increases in the prices of traded and non-traded goods.

Similar equations can be written for country B, which then allows us to obtain:

$$\dot{P}_A - \dot{P}_B = (1-b_1)(\dot{QT}_A - \dot{QN}_A) - (1-b_2)(\dot{QT}_B - \dot{QN}_B) \qquad (20A.6)$$

where $(1-b_2)$ represents the weight of non-traded goods in B.

Now in this simple formulation the rate of increase in the price of traded goods is the same (zero) in the two countries. At the same time, the overall rates of inflation can differ for two distinct reasons. First, if the relative productivity growth in the two sectors is different across countries, for example, if $b_1 = b_2$ and the productivity margin is greater in A than in B, the rate of inflation will be relatively higher in A. Second, if the margin is the same in the two countries, A's rate of inflation can still be higher if $(1-b_1)>(1-b_2)$ (that is, the weight of non-traded goods is greater in A than in B). The reason is that with lower productivity growth in the non-traded goods sector, the increase in unit labour costs will be greater (positive) in this sector; hence, the increase in overall prices will be greater in A.

Annex 2

This Annex demonstrates more rigorously the effects on exchange rates of changes in foreign output, assuming lags over two periods in the effects of exchange rate changes on the current account. Given the very limited aims here the neo-Keynesian model can now be represented by five equations (dropping all irrelevant variables).

$$\Delta Yr = \Delta Ar + \Delta CA \tag{20B.1}$$

$$\Delta Ar = \alpha_1 \Delta \mathrm{Yr} \tag{20B.2}$$

$$\Delta CA = \alpha_{20}\Delta Yf - \alpha_9 \Delta Yr + ML_1 \Delta E + ML_2 \Delta E_{-1} \tag{20B.3}$$

The change in the current account is explained by foreign output, domestic output and the current and lagged exchange rate. ML_1 and ML_2 represent, respectively, the first and second period effects on the current account of a change in the exchange rate. $ML_1 + ML_2$ represents the long-run effect.

$$\Delta K = \alpha_{12}(\Delta E - \Delta Ee) \tag{20B.4}$$

This represents Equation (20.1) in the text, recalling that the domestic interest rate is held fixed.

$$\Delta B = \Delta CA + \Delta K \tag{20B.5}$$

We can substitute Equations (20B.3) and (20B.4) into Equation (20B.5) and set $\Delta B = 0$. We can also substitute Equations (20B.2) and (20B.3) into Equation (20B.1). We are then reduced to a system of two equations which jointly determine output and the exchange rate.

The solution for the exchange rate is:

$$\Delta E = -\frac{\alpha_{20}(1-\alpha_1)}{Z}\Delta Yf + \frac{\alpha_{12}(1-\alpha_1+\alpha_9)}{Z}\Delta Ee - \frac{ML_2(1-\alpha_1)}{Z}\Delta E_{-1} \tag{20B.6}$$

where $Z = \alpha_{12}(1-\alpha_1+\alpha_9) + ML_1(1-\alpha_1)$.

With neutral exchange rate expectations, $\Delta E = \Delta Ee$, the short-run solution becomes:

$$\Delta E = -\frac{\alpha_{20}}{ML_1}\Delta Yf - \frac{ML_2}{ML_1}\Delta E_{-1} \tag{20B.7}$$

After full adjustment the solution is:

$$\Delta E = -\frac{\alpha_{20}}{ML_1 + ML_2}\Delta Yf \tag{20B.8}$$

To obtain a 'short-run' solution with rational expectations, we substitute the full adjustment solution, Equation (20B.8), for ΔEe in Equation (20B.6). If there is perfect capital mobility $\alpha_{12} \to \infty$, the solution becomes identical to Equation (20B.8). In other words, the overshoot as well as the instability is removed.

Notes for Chapter 20

1 Two surveys of the literature are: P. Isard (1978); S. Schadler (1977).
2 This section focuses only on the relative version and disregards the absolute version of the theory. Two good treatments of PPP may be found in: L. Officer (1976); L. Yeager (1976), Chapter 11.
3 For some discussion of these issues see: J. Artus (1978); N. Thygesen (1978); I. Kravis and R. Lipsey (1978); J. Frenkel (1978).
4 For illustrations of this see: B. Balassa (1964) and R. I. McKinnon (1971).
5 For some empirical work on this see: K. Clements and P. Nguyen (1979).
6 For examples of these in the literature see: H. Stoll (1968); J. Kesselman (1971); J. Artus (1978); B. McCallum (1977a); R. Haas and W. Alexander (1979).
7 For an example see H. Stoll (1968).
8 For an example of the use of extrapolative expectations see J. Kesselman (1971).
9 See, for example, J. Artus (1978).
10 For an example of this see R. Haas and W. Alexander (1979).
11 For an example see B. McCallum (1977a).
12 The case of a decline in foreign output is discussed in some detail in Chapter 25, as an illustration of the way in which vicious circles might be generated under flexible exchange rates.
13 For a model along these lines see R. Dornbusch (1976). Of course in reality the exchange rate will not behave so smoothly and will also be affected by some of the same influences discussed previously.
14 The model is an adaptation and extension of the monetarist model in Chapter 13. The literature on this is very extensive. See: J. Bilson (1978); S. Kohlhagen (1979); J. Frenkel (1978); T. Humphrey and T. Lawler (1977); K. Clements and J. Frenkel (1980); J. Frenkel and K. Clements (1978); R. J. Hodrick (1978); M. E. Kreinin and L. H. Officer (1978).
15 P. Cagan (1956).
16

$$r_A - r_B = \frac{Ee - E}{E}$$

or

$$\Delta r_A - \Delta r_B = \frac{1}{E}\Delta Ee - \frac{Ee}{E^2}\Delta E$$

so

$$\Delta r_A - \Delta r_B = \left(\frac{Ee}{E}\right)\frac{\Delta Ee}{Ee} - \left(\frac{Ee}{E}\right)\frac{\Delta E}{E}$$

which is the same as Equation (20.10) if we assume that Ee/E approximates unity.

17 The assumption is not too unrealistic, since we are dealing here not with imports/exports but all tradables including importables and exportables.

18 Our own monetarist model also identified real changes in the demand for traded and non-traded goods as an *implicit* determinant of exchange rates; these changes however tend to be played down by monetarists.

19 The difference between a 'Keynesian' and a 'monetarist' overshoot is that in the latter case, in the initial period, there is a substantial price effect (for traded goods) flowing from the devaluation.

20 P. J. K. Kouri (1976); W. Branson, W. Halttunen and P. Masson (1977); R. Dornbusch (1978).

21 As in R. Dornbusch (1978).

22 The foreign country can be represented along similar lines but this is omitted in the interest of expositional simplicity.

23 In this case wealth is unchanged with increased foreign asset holdings offset by the revaluation. The reason for the outcome is evident from Equations (20.19)–(20.21). With *Mo* and *B* given, the value of *We* cannot change and, at the same time, equilibrate both money and bond markets.

24 But these, however, are assumed to affect the exchange rate through a wealth effect.

25 For example, see P. Isard (1978), Appendix.

Chapter 21

Exchange Rate Behaviour – the Evidence

Introduction

The previous chapter provided the theoretical framework for the analysis of exchange rate behaviour. This chapter will review the facts on exchange rate behaviour and will make some attempt to interpret and explain this behaviour, drawing largely on our previous analysis.

Exchange Rate Instability

There are, in principle, several ways of measuring exchange rate instability. First, one can calculate standard deviations either of levels of exchange rates or of percentage changes in exchange rates. These two measures will give different results if there is a noticeable trend in the series. For example, if there were a steady trend in the series the second measure would show very little instability while the first would indicate a good deal of instability. Since we are more interested in deviations from trends the second measure appears to be the more appropriate one. In other words, one can view exchange rate movements in this context as deviations from a secular 'crawl'.

Second, there are at least four relevant exchange rates one might use: bilateral exchange rates (between any two currencies), effective exchange rates,[1] real bilateral exchange rates and real effective exchange rates.[2] One's choice from these depends very much on the purpose of the exercise. If one were concerned about exposure in particular currencies or in a (trade weighted) bundle of currencies clearly the bilateral or effective rates would be the appropriate ones to use. On the other hand, if one were more concerned with changes in the competitive position of a country vis-à-vis either the rest of the world or a particular economy, these exchange rates adjusted for relative prices (the real rates) would be the more appropriate choice. Changes in the competitive position are particularly important in that they provide signals for resource movements and hence may be indicative of potential disturbances to the economy. Changes in real exchange rates may also be the more relevant concept if one were concerned, for example, with implications for trade and uncertainty of a more flexible exchange rate regime.

Table 21.1 shows the standard deviations of the monthly percentage changes in the bilateral and effective rates for each year since 1973. There are two features of this table worth noting. First, with the exception of Canada, exchange rates are significantly more volatile on a bilateral basis than on an effective basis. In other words, instability vis-à-vis one currency (the US dollar) is at least partially offset by opposite instability vis-à-vis other currencies with which the country

Table 21.1 Standard deviations of (monthly) percentage changes in bilateral[a] and effective exchange rates – March 1973 to December 1978 (inclusive)

Country	*1973*	*1974*	*1975*	*1976*	*1977*	*1978*
Canada	0.46	0.85	0.79	2.2	1.2	1.13
	(0.88)	(0.53)	(0.91)	(1.34)	(0.98)	(1.49)
France	3.74	3.49	3.31	1.48	0.93	4.52
	(2.03)	(1.45)	(1.42)	(1.20)	(0.44)	(1.54)
Germany	4.83	3.00	3.41	1.30	1.90	5.00
	(3.22)	(1.60)	(1.04)	(1.02)	(0.93)	(1.50)
Italy	2.28	3.00	2.09	4.33	0.37	2.87
	(2.30)	(1.03)	(0.92)	(3.40)	(0.67)	(0.69)
Japan	1.63	2.93	1.53	0.97	1.62	5.52
	(1.40)	(1.56)	(0.94)	(0.98)	(1.63)	(3.23)
United Kingdom	1.96	1.67	2.07	2.99	1.85	3.59
	(1.69)	(0.74)	(0.93)	(2.46)	(1.08)	(1.41)
United States	(2.19)	(1.25)	(1.23)	(0.47)	(0.81)	(1.55)

Source: International Monetary Fund, *International Financial Statistics.*
[a]vis-à-vis US dollar.
Numbers in parentheses are for effective exchange rates.

trades. Second, 1976 (for sterling, the lira and the Canadian dollar) and 1978 (for most major currencies) stand out as years when exchange markets were relatively disturbed.

Table 21.2 shows the variations in the volume of intervention for each year for each of the countries.[3] This table bears comparison with Table 21.1. On the one hand, given the fundamental instability in exchange rates, increased intervention will tend to moderate the movements in exchange rates, so one would expect the relationship between exchange rate instability and intervention to be negative. On the other hand, the greater the fundamental instability in exchange rates, the greater may be the need to intervene; hence the relationship

Table 21.2 Volume of intervention[a] industrial countries – March 1973 to 1978

Country	*1973*	*1974*	*1975*	*1976*	*1977*	*1978*
Canada	73	94	94	250	199	430
	(2.9)	(2.7)	(2.6)	(6.3)	(4.7)	(9.3)
France	407	120	369	307	94	360
	(10.9)	(2.2)	(6.8)	(4.8)	(1.3)	(4.4)
Germany	1111	572	543	815	675	1547
	(20.2)	(8.2)	(7.2)	(9.2)	(6.6)	(12.7)
Italy	283	680	330	426	553	580
	(10.0)	(16.6)	(8.6)	(9.8)	(11.6)	(10.3)
Japan	689	343	246	336	554	1226
	(18.1)	(5.5)	(4.3)	(5.2)	(7.8)	(15.3)
United Kingdom	239	327	188	577	1439	527
	(6.3)	(6.0)	(3.5)	(10.2)	(22.3)	(6.7)

Source: International Monetary Fund, *International Financial Statistics.*
[a]The first line (for each country) gives the mean (without regard to sign) of the monthly change in reserves in each year (in millions of US dollars).
The line below (numbers in parentheses) gives the mean as above divided by the value of imports in US dollars for that year.

might, in these circumstances, be positive. It is, of course, difficult to disentangle these opposing influences from the crude data. The latter influence is clearly evident in Japan and Germany in 1978 when exchange markets were much more unstable and the volume of intervention actually increased substantially. In Canada, too, the years when exchange markets were most unstable (1976–78) were also those when the volume of intervention was apparently greatest. However, the opposite influence appears in Germany in 1976, in Italy in 1977 and, perhaps, in the UK in 1977.

Table 21.3 shows the standard deviations of the quarterly percentage changes in bilateral, effective and (alternative) real exchange rates for the period 1973(1) to 1977(4). It shows that, in general, the standard deviation of the quarterly movements is greatest for bilateral rates and lowest for real rates (on a unit cost basis). This indicates that instability in exchange rates tends to be partially offset by changes in relative prices.

Finally, it is of some interest to compare the instability in exchange rates with the instability in other macro-economic series. This provides an indication of whether there is 'excessive' exchange rate instability. For example, the author computed standard deviations of per cent changes in the volume of money (UK and USA) in commodity prices, in share prices (UK) and in Euro-dollar interest rates for the period 1976 (1) to 1979 (4). These were compared with standard deviations of per cent changes in various exchange rate series for the same

Table 21.3 Standard deviation of quarterly percentage changes in exchange rates – 1973 (1) to 1977 (4)

Country	*Bilateral (vis-à-vis US dollar)*	*Effective*	*Real Bilateral (vis-à-vis US dollar) (Unit Costs)*	*Real effective*[a] *(Unit Costs)*
Canada	1.95	2.17	1.74	2.42
France	5.34	3.11	4.05	2.34
Germany	6.54	3.50	5.14	2.77
Italy	5.91	3.57	4.16	3.51
Japan	3.53	2.93	3.80	2.81
United Kingdom	4.69	3.20	3.51	2.66
United States	–	2.64	–	2.36

Sources: Bilateral and Effective Rates – International Monetary Fund, *International Financial Statistics.*
Quarterly Real Exchange Rates (as described above) are taken from the OECD (1978b). Three series were constructed by the OECD; one based on unit costs, another on export unit values and a third on consumer prices. Only unit costs were used. The weights used by the OECD were those of the IMF.

[a]There are two steps in the construction of a real effective exchange rate. The first step is to convert each country's price index in local currency into a common currency (US dollar terms). The second step is to calculate a ratio for each country of the local price index in dollar terms to the trade weighted price index in dollar terms of the rest of the world. The resultant ratio is the index of the real effective exchange rate.
A real bilateral exchange rate (vis-à-vis the USA) is simply the ratio of each country's price index in dollar terms to the US price index.

period. The conclusion is that while the instability in the money series is comparable with the instability in exchange rates the instability in share prices, in Euro-dollar interest rates and in commodity prices far exceeds the instability in exchange rates.

Explaining Exchange Rate Behaviour

A review of the empirical literature suggests that there have been four approaches to explaining exchange rate behaviour, corresponding, in effect, to the theoretical approaches identified in the previous chapter. The first draws on PPP. The second draws on a Keynesian-type analysis. The third draws on a monetarist framework while the fourth draws on a 'portfolio balance' framework. This chapter will briefly evaluate these studies and try and determine whether they have provided real insights into exchange rate behaviour in recent years.

Purchasing Power Parity

Consider, first, the evidence for PPP. There is now a very considerable literature that attempts to test the empirical validity, in the longer run, of the relative version of PPP.[4] The findings of this literature may be summarised as follows. Nearly all of it finds some evidence in support of the theory for the longer run. The theory appears to hold somewhat better for effective (trade-weighted) rates (vis-à-vis trade-weighted relative inflation) than for bilateral rates; also it holds up better for export and wholesale price indices than for cost-of-living indices.[5]

Figures 21.1 to 21.6 show the trends in the bilateral exchange rates (E), the price ratios (Pd/P_{US}) and the real exchange rate (Er) for several currencies, using March 1973 as the base and October 1979 as the terminal date. The real exchange rate is calculated as the ratio of the exchange rate (defined in each case as units of domestic currency per US dollar) to the ratio of domestic to US wholesale prices (or their nearest equivalent), so an increase (decrease) in the real exchange rate signifies that the country's competitive position improves (deteriorates) vis-à-vis the USA.

Figure 21.1 *Canada exchange rates and relative prices*

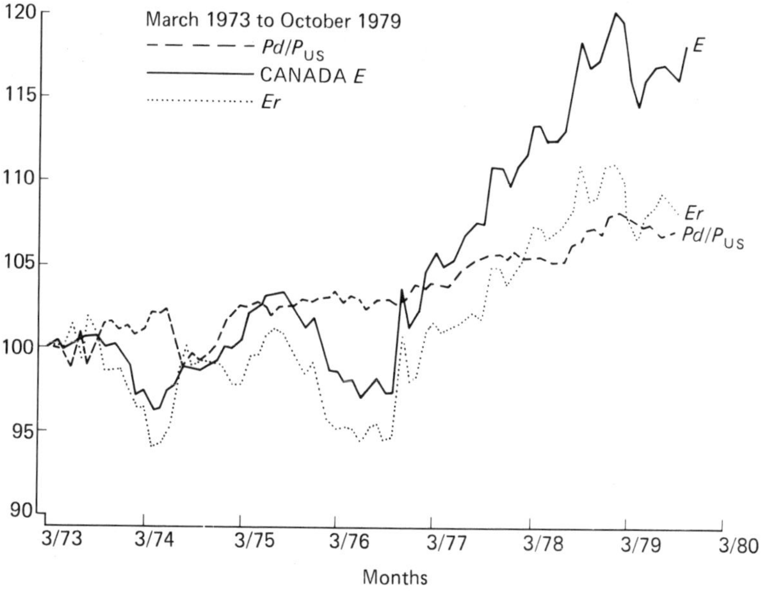

Source: International Monetary Fund, *International Financial Statistics.*

Figure 21.2 *France exchange rates and relative prices*

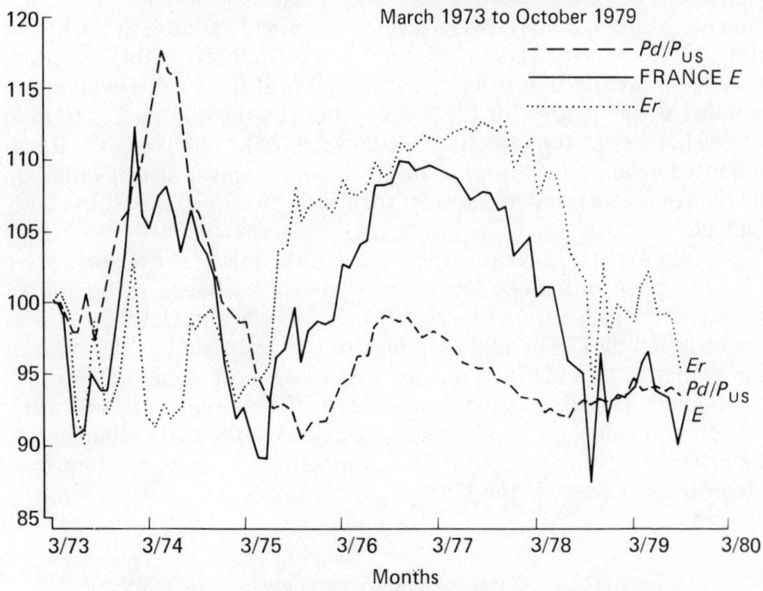

Source: International Monetary Fund, *International Financial Statistics.*

Figure 21.3 *Germany exchange rates and relative prices*

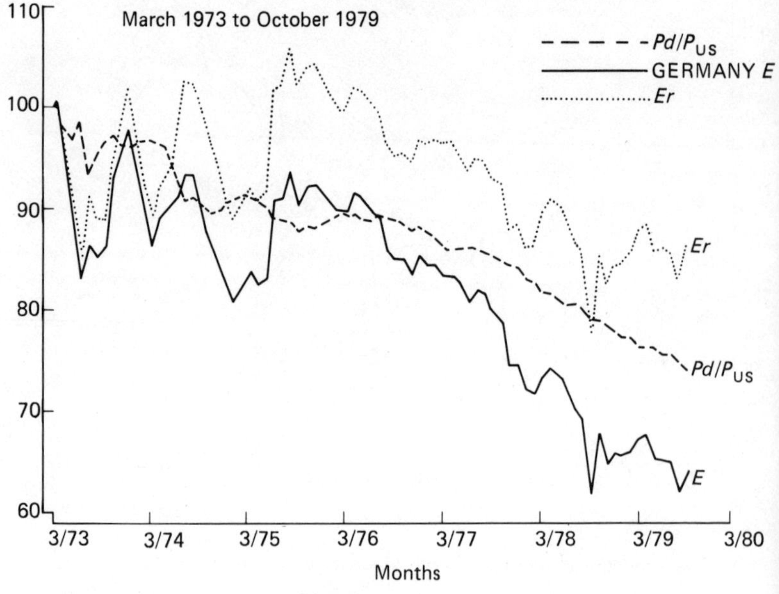

Source: International Monetary Fund, *International Financial Statistics.*

Figure 21.4 *Italy exchange rates and relative prices*

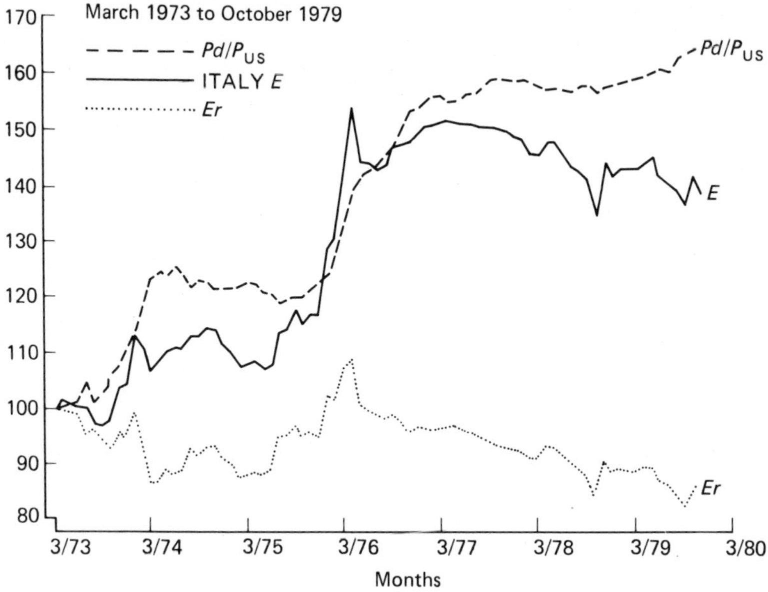

Source: International Monetary Fund, *International Financial Statistics.*

Figure 21.5 *Japan exchange rates and relative prices*

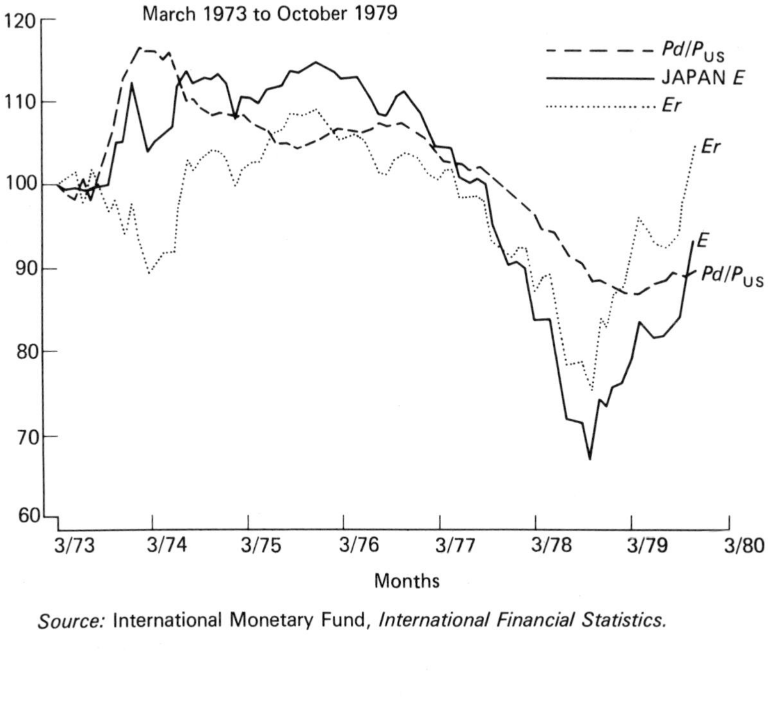

Source: International Monetary Fund, *International Financial Statistics.*

Figure 21.6 *UK exchange rates and relative prices*

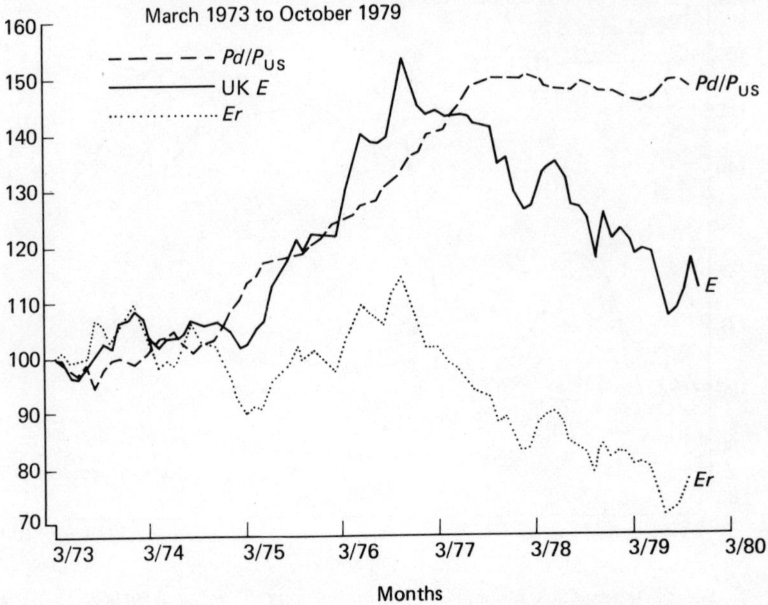

Source: International Monetary Fund, *International Financial Statistics.*

Several features of the figures are worth noting. First, it is evident that countries whose prices have tended to rise over the period relative to the USA (Canada, Italy and the UK) have also tended to devalue vis-à-vis the dollar. By contrast, countries whose prices have tended to fall relative to the USA (France, Germany and Japan) have also tended to revalue vis-à-vis the dollar. Second, with the exception of Canada (where the reverse occurred) all countries experienced a substantial fall in the real exchange rate during 1977/78. Third, in both France and Japan the real exchange rate, after substantial fluctuation over the period, had returned to its March 1973 level by mid–late 1979. By contrast, after 1977 the real exchange rate rose substantially in Canada and fell substantially in Italy, Germany and the UK. Possible reasons for some of these trends are continuing political uncertainties in Canada, the North Sea oil developments in the UK and reserve diversification.

Monetarist and Portfolio-Balance Approaches

The key monetarist equation, which has provided the starting point for a considerable amount of econometric work on exchange rate determination, is:[6]

$$\dot{E} = (\dot{Mo}_A - \dot{Mo}_B) - \alpha_1(\dot{Yr}_A - \dot{Yr}_B) + \alpha_2(\Delta r_A - \Delta r_B) \tag{21.1}$$

Notation

subscript A = country A
subscript B = country B
$\dot{E}$ = rate of change in the exchange rate (units of domestic currency per unit of foreign currency)
$\dot{Mo}$ = rate of growth in the money supply
r = domestic interest rate
$\dot{Yr}$ = rate of change in real GNP

Numerous variants on this basic equation have been estimated. Sometimes the equation is estimated in a form very similar to this; sometimes proxies for exchange rate expectations are used in lieu of the interest-rate differentials; sometimes again PPP is allowed to hold with a lag or some lag is allowed in the money demand equation; sometimes, too, non-traded prices are explicitly allowed for.

This econometric analysis is too large, too complex and too diverse to summarise in detail here.[7] One recent reviewer of this work, Mussa,[8] concluded that, by and large, it showed that 'the behaviour of exchange rates is consistent with the monetary model and that this model is of assistance in explaining a significant fraction of exchange rate movements'.[9] Another review,[10] however, concluded that the results were mixed, conforming only 'in part' to a priori expectations. We have ourselves already expressed some skepticism about some of the assumptions underlying the more extreme versions of the approach (see also p. 263). At this stage, then, it is best to suspend judgement till the issues are clarified and still more discriminating work is forthcoming.

There have also been some recent attempts to apply econometrics to the portfolio balance approach.[11] To illustrate, consider our own presentation of the model in Chapter 20. Referring once again to Table 20.1 it is easy to see that, in the context of a bilateral exchange rate, the foreign interest rate could be solved in terms of the stock of money, net external assets and (own) domestic assets held by foreigners. The solution, then, for the bilateral exchange rate would have domestic and foreign money, domestic and foreign net external asset holdings and, finally, domestic and foreign holdings of home assets. An example of a study of this kind is that of Branson–Halttunen–Masson.[12] They try to explain the mark–dollar rate for the period August 1971 to December 1976 in terms of the German and US money stocks and the German and US net private foreign asset stocks (defined as cumulations of current account balances of each country on benchmark observations minus holdings of central banks), deliberately excluding home assets largely because (as we have seen) their effects on the exchange rate are ambiguous. Their results are fairly good and consistent with expectations. The approach is promising but the literature is still in its infancy and there are serious data problems associated with it.

Keynesian Analysis – Import and Export Demand Elasticities

It will be recalled that an important element in exchange rate determination within a Keynesian framework was the length of the lag in the adjustment of the trade balance to a change in the exchange rate and the possibilities for perverse short-term effects. What, then, is the evidence on short- and long-term import and export demand elasticities? There is something of a consensus now that the lags are fairly long and that in several economies the short-term elasticities are sufficiently low to generate perverse initial outcomes.[13] Table 21.4 sets out the IMF estimates for several developed countries. Of the fourteen countries in the table there are eight where the sum of the short-run demand elasticities is significantly below 1, one (Switzerland) where the sum is marginal and only five where the sum is significantly greater than 1. In a majority of the developed countries, it thus seems that over the first year or so one can expect a change in the exchange rate to have perverse effects on the trade balance. This is a most important result which in itself would go part of the way towards explaining some, at least, of the observed instability in exchange rates.

Keynesian Analysis – The Mark–Dollar Rate

Let us see, now, if we can apply a Keynesian framework to explain the month to month movement in a particular bilateral exchange rate: the mark–dollar rate.

A Keynesian would start by trying to explain the current and capital accounts of the balance of payments. The current account would be explained by relative prices, the exchange rate and relative output (see Chapter 11). The capital account would be largely explained by the interest rate differential adjusted for the expected change in the exchange rate, as in Equation (20.1). With the balance of payments equal to the sum of the current and capital accounts this simple Keynesian framework allows us to explain the exchange rate in terms of: (1) relative output, (2) relative prices, (3) the interest rate differential, (4) the expected exchange rate and (5) an intervention variable (to take account of the volume of intervention in the foreign exchange market). (See also the Annex for a more formal treatment of this.)[14]

We have already seen that relative prices are helpful in explaining long-term trends in the exchange rate. A useful starting point in any analysis of exchange rate behaviour is to focus on the short-run (monthly) movements in the bilateral real exchange rate (that is, the dollar–mark exchange rate divided by the wholesale price

Table 21.4 Point estimates of foreign trade price elasticities of demand in the IMF world trade model[a]

Country	Imports		Exports		Sum	
	Short-run	Long-run	Short-run	Long-run	Short-run	Long-run
Canada	−0.69	−0.69	–	–	−0.69	−0.69
United States	−0.03	−1.07	−0.20	−1.05	−0.23	−2.12
Japan	−0.25	−0.37	−1.68	−1.68	−1.93	−2.05
France	−0.49	−0.49	−1.23	−1.53	−1.72	−2.02
Germany	−0.28	−0.58	−0.03	−0.60	−0.31	−1.18
Italy	−0.09	−0.09	–	–	−0.09	−0.09
United Kingdom	−0.25	−0.25	−0.10	−0.45	−0.35	−0.70
Belgium	−0.43	−0.43	−1.15	−2.45	−1.58	−2.88
Denmark	−0.16	−1.10	−0.47	−0.53	−0.63	−1.63
Netherlands	−0.04	−0.04	−0.08	−1.03	−0.12	−1.07
Austria	−0.03	−0.03	−0.66	−0.89	−0.69	−0.92
Norway	−0.75	−2.45	−0.95	−1.85	−1.70	−4.30
Sweden	−1.60	−1.60	−1.49	−1.50	−3.09	−3.10
Switzerland	−0.02	−0.02	−0.96	−1.48	−0.98	−1.50
Average	−0.37	−0.66	−0.64	−1.07	−1.01	−1.73

Source: J. R. Artus and J. H. Young (1979).

[a]The short-run response elasticity is the coefficient on the average of the relative price term over the preceding two half-years; the long-run response elasticity is based on the cumulative response over four years.

ratio – Germany over the USA). The trend in this series is shown in the top panel of Figure 21.7.

In attempting to explain this series within a Keynesian framework we concentrate on a number of key variables. These are: the output ratio, the interest rate differential and the US current account which we use as a proxy to represent expectations. These are all shown in that order in the figure, below the real exchange rate. The expectation would be that an increase in the differential $(rf-r)$, or an increase in the ratio (Yrd/Yrf) or, again, an improvement in the US current

Figure 21.7 (overleaf) *Notation*

Er = exchange rate (marks per US dollar) multiplied by the US wholesale price and divided by the German wholesale price (all in index form), March 1973 = 100

rf-r = 3-month Euro-dollar rate less German 3-month interbank deposit rate

Yrd/Yrf = ratio of German to US industrial production indices

CA = US current account (quarterly)

Mo_1d/Mo_1f = ratio of narrow money Germany to US (in index) – unbroken lines, March 1973 = 100

Mo_2d/Mo_2f = ratio of broad money Germany to US (in index) – broken lines, March 1973 = 100

Figure 21.7 *Determinants of the real Mark-Dollar exchange rate 1973–78*

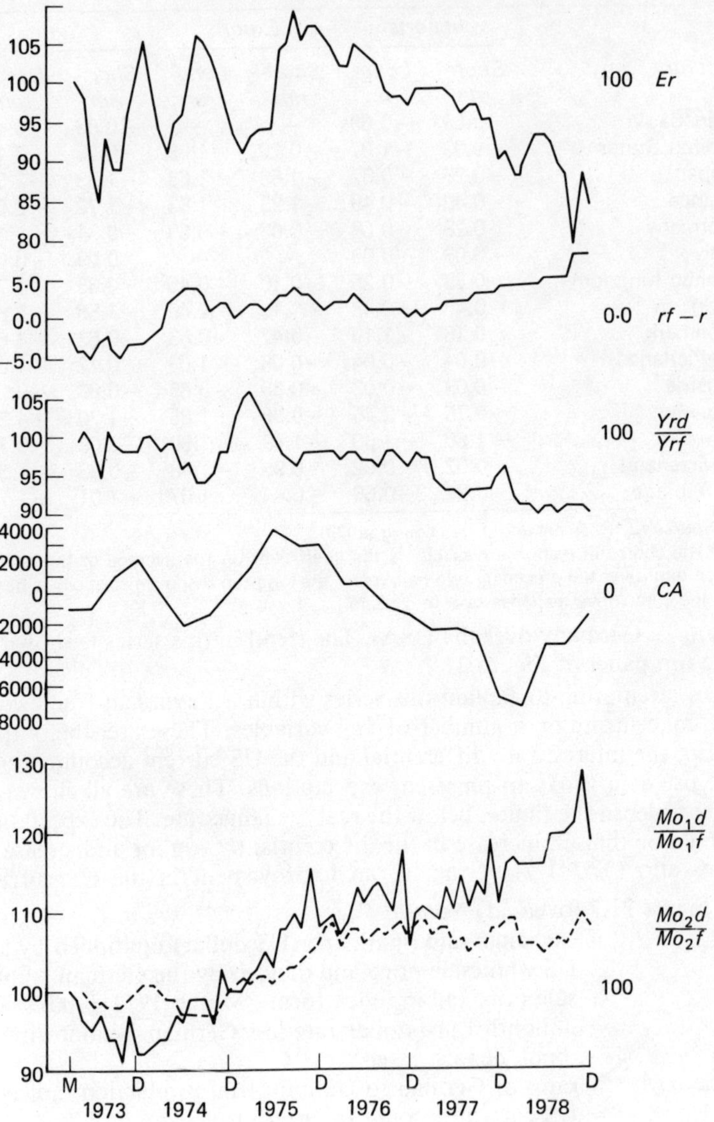

Sources: International Monetary Fund, *International Financial Statistics*; Monthly Bulletin, U.S. Federal Reserve; World Financial Markets, The Morgan Guaranty Trust Company of New York.

account (*CA*) will – other things being equal – tend to strengthen the dollar vis-à-vis the mark (that is, increase the real exchange rate).

The swings in the real exchange rate are easily identifiable and the whole period can be broken down into a number of distinctive sub-periods. These are:

Period	*Trend in Real Exchange Rate*[15]
May 1973–July 1973	Down
July 1973–January 1974	Up
January 1974–April 1974	Down
April 1974–September 1974	Up
September 1974–February 1975	Down
February 1975–September 1975	Up
September 1975–October 1976	Down
October 1976–July 1977	Stable
July 1977–November 1978	Down
November 1978–	Up

A brief account of each sub-period follows. The first decline in May–July 1973 can be largely explained in terms of the relative tightening of monetary policy in Germany and the political uncertainties in the US. The sharp reversal of the following six to seven months is largely accounted for in terms of the continuing surplus in the US current account, the relative easing of German monetary policy, the firm policy announcements in support of the dollar and, finally, a reaction to the sharp earlier fall.

The fall in the real exchange rate between February and April 1974 can be attributed to a number of factors. First, there was some reaction to the previous upswing which again was felt to have been overdone. Second, there was the oil price shock whose effects on the US current account were beginning to manifest themselves. Third, there was the removal in the USA of controls over the outflows of capital and, as well, some easing of controls over the inflows of capital into Germany. Fourth, the political scene in the USA continued to be unsettled. Finally, it is particularly interesting to note that this trend persisted despite a progressive tightening of US monetary policy relative to Germany, suggesting that expectations unfavourable to the US dollar were dominant, with relative interest rates now adjusting to expectations.

Both the upswing in May to September 1974 and the downswing in September 1974 to February 1975 can be largely explained by relative monetary policies. The downswing came, however, in the face of a sharp rise in Germany's output relative to the USA.

The upswing in February to September 1975 was, again, substantially influenced by relative monetary policies but now also by the stronger US current account position, which had begun to make some impression, and also by the announcement of an informal agreement between the USA and Germany to counteract any downward movement of the dollar by market intervention. This upswing came in the face of a sharp recovery in US output relative to Germany.

The downswing in the year beginning October 1975 can be attributed, in part, to the interest rate differential and, in part, to the deteriorating US current account. Then, between October 1976 and July 1977 the real exchange rate fluctuated very little. Figure 21.7 suggests that the effects of the small change in the interest differential favouring the USA may have been offset by the relatively greater acceleration in output in the USA and the continuing deterioration in the US current account.

The period running from July/August 1977 to November 1978 is in many ways the most interesting one. Apart from brief interruptions (usually following some announcement by the USA of some dollar-support measures),[16] there was a protracted and sharp decline in the real exchange rate. A striking feature of the period is that the decline took place in the face of a strong improvement in the Euro-dollar interest rate vis-à-vis the interest rate in Germany. These facts suggest that, in this period, at any rate, expectations and speculation were dominant and that now interest rate differentials were offsetting the unfavourable expectations about the US dollar.

The period is dominated by the performance of the US current account which had, in fact, begun to move into deficit by the second half of 1976. The continued deterioration of the US current account reflected several considerations, including the continued rapid output recovery in the USA, the declining competitive position of the USA, the huge increase in its oil imports[17] and, also, certain structural factors such as the increased competition from the newly industrialised developing countries. The associated collapse in the US dollar also led to some switch out of the dollar, held as a reserve currency (by the OPEC and other developing countries).

The recovery in the US dollar did not come till early November 1978 and continued into the early months of 1979. The dramatic turnaround followed the announcement of several measures on 1 November 1978. These included a one per cent increase in the discount rate (for purely external reasons) and the co-ordinated mobilisation of substantial funds to support the dollar.

An Econometric Analysis of the Mark–Dollar Rate

On the strength of this casual analysis some econometric work was undertaken. Taking the monthly log of the real exchange rate (*Er*) as the dependent variable the principal independent variables used were (1) the log of the output ratio (current and lagged) (*Yrd/Yrf*), (2) the interest rate differential (*rf-r*), (3) the moving average of the US current account in the previous three months (*CA*) and (4) the log of the real exchange rate lagged one period.

The last three variables combined were able to account for a substantial proportion of the movement in the real exchange rate. The result of this regression is:

$$\underset{}{\ln Er =} \underset{(-1.5)}{-0.01} + \underset{(1.0)}{0.17(rf\text{-}r)} + \underset{(2.6)}{0.49CA} + \underset{(10.3)}{0.8\ln Er_{-1}} \qquad R^{-2} = 0.71$$

The significance of the lagged dependent variable possibly suggests some role for bandwaggon effects. The interest rate differential has the right sign but it is not significant, whereas the US current account is significant in the equation and has the right sign.

Monetarist Analysis – The Mark–Dollar Rate

It would be instructive to see if a monetarist analysis might have been helpful in explaining the exchange rate movement. Figure 21.3 shows the trends in the bilateral exchange rate, while Figure 21.7 shows the key monetarist variables represented by (1) the output ratio and (2) the ratios of the volume of money (narrow and broad).

It is difficult to explain the long-term trend in the bilateral exchange rate in terms of monetarist analysis. From March 1973 to the end of 1978 the mark revalued substantially vis-à-vis the US dollar, yet monetary growth was faster in Germany and, in addition, the growth of output was faster in the USA over that time. These two influences combined should have led to a secular fall in the mark, not to a rise.[18] The monetarist explanation also appears inadequate in trying to account for the 1978 collapse of the US dollar. From about mid-1977 to mid-1978 (broad) monetary growth was about as rapid in Germany as in the USA. In that same period (narrow) money actually grew more rapidly in Germany. Output, too, continued to grow more rapidly in the USA. As already noted, it is evident that expectations adverse to the US dollar became dominant from mid-1977; but the switch in expectations could hardly be accounted for by relative monetary growth or relative output growth.

Conclusions on the Mark–Dollar Rate

A number of tentative conclusions may now be drawn from our historical review. First, the notion that monetary independence can be secured under flexible exchange rates needs to be qualified, particularly in the light of the 1978 experience. On the one hand, there were two occasions (in January and November 1978) when the USA was forced to raise its discount rate predominantly for external reasons. On the other hand, Germany, by intervening heavily in foreign exchange markets during 1978[19] and refusing to sterilise, allowed its monetary growth to exceed its target for the year.

Second, it appears that in relatively stable periods interest rate differentials play a key role in determining real exchange rates. However, there were two conspicuous occasions (in early 1974 and 1978) when exchange rate movements appeared to be dominated by expectations and on those occasions interest rate differentials served the role of offsetting the changed expectations. In other words, real exchange rates moved in line with expectations but in a direction opposite to interest rate differentials.

Third, the cyclical swings in the real exchange rate provide suggestive evidence of 'bandwaggon' effects. In other words, once a swing in one direction became evident it would, on occasion, be reinforced by a change in expectations. This would appear to confirm the view of a number of commentators that there are insufficient investors with available funds willing to take open positions on the strength of longer-term exchange rate expectations.[20]

Fourth, trends in one direction tend to be reversed only when there is clear evidence of a substantial change in policy or in the underlying determinants. Announcements of small changes in policy or of a determination to maintain orderly exchange markets will tend to stabilise markets, but only temporarily. Fifth, and finally, the current account of the USA appears to have played a key role in the formation of expectations about exchange rates. Indeed from early 1975 to mid-1978 the medium-term movement in the real exchange rate has largely paralleled the movement of the US current account.

Speculation and Exchange Rate Instability

By way of conclusion is it possible now to say anything about the role of speculation in exchange rate instability?

To begin, what does it mean to say that speculation is, on balance, stabilising or destabilising? Most economists would answer this by saying that when the exchange rate is more (less) variable than it would have been in the absence of speculation, speculation could be said to be destabilising (stabilising). But what does the absence of speculation mean? Does it mean, for example, that expectations are formed neutrally? These issues are very difficult and cannot be pursued in detail here.[21] It is sufficient to mention some selective approaches to this question and some empirical findings.

If one treats the forward premium/discount as an approximation to exchange rate expectations then one possible way of determining whether speculation is stabilising or destabilising over a longer period is to compare the volatility of spot movements with the volatility of the forward premium/discount. If spot rates are more (less) volatile than forward premium/discount then this suggests that speculation is relatively stabilising (destabilising). Table 21.5 provides data on standard deviations of percentage changes in monthly spot rates and forward premia/discount for different time periods. By the criterion applied here speculation on the mark would have been 'on balance' stabilising.

A quite different attack on this whole problem draws on the weak version of the efficient markets hypothesis. According to this, exchange markets are efficient if speculators exploit all the information available from past movements in exchange rates in a way that ensures that no abnormal profits remain to be earned. The issue is important. If markets are efficient in this sense then it means that there is some presumption that speculation would be stabilising on balance; at the same time, the case for short-term intervention by the monetary authorities might be weakened.

Some efficient market tests centering on the forward rate have already been described (see Chapter 19). There are, in addition, several other kinds of tests. Typical of these are those that apply various simple trading rules to the buying and selling of currencies to see whether these rules yield abnormal profits. For example, one rule states that when a given currency appreciates (depreciates) *x* per cent from a previous low (high), switch funds into (out of) that currency. An alternative rule states that where the currency moves *x* per cent above (below) the moving average the speculator should move into (out of) the currency. The objective of these rules is to try and exploit changes in market tendencies. One of the most recent studies of this kind is that of Cornell–Dietrich,[22] who apply the above-mentioned

Table 21.5 Standard deviation of percentage changes in monthly spot rates and forward premia/discount – March 1973 to July 1978 – mark–dollar

	1973–78	*1973–75*	*1976–78*
% change spot rate	3.044	3.884	1.720
Forward premium/discount	1.897	2.179	1.545

rules to six currencies vis-à-vis the US dollar for the period March 1973 to September 1975. They conclude that the markets for the pound, the Canadian dollar and the yen were efficient but that the markets for the mark, the Dutch guilder and the Swiss franc were inefficient. Several other studies confirm the inconclusiveness of the tests and the enormous statistical difficulties in carrying them out.[23] Difficulties here include defining the relevant time period, calculating transaction costs and relative rates of return on investment in different currencies, allowing for the costs of discovering the best rules and determining what constitutes an abnormal return. In general, outcomes tend to be sensitive to these considerations.

Still another attack on the problem has been undertaken by Kohlhagen.[24] His first step is to estimate one variant of the monetarist equation explaining the log of a bilateral exchange rate in terms of the log of the relative real income, the log of the relative money supplies and the forward premium or discount (which is intended to capture speculative expectations). He then compares the variance of each observed exchange rate with each derived exchange rate that would have occurred without speculation (that is, with the influence of the forward premium or discount omitted). If the former is smaller (greater) than the latter, speculation is said to be stabilising (destabilising). He applies this framework to three bilateral exchange rates (the mark–franc, the dollar–franc and the mark–dollar) for the years 1973–75. His results are mixed; speculation was destabilising in the two franc markets and stabilising for the mark. While these particular results should not be taken too seriously, the method is, nevertheless, interesting and may be applied to other general frameworks and to other methods of representing expectations.

Finally, Artus[25] estimates, as part of a larger financial model for Germany, an equation explaining the percentage change in the mark–dollar forward rate (proxying the expected future value of the spot rate) in terms of the percentage change in the spot rate and the expected relative rate of inflation. He finds the coefficient of the percentage change in the spot rate to be +0.7, implying that investors revise their expectations, in part at least, in the same direction as the exchange rate change. Artus interprets his findings as implying unstable expectations, concluding that 'up to the present time [1976] the experience of the Federal Republic of Germany with floating does not bear out the faith that many economists have had in the stabilising role of short-term capital flows'.

These varying results and approaches demonstrate how little is really known about the formation of expectations and how difficult it is to evaluate whether speculation has served to stabilise or destabilise exchange rate movements.

Annex – Keynesian and Monetarist Models of Exchange Rate Determination – the Technical Links

Notation

subscript A = country A
subscript B = country B
CA = current account of the balance of payments

$\dot{E}$ = rate of change in the exchange rate
$\dot{E}e$ = rate of change in the expected exchange rate
K = net capital flows
$M\dot{o}$ = rate of growth in the money supply
$\dot{P}$ = overall rate of inflation
r = domestic interest rate
X = volume of exports
$Y\dot{r}$ = rate of change in real GNP

Two key models labelled Keynesian and monetarist were presented in this and the previous chapter. This Annex will now attempt, briefly, to demonstrate the technical links between the two models.

To simplify, we take the extreme monetarist version which assumes all goods are traded goods. In Equation (20.16) this means setting $\alpha_{14}=\alpha_{20}=1$. This then yields:

$$\dot{E}=\frac{1}{1+\alpha_2}(M\dot{o}_A-M\dot{o}_B)+\frac{\alpha_2}{1+\alpha_2}\dot{E}e-\frac{\alpha_1}{1+\alpha_2}(Y\dot{r}_A-Y\dot{r}_B) \quad (21A.1)$$

In the Keynesian model we need to derive a current account as well as a capital account equation. If we deflate the change in each of these accounts by, say, the value of exports (X) and assume that the current account is initially in equilibrium we have, for the current account (CA):

$$\frac{\Delta CA}{X}=-\alpha_3(\dot{P}_A-\dot{P}_B-\dot{E})+\alpha_4 Y\dot{r}_B-\alpha_5 Y\dot{r}_A \quad (21A.2)$$

and for the capital account (K):

$$\frac{\Delta K}{X}=\alpha_6\Delta r_A-\alpha_6\Delta r_B+\alpha_6\dot{E}-\alpha_6\dot{E}e \quad (21A.3)$$

If we sum these two and set the change in the balance of payments as zero we can solve for the percentage change in the exchange rate. Since the solution is in rate of change terms we can also, realistically, set $\alpha_4=\alpha_5$.

$$\dot{E}=\frac{\alpha_3}{\alpha_3+\alpha_6}(\dot{P}_A-\dot{P}_B)-\frac{\alpha_4}{\alpha_3+\alpha_6}(Y\dot{r}_B-Y\dot{r}_A)$$

$$-\frac{\alpha_6}{\alpha_3+\alpha_6}(\Delta r_A-\Delta r_B)+\frac{\alpha_6}{\alpha_3+\alpha_6}\dot{E}e \quad (21A.4)$$

We can now use the two money demand equations, (20.8) and (20.9), to derive:

$$\dot{Mo}_A - \dot{Mo}_B = (\dot{P}_A - \dot{P}_B) + \alpha_1(\dot{Yr}_A - \dot{Yr}_B) - \alpha_2(\Delta r_A - \Delta r_B) \quad (21A.5)$$

If we solve for the interest rate differences and then substitute into Equation (21A.4) we have:

$$\dot{E} = \frac{\alpha_6}{\alpha_2(\alpha_3+\alpha_6)}(\dot{Mo}_A - \dot{Mo}_B) + \frac{\alpha_2\alpha_3-\alpha_6}{\alpha_2(\alpha_3+\alpha_6)}(\dot{P}_A - \dot{P}_B)$$

$$+\frac{\alpha_2\alpha_4-\alpha_1\alpha_6}{\alpha_2(\alpha_3+\alpha_6)}(\dot{Yr}_A - \dot{Yr}_B) + \frac{\alpha_6}{\alpha_3+\alpha_6}\dot{E}e \quad (21A.6)$$

To demonstrate the technical links between the two models we now impose two key monetarist assumptions on the Keynesian solution represented by Equation (21A.6): first, that PPP holds so $\dot{E} = \dot{P}_A - \dot{P}_B$, and second, that there is perfect capital mobility so $\alpha_6 \rightarrow \infty$. The solution is Equation (21A.1) above, the monetarist equation. In short, the monetarist equation turns out to be a special case of the Keynesian equation.

Notes for Chapter 21

1 An effective exchange rate index for any one currency is simply a weighted average of all bilateral rates with currencies with which the country trades. There are basically two ways to calculate the weights. One is based on average bilateral trade. For example, vis-à-vis economy B the weight would be the sum of exports to and imports from B divided by the total value of exports plus imports in a particular year. These weights will change as the importance of trade with particular economies changes. A second method of calculating weights is much more complicated and requires knowledge of elasticities of demand for imports and exports vis-à-vis particular economies. As an example, suppose two economies carry the same bilateral weights; then if (all other things being equal) a devaluation vis-à-vis one is exactly offset by an equal revaluation vis-à-vis the other, the effective exchange rate based on bilateral weights would show no change. It may be, however, that the trade balance effects do not necessarily offset each other (for example, if demand elasticities are high vis-à-vis the one country and low vis-à-vis the other, equal and opposite exchange rate changes with two currencies will not leave the trade balance unchanged). On the criterion of equal trade balance effects the weights of the two currencies will have to be different, a higher weight being assigned to the currency with the higher demand elasticities. The IMF, in its effective exchange rate series, calculates weights on this second basis. These weights are derived from their world trade model (MERM). For details of these and other possible trade weights see R. Rhomberg (1976).

2 A real exchange rate, as distinct from a nominal exchange rate, is simply the nominal exchange rate adjusted for appropriate relative prices.

3 The measure used for intervention is rough and open to several objections (for example, it does not discount valuation effects, nor the effects of official borrowings or swap operations). The second measure (in parentheses) allows some rough comparability across countries.
4 The evidence bearing on the monetarist version of PPP (the law of one price for traded goods) was reviewed in Chapter 14. See also: L. Officer (1976); L. Yeager (1976); D. King (1977); J. Frenkel (1978); N. Thygesen (1978); J. Hodgson and P. Phelps (1975).
5 On the issue of causation the evidence is confusing. Compare, for example, J. Hodgson and P. Phelps (1975), J. Frenkel (1978) and D. King (1977).
6 If it is assumed that all goods are traded goods then PPP is represented as $\dot{P}_A - \dot{P}_B = \dot{E}$. If Equation (20.7) is subtracted from Equation (20.6) and PPP substituted into the solution, Equation (21.1) is easily obtained.
7 See the references cited in the previous chapter.
8 M. Mussa (1979).
9 M. Mussa (1979), p. 45.
10 M. E. Kreinin and L. H. Officer (1978).
11 W. Branson, H. Halttunen and P. Masson (1977); M. Porter (1977); M. Dooley and P. Isard (1978).
12 W. Branson, H. Halttunen and P. Masson (1977).
13 For a survey of the econometric work in the area see R. M. Stern, J. Francis and B. Schumacher (1976).
14 Variations on this basic Keynesian framework can be found in J. Hodgson (1972); L. Thomas (1973); H. Goldstein (1979).
15 An upward (downward) trend means that the US dollar is up (down).
16 For example, in early January 1978 there was an announcement that the USA and Germany had arranged a special swap line. A few days later, for predominantly external reasons, the official US discount rate was raised by a ½ per cent. The market then reversed itself but not for long.
17 The continuing lack of an energy policy in the USA also contributed to adverse expectations.
18 Yet US prices over the same period grew more rapidly than Germany's. Monetarists explain this in terms of financial innovations in the USA which led to a secular fall in the demand for money in the USA relative to Germany. See J. Bilson (1979b).
19 The desire to moderate the revaluation was also motivated by the slackness in the economy.
20 See: J. R. Artus and J. H. Young (1979); P. Isard (1978); R. I. McKinnon (1976b); N. S. Fieleke (1979).
21 For a detailed discussion of the issues see S. Kohlhagen (1979).
22 W. Cornell and J. Dietrich (1978).
23 R. Levich (1979a); S. Black (1978); M. Dooley and J. Shafer (1976).
24 S. Kohlhagen (1979).
25 J. R. Artus (1976).

Part Five

Choice of Exchange Rate Regime

Chapter 22

The Effectiveness of Macro-Policy

Introduction

One criterion by which to choose between a fixed and a flexible rate regime is in terms of the relative effectiveness of monetary and fiscal policies. This chapter addresses itself to these issues.[1]

In Chapter 11 we distinguished three monetary regimes: a fixed rate regime based on the IMF (MR), a fixed rate regime based on the gold standard (GR) and a flexible rate regime (FR). The adjustment mechanism associated with each of these regimes was embodied in the model presented in that chapter. In Chapter 14 we also argued that the aggregate demand component of the model provided the appropriate framework for short-term analysis while the complete model, with price and wage adjustment, was the appropriate framework for longer-term analysis.

Given our concern in this chapter with short-term demand management, we now use the aggregate demand component of the model to inquire, for each of the three exchange rate regimes we identified, how a given change in monetary and fiscal policy influences, in the short run, the level of output. The regime which then generates the largest change in output for any given change in macro-policy is taken (other things being equal) to be the preferred regime.

The Relative Effectiveness of Monetary Policy

Consider, first, the effects of an exogenous open market purchase under the three regimes (GR, MR and FR) and assume, initially, that capital is completely immobile, so the *B* schedule is vertical (see Figure 22.1).

Suppose that at the start of our analysis all markets are in equilibrium at Yr_0. Now an increase in the volume of money will shift the *LM* schedule to the right to LM_1, raising the level of income to Yr_1.

At Yr_1 there will be a current account deficit represented by *ab*. If the monetary authorities sterilise the monetary effects of this deficit, say, by additional open market purchases, the level of output can be sustained, in the short term, at Yr_1, which then represents the solution for the MR regime. With this solution the goods and money markets are in equilibrium but the foreign exchange market remains in disequilibrium.

If there is no sterilisation, as in the GR regime, the volume of money would be allowed to shrink in line with the deficit, and this continues until the original level of output Yr_0 is restored. At this point, all three markets return to equilibrium at the original intersection of the three schedules. Monetary policy will have been completely unsuccessful while, at the same time, there will be a loss of reserves from the current account deficit exactly equal to the original open market purchase.

Figure 22.1 *Monetary policy with zero capital mobility*

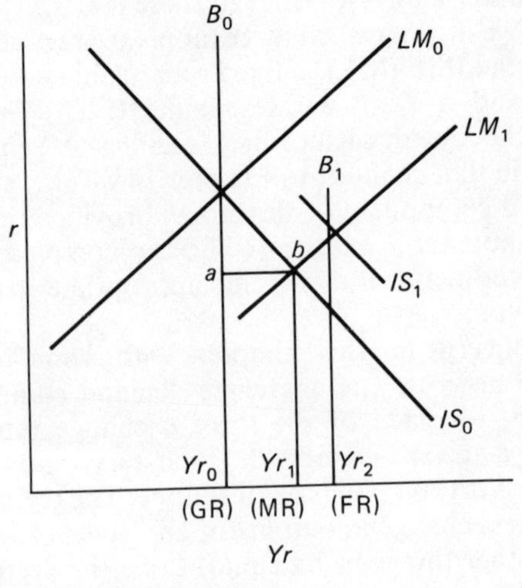

With flexible exchange rates (FR) the deficit cannot influence the money supply since there is no central bank intervention, but now the exchange rate devalues. Assuming the Marshall–Lerner condition holds, this shifts the *IS* schedule to the right, lifting further the level of income. As a result of the devaluation the *B* schedule also shifts to B_1. In the end all markets are again in equilibrium and the final solution must be a point at which all three schedules intersect, as at Yr_2.

With zero capital mobility, then, monetary policy is most effective for FR, has some effectiveness for MR and is completely ineffective for GR.

Now consider the case where there is some capital mobility (see Figure 22.2). An expansionary monetary policy will again raise the level of income to Yr_1; now, however, the deficit (*ab*) will be larger than previously (*cb*) because with lower interest rates there are also outflows of capital. In the MR regime the economy will settle at Yr_1 and the monetary authorities will now have to undertake larger sterilisation operations (for example, by making larger purchases of government securities) so as to preserve the new higher volume of money.

In the GR regime the volume of money will be allowed to fall and again equilibrium can only be restored at the original level of output. Monetary policy will again be completely ineffective, the only difference being that with the larger initial deficit the movement to equilibrium will be accelerated and the final solution will be reached sooner.

Figure 22.2 *Monetary policy with some capital mobility*

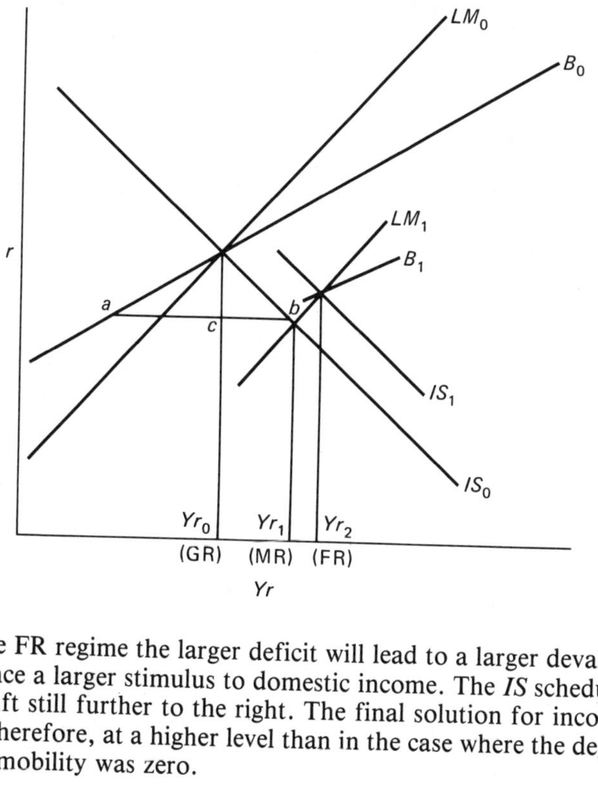

In the FR regime the larger deficit will lead to a larger devaluation and hence a larger stimulus to domestic income. The *IS* schedule will now shift still further to the right. The final solution for income for FR is, therefore, at a higher level than in the case where the degree of capital mobility was zero.

Finally, consider the case where capital mobility is perfect (see Figure 22.3). We have already seen[2] that as this limit is approached sterilisation operations become self-defeating and the monetary authorities lose control over the volume of money. At this point, the MR and GR regimes become identical. Monetary policy is now totally ineffective in the two regimes. Given, too, that capital markets tend to adjust rapidly, any attempt to implement an independent monetary policy will be very quickly offset by an equivalent outflow of capital without any transitory impact on income.

By contrast, with FR, monetary policy is now very powerful. The reason for this is the following. The lower interest rate raises income; so long as the interest rate is below the foreign interest rate, the exchange rate devalues and income increases pushing up the demand for money and interest rates until interest rates return to their original level. Output must, at that point, have increased in the same proportion as the volume of money, replicating, in effect, 'quantity theory' results.[3]

Figure 22.3 *Monetary policy with perfect capital mobility*

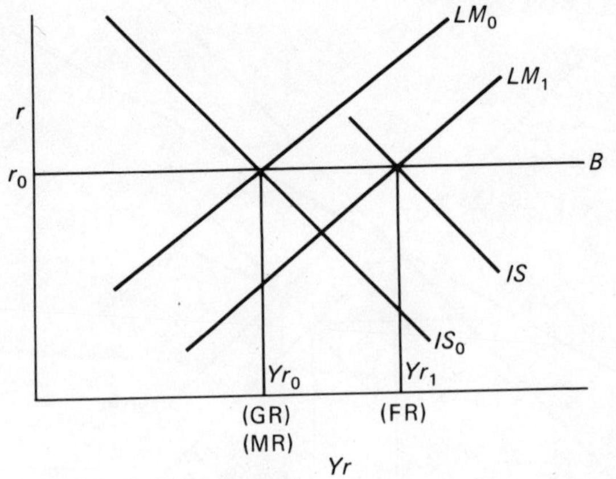

The Relative Effectiveness of Fiscal Policy

Consider, now, the effects of an increase in government expenditure and assume again that initially capital is completely immobile (see Figure 22.4).

The increase in expenditure will shift the *IS* schedule to the right and raise the level of income to Yr_1, which now represents the solution for the MR regime. At Yr_1 the monetary authorities will counteract the effects of the current account deficit, represented by *ab*, on the volume of money.

In the GR regime the deficit will reduce the money supply, so the LM schedule will shift to the left. This must continue until the deficit has been eliminated and income reverts to its original level. At this point, all the expansionary effects of the increased government expenditure will have been completely offset by reduced private expenditure, induced, in this case, by the rise in the interest rate from r_0 to r_1.

In the FR regime the deficit will induce a devaluation of the exchange rate, shift *IS* further to the right (to IS_2) and lift the level of income to Yr_2. The devaluation will also shift the *B* schedule to the right to meet the *IS* and *LM* schedules.

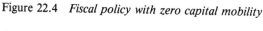

Figure 22.4 *Fiscal policy with zero capital mobility*

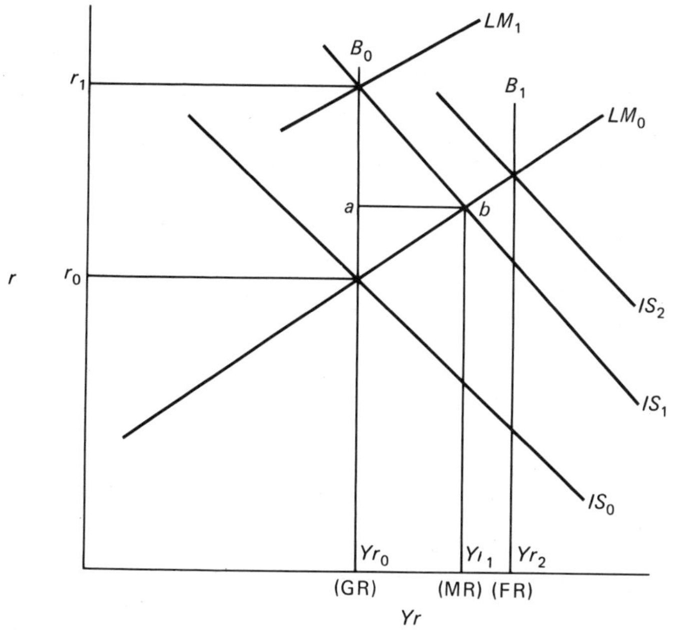

Consider, now, what happens as capital mobility increases. It is most important here to distinguish between a relatively 'low' degree of capital mobility, defined as a situation where the *B* schedule is to the left of the *LM* schedule in the upper range (as, for example, B_1 in Figure 22.5), and a relatively 'high' degree of capital mobility, where the *B* schedule has moved beyond *LM* (to the right of *LM*) (as, for example, in B_2). So long as the degree of capital mobility is relatively low, fiscal expansion will open up an overall deficit in the balance of payments (equal to *ab* in Figure 22.5). The reason is that although there is now some capital inflow in response to the higher interest rate, these inflows are not sufficient to offset the current account deficit associated with the higher level of income. When *B* coincides with *LM* the overall balance of payments is in equilibrium, the surplus in the capital account now exactly offsetting the deficit in the current account. Beyond *LM* (at B_2) fiscal expansion actually improves the balance of payments (opening up a surplus equal to *bc*). Now the associated inflow of capital more than offsets the current account deficit.

With low capital mobility (as defined) the rankings for the three regimes are similar to the case where capital mobility is zero. The relative effectiveness of fiscal policy, however, is changed. Fiscal policy now has some effectiveness in the GR regime because the current account deficit associated with the increase in output can be offset by some capital inflow. By contrast, fiscal policy is less effective with FR because the deficit is smaller and hence the devaluation will be weaker. At the same time, in the MR regime, the effectiveness of fiscal policy remains the same.

Figure 22.5 *Fiscal policy and capital mobility*

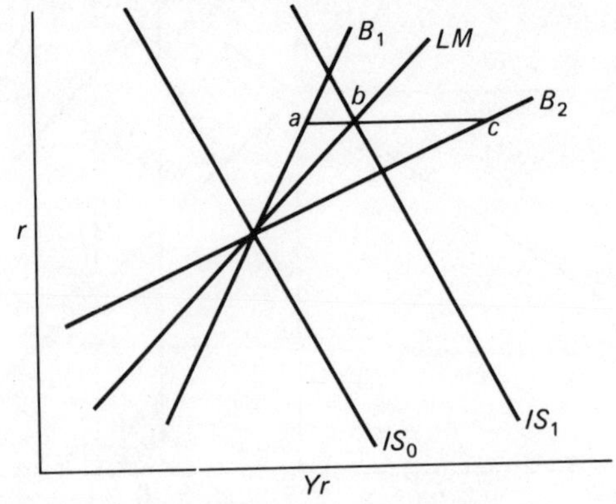

What happens when the degree of capital mobility is relatively high (that is, when the *B* schedule has shifted beyond *LM*)? (See Figure 22.6.) In the MR regime the solution will be at Yr_2, with the surplus (*ab*) sterilised by, say, open market sales. In the GR regime the surplus will add to the domestic money supply, shift the *LM* schedule to the right (to, say, LM_1) and raise the level of income to Yr_3. With FR the exchange rate will revalue, *B* will shift to the left to B_1, the *IS* schedule will shift to the left to IS_2 and the level of income will now drop to Yr_1. Fiscal policy is, then, most effective for GR and least effective for FR, with MR in the intermediate position.

Figure 22.6 *Fiscal policy with high capital mobility*

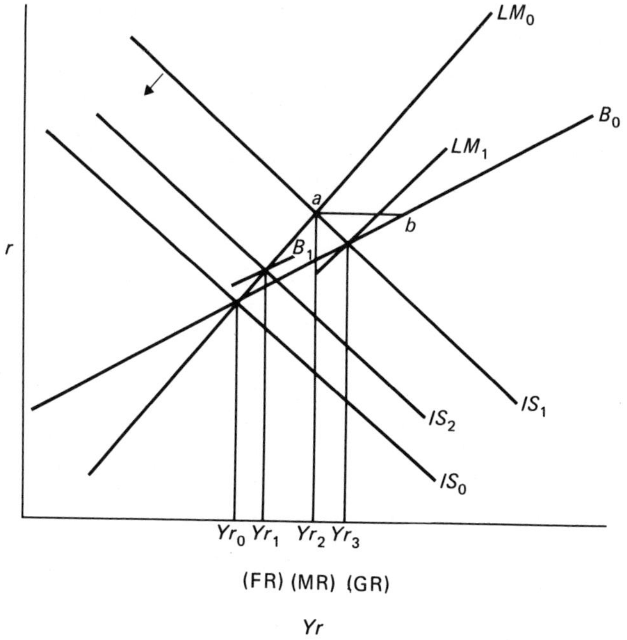

Figure 22.7 *Fiscal policy with perfect capital mobility*

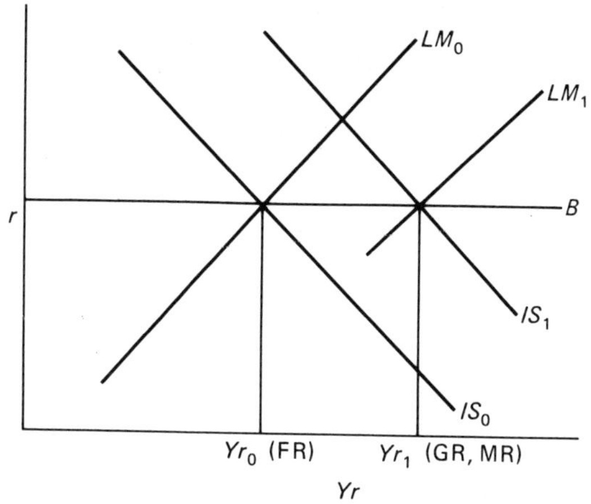

Finally, if capital mobility is perfect, fiscal policy becomes very potent under fixed rates (for both MR and GR) (see Figure 22.7). Fiscal expansion now opens up a surplus, increasing the volume of money to accommodate the increase in output (to Yr_1) at a fixed interest rate. By contrast, fiscal policy is completely ineffective under FR. So long as income and the interest rate are above their original levels, the currency will continue to revalue until the original income and interest rate are restored. In this case, the reduction in the trade balance will have completely offset the increase in government expenditure. In other words, with money supply fixed, by definition, and interest rates unchanged, income cannot change in this model.

Summary, Conclusions and Qualifications

In the model that we have used monetary policy is always more effective with flexible exchange rates than with fixed rates and the advantage of flexible exchange rates increases the higher the degree of capital mobility. Monetary policy is always completely ineffective with fixed rates if there is no sterilisation, whatever the degree of capital mobility. If capital mobility is perfect sterilisation is no longer feasible and monetary policy is then completely ineffective under fixed rates. On the other hand, with perfect capital mobility monetary policy is very effective under flexible exchange rates.

With low capital mobility fiscal policy is most effective under flexible exchange rates and least effective under fixed rates without sterilisation. With high capital mobility the rankings are reversed, fiscal policy being most effective with fixed rates without sterilisation and least effective with flexible rates. With perfect capital mobility fiscal policy is completely ineffective with flexible exchange rates and very effective with fixed rates.[4]

With low capital mobility, then, both monetary and fiscal policies are most effective under flexible exchange rates. From the standpoint of macro-policy, therefore, it would appear that a flexible rate system is to be preferred in these conditions. However, with high capital mobility there is a trade-off: flexible rates will improve the performance of monetary policy but weaken the performance of fiscal policy. With perfect capital mobility monetary policy is not usable under fixed rates and fiscal policy is not usable under flexible rates. If, therefore, capital mobility is high the choice of exchange rate regime will depend on which macro-instrument (monetary or fiscal) is judged to be the more useful and dependable. If monetary policy, for example, is viewed as being the more flexible instrument then its loss would be relatively more severe and there would be a case for flexible rates.

Realistically, we now need to make several qualifications to our conclusions. First, it needs to be emphasised that our results are derived from a specific model and hence are subject to any limitations associated with the model. For example, when certain extensions or changes are made to the model some of our results may be reversed. Three instances of this will be given. Suppose that, over the short term of, say, a few months, the Marshall–Lerner condition did not hold. Then monetary expansion under FR would force a devaluation; this, however, would not correct the deficit but would increase it. This larger deficit would need to be offset by a capital inflow, which could be forthcoming if the devaluation were sufficient to induce an expectation of a revaluation. In this case with a larger current account deficit over this short-term horizon, monetary policy would be less powerful under FR than under MR.[5] As we have already seen (in Chapter 21), this case may be of more than academic interest.

Again, we have made no allowance for the price effects (immediate as well as those flowing from subsequent wage adjustments) of exchange rate changes, in part because we have simplified by deflating money balances by the domestic rather than the overall price level[6] and in part, too, because we have argued that labour markets adjust slowly. When, however, allowance is made for price changes, a devaluation will lead to some increases in prices which are absent with fixed rates. Hence, some of the monetary expansion will be absorbed in prices, weakening the real effects under flexible exchange rates (see also Chapter 29).

Still another instance where our result might be reversed would be the case where capital flows are influenced not only by relative interest rates but also (positively) by levels of income. The argument here is that as income increases this induces inflows of capital to take advantage of higher levels of activity and expected profitability. If this income effect were sufficiently powerful monetary expansion might, on balance, improve the overall balance of payments; in other words, the inflow of capital would have more than offset the deterioration, due to the combined effects of lower interest rates (on capital flows) and higher levels of income (on the current account). Again, here, the associated revaluation would force a lower level of output under FR than under MR. Unlike the immediately preceding examples, however, this case is likely to be of only academic interest.

Second, a good case could be made for the view that, in general, the effects of both monetary and fiscal policies are likely to be even less predictable under FR than under MR. The reason is that there is additional uncertainty associated with the response of the exchange rate and, as well, with the effects of the change in the exchange rate on economic activity. This suggests that any advantage associated with greater (mean) leverage under FR might be offset, partially or fully, by an increased uncertainty about the shorter-term effects.

Third, it would be possible to argue that, provided monetary and fiscal policies had some effectiveness, similar outcomes might always be achieved by applying the policy more vigorously in the regime with the weaker effect. For example, suppose it is true that a given increase in the volume of money has a weaker effect on output under fixed than under flexible exchange rates; nevertheless, the same result may be achieved with fixed rates by simply increasing the volume of money by a greater amount. There may, however, be costs associated with more vigorous use of, say, money supply policy. These may take several forms: the greater volatility of interest rates, the greater volatility of reserves, the greater volatility of commercial banks' profits and, finally, the possibly greater uncertainty associated with larger money supply changes.

Fourth, with short-term fine-tuning currently in disfavour this basis for choosing the exchange rate regime would appear, on the face of it, to be less important. This is true to some degree. However, if fine-tuning were, in fact, abandoned and the monetary authorities chose to implement a relatively stable monetary growth policy they may have difficulties controlling the money supply if the exchange rate were fixed and capital mobility were very high. In this case, the monetary authorities' hands would be tied: a neutral monetary policy in this context would have to mean a constant contribution to monetary growth from increases in the domestic assets of the central bank. So, even without demand management, fixed rates under certain conditions may make it difficult for the monetary authorities to implement their chosen neutral monetary policy.

Fifth, the argument that flexible exchange rates secure monetary independence if capital mobility is relatively high is not entirely borne out by the recent experience with flexible rates. As we have shown, to secure this independence the monetary authorities must be prepared to tolerate substantial fluctuations in exchange rates over a relatively short period. They have, however, found this largely unacceptable. What this means, then, is that whereas the constraint on independent monetary policy with fixed rates is the associated movement in reserves, the constraint with flexible rates is the associated movement in exchange rates. So, with fixed rates and high capital mobility the monetary authorities lose control over the volume of money; by contrast, with flexible rates, under the same conditions, they have control but are largely unwilling to exercise it fully.

Sixth, and finally, we concluded that monetary policy was difficult to implement in a world of fixed rates when capital mobility was high. This, however, need not be an argument for flexible exchange rates, but rather an argument for reducing the degree of capital mobility (for example, by controls over capital movements) so as to make monetary policy more effective.

Table 22A.1 Solutions for monetary and fiscal policies

	Monetary Regime		
Exogenous change	*MR*	*GR*	*FR*
ΔMo (ΔD)	$\frac{\alpha_3}{\alpha_6(1-\alpha_1+\alpha_9)+\alpha_3\alpha_4}$	0	$\frac{\alpha_{12}+\alpha_3}{\alpha_6(1-\alpha_1)+\alpha_4(\alpha_{12}+\alpha_3)}$
ΔGr	$\frac{\alpha_6}{\alpha_6(1-\alpha_1+\alpha_9)+\alpha_3\alpha_4}$	$\frac{\alpha_{12}}{\alpha_{12}(1-\alpha_1+\alpha_9)+\alpha_9\alpha_3}$	$\frac{\alpha_6}{\alpha_6(1-\alpha_1)+\alpha_4(\alpha_{12}+\alpha_3)}$

Annex

Notation

D = domestic assets of the central bank
Gr = real government expenditure
K = net capital flows
M = volume of imports
Mo = money supply
r = domestic interest rate
Yr = real GNP

This Annex will derive, mathematically, the results described in the text. Table 22A.1 shows the solutions for monetary and fiscal policies under the three monetary regimes. These solutions are derived from the aggregate demand model in Chapter 11.

Consider, first, the case of monetary expansion. With GR, the solution is shown as 'zero' as described in the text. It is easily shown, too, that the solution for FR is larger than that for MR. Since α_{12} (the degree of capital mobility) does not enter into the solution for MR the effectiveness of monetary policy is independent of the degree of capital mobility except, of course, in the case where α_{12} approaches infinity when the solution is the same as GR. With FR, however, it is easily established that the effectiveness of monetary policy increases as the degree of capital mobility increases.

The case of fiscal expansion is slightly more complicated. Low capital mobility is represented by the case where $\alpha_9\alpha_6 > \alpha_{12}\alpha_4$ whereas for high capital mobility $\alpha_{12}\alpha_4 > \alpha_9\alpha_6$. The reason for this is the following. $\alpha_9 = \Delta M/\Delta Yr$ where, with exports exogenous, ΔM is the change in the current account.

$$\alpha_{12} = \frac{\Delta K}{\Delta r} \qquad \alpha_4 = \frac{\Delta Mo}{\Delta Yr} \qquad \alpha_6 = \frac{\Delta Mo}{\Delta r}$$

For low capital mobility the condition reduces to

$$\frac{\Delta M}{\Delta Yr} > \frac{\Delta K}{\Delta Yr}$$

and for high capital mobility it reduces to

$$\frac{\Delta K}{\Delta Yr} > \frac{\Delta M}{\Delta Yr}$$

This amounts to saying that for low (high) capital mobility the increase in output has a bigger (smaller) effect on the current account than on the capital account.

It is easily shown that when $\alpha_9\alpha_6 > \alpha_{12}\alpha_4$ (the low capital mobility case), FR > MR > GR and when $\alpha_{12}\alpha_4 > \alpha_9\alpha_6$ (the high capital mobility case), GR > MR > FR.

To demonstrate the results in the text we need to show how capital mobility affects the solutions. For the MR regime the solution is independent of capital mobility (except again as α_{12} approaches infinity). For GR the solution is:

$$\frac{1}{1-\alpha_1+\alpha_9+(\alpha_9\alpha_3/\alpha_{12})}$$

which shows that the higher the capital mobility, the higher is the expression. When $\alpha_{12}=0$ the expression becomes zero. When α_{12} approaches infinity the expression becomes:

$$\frac{1}{1-\alpha_1+\alpha_9}$$

which is the standard Keynesian open economy multiplier with fixed interest rates. For FR the solution is:

$$\frac{\alpha_6}{\alpha_6(1-\alpha_1)+\alpha_4(\alpha_{12}+\alpha_3)}$$

which becomes smaller the higher is α_{12}. At the limit when α_{12} approaches infinity, the expression becomes zero, as in the text.

Notes for Chapter 22

1 Selected literature on this includes: J. Fleming (1962); R. Mundell (1963); R. Stern (1973); J. Helliwell (1969); A. Krueger (1965); M. v. Whitman (1970); R. Mundell (1968), Chapter 5; V. Argy (1969); J. J. Polak and V. Argy (1971); A. Swoboda (1972).

2 See Chapter 14.

3 This can be seen intuitively if we take velocity *Yr/Mo* to be a (positive) function of the interest rate. With the interest rate fixed and the volume of money increasing the only way velocity would be unchanged would be if output increased in the same proportion as the volume of money.

4 The result – for flexible exchange rates and perfect capital mobility – that monetary policy has quantity theory results while fiscal policy is completely ineffective is an interesting illustration of how 'monetarist' results may be generated with what is essentially a Keynesian model.

5 This is essentially the argument in J. Niehans (1975).

6 If money balances were deflated by the overall price level a devaluation (revaluation) would raise (lower) the price level, increase (reduce) the demand for money and, hence, shift the *LM* schedule to the left (right).

Chapter 23

Insulation of the Domestic Economy from Random Disturbances

Introduction

In the previous chapter we were concerned with evaluating the effectiveness of monetary and fiscal policies, for demand management, under conditions of fixed as well as flexible exchange rates. As we indicated, there is now growing skepticism about the usefulness of demand-management policies and increased acceptance of the view that both monetary and fiscal policies ought to be directed towards longer-run goals.

This suggests a quite different and an alternative approach to the problem of the choice between fixed and flexible exchange rates. We can now assume, as a starting point, that monetary–fiscal policies are effectively neutralised (fine-tuning is abandoned) and then evaluate the degree to which alternative exchange rate regimes insulate the economy from various types of random disturbances.[1]

In our analysis, we will draw on exactly the same underlying framework that we used in the previous chapter. Again we use the short-term (aggregate demand) model and again we have three regimes: two fixed exchange rate regimes (with and without sterilisation) and a flexible rate regime. We now need to define the major types of disturbances to which an economy might be exposed. In the analysis we recognise the following types of disturbances:

(1) a domestic expenditure shock,
(2) a domestic demand for money shock,
(3) a domestic price (wage) shock,
(4) a foreign price shock,
(5) a capital flow shock (which takes the form either of a direct inflow or of a change in the foreign interest rate)
(6) a foreign real demand shock.

Table 23.1 Relative insulation from various disturbances for three monetary regimes (rankings – most stabilising first)

Shocks	*Low capital mobility*	*High capital mobility*
DOMESTIC		
1. Expenditure	GR, MR, FR	FR, MR, GR
2. Demand for money	GR, MR, FR	GR, MR, FR
3. Domestic price (wage)[a]	FR, MR, GR (GR, MR, FR)	FR, MR, GR (GR, MR,FR)
EXTERNAL		
4. Foreign price	FR, MR, GR	FR, MR, GR
5(a). Capital flows (direct inflow)	MR (FR, GR)	MR (FR, GR)
5(b). Capital flows (foreign interest rate)	MR (FR, GR)	MR (FR, GR)
6. Foreign real demand	FR, MR, GR	FR, MR, GR

[a]Results in parentheses represent the cases where the outcome is a surplus in the balance of payments – see text.

These six disturbances fall neatly into two categories: the first three originate domestically while the last three originate overseas. A further useful distinction is between real shocks represented by (1) and (6), financial shocks represented by (2) and (5) and supply (price) shocks represented by (3) and possibly (4).

The objective of the exercise is to determine the degree to which output is affected by each disturbance for each of the three exchange rate regimes. The choice of exchange rate regime, in this context, is based on the degree to which domestic output is insulated by the disturbances. The regime which, on balance, minimises the effects on domestic output from exogenous disturbances is, all other things being equal, to be preferred.

The Analytical Results

The results of the analysis are summarised in Table 23.1,[2] and a mathematical annex shows how these results are arrived at.

Consider, first, a domestic expenditure shock. The case exactly parallels that of fiscal expansion. For reasons already explained in the previous chapter, if capital mobility is low the effects will be weakest

Figure 23.1 *A domestic price shock with a deficit*

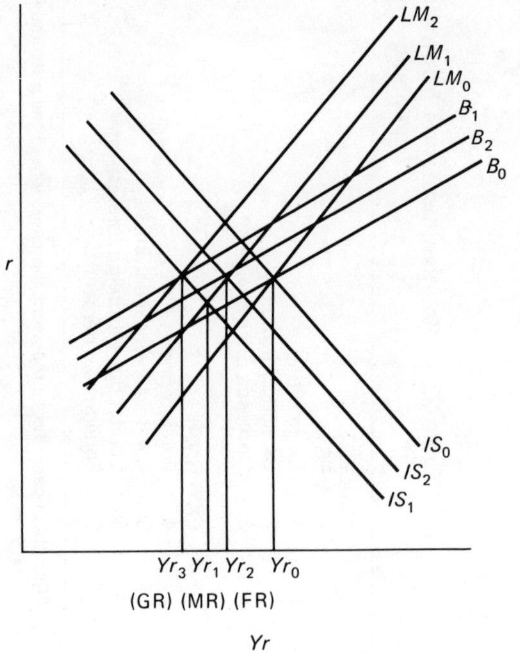

under GR and strongest under FR, while if capital mobility is high the effects will be weakest under FR and strongest under GR.

An increase in the demand for money, which shifts the *LM* schedule to the left, raises interest rates and reduces output. This, in turn, improves the balance of payments. With GR the improvement will increase the volume of money and attenuate the drop in output. With FR the surplus leads to a revaluation which aggravates the fall in output. Hence, for this particular disturbance, GR is the best stabiliser while FR is the worst stabiliser. It is also evident that the higher the degree of capital mobility the greater the insulation with GR and the weaker the insulation with FR.

For a domestic price shock the rankings are ambiguous. This case is illustrated in Figure 23.1. If the Marshall–Lerner condition holds the *IS* schedule will shift to the left (to IS_1) depressing economic activity. At the same time the *LM* schedule will also shift to the left (to LM_1), since now with domestic prices higher the demand for money will increase. Also, the *B* schedule will shift to B_1 because with a higher domestic price level a lower output level (or a higher interest rate) is required to restore equilibrium to the balance of payments. What happens to the balance of payments depends on the strength of the shift in the *IS* schedule relative to the shift in the *LM* schedule. If the shift in the *IS* schedule is dominant the balance of payments will move into deficit. If, on the other hand, the real balance effect is dominant economic activity will fall sufficiently to turn the balance of payments into a surplus.

With fixed rates and sterilisation (MR) economic activity will fall from Yr_0 to Yr_1. If a deficit emerges (as in Figure 23.1), with FR there will be a devaluation, the *IS* and *B* schedules will shift to the right and output will settle at Yr_2; with GR the volume of money will fall shifting the *LM* schedule to LM_2 and reducing economic activity further (to Yr_3). If, on the other hand, a surplus emerges the rankings of FR and GR would be reversed.

An increase in (non-oil) foreign prices will increase domestic demand and the balance of payments will move into surplus. With FR any potential increase in economic activity will be offset by the revaluation. By contrast, with GR the increase in economic activity will be aggravated. Hence, in this case, FR insulates best while GR insulates worst.

We distinguish two capital inflow shocks: one takes the form of a fall in the foreign interest rate and the other takes the form of an exogenous net inflow of capital. The outcomes are different in these two cases. If sterilisation is possible any inflow, from whatever source, will have no effect on the volume of money. The MR regime, therefore, in this case, will provide perfect insulation and will perform best. With GR a fall in the foreign interest rate will lead to an increase in the volume of money, forcing down the domestic interest rate and raising economic activity. In this case, the easier monetary policy overseas will have been imported. The higher the degree of capital mobility the bigger the inflow and the bigger the increase in economic activity. By contrast, with an exogenous net inflow (and the same foreign interest rate), the higher the degree of capital mobility the less is the effect on economic activity because any drop in the domestic interest rate will now induce an offsetting outflow of capital. In the limit, for example, when capital mobility is perfect, there will in fact be perfect insulation.

With FR a drop in the foreign interest rate leads to a revaluation which now reduces economic activity. In this case, the higher the capital mobility the larger is the reduction in economic activity because the larger will be the revaluation. With an exogenous net inflow the revaluation will again lower economic activity; however, the lower economic activity will force down the domestic interest rate; this, in turn, will induce an outflow of capital, weakening the exchange rate and attenuating the fall in activity. Now the higher the capital mobility the weaker the effect on economic activity; at the limit with perfect capital mobility there will again be perfect insulation.

To summarise: the regime that performs best for a capital inflow shock is the MR regime, while it is impossible to determine which of the other two regimes performs better. It is interesting to note that all three regimes are perfect insulators for exogenous capital inflows when capital mobility is perfect.

Finally, an increase in foreign demand leads to some increase in output and a surplus in the balance of payments. With FR, the associated revaluation will offset the potentially stimulating effects of the expansion in exports. With GR, the surplus will lead to some increase in the volume of money, which will aggravate the stimulus to income. Hence, for this disturbance FR is the best insulator and GR the worst.

At this point, it is useful to inquire how our results, for flexible rates, would be affected if speculation were assumed to be stabilising.[3] Since we are dealing with random disturbances it is appropriate to take the case where the effects on exchange rates are judged to be transitory, so some reversal is anticipated in subsequent periods. The results may easily be summarised. Clearly, stabilising speculation will dampen the fluctuation in the exchange rate. For example, if there is a devaluation (revaluation) and a revaluation (devaluation) is anticipated, the speculative inflow (outflow) will serve to attenuate the fall (rise) in the currency. It follows that wherever FR tended to be a relatively good insulator from a disturbance the relative insulation will now be weakened; on the other hand, wherever FR was relatively destabilising for a particular disturbance the relative instability will also be weakened.

Consider, for example, the case of a real foreign demand shock. The associated revaluation will create expectations of a devaluation; the induced outflow of capital will now permit some improvement in the current account and hence some increase in income. The FR regime will not, therefore, in this case, provide complete insulation. Interestingly, stabilising speculation actually destabilises output. A parallel example is the case where there is a private expenditure shock and capital mobility is high. Now the expected devaluation will weaken the revaluation and hence the degree of insulation. Again, stabilising speculation is destabilising to output. On the other hand, for an increase in the demand for money the revaluation and hence the relative instability will be weakened; or again if there is an expenditure shock and capital mobility is low, the associated expected revaluation will be stabilising to output.

An Evaluation of the Results

Are any general conclusions possible from our analysis? If we distinguish domestic from external shocks there is some (small) presumption in the results that if the external economy is relatively more unstable (stable) than the home economy, a FR regime would perform better (worse) than a GR regime. This particular conclusion is, in fact, virtually unambiguous if capital mobility is relatively low and a domestic price shock led to a balance of payments surplus.

Perhaps the safest conclusion one can draw from Table 23.1 is that when capital mobility is relatively high FR scores well in terms of rankings. For four out of six disturbances, FR performs best (provided a domestic price shock generates a deficit). The two cases where FR performs relatively poorly are where the shocks are financial. The GR regime appears to perform most poorly, registering the worst performance for every shock, bar one (the demand for money shock). The MR regime comes off second best; it is ranked in the middle position in every instance, bar one (capital flows) where it in fact performs best.

One might ask, at this point, what bearing 'openness' has on the choice between fixed and flexible rates from the standpoint of insulation. Increased openness will, under fixed rates, magnify the effects of certain disturbances and weaken the impact of others. For example, a given percentage change in foreign prices, or in foreign output, will have a larger domestic impact the more open the economy. To take a specific illustration, if foreign output and imports increased by 10 per cent, the larger the share of exports in GNP the bigger will be the percentage change in domestic output.

By contrast, a given change in domestic expenditure, or in the demand for money or in capital flows will have a weaker domestic impact the more open the economy. The reason is that for any given change in domestic demand the leakage into imports is larger and, hence, the effect on domestic activity weaker.

The only conclusion one can draw from these results is that there is, perhaps, some presumption that if external disturbances are dominant, the more open the economy the greater (smaller) is the relative advantage (disadvantage) of flexible rates, while if domestic disturbances are dominant the more open the economy the greater (smaller) is the relative advantage (disadvantage) of fixed rates.

An interesting paper by Stein[4] bears on some of the issues we have been discussing. It suggests that, other things being equal, a flexible rate (fixed rate) regime might be the more efficient if a balance of payments surplus (deficit) tends to be associated with upswings in economic activity while a balance of payments deficit (surplus) tends to be associated with downswings. The principle here is that the regime that appears to act in a contra-cyclical fashion would be favoured. If, for example, an upswing was associated with a surplus then a flexible rate regime, by forcing a revaluation in the circumstances, would serve to dampen the upswing. Our own results are, in fact, entirely consistent with Stein's criterion. In every case where we concluded that, say, a FR was to be preferred, rising (falling) economic activity happened to be associated with a surplus (deficit); and where we concluded that a fixed rate was to be preferred, rising (falling) activity was associated with a deficit (surplus). All this suggests that a direct empirical test of the kind of analysis we have undertaken might be provided by observations of the cyclical movements in the balance of payments vis-à-vis the level of economic activity. A refined application of the Stein test was, in fact, attempted for several countries by Tower and Courtney.[5] The difficulties, unfortunately, proved immense and the results quite inconclusive.

Annex

Notation

edm = elasticity of demand for imports
edx = elasticity of demand for exports
Mo = money supply
Pd = domestic price level
Pf = foreign prices denominated in foreign currency
rf = foreign interest rate
X = volume of exports
Yf = foreign real GNP

Table 23A.1 Multipliers for various random disturbances

	Monetary regime		
Disturbance	*MR*	*GR*	*FR*
1. ΔA_1 (Expenditure)	$\frac{\alpha_6}{\alpha_6(1-\alpha_1+\alpha_9)+\alpha_3\alpha_4}$	$\frac{\alpha_{12}}{\alpha_{12}(1-\alpha_1+\alpha_9)+\alpha_9\alpha_3}$	$\frac{\alpha_6}{\alpha_6(1-\alpha_1)+\alpha_4(\alpha_{12}+\alpha_3)}$
2. ΔA_2 (Demand for money)	$-\frac{\alpha_3}{\alpha_6(1-\alpha_1+\alpha_9)+\alpha_3\alpha_4}$	0	$-\frac{\alpha_{12}+\alpha_3}{\alpha_6(1-\alpha_1)+\alpha_4(\alpha_{12}+\alpha_3)}$
3. ΔPd (Domestic price)	$-\frac{\alpha_6 ML+\alpha_3 Mo}{\alpha_6(1-\alpha_1+\alpha_9)+\alpha_3\alpha_4}$	$-\frac{ML(\alpha_{12}+\alpha_3)}{\alpha_{12}(1-\alpha_1+\alpha_9)+\alpha_9\alpha_3}$	$-\frac{Mo(\alpha_3+\alpha_{12})}{\alpha_6(1-\alpha_1)+\alpha_4(\alpha_{12}+\alpha_3)}$
4. ΔPf (Foreign price)	$\frac{\alpha_6 ML}{\alpha_6(1-\alpha_1+\alpha_9)+\alpha_3\alpha_4}$	$\frac{ML(\alpha_{12}+\alpha_3)}{\alpha_{12}(1-\alpha_1+\alpha_9)+\alpha_9\alpha_3}$	0
5(a). ΔA_5 (Exogenous capital inflow)	0	$\frac{\alpha_3}{\alpha_{12}(1-\alpha_1+\alpha_9)+\alpha_9\alpha_3}$	$\frac{-\alpha_6}{-\alpha_6(1-\alpha_1)+\alpha_4(\alpha_{12}+\alpha_3)}$
5(b). Δrf (Foreign interest rate)	0	$-\frac{\alpha_3\alpha_{12}}{\alpha_{12}(1-\alpha_1+\alpha_9)+\alpha_9\alpha_3}$	$\frac{\alpha_6\alpha_{12}}{\alpha_6(1-\alpha_1)+\alpha_4(\alpha_{12}+\alpha_3)}$
6. ΔYf (Real foreign demand)	$\frac{\alpha_6\alpha_{20}}{\alpha_6(1-\alpha_1+\alpha_9)+\alpha_3\alpha_4}$	$\frac{\alpha_{20}(\alpha_3+\alpha_{12})}{\alpha_{12}(1-\alpha_1+\alpha_9)+\alpha_9\alpha_3}$	0

$ML = X(edx+edm-1)$ – see Chapter 11.

The model is easily amended to accommodate our disturbances. For a domestic expenditure shock a disturbance term (A_1) is added to the real absorption equation (Equation 11.3) of the model. It is evident that it gives results similar to changes in government expenditure. For a demand for money shock a disturbance term (A_2) is added to the demand for money equation (Equation 11.8). For a domestic or foreign price shock we simply treat changes in domestic or foreign prices as exogenous (as in the aggregate demand component of the model). For an exogenous inflow we add a disturbance term (A_5) to Equation (11.13) (the capital flow equation). The change in the foreign interest rate (Δrf) is treated as exogenous in the model. The real foreign demand disturbance is represented in Equation (11.4) of the model by foreign output (Yf).

The multipliers are all calculated for 'full equilibrium'. This is justified on the ground that we are only interested here in the relative multipliers. Full equilibrium, however, might not be attained in the time horizon envisaged. For example, for the GR regime the solution assumes that the balance of payments is restored to equilibrium but this would, of course, take time.

Table 23A.1 shows the multipliers for the various disturbances as defined above and in the text.

For an expenditure change (ΔA_1) the result is the same as for a change in fiscal policy. This result is explained in the Annex to Chapter 22. For ΔA_2, FR>MR>GR.[6] For ΔPd the result is ambiguous as indicated in the text. For ΔPf, GR>MR>FR. For ΔA_5, $\genfrac{}{}{0pt}{}{\text{GR}}{\text{FR}}$>MR. For ΔYf, GR>MR>FR.

For ΔA_5 (the exogenous capital flow shock) one result noted in the text can be demonstrated. If $\alpha_{12} \rightarrow \infty$ (perfect capital mobility) the multiplier for all three regimes is zero.

Notes for Chapter 23

1 See S. Turnovsky (1976); V. Argy (1975). Neutral monetary policy with the GR regime means holding the domestic assets of the central bank fixed or in a growth context their contribution to monetary growth fixed. With MR and FR neutral monetary policy means following a Friedmanite monetary rule.

2 The analysis disregards the possibility of covariation among the disturbances. An obvious covariation, for example, would be an increase in private expenditure being associated with a reduction in the demand for money.

3 See, on this, V. E. Argy and M. G. Porter (1972).

4 J. Stein (1963).

5 E. Tower and M. Courtney (1974).

6 For GR the multiplier is shown as zero. This, of course, is the 'long-run' result whatever the degree of capital mobility. However, if capital mobility is low there will be some transitional change in output. If capital mobility is infinite a change in the demand for money is fully and quickly accommodated with no effects on output.

Chapter 24

Exchange Rate Regime – World Inflation and Unemployment

Introduction

An important consideration in the choice between fixed and flexible exchange rates is the effect that the alternative exchange regimes would have on world inflation, world unemployment and their distribution. This chapter addresses itself to this question.[1]

Flexible Exchange Rates and Inflation – Some Arguments

Asymmetries

To begin, there are several arguments based on various asymmetries that suggest differences in inflationary outcomes for fixed and flexible rate regimes.[2] One asymmetry turns on the notion that with fixed rates the burden of adjustment tends to fall on deficit rather than surplus countries, injecting a deflationary bias on the world economy which in turn will tend to moderate world inflation. Again, various asymmetries have been put forward which are alleged to reinforce inflationary tendencies under flexible rates.

First, it is contended that for any one country or across countries there may be ratchet effects – devaluations raising prices by more than revaluations reduce them. This argument rests partly on the assumption that wages and prices rarely take a downward trend and partly on the alleged tendency of importers to pass on higher import prices in a devaluation but to profiteer in a revaluation. The first possibility cannot be realistically maintained in a world where the rate of inflation is positive, so revaluations would simply reduce the rate of inflation, without requiring an actual fall in prices. The second may hold but it is unlikely to be significant or persistent.[3]

Second, it is also contended that a country that is devaluing (for instance, because of an unfavourable structural change or an outflow of capital) will allow the inflationary effects, while the country that is revaluing will attempt to counter the deflationary effects and hence inject an inflationary bias in the world economy.[4] This argument may carry some (marginal) conviction in a world where overriding priority is attached to unemployment, but appears particularly unconvincing in a world (since 1974) where priorities have shifted dramatically towards controlling inflation.

Flexible Rates and Structural Unemployment

It is also sometimes argued that flexible exchange rates may create more structural unemployment by signalling more frequent shifts in resources between traded and non-traded goods.[5] If governments attempted to eliminate this structural unemployment by expansionary policies, the associated bottlenecks would generate additional inflation under flexible rates. Alternatively, if Phillips curves were non-linear the greater variability in demand might lift the rate of inflation in the economy as a whole.

Flexible Exchange Rates, the Demand for Reserves and Inflation

Another argument bearing on the potential inflationary effects of alternative exchange rate regimes is that a switch to flexible exchange rates (without, say, intervention) will result in an excess supply of international reserves, and that this excess supply could, in certain circumstances, generate some additional world inflation. It is important here to distinguish the different reserve assets. We can dismiss the case of SDRs first because their (presumed) withdrawal (by the IMF) would leave the world economy unchanged (the reduction in demand would be exactly matched by a reduction in supply). What happens in the case of reserve currencies? Countries with excess reserve currencies might inflate vis-à-vis the reserve currency countries and in this way liquidate the reserve currencies. This case, however, is unconvincing. More realistically, the countries with excess reserve currencies would revalue vis-à-vis the reserve currencies, setting in motion a process of excess demand and inflation in the reserve currency countries and deflation in the rest of the world. This is a particular illustration of the asymmetry already discussed previously. Finally, what happens if gold is sold on the market? If a central bank sold gold to residents of another country, it would be exchanging gold for foreign currency, which it could then sell on the market, revaluing its own currency vis-à-vis the foreign currency it initially acquired. This suggests, on a general scale, that the currencies of the countries whose residents buy the gold will devalue relative to the rest of the world, with the consequences already discussed.

Flexible Rates and the Cost of Trading

Still another relevant argument is the one that the additional uncertainty associated with trade will add to the costs of trade and hence to the prices of traded goods. There is first (and unarguably) the 'insurance' cost of covering in the forward market. This is measured by the bid–ask margins, which have tended to increase with more flexible rates.[6] Without cover, however, the variance of trading profits may increase, reducing the incentives to produce in the sector and hence forcing some increase in the price of traded goods. But, as we show in a later chapter (p. 304),[7] it is not evident that trading profits will become more variable with flexible exchange rates.

Some Conclusions

Our conclusion thus far is that none of the arguments alleging a greater potential for inflation under flexible exchange rates is particularly strong or convincing. Moreover, except in one or two instances (the argument from a deflationary bias or the argument regarding structural unemployment), they would in any case lead to once-over effects on the price level only.

It is worth noting, however, that while flexible rates, according to the arguments reviewed so far, may have no significant effects on inflation, they almost certainly increase the amplitude of price movements. This tendency will be the more pronounced the greater the degree of wage indexation. In turn, this creates greater uncertainty, which itself imposes a cost on the community.

Phillips Curve Analysis

We now turn to a more formal analysis of the problem. The focus shifts to the longer-run choice between fixed and flexible exchange rates: a flexible rate regime (pure or managed) will now be contrasted with a longer-run fixed rate regime (of the Bretton Woods type) where exchange rates adjust only very infrequently.

We begin with a relatively simple (but nevertheless useful) framework, which will be refined subsequently. Assume to begin with that:

(1) In a fixed rate world the rate of inflation is the same across countries.
(2) This uniform rate of inflation is independently determined by the largest and most powerful industrial country (the key country).
(3) The key country's rate of inflation is independent of the exchange rate regime.

(4) Each country has a long-run Phillips curve, tracing a traditional negative relationship between its rate of inflation and its unemployment rate.
(5) Under flexible exchange rates each country is free to determine its optimal combination of inflation and unemployment, on the basis of its own 'community indifference curves'.

The analytical argument will be developed in two steps. We first take the case where the key country has a relatively low rate of inflation and then examine the case where it has a relatively high rate of inflation.

Case 1 – Key Country Has a Relatively Low Inflation Rate

What does it mean to say that the key country has a relatively low inflation? It means, in effect, that given a country's Phillips curve and its own indifference curves, reflecting its preferences, the key country's optimal inflation is below the optimal of, say, a majority of other industrial countries.

It is convenient to distinguish two possible reasons for this. First, the key country (KC) may share a common Phillips curve with the rest of the world (ROW) but, on the other hand, its indifference curves reflect a relatively stronger preference for low inflation and high unemployment. This case is illustrated in Figure 24.1. It is assumed that the KC prefers a position *P* on the Phillips curve (PC), which it shares with the rest of the world. A majority of the rest of the world, on the other hand, prefer the position *F* on the schedule.[8] The two vertical lines represent the situations with flexible rates, with the ROW combining an inflation rate of *F* with an unemployment rate of *OQ* while the KC will choose an inflation rate of *P* and an unemployment rate of *OP*. The horizontal line *OP* represents the fixed rate (MR) case with the uniform inflation rate of *P* determined by the KC.

In this case, flexible rates yield a higher world rate of inflation (a weighted average of *P* and *F*) but a lower world rate of unemployment (a weighted average of *OP* and *OQ*). The 'excess' unemployment under fixed rates is represented by *QP*. The dispersion of unemployment and inflation are both greater under flexible rates.

Second, the key country may have a lower relative inflation rate, as defined, not because it has different preferences (indeed it is assumed to share indifference curves with the ROW) but because its Phillips curve is differently situated. This case is illustrated in Figure 24.2. *OQ* traces the optimal combinations of inflation and unemployment traced by intersections of Phillips curves with progressively higher indifference curves (not drawn) reflecting community preferences. The outcomes are much the same as in the previous case with *F* and *G* the preferred positions now for the KC and the ROW, respectively. With

Figure 24.1 *Common Phillips curves and different preferences*

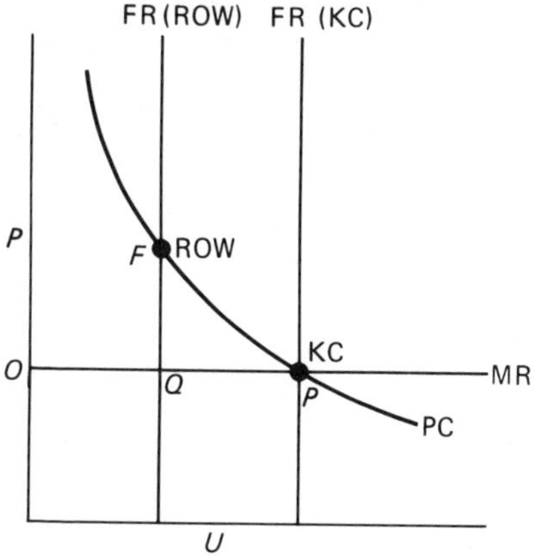

fixed rates the rest of the world would have to assume an excess unemployment rate of *BC*. It should be noted that now, as distinct from the previous case, the dispersion of unemployment is greater under fixed rates while the dispersion of inflation is greater under flexible rates.

Finally, a mixed case where the positions of the Phillips curves are different and also the indifference curves are different is easily illustrated. It is possible for the KC to have an unfavourable Phillips curve (that is, to the right of the ROW) and yet to have a relatively low inflation if its preferences lean strongly towards keeping inflation down, albeit at a higher cost in terms of unemployment. This case is shown in Figure 24.3. The dispersion of both inflation and unemployment is now greater under flexible than under fixed rates.

Case 2 – Key Country Has a Relatively High Inflation Rate

Here the conclusions are largely reversed. The key country may have a relatively higher rate of inflation because its preferences are different and/or because its Phillips curve is differently situated. In this case world inflation will be higher under fixed than under flexible rates, while the dispersion of the inflation rate will continue to be higher under flexible than under fixed rates. World unemployment will now be lower under fixed rates, while the dispersion of unemployment may be higher or lower under fixed rates.

Our conclusion then is that in so far as a flexible rate regime allows each individual country to choose its optimal combination of inflation and unemployment (all other things being equal) this would have to constitute one argument favouring flexible exchange rates.

Figure 24.2 *Shared indifference curves and different Phillips curves*

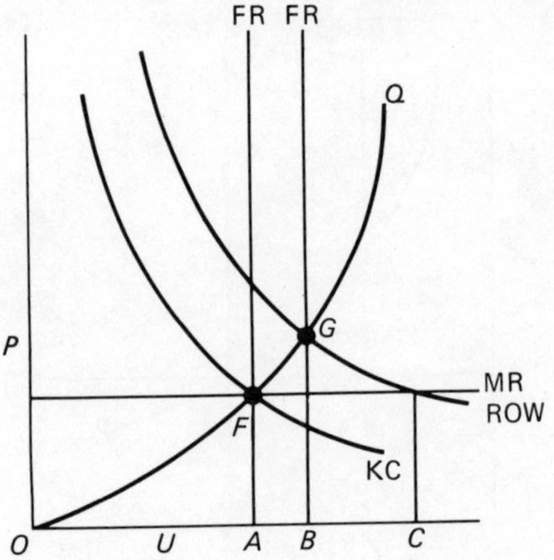

Figure 24.3 *Different Phillips curves and preferences*

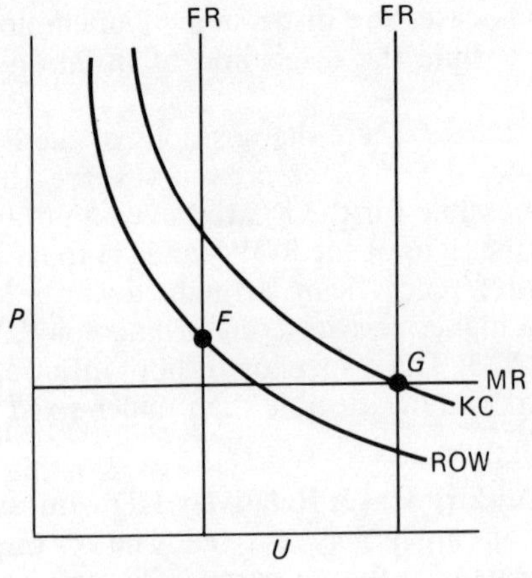

Application of Framework to Early–Later 1960s

The analysis developed above is not an unrealistic representation of the situation in the industrial world in the early to mid-late 1960s. First, the USA was the key country by dint of two factors: its economic superiority and the use of the US dollar as the reserve currency of the system. The latter effectively meant that the USA did not have a balance of payments constraint, while, on the other hand, other countries were forced in the longer run to adapt to the USA.[9] Second, the inflation differentials were, in fact, relatively small, so

Table 24.1 Standard deviations of inflation rates – fifteen industrial countries

Year	*Mean rate of inflation*	*Standard deviation*
1961	2.2	1.3
1962	3.8	2.1
1963	3.7	2.1
1964	3.6	1.4
1965	4.1	1.4
1966	4.1	1.5
1967	3.6	1.5
1968	3.6	1.7
1969	4.0	1.7
1970	5.4	2.0
1971	5.7	1.6
1972	5.9	1.1
1973	8.1	1.6
1974	12.4	4.3
1975	11.5	4.4
1976	9.1	3.9
1977	8.5	4.1

Source: International Monetary Fund, *International Financial Statistics* (May 1977) – Consumer Prices.

our assumption that inflation rates were equalised across countries is a reasonable approximation (see Table 24.1). Third, certainly until the later 1960s nearly all industrial countries did appear to have clearly defined Phillips curves.[10] The evidence reveals that during the 1960s the USA and Canada had the most unfavourable (outlying) Phillips curves, Germany and Japan the most favourable, while France and the UK were in an intermediate position.[11] Fourth, during the 1960s there was a large movement by the USA along its Phillips curve (due overwhelmingly to the shift in preference of the Democratic Administrations) towards a significantly lower rate of unemployment and a higher rate of inflation.

Taking all these facts into account, we may now place the following interpretation on developments in the period. In the very early 1960s, when the US inflation rate was very low and its unemployment rate high, the fixed rate regime helped to keep world inflation down (and possibly world unemployment up). The situation, however, changed dramatically in the later 1960s. Then, with the US inflation rate significantly higher, the fixed rate regime may have helped to raise the world inflation rate. Under those conditions, as we have seen, a flexible rate regime might have served to reduce the world inflation rate.

The Case of the Vertical Phillips Curve

What are the implications of a vertical long-run Phillips curve for the choice between fixed and flexible exchange rates? To begin with countries are no longer free to choose their optimal combination of inflation and unemployment. With unemployment largely predetermined (at the natural rate) countries would then be able to choose only their rates of inflation. In so far as inflation preferences across countries were different, a fixed rate regime might still entail some costs. Nevertheless, it would appear that the case for (permanently) fixed rates would have strengthened significantly. (See Chapter 27.)

Notes for Chapter 24

1 A. D. Crockett and M. Goldstein (1976); W. M. Corden (1977), Chapters 4 and 5; E. M. Claasen (1976); J. Fried (1973).
2 See W. M. Corden (1977), Chapter 5.
3 See M. Goldstein (1977).
4 This same argument cannot be used to prove an inflationary bias under fixed rates because in this case there are deficits (and changes in international reserves) to contend with.
5 See A. Lanyi (1969); see also R. Cooper (1972).
6 See A. D. Crockett and M. Goldstein (1976) who show that the additional costs are almost trivial.
7 For a discussion of this see Chapter 25.
8 Of course, more realistically, some countries will be to the left of *P* and some to the right, with the latter in the majority.
9 This may be too strong. Our assumption (3) above probably did not hold in this extreme form. The US role was not entirely passive; there is some evidence (for instance, in the early 1960s) that the USA did take account of her balance of payments position in determining her macro-policy.
10 This, however, is almost certainly spurious and may simply reflect the fact that the mean expected rate of inflation was fairly stable over that period. What is relevant here for the discussion is whether the countries could have secured permanent changes in their unemployment rates by opting for significantly different rates of inflation. See Chapter 12 for a further discussion of these issues.
11 See E. Spitaeller (1971).

Chapter 25

Exchange Rate Flexibility, Trade, Reserve Demand and Vicious Circles

Introduction

This chapter looks at some additional considerations in the choice between fixed and flexible rates. First, it examines the argument that greater flexibility reduces trade and that this represents a cost of greater exchange rate flexibility. Second, it examines the argument that greater flexibility reduces the need for international reserves and that this is a benefit flowing from greater flexibility. Third, it examines the argument that the adoption of flexible exchange rates may lead to vicious (virtuous) circles of devaluation–inflation (revaluation–deflation) and that this represents a cost associated with a flexible rate regime.

Notation used in this chapter

E = exchange rate (units of domestic currency per unit of foreign currency)
Gr = real government expenditure
Mo = money supply
P = overall price level
Pd = domestic price level
W = nominal wage rate
Yf = foreign real GNP
Yr = real GNP
ML = Marshall–Lerner condition

Exchange Rate Flexibility and Trade

There are two key issues here. First, how does greater exchange rate flexibility affect the volume of trade? Second, given the impact of increased flexibility on trade, what are the implications for welfare? The volume of trade can be influenced in two ways by increased exchange rate flexibility: by adding to the direct costs of trade and/or by increasing the variance of expected profits from trade.

Exchange rate risk is made up of an insurable component (the forward cover for particular short term transactions) and a component that is not normally insurable (associated with a commitment in a particular activity, for example, risk due to longer-term fluctuations in rates, short-term valuation effects).[1] A greater amplitude of exchange rate movement will increase the cost of forward cover and hence the direct costs of trade. This cost of forward cover is measurable by the bid–ask spread,[2] which itself has increased significantly in recent years.[3] The cost, however, tends to be very small: Crockett and Goldstein, for example, mention a spread of something of the order of 1/10th of 1 per cent of the transaction price.[4] This suggests that, by itself, its impact on the volume of trade would have been very small.

How does exchange rate flexibility affect the variance of expected profits from trade? To evaluate this question one has to compare a situation where exchange rates are relatively fixed with a situation where exchange rates have become more flexible. First, it may just be that increased flexibility will serve to offset price differentials to a greater degree, so reducing the variance in real exchange rates. In this case, other things being equal, the variance of expected profits from trade might actually be reduced with increased exchange rate flexibility, and this might offset the (small) additional cost of forward cover. However, the evidence (and intuition) would appear to be against this. Real exchange rates have been more volatile in the floating period than in the fixed rate period. Second, as Friedman[5] notes, there may be greater exchange rate uncertainty, with more flexible rates, but there are other kinds of uncertainties, bearing on trade, with relatively fixed rates. For example, there may be greater uncertainty associated with commercial policy or exchange controls, or stop–go policies to correct payments disequilibria. Hence, the variance of expected profits with trade may not increase with increased flexibility. Third, the (uninsured) longer-term exchange rate risk need not be greater with more flexible rates, since what is relevant here is longer-run uncertainty about exchange rates and this might not be different in the two regimes.

The conclusion we reach is the following. If one is comparing an adjustable peg type regime with, say, a pure float it is not clear that trade will be adversely affected by the latter. If, however, one is comparing degrees of managed floats then our analysis suggests that, provided intervention serves to attenuate the fluctuation in exchange rates, the more flexible the exchange rates the smaller is likely to be the volume of trade. This is so because the extra cost of forward cover and the greater volatility in real rates will now be the dominant influences. It is, in fact, very difficult to secure evidence on the effects of flexibility on trade but what evidence is available suggests that increased exchange rate flexibility does not appear to have affected trade adversely in any significant way.[6]

If it is difficult to determine exactly how flexibility affects the volume of trade it is even harder to evaluate how welfare is affected. Lanyi[7] makes one or two telling points in this regard. Assuming that increased exchange rate flexibility reduces trade, why is the community necessarily worse off? Relatively fixed rates entail, in effect, a subsidy to trade but a subsidy leads to a misallocation of resources (subject to the usual second-best reservations) unless there are offsetting externalities. Hence, to argue that increased exchange rate flexibility actually misallocates resources because it reduces trade one would need to make some case for externalities from subsidising trade. Lanyi gives two examples of potential externalities with relatively fixed rates. First, that the consumer will have a wider range of choice of products. Second, that there may be increased foreign competition which, in turn, stimulates managerial efficiency as well as technical and product innovations.

Essentially the argument here is that, if there were no significant externalities, the increased social cost of forward cover from increased flexibility might in any case be more than offset by the benefit from an improved allocation of resources.[8]

Exchange Rate Flexibility and the Demand for International Reserves

There are again two issues present: first, the relationship between increased flexibility and the demand for reserves, and second, the effect of any change in the demand for reserves on a country's, and the world's, real welfare.

It is, of course, a truism that in a free float the demand for reserves is zero; hence it goes without saying that there will be a net reduction in the demand for reserves if there is a switch from some intervention to zero intervention. On the face of it, it would also appear intuitively reasonable to contend that there would be a negative relationship between flexibility and the demand for reserves, so the greater the exchange rate flexibility the less will tend to be the demand for reserves. This intuition is probably correct; it may, however, be useful to cite two (admittedly extreme) instances where this intuition would not hold.

The first instance is ascribed to Williamson[9] who constructs a special model designed to demonstrate how, under certain conditions, increased flexibility will increase the need for reserves. The special case is one where there is a perverse Marshall–Lerner condition (J curve) and speculation is totally absent (or it is neutral). Consider a disturbance to the current account (resulting, say, from an increase in foreign demand) and contrast three cases: the pure float, the fixed rate case and the intermediate case. In the conditions assumed (about speculation) the pure float is clearly unstable: the exchange rate will move upwards endlessly. In itself this case is not very interesting nor very realistic. In the fixed rate case the monetary authorities would buy foreign exchange to the extent of an improvement in the current account. In the third case there would be some revaluation but initially this revaluation would improve the current account further; the monetary authorities would then step in and buy a larger volume of reserves, to stabilise the situation. In a sense they would be acting out the part of stabilising private speculation. In the next period, however, the current account would deteriorate – there would be a devaluation which in itself would aggravate the loss of reserves. In this third case, then, with some exchange rate flexibility the instability in reserves is greater than in the fixed rate case, so the monetary authorities would now want to hold a larger stock of international reserves.

A second instance is the case where speculation is now destabilising.[10] A revaluation will lead to an expectation of a further revaluation, inducing a net inflow of capital that will add further to reserves. By contrast, a devaluation will lead to an expectation of a further devaluation, inducing an outflow, which will result in an additional loss of reserves. Greater flexibility upwards and downwards may thus result in greater reserve instability.

Although one has to concede the theoretical possibility that increased flexibility may, for some conditions, increase the need for reserves the more realistic case would be the one where the relationship is a negative one.

Realistically, then, one would expect a reduction in the demand for reserves in the more recent period, all other things being equal. Is there evidence of this?

One way to proceed is to look at trends in reserve use, as an indication of the change in the need for reserves. This is the approach in Williamson[11] and Suss.[12] Suss, for example, compares reserve use calculated in three different ways,[13] for fourteen developed countries, in the years 1968–72 with reserve use in the years March 1973–June 1975. Suss's finding was that for seven of the fourteen countries there was an unambiguous (by all three tests) reduction in reserve use in the floating period, while for three there was an unambiguous increase in reserve use. In the remaining countries the outcomes were ambiguous, depending on the measure used. Thus, there is some empirical support for the view that on balance reserve use would have diminished in the floating period. At the same time, it needs to be noted that a reserve use measure is open to the objection that more unstable conditions might lead to greater reserve use, even though the need for reserves may have declined with increased flexibility.

A potentially more acceptable way of proceeding is to try and estimate an equation that would explain the demand for reserves over a given time period. This has the merit that it would at least allow us to isolate influences on the demand for reserves other than exchange rate flexibility. This is the approach in Heller and Khan.[14] Their equation, using quarterly data, for various groups of countries for the period 1964–72, explains reserve holdings (with some lag) by three variables: the ratio of imports to domestic income,[15] the level of imports and a measure of variability of the balance of payments (reserves). To determine whether floating produced a structural change in the demand for reserves they carry out a number of stability tests. They were able to conclude, on the basis of these tests, that for industrial countries there was a once-and-for-all downward shift in the function late in 1973, suggesting a (lagged) reduction in the demand for reserves following the move to the float.[16] By contrast, they found that for non-oil developing countries there was an apparent increase in the demand for reserves (possibly associated with the increased uncertainty and the fact that these countries have continued to peg their currencies to some other major currency).

The evidence, then, on balance supports the hypothesis that increased flexibility has tended to reduce the demand for reserves.

Having concluded that increased flexibility probably reduces the demand for reserves we now need to ask how any reduction in the demand for reserves affects a country's, and the world's, real welfare. We focus here only on foreign exchange. Consider an individual country holding an excess supply of foreign exchange. This can now be invested long-term so that the difference between the short- and long-term interest rates on these holdings represents the gain to the country. Some very rough calculation may, in fact, be made of these potential gains. For example, if we assume, as an extreme case, that an additional three percentage points were earned by all foreign exchange in 1975, the gain as a percentage of GNP turns out to be very small indeed – of the order of 0.18 per cent for Germany, 0.08 per cent for Japan and 0.02 per cent for Italy.

Are these gains at the expense of the USA and the UK? The issues are complex. For example, if, at one extreme, these countries enjoy no seignorage from the reserve currency they might not be worse off after liquidation of some at least of these reserve assets.[17] If, however, there is some seignorage accruing then these countries will be worse off'.

Exchange Rate Flexibility and Vicious Circles

The argument is frequently advanced that, in a flexible rate world, certain disturbances to an economy's balance of payments may, under some conditions, expose that country to a vicious (virtuous) circle of devaluation–inflation (revaluation–deflation).[18]

To evaluate the argument consider the case of a permanent reduction in the demand for a country's exports and suppose that a 10 per cent change in the real exchange rate is required to restore equilibrium to the current account. Suppose, also, that there is no money illusion (wages adjust fully to changes in prices) and that the interest rate is fixed (the monetary authorities follow an accommodating policy). To illustrate what happens in this case we make the following assumptions. First, the overall price level is composed of domestic prices and foreign prices (now represented by the exchange rate), with domestic prices carrying a weight of 80 per cent and foreign prices a weight of 20 per cent.[19] Second, wages adjust fully with a one period lag to the overall price level. Third, domestic prices adjust instantaneously to changes in wages. Fourth, as noted above, the exchange rate must adjust so as to bring about a real change of 10 per cent. These four assumptions can be represented, respectively, by the following equations:

$$\Delta P = 0.8\Delta Pd + 0.2\Delta E \qquad (25.1)$$

$$\Delta W = \Delta P_{-1} \qquad (25.2)$$

$$\Delta Pd = \Delta W \qquad (25.3)$$

$$\Delta E = \Delta Pd \qquad (25.4)$$

where $\Delta E - \Delta Pd$ is the real exchange rate.

To be able to focus on the balance of payments adjustment mechanism as prices and wages adjust we also abstract from any transitional movement in output. The adjustment sequence is shown in Table 25.1. At the start of period 0 (say a quarter) there is a 10 per cent devaluation which, in turn, leads to a 2 per cent increase in the overall price level (Equation 25.1). During this period, before there is any adjustment in wages, the real exchange rate will have improved by 10 per cent. At the start of period 1 wages and domestic prices will adjust upwards by 2 per cent (Equations 25.2 and 25.3), but since this reduces the real exchange rate by some 2 per cent there will be a further devaluation of 2 per cent to restore the 10 per cent change in the real exchange rate (Equation 25.4). The combination of the devaluation and the increase in domestic prices will raise the overall price level in period 1 by a further 2 per cent. At the start of period 2

Table 25.1 Adjustment under flexible exchange rates to a permanent reduction in real foreign demand for a country's exports[a]

Period (quarters)	*Change in overall prices*	*Change in wages and domestic prices*	*Change in real exchange rate*	*Change in exchange rate*
0	+2%	—	+10%	+10%
1	+2%	+2%	0	+ 2%
2	+2%	+2%	0	+ 2%
3	+2%	+2%	0	+ 2%

[a]See equations in text.

wages and domestic prices will rise by another 2 per cent and there will be a further devaluation of 2 per cent, altogether raising the overall price level by still another 2 per cent. It is obvious that this sequence will be sustained, with prices rising, in this example, by 2 per cent in each quarter. Over the whole of this first year the overall price level will have risen by 8 per cent while domestic prices and wages will have risen by 6 per cent, so real wages will have fallen by 2 per cent (the weight of foreign prices multiplied by the 10 per cent devaluation). This fall of 2 per cent will be sustained (on a once-over basis) indefinitely. In all subsequent periods wages and domestic prices will rise at the same rate (8 per cent) as the exchange rate.

This example suggests the following conclusions. For the conditions assumed, so long as wages adjust with some lag the real wage rate will fall permanently. However, the rate of inflation and monetary growth will be permanently higher (in our example by 8 per cent). At the same time, there will be an annual rate of devaluation (in our example of 8 per cent). The analysis also suggests that the annual rate of inflation required to secure a given reduction in real wages and a permanent change in the real exchange rate will depend on the speed of adjustment in the labour market. The speedier the adjustment the higher will have to be the rate of inflation. It is worth noting, too, that although the new rate of inflation and the rate of devaluation are both stable, the price level and the exchange rate will rise indefinitely and, in this sense, there is a vicious circle involved. The economy, in other words, is in permanent disequilibrium.

An important question which we now need to ask is whether this vicious circle, which we have identified for flexible rates, could be avoided with fixed rates. The issues are difficult because we need to define the conditions under which adjustment will take place with fixed rates. Suppose, for example, that we imposed the same two conditions (zero money illusion and a fixed interest rate) on the fixed rate case. Assume, too, realistically, that the foreign exchange market is restored to equilibrium in the long run. What will be the adjustment in this case to a permanent drop in real foreign demand?

Adapting the complete model in Chapter 11 it can be shown (see Annex) that the final outcome requires a drop in output and, in addition, a rise in the real exchange rate (with domestic prices falling relative to foreign prices). With flexible exchange rates, then, we have a disequilibrium situation and a permanently higher rate of inflation, while, with fixed rates, we have a permanently higher unemployment rate.

If, however, higher unemployment is assumed to be tolerated with fixed rates, presumably it would also be tolerated with flexible rates. In this case, the monetary authorities need not follow an accommodating policy with flexible rates. They would then allow the interest rate and unemployment to rise, and in this way avoid the continuing rise in prices. If a country wished to avoid a vicious circle and if the real wage rate were fixed, it would appear that it might have to assume some unemployment, whatever the exchange rate regime. In this case, in the situation being considered, there might be little advantage in using the exchange rate as a mechanism of adjustment.

Does the evidence support the argument that there is now little if any money illusion and hence that a devaluation will in the long run be fully offset by a rise in domestic prices? A recent survey of the evidence by the OPTICA group arrived at this important conclusion:

> The OPTICA group has found its review of selected empirical evidence on the origins and consequences of exchange-rate changes to confirm the view that a country's exchange rate is, in the European economies in the late 1970s, very largely a nominal phenomenon. . . . While the impact on real variables is not completely negligible over short periods – and may be enlarged by government action on prices and incomes – the usefulness of exchange-rate changes in effecting macroeconomic adjustments seems more limited than is generally believed. Particularly as regards external adjustment, the time period between the initial change in the current account in the 'wrong' direction (the J-curve effect) and the ultimate phase when domestic costs and prices have fully embodied the exchange-rate change, appears to have shortened so much as to make such changes undesirable.[20]

Annex

The model in Chapter 11 can easily be adapted to accommodate this case. The first step is to set $\Delta r = 0$. Foreign exchange marke equilibrium also requires now that the current account be restored to balance. Equations (11.7), (11.10), (11.14) and (11.19) can be amended to take account of these adjustments. We then have four equations which determine *Yr, Pd, Mo, Gr*. Fiscal policy is now endogenous because if the current account is to be restored to equilibrium fiscal policy must be manipulated to ensure this.

The solutions for *Yr, Pd* and *Gr* are, respectively:

$$\Delta Yr = \frac{\alpha_{20}\alpha_{15}(1-\alpha_{14})}{ML+\alpha_9\alpha_{15}(1-\alpha_{14})}\Delta Yf$$

$$\Delta Pd = \frac{\alpha_{20}}{ML+\alpha_9\alpha_{15}(1-\alpha_{14})}\Delta Yf$$

$$\Delta Gr = \frac{\alpha_{20}\alpha_{15}(1-\alpha_{14})(1-\alpha_1)}{ML+\alpha_9\alpha_{15}(1-\alpha_{14})}\Delta Yf$$

This demonstrates that a fall in foreign output, given the interest rate and the constraint that the current account must be in balance, requires a fall in output and prices and, also, a deflationary fiscal policy. With output and prices falling, it is easy to see, too, that to maintain the same interest rate the volume of money will need to fall.

It is easy to show that these solutions will equilibrate all four markets. The goods market is in equilibrium because the drop in government expenditure combined with the drop in foreign output will only be partially offset by the increase in the real exchange rate. The money market is in equilibrium because the fall in the volume of money will accommodate the fall in output and prices. The current account is in equilibrium because the fall in foreign output will now be exactly offset by the combined effects of the drop in output and the improvement in the real exchange rate. Finally, the drop in output is consistent with equilibrium in the labour market because while the real wage rate to suppliers of labour will be fixed, the real wage rate to producers will now have risen.

Notes for Chapter 25

1 See A. Lanyi (1969), p. 5; R. Z. Aliber (1976).

2 The mean of the bid–ask spread might be taken as (roughly) the mean expected rate, so the greater the uncertainty the larger will need to be the margin of profitability. See also Chapter 19.

3 See A. D. Crockett and M. Goldstein (1976). R. Z. Aliber (1976) shows how exchange risk, measured by the mean forecast error between the forward rate and the spot rate at maturity and by the standard deviations of those forecast errors, increased by a factor of five to ten.

4 A. D. Crockett and M. Goldstein (1976).
5 M. Friedman (1953).
6 One way in which this is tested is to introduce a measure of exchange uncertainty in an equation explaining import and export volume. This measure has not been significant. See J. R. Artus and J. H. Young (1979).
7 A. Lanyi (1969), p. 8.
8 The literature has tended to pay far more attention to the effects of exchange rate flexibility on trade than to the effects of flexibility on capital flows. The issues here almost exactly parallel those for trade and will not be pursued. Again, one needs to examine, first, the effects of flexibility on portfolio and direct investment and, second, the implications of these effects for welfare. For reasons which parallel those for trade the answers to both of these questions remain highly contentious. See A. Lanyi (1969) and L. Yeager (1976), Chapter 13.
9 J. Williamson (1976). See also S. W. Black (1976). Williamson provides a mathematical demonstration of the argument.
10 G. Haberler (1977).
11 J. Williamson (1976).
12 E. C. Suss (1976).
13 The three calculations are: (1) the average of the absolute values of the monthly percentage changes in a country's reserves, corrected for the change in world reserves; (2) the standard deviation of the percentage changes in a country's monthly reserves corrected for the change in world reserves about the mean value; (3) the ratio of the average change in reserves to the average basic balance.
14 H. R. Heller and M. S. Khan (1978).
15 As they point out, the relationship between the import ratio and the demand for reserves is ambiguous. For example, if the ratio represents the marginal propensity to import then the more open the economy the less the need for reserves because adjustment by deflation will be less costly. On the other hand, the higher the ratio the more 'open' the economy and so the greater the need for reserves. As it happens they find a negative sign, suggesting that the first influence might be dominant.
16 One ambiguous aspect of the study is that a reduction in the demand for reserves would show up in a reduction in reserve use, so the independent variable representing reserve variability would presumably already have captured some, although (as we have seen) not all, of the change in the demand for reserves.
17 In effect the larger commitments overseas would be offset by the diminished costs of intermediation.
18 See J. Artus and A. D. Crockett (1978); T. D. Willett (1977). See also J. Bilson (1979a); G. Basevi and P. De Grauwe (1977).
19 To simplify we also assume that imports are composed of final goods only, not inputs.
20 As summarised in N. Thygesen (1978). To take a concrete example from the UK: in the London Business School model there is full offset after some five to six years. After two years some 60 per cent of a devaluation shows up in wages and domestic prices.

Chapter 26

Costs and Benefits of a Managed Float

Introduction

In this chapter we deal with the case for and against short-term central bank intervention in the foreign exchange market. We proceed in two steps. First, in the wake of our findings to this point we ask what light they throw on the case for intervention. Second, we examine, briefly, the various rules for intervention that have been proposed to date.

The Theoretical Case for Short-term Intervention

One of the more difficult and important policy issues today is to identify the conditions under which short-term intervention by the monetary authorities will be in the economic interest of the community. In other words, we would like to know whether a theoretical case can be made for some management of the exchange rate. The analysis in the previous chapters allows us to identify a number of potential benefits flowing from market intervention.

First, intervention may serve under certain conditions to reduce the volatility of output. There are two ways in which this might be achieved. Macro-policy may be rendered more effective by intervention or, again, intervention may serve to insulate an economy more effectively from random disturbances. To take two specific examples: we showed that fiscal policy might be more effective, if capital mobility is high, with fixed than with flexible exchange rates. We also showed that for certain conditions (for example, in the face of real domestic shocks combined with low capital mobility, domestic demand for money shocks or capital flows shocks), intervention may insulate the economy more effectively than flexible exchange rates.

Second, intervention may, in certain circumstances, also serve to reduce the level of prices (for instance, in the face of a variety of asymmetries or of a 'vicious circle' situation) and perhaps, too, the volatility in the price level.

Third, if private markets are less efficient than central banks, in the sense that they do not exploit in the same degree all the available information about the fundamental determinants of exchange rates, intervention may reduce the ultimate volatility in exchange rates. As we have seen, however (see Chapters 19 and 21), the evidence on this is ambiguous; in other words, we are not sure how efficient the foreign exchange market really is.

On the other hand, the cost of intervention is the cost of holding some reserves (or from borrowing) in order to implement the intervention policy. If these costs are below the net potential benefits identified above, some intervention is theoretically in the interest of the community.

Unfortunately, the moment one ventures beyond an academic exercise in cost–benefit analysis some very serious problems begin to surface. First of all, the potential benefits identified may not be additive and may conflict with one another. Second, our review of the potential benefits provides no 'rule of thumb' or guidance as to how these potential benefits might be exploited in reality.

Consider, first, the possibility of potential conflict in the benefits that flow from intervention. One instance will be given of how a conflict may emerge in intervention policy between the desire to reduce fluctuations in output and the desire to reduce exchange rate volatility by drawing on information not fully exploited by the private sector.

Consider the case again of an increase in real foreign demand, with 'neutral' exchange rate expectations. We have seen that associated revaluations of the currency will normally serve to insulate the domestic economy from the foreign disturbance. If, however, there are lags in the adjustment of the trade balance to a change in the exchange rate and if speculation is insufficiently stabilising the exchange rate will 'overshoot', revaluing 'excessively', initially, and then reversing itself in subsequent periods. In this event, intervention may serve to dampen the fluctuation in the exchange rate but at the cost of some additional fluctuation in output. For example, if the monetary authorities sold foreign currency to reduce the initial revaluation and subsequently bought the foreign currency (at some profit to themselves) the current account would improve initially but subsequently deteriorate and this would entail some initial increase in output that would be reversed in later periods.

Even bearing in mind these qualifications, there would probably still be a residual case for intervention. It is, however, one thing to establish a theoretical case for intervention and quite another to demonstrate that intervention in practice could or would be beneficial. In the real world the exchange rate is exposed to a great variety of disturbances, some of which might best be countered by allowing the exchange rate to move freely while others would best be countered by intervention.[1] But, in practice, it may be difficult to associate exchange rate movements with particular disturbances. In other words, in a world of very imperfect information the scope for successful intervention would appear to be more modest. It is in this context that one should evaluate rules for intervention. These rules might be viewed as 'second-best' methods of securing the potential benefits from intervention.

Rules for Intervention

Since the advent of managed floats there have been several attempts to establish guidelines or rules for intervention.[2] These guidelines fall into two classes. First, there are those that mandate some form of 'leaning against the wind'. Second, there are those that propose 'exchange rate targets' with intervention guided by these targets.

In its simplest form 'a leaning against the wind' rule would require monetary authorities to intervene so as to partially resist market forces and stabilise the exchange rate.[3] The underlying rationale provided for the rule is that private operators cannot be relied on to achieve this result. Even if this were true, we have seen that there will be circumstances where such a rule might run counter to some other desired objective of policy (for instance, stabilising output).

This rule is embodied in the first two of the 1974 IMF Guidelines for Countries Authorised to Adopt Floating Rates[4] (since superseded by the Surveillance Document).[5] These were:

(1) A member with a floating exchange rate should intervene on the foreign exchange market as necessary to prevent or moderate sharp and disruptive fluctuations from day to day and from week to week in the exchange value of its currency.
(2) Subject to (3)(b), a member with a floating rate may act, through intervention or otherwise, to moderate movements in the exchange value of its currency from month to month and quarter to quarter, and is encouraged to do so, if necessary, where factors recognised to be temporary are at work. Subject to (1) and (3)(a), the member should not normally act aggressively with respect to the exchange value of its currency (i.e. should not so act as to depress that value when it is falling, or to enhance that value when it is rising).

One difficulty with this rule, in its simplest form, is that it is open to abuse. For example, countries might manage the exchange rate to their advantage by an asymmetrical intervention policy or, again, might resist market forces too vigorously. To safeguard against these possibilities Mikesell and Goldstein proposed a number of additional guidelines.[6] These include a rule that net reserve changes in a given direction should not persist for more than three consecutive months (except when reserve levels were believed to be excessive or deficient) and another rule that would require monetary authorities to restore their original reserve position within a reasonable period of time. Tosini, however, criticises these supplementary guidelines on several grounds:[7] she feels that they would be hard to implement, that any reserve reconstitution provision might provoke one-way speculation, discourage intervention and so aggravate exchange rate movement, and that they might encourage monetary authorities to resort to other means of manipulating exchange rates (for instance, by capital controls which, by limiting the movement of capital, may again lead to increased exchange rate instability).

The target approach to intervention involves two steps: first, the determination of the 'target' exchange rate and second, the rules for intervention in relation to the target. Ethier and Bloomfield[8] have advanced a number of proposals that fall within this approach.[9] In their latest[10] study they propose three rules to guide intervention. These are:

(a) No country would be permitted to sell its own currency at a price below the floor of its reference rate band or to buy its own currency at a price above the ceiling of its reference rate band.
(b) The structure of reference rates, expressed in SDRs, would be periodically revised by the IMF through a multilateral consultation with the participants which would utilize all available information and at which the participants would communicate their intentions for all relevant policy measures.
(c) No country would be permitted deliberately to deviate from its stated targets, for a stipulated collection of policy measures other than exchange market intervention, in a direction that would tend to depreciate its currency when the exchange rate was below the floor of its reference rate band, or that would tend to appreciate its currency when the exchange rate was above the ceiling of its reference rate band.

To begin with, countries would have a target exchange rate (the reference rate) determined as in (b)[11] and a band (which may be zero) around that target. Within the band they may or may not intervene as they wish. Outside the band, however, they may intervene if they choose but in only one direction. For example, outside the upper point of the band, monetary authorities can either intervene to resist any further upward movement by market forces or allow market forces to push the exchange rate further upwards. They may not, however, intervene to resist any downward movement (towards the reference rate) or to push the rate further upward by buying their own currency (selling foreign exchange). Again, outside the lower point they may allow market forces to push the exchange rate further in a downward direction, or resist the downward movement, but they may not intervene to resist any upward movement towards the reference rate or to push the rate further downward by selling their own currency (buying foreign exchange).

The difference between these proposals and the arrangements under the Bretton Woods System can be stated quite simply. In the Bretton Woods System intervention at the upper and lower points was mandatory. Within the band, however, the monetary authorities had some freedom of choice. In the Ethier–Bloomfield proposals they may allow a free float, so the rate can move outside the band, but they may also, if they choose, resist any movement outside the band. Moreover, the target exchange rate would, of course, be changed much more frequently than in the Bretton Woods System.

Several advantages are claimed for these proposals. First, they allow a choice between a free float and some intervention to moderate movements in exchange rates (as in the 'leaning against the wind' rule). Second, rule (a) is designed to prohibit aggressive exchange rate behaviour[12] and destabilising official intervention.[13] Third, rule (c)[14] is designed to prohibit a resort to other means of influencing exchange rate behaviour in an aggressive fashion. Fourth, by providing a reference point (the exchange rate target) the proposals may help to stabilise exchange rate speculation. Fifth, exchange rate targets may be altered without associated disruptive capital movements, since the actual exchange rate, which is likely to differ from the reference rate, need not itself be affected.

These ideas have considerable merit. However, they might not be easy to implement. Currently (mid-1979) while the IMF has its own refined calculations of appropriate (longer-run) exchange rates,[15] these calculations are not publicly available, nor, if they were, would they be necessarily accepted, given the difficulties associated with the exercise. Moreover, the idea that aggressive behaviour by means other than intervention is effectively prohibited by rule (c) is altogether too optimistic. There is, for example, nothing in rule (c) to prohibit countries from officially announcing policy targets which in themselves would constitute aggressive behaviour.

One other distinctive proposal (the Optica Plan)[16] that also falls within this second class of rules may be briefly mentioned. The target exchange rate would be based on a purchasing power parity rule[17] (calculated from wholesale prices). High inflation-depreciating countries would have to intervene at the lower end of a band to stop any further depreciation but they would not be allowed to intervene to stop an appreciation above the upper end of the band, if market forces pushed the exchange rate in that direction. By contrast, low inflation-appreciating countries would have to intervene at the upper end to stop any further appreciation but again they could not intervene to stop a depreciation below the lower end if market forces pushed the rate in that direction. This asymmetrical rule was intended to avert the risks of vicious or virtuous circles in exchange rate and price behaviour.[18]

Notes for Chapter 26

1 For a more general discussion of this question see Chapter 32.
2 R. F. Mikesell and H. N. Goldstein (1975); IMF (1974b) (also reproduced in R. F. Mikesell and H. N. Goldstein, 1975); W. Ethier and A. I. Bloomfield (1975); P. A. Tosini (1977); J. Williamson (1975); W. Ethier and A. I. Bloomfield (1978); Commission of the European Communities (1977), Chapter 2; N. Thygesen (1978).
3 This represents to a iarge extent the actual practice of many industrial countries. For econometric substantiation of this see J. R. Artus (1976); P. J. Quirk (1977).
4 See IMF Committee of Twenty (1974a), pp. 34–7.
5 See Chapter 10.
6 R. F. Mikesell and H. N. Goldstein (1975), p. 5.
7 P. A. Tosini (1977), pp. 14–16. See also the discussion of the reserve indicator proposal in Chapter 10.
8 See also the discussion of IMF surveillance in Chapter 10.
9 See also the 'Guidelines for Countries Authorized to Adopt Floating Rates', IMF (1974b), which also adopt something like a target approach.
10 W. Ethier and A. I. Bloomfield (1978), pp. 229–30.
11 For a discussion of how this might be arrived at see J. R. Artus (1978).
12 In fact countries have not really attempted to secure a competitive advantage because in recent years they have been particularly concerned about the inflationary implications of a devaluation.
13 In theory a band does allow some scope for exchange rate 'manipulation' but this can be counteracted by a change in the reference rate.
14 Rule (c) was an addition introduced in their later contribution in 1978.
15 See J. R. Artus (1978).
16 See Commission of the European Communities (1977); see also N. Thygesen (1978).
17 See the discussion of the limitations of PPP in Chapter 20.
18 For some theoretical analysis of this see G. Basevi and P. De Grauwe (1977).

Chapter 27

Monetary Unions – Analysis and Application to the EEC

Introduction

Thus far we have been concerned with the benefits and costs of fixed and flexible exchange rates from the standpoint either of a single country or of the world as a whole. We now turn our attention to the question of the benefits and costs associated with the formation of a monetary union.[1] As we will see, the theory of monetary unions is a special case of the kind of analysis we have already undertaken in previous chapters. We want, now, to see if we can decide what kinds of considerations are important in determining which countries, if any, should join together in a monetary union.

From the outset it is important to make a distinction between two types of monetary unions, corresponding, in effect, to stages on the way to unification. The first of these is the weak union; the second is the strong union.

In a weak union, each member maintains its independent currency, but exchange rates are fixed between member countries while, at the same time, free to move vis-à-vis the rest of the world. Also, each participant is assumed to retain some restrictions on the movement of capital within the union. Again, while there may be some pooling of members' international reserves, each participant retains an independent balance of payments. Finally, short-term independent monetary and fiscal policies continue to be possible.

By contrast, a strong union is assumed to have a common currency circulating and a common central bank. Each member now no longer has an independent balance of payments vis-à-vis other members of the union. At the same time, capital markets are unified and independent monetary policy becomes impossible. Some independent fiscal policy, however, continues to be feasible. In effect, for most practical purposes, the member countries may now be viewed as regions or states within one national entity.

In evaluating the benefits of monetary unification a useful distinction to make is between the political–social benefits and the economic benefits. The political benefits come from the lessening of national divisions or international tensions and the strengthening of countervailing power vis-à-vis other economic blocs. The social benefits would flow from greater mobility across the frontiers resulting in stronger cultural links.

There are three principal economic benefits claimed for a union.[2] Assume, to begin, that we have a strong union, as we have defined it. The first economic benefit flows from the fact that money becomes more efficient in its function as a medium of exchange. The common currency now commands a wider range of goods and this eliminates the costs of conversion, of portfolio revaluations and, also, of forward cover.[3] This benefit is clearly related to the volume of intra-trade (which, of course, is itself likely to increase with monetary integration) so the more open the economies, the larger will be the gain from this source. A related potential benefit is that there may be some additional economies of scale in banking within the union.

The second economic benefit stems from the reduced need for reserves. For a strong union this benefit derives from three factors: the elimination of intra-union trade (which reduces the openness of the large unit compared to its individual parts), compensating disturbances to the balance of payments of member countries vis-à-vis the rest of the world, and the credit arrangements within the union. These benefits will be larger the more open the economy[4] and also the greater the product differentiation within the union (because there is more likely to be a tendency to offset demand shocks).

A further related benefit flows from the possibility that the union's common currency might serve as a reserve currency to the rest of the world. In this case the union would effectively be 'borrowing' on a permanent basis from the rest of the world, and using the funds to invest long term or to absorb resources from the rest of the world.[5]

A third economic gain may come about from the effects of the removal of speculation, exchange rate uncertainty and capital restrictions on intra-union trade, capital flows, domestic production and investment.[6]

Whatever their actual magnitude the three economic gains identified would be significantly lessened for the weak union. There would now continue to be costs of conversion (although these would be less than without the union), reserves for intra-trade would still be needed, while some exchange rate uncertainty would remain.

While it is relatively easy to define the potential benefits it is much more difficult to determine what the potential costs are. We identify, in our analysis, three distinct kinds of potential costs of joining a monetary union. First, there are the potential relative costs of adjustment under fixed rates to longer-term divergences between participating countries. Second, there are the potential relative costs of adjustment under fixed rates to short-term random disturbances. Third, there are the possible costs associated with the renunciation of independent monetary policies for demand management. Each of these will now be dealt with in more detail.

Potential Costs of Adjustment to Longer-term Divergences

Two cases are worth distinguishing here. The first is the case where there are different propensities to inflate in the participating countries. The second is the case where there are structural shifts in demand (or in capital flows) between member countries.

Differences in Propensities to Inflate

Suppose, first, that each country in the potential union had its own Phillips curve. Then, in the absence of a union, each country would choose its own optimal combination of inflation and unemployment, and any emerging differences in the rate of inflation would be offset by exchange rate changes.[7] Suppose, now, a weak monetary union were formed and a common rate of inflation had to be established. What costs would be imposed on participants? Each country would be forced away from its preferred trade-off position. The associated costs would be a function of the differences in preferred positions and the extent to which the Phillips curves were differently situated (for example, because of differences in trade union aggressiveness or differences in structural unemployment).[8] The more homogeneous the preferences and the more alike the Phillips curves the smaller would be the costs.

It could be contended, however, that these costs would fall off as the monetary union consolidated; preferences may converge and initial differences in the positions of the Phillips curves may gradually be eliminated. For example, differences in trade union aggressiveness may gradually disappear while differences in structural unemployment may be alleviated by special regional policies implemented after the union is formed. Also, these costs might be alleviated the more mobile labour is within the union, with labour moving out of the relatively high unemployment regions and into the relatively low unemployment regions. But even this might not help in some conditions. Suppose that in one country, in order to hold down the rate of inflation to the union level (for instance, to offset relative trade union aggressiveness) a higher rate of unemployment is required. If the unemployed left, pressures will surface again and a still higher rate of unemployment may be required, generating a vicious circle.

If there is no long-run money illusion and the Phillips curve is vertical, the costs of a monetary union are reduced.[9] It would be wrong, however, to conclude that in this case the costs disappear altogether. Several kinds of costs are possible. First, there may be transitional costs. The relatively high inflation country will have to lower its inflation rate and this would almost certainly result in some transitional unemployment. A key question here is the duration of the adjustment process. If adjustment to a lower point on the vertical Phillips curve takes a very long time (for example, many years), the costs for all practical purposes could then be not too dissimilar to the case where there is a long-run trade-off. Second, there may be (transitional) social costs. A relatively high inflation may be the means by which social frictions, industrial unrest and class warfare are minimised.

Third, there may be 'frictional administrative' costs in implementing a fixed rate regime of this kind. Suppose all participating countries agreed on a common rate of inflation, say, for traded goods. This then translates into a common rate of increase in unit labour costs for traded goods. The next step is to forecast long-run rates of growth of productivity in the traded and non-traded goods sectors. Given the required growth in unit labour costs in traded goods, this gives the required growth of wages in the two sectors (assumed to be the same) and, also, the implicit rate of inflation in the non-traded goods sector and in the economy as a whole. Finally, it is necessary to ensure that growth in the volume of money will be consistent with these outcomes. This requires, additionally, an estimate of the long-run growth of output and the likely trends in velocity. Given these and the estimate of the overall rate of inflation, the long-run rate of growth in the volume of money for each country can be derived directly.

Clearly each of these steps is subject to error. For example, estimates of productivity or velocity may be inaccurate, possibly throwing out the inflationary outcome. Moreover, an 'incomes policy' (the appropriate growth of wages) is clearly implied but this may be difficult to secure. There will also almost certainly be costs associated with the correction of errors.

In the case of a strong union the common central bank will determine the appropriate long-run rate of growth of money for the union as a whole on the basis of the union's common rate of inflation, its long-run real growth rate and its anticipated percentage change in velocity. What would happen if there were significant differences within the union in the long run in the percentage increases in velocity or in real output growth? Adjustment here would take the form of automatic flows of capital from regions with relatively high percentage increases in velocity (relatively low rates of growth of output) towards regions with relatively low percentage increases in velocity (relatively high rates of growth of output) (that is, from regions with relative excess supply to regions with excess demand for money). Relative monetary growth would, in other words, automatically adjust.

A potentially more serious source of friction is the case where there are significant differences in the rate of growth of labour productivity and, at the same time, in the wake of the monetary union, equivalent rates of growth of nominal wages. It follows that rates of growth in unit labour costs will tend to rise faster in the low productivity countries. With their competitive positions progressively declining there may be growing unemployment in these regions. There is a possibility here of generating, in the low productivity region, a vicious spiral of growing unemployment, persistent capital outflows and progressively lower scale production. It is not satisfactory to argue that unemployment would be eased by migration to the high productivity regions: population decline and stagnation in some of the participating nations would be viewed with very serious concern.

Structural Demand Shifts

Suppose now, to take a different case, demand switches from one potential union member to another. We need to ask again what form adjustment would take with and without the union.

In the absence of a union we assume there would have been some adjustment in the exchange rate. If there is some money illusion the exchange rate adjustment would have corrected the balance of payments disequilibrium and, in addition (in large part), any potential unemployment/inflation in the respective countries.[10] If, however, there is no money illusion the analysis is much more complicated. The outcome, as we have seen,[11] depends essentially, in this case, on whether interest rates are assumed unchanged and on the speed of adjustment in labour markets. If interest rates are fixed and if labour markets adjust quickly, the country that experiences the drop in demand may have to take a significantly higher rate of inflation to correct the imbalance.

An important consideration here is that the likelihood of money illusion may well depend on how open the economies are vis-à-vis one another. If trade within the potential union is very large, then an exchange rate change will have a significant initial price effect and is, therefore, more likely to trigger a wage adjustment. Again, the more open the economy the greater the case for a monetary union, since now the effectiveness of the exchange rate as an instrument of policy is diminished.

Now consider the adjustment mechanism in the face of a demand switch, within a weak union. If the country affected adversely allows some deflation, the degree of unemployment required will depend on how open the economy is. The more open the economy the larger the balance of payments adjustment for any given reduction in output, so the costs of a monetary union are again reduced the more open the economy.

Labour mobility, too, may facilitate the adjustment. Mundell,[12] for example, argued that the emerging unemployment as well as the deficit could be corrected by migration to the economy experiencing the excess demand. However, many subsequent commentators pointed out that labour is not likely to be mobile to this degree across frontiers and that, in any event, there are substantial costs associated with migration, not the least being the social and psychological costs of settling into a different cultural environment.[13]

Official capital transfers could also ease the adjustment process; private capital, on the other hand, may ease or aggravate the situation. The drop in demand, for example, may provoke outflows of capital.

If an incomes policy were successful in changing relative prices the adjustment would again be facilitated. With prices moving upwards over time all that would be needed would be that the rate of price change should slow down on a once-over basis in the economy experiencing the drop in demand.

In a weak union the balance of payments positions need to be corrected in the longer run; in the strong union the balance of payments is not a concern. Thus, regional policies to expand domestic employment are more plausible for a strong than for a weak union.

The important conclusion that emerges here is that, in the face of a structural change of the kind we are examining, independence does allow greater freedom of choice from a policy menu in confronting the situation and, in this sense, is to be preferred.

Random Disturbances, Costs of Adjustment and the Union

It is useful to begin by distinguishing micro- from macro-disturbances. Micro-disturbances affect individual commodity groups while macro-disturbances affect the demand for all goods. Kenen[14] has argued that the more diversified the economy, the more insulated it will tend to be from micro-shocks; it follows that the need for exchange rate flexibility, as a protection against such shocks, will be diminished. Hence, the case for a union is strengthened the more diversified internally the economies are.[15]

Macro-random disturbances are likely to be of greater significance. In order to evaluate this case we need to assume that there are differences among the potential union members in the extent of instability originating domestically. We need to ask how the participating countries would be affected by forming a union of the weak or strong variety. With this aim we assume, for simplicity, a two-country world where, initially, the countries are of roughly equal size, and then contrast three distinct cases. First, the case where the two countries are independent and the exchange rate is flexible (Regime 1). Second, the case where the two countries have now formed a weak monetary union. Here, capital mobility is higher than in the previous case (with some relaxation of exchange controls) but the two countries continue to enjoy some short-term monetary independence and are able to sterilise the balance of payments effects on domestic liquidity (Regime 2). Third, the case where the two countries have formed a strong union, share a common currency and there is perfect capital mobility (Regime 3).

The next step is to identify the types of disturbances that would be relevant to our analysis. We identify three types of disturbances: a monetary disturbance (including random money supply or money demand shocks), a real disturbance (expenditure changes), and a demand switch (from one country to the other).[16] We assume that, initially, the shocks retain the same character[17] in all three regimes. The key question we need to answer for each of the regimes is: To what degree does the regime allow a country independence from disturbances? The country will opt for that regime that best shelters it from the disturbances originating within the potential union.

The underlying model is again the short-term one, which is now extended to a two-country world.[18] The two countries are labelled A and B and in what follows we assume that A's economy is the more unstable one.

Table 27.1 summarises the preferences that A and B would have for the three regimes for different disturbances and under different assumed conditions.

We will now attempt a verbal explanation of these results. To aid in understanding these we need to bear in mind that we are assuming that the two countries, of equal size, share common structural relationships (for example, propensities to spend, interest sensitivity of the demand for money). For any given disturbance, the change in world output will be the same, whatever the regime. The regime, however, determines how the change in world output is distributed between the two economies. For monetary and real disturbances (originating in A, the unstable economy) A will prefer the regime that allows it to transmit the largest share of its own instability to B, while B will prefer the regime that gives it the most independence from A's instability.

Consider, first, the case where there is monetary expansion in A (or, equivalently, a fall in the demand for money) and suppose capital mobility were zero in Regime 1, which means that the current account

Table 27.1 A's and B's preferences for three regimes for different disturbances

	Monetary disturbance[a]		*Real disturbance*[a]		*Demand switch*
	Low capital mobility	*High capital mobility*	*Low capital mobility*[b]	*High capital mobility*[b]	
A's preferences	3>2>1	3>2>1	2>3 1 2>1>3	1>2>3 1>2>3	1> 2 3
B's preferences	1>2>3	2>3 (1?)	1 3 >2 1>2 (3?)	3>2>1 2>1 (3?)	1> 2 3

[a]Originating in A (assumed to be the more unstable economy).
Regime 1 is the independent one. Regime 2 is the weak union. Regime 3 is the strong union.
Low/high capital mobility refers to Regime 1.
[b]The upper (lower) result is the case where output in B increases (falls) in the strong union from A's expansion.

must be restored to balance. The monetary expansion will open up a potential current account deficit in A and a potential current account surplus in B, which will need to be eliminated by a devaluation of A's currency. B's economy, in this case, is completely sheltered from A's disturbance, the increase in demand for her goods being exactly offset by the revaluation of her currency.

In Regime 2, with assumed sterilisation, monetary expansion will increase output in A, increase the demand for B's goods and so lift output, as well, in B. With perfect capital mobility (Regime 3) there will now be money flows from A into B until interest rates are equalised in the two countries. Output in B will expand beyond the level in Regime 2 while output in A will fall below the level in Regime 2. Indeed, in this case, given the underlying assumptions, the increase in output will be shared equally between A and B.

With very low capital mobility, B's economy is most sheltered from A's monetary disturbance in Regime 1 (independence) and least sheltered in Regime 3. So B's preferences will be in that order (see Table 27.1). A, on the other hand, will have reverse preferences, opting for that regime (3) which allows it to export the largest share of its own instability.

With some capital mobility in Regime 1 the outcomes are a little more complicated. Monetary expansion in A (or a reduction in the demand for money) will now lower A's interest rates and a capital outflow will ensue. To secure equilibrium to the overall balance of payments A's current account must actually improve to offset the capital account deficit. The counterpart of A's current account surplus is B's deficit, which implies that net demand has fallen in B, so B's output actually falls. Monetary expansion in A then leads to an increase in A's output but a decrease in B's output. The more mobile the capital the greater will be the increase in A's output and the greater the decrease in B's output.

With the outcomes for Regimes 2 and 3 unchanged A's preferences are again clear-cut. Now, as capital mobility increases, A is even worse off under Regime 1 since its output must correspondingly increase further to offset the drop in output in B. B's preferences are, by contrast, less determinate. While B will unambiguously prefer Regime 2 to Regime 3, its own standing in Regime 3 is uncertain. Of course, it experiences some reduction in output, which, on a priori grounds, cannot be compared with its increase in output under the two other regimes.

Now consider the case of an increase in expenditure in A. If capital mobility for Regime 1 were again zero, A's potential current account deficit would be liquidated by a devaluation of its currency, allowing B's economy to be sheltered from A's disturbance. In Regime 2 the increase in expenditure will lead to some increase in the demand for B's products and so to some sympathetic increase in B's output. In Regime 3 the outcome is more complex. Taking the solution in Regime 2 as the starting point, output in A will have risen by more than output in B. Interest rates, therefore, will be higher in A than in B, and money will flow from B to A. As the volume of money falls in B its output will also fall. B's ultimate position is ambiguous because, on the one hand, the expansion in output in A pushes up its own level of activity but, on the other hand, with the volume of money down and its interest rates being forced up its economic activity will be depressed. In equilibrium the world interest rate in A and B will be higher because the world volume of money will be the same but world output will be higher.

With some capital mobility in Regime 1 the outcomes are again different. An increase in expenditure in A will now, in equilibrium, lead to a current account deficit that will be offset by a capital account surplus. In B the counterpart is a current account surplus, which implies some increase in B's output. So in this case expansion in A will also result in an expansion in B. The more mobile capital is the larger will be A's current account deficit (to offset the larger inflow of capital); hence the bigger B's surplus and the bigger the expansion of output in B. Again, we find that capital mobility reduces the degree of B's independence from A's disturbances.

In determining preferences for real expenditure disturbances, there are two important relevant considerations: the mobility of capital and whether output increases or decreases in B for Regime 3 (see Table 27.1). Suppose, for example, output fell in B in Regime 3. Then with low capital mobility A will experience its biggest increase in output in Regime 3 and its smallest increase in Regime 2. With high capital mobility its own output will fall below the level in Regime 2 (because now there will be a revaluation of A's currency) so its first preference will now be Regime 1. B's preferences will be uncertain under these same conditions. For low capital mobility it will unambiguously prefer Regime 1 to 2 and for high capital mobility it will unambiguously prefer Regime 2 to 1 (because with Regime 1 there will now be an additional stimulus from the devaluation of its own currency). However, with its own output falling in Regime 3 its position vis-à-vis the other regimes is ambiguous.

If output, on balance, were to increase in B in Regime 3, the preferences are unambiguous where capital mobility is high. For example, A will unambiguously rank Regime 1 first (because the associated revaluation of A's currency will force some reduction in its own activity below the level in Regime 2) and Regime 3 last, because now in Regime 3, with additional money flowing into the economy, output will be above the level in Regime 2. B's preferences will, by contrast, be the reverse.

For a demand switch disturbance (which could originate in either country) the two economies will prefer Regime 1, which allows some offset to the disturbance through an adjustment in the exchange rate.

What, then, are we to conclude from the analysis? Provided capital mobility is relatively low, B does have a clear preference for independence while A may have some leaning towards some monetary union (which allows it to export its disturbances). For high capital mobility B's position is more ambiguous while A unambiguously prefers a union for a monetary disturbance but independence for a real disturbance. To sum up, there is some support for the argument that the more unstable economy will prefer some union while the more stable economy will prefer independence.

The relative size of the member countries may be important in this case. A very small and unstable economy may enjoy substantial gains from joining a stable union. Her instability will now be spread (negligibly) across the other countries while, at the same time, she may be able to enjoy the other countries' stability. Also the resistance of the other members to accommodating the small unit will be diminished.

An important qualification to this discussion is the implicit assumption that domestic instability is exogenous and independent of whether or not countries join together in a union. It may, for example, be the case that there will be some convergence in the relative instability after the monetary union is formed.

Costs of Renouncing some Independent Demand-management Policies

In a weak monetary union there may be some (limited) scope for short-term independent monetary and fiscal policies. However, a switch from independence to a weak monetary union would tend to weaken the effectiveness of monetary policies but may weaken or strengthen the effectiveness of fiscal policies (depending on whether capital mobility was low or high with flexible rates).[19]

In a strong union monetary independence is impossible by definition while fiscal policy continues to be feasible and indeed would be strengthened further. The issues here are very broad and complex depending on the relative uses of monetary/fiscal policies, their short-term effectiveness and also on the need (if any) for counteracting policies.[20]

Summary and Conclusions – Theoretical Analysis

We have reviewed the benefits and costs of a monetary union. We now need to summarise the key considerations that determine how large these costs and benefits might be. It is possible to conclude from our analysis that the costs would be smaller (and/or the benefits larger) if:

(1) The differences in the rates of growth of labour productivity are not large.

(2) There is no money illusion in the economy and there is no long-run trade-off between inflation and unemployment.

(3) Intra-trade is large (the economies are relatively open).[21] Our own analysis suggests that openness (1) increases the gains from the more efficient use of money, (2) increases the gains from the diminished demand for international reserves, (3) reduces money illusion within the potential union rendering exchange rate adjustment more costly and (4) reduces the cost of adjustment under fixed rates. On the other hand, we have seen that openness may increase a country's exposure to external shocks under fixed rates and this may argue against a union for a relatively stable economy. Also diversification tends to reduce the degree of openness but diversification, as we saw, strengthened the case for a union. Nevertheless, on balance, McKinnon's claim that openness strengthens the case for a union would appear to be vindicated.

(4) The differences in the propensities to inflate were relatively small. The greater the differences, the greater will tend to be the emerging social tensions, the greater the conflict over appropriate

common rates of inflation and the greater the risks of unemployment emerging in those regions with a relatively high propensity to inflate.

(5) The differences in the degree of domestic instability were relatively small. In this case countries share in the outcomes of each other's disturbances and do not have to be exposed to an 'excessive' degree of external instability.

(6) Finally, there was a significant degree of labour mobility within the union. While it must be recognised that (in contrast to Mundell's original view) there are substantial costs associated with the 'involuntary' movement of labour across frontiers, the costs of adjustment are nevertheless eased by a labour force that is mobile.

European Monetary Integration

Developments to 1978[22]

In December 1969 the EEC Heads of State decided that steps should be taken to proceed with the formation of a monetary union. A committee headed by Werner was assigned the task of investigating the viability of proceeding with a union. The committee's report, which appeared in October 1970, made several recommendations. It envisaged a ten-year horizon, over which there would be a gradual advance towards complete monetary unification, which it judged to be attainable by 1980. It proposed a progression towards this aim in three stages. The first stage, which was spelt out in some detail, was to last three years to the end of 1973. Initially, attention was to centre on limiting exchange rate fluctuations among member countries, on extending facilities for short- and medium-term credit, on relaxing intra-EEC exchange controls and on greater co-operation in economic policies.[23] In the later stages, exchange rates would become permanently fixed, capital markets would be progressively unified, reserves would be pooled and policies would become fully co-ordinated.

In March 1971 the EEC Council of Ministers endorsed the Werner Report, in substance,[24] and decided to implement some modest steps in the direction of a union, including the provision of medium-term credit facilities and, from June 1971, a reduction in the maximum spread for intra-EEC exchange rate margins from the prevailing 1.5 to 1.2 percentage points. In the event, exchange markets became very unstable from May 1971 and the exchange rate provision was never implemented.

A more important step was taken in April 1972, when it was decided that from July 1972 the maximum spread was to be 2.25 per cent, half the new Smithsonian allowable spread of 4.5 per cent. This was the origin of what came to be labelled the snake in the tunnel (the tunnel being the larger spread allowable with outside currencies). The participants in the agreement were Germany, France, Italy, the Benelux countries, the UK, Ireland, Norway and Denmark (the last four being then prospective EEC members),[25] but by June 1972, with sterling under attack, the UK and Ireland left the snake. Italy left in February 1973 and by March 1973 there was effectively no tunnel and the remaining members then floated against outside currencies. Sweden joined in March 1973 but France left the snake in January 1974, returning in July 1975 but leaving again in March 1976. Sweden left in 1977. By 1978 the only members left were Germany, the Benelux, Denmark and Norway.

This initial experiment with monetary unification must be judged to have been largely a failure. Not only did the membership change over the years but there were also, on several occasions, exchange rate adjustments within the union that went beyond the allowable spreads. A report in 1975, prepared by a study group headed by Marjolin, concluded that monetary and economic policies had become even more divergent and that 'Europe is no nearer to European Monetary Unification than in 1969. In fact, if there has been any movement it has been backward'. It reaffirmed the key importance of close economic co-ordination and asserted that in its absence there was no point in trying to pursue monetary unification further.

Table 27.2 shows the standard deviation of inflation rates as well as monetary growth for the snake countries (excluding Denmark) as well as for the EEC as a whole. It is evident that beginning in 1973 the

Table 27.2 Standard deviations monetary growth (*M*1) and inflation rates (*P*) (consumer prices)

Year	*EEC countries*		*Snake countries*[a] *excluding Denmark*	
	*M*1	*P*	*M*1	*P*
1970	8.6	1.2	2.7	0.2
1971	4.5	1.9	3.4	1.6
1972	2.1	1.0	2.7	1.4
1973	5.5	1.5	3.7	0.6
1974	5.3	4.4	2.0	2.8
1975	3.7	6.3	3.7	3.5
1976	3.9	4.9	0.8	2.6
1977	4.7	5.3	3.1	1.7

Source: P. De Grauwe and T. Peters, 'The EMS, Europe and the dollar', *The Banker*, April 1979, pp. 39–45.

[a]Benelux, Germany and Norway.

standard deviations are substantially smaller for snake countries than for the EEC as a whole.

The early attempt at monetary unification may be said to have failed for several reasons, including, principally, the upheavals in the international monetary system, the oil crisis and the very weak efforts at macro-co-ordination.

The New Step Forward in 1978[26]

In late 1977 Roy Jenkins, the President of the Commission, revived the idea of a monetary union, recommended new initiatives in that direction and supported the concept of a common European currency. The proposal fell on receptive ears. As it happened, several factors during 1978 appeared to be conspiring to strengthen the case for a union: dissatisfaction with the ways in which exchange markets were functioning, the alarm over the collapse of the US dollar in the second half of 1978, the growing view that the uncertainties associated with exchange rate instability were having an adverse effect on employment, trade and investment and the specific concern over the inflationary effects of currency devaluations, and finally some convergence during 1978 in inflation and monetary performances.

Extensive negotiations during 1978 led, in December 1978, to the resolution to implement a new European Monetary System. This system came into force in March 1979. All member countries, with the exception of the UK (who indicated it might join at a later date) agreed to participate in the scheme.[27] Its main features are the following:

(1) Creation of a European currency unit (ECU) which is to be at the heart of the system.[28] The ECU is made up of a basket of given amounts of the nine currencies in the EEC.
(2) Each currency in the scheme has a central rate which is expressed in terms of ECUs. With the exception of Italy each currency is allowed a margin of ±2.25 per cent around the central rate. Italy opted for a wider margin of ±6 per cent. Changes in central rates may be made by 'mutual agreement'.
(3) An interesting innovation is the adoption of a 'divergence indicator'. A complicated formula serves to flash a signal that the currency is approaching its outward limits. At this point a presumption is created that some corrective measures would need to be taken. These corrective measures may take many forms, including appropriate domestic monetary policies and/or changes in central rates. Central rates would be altered when fundamental conditions (for example, rates of increase in costs and prices) in one country had drifted away from the other members.
(4) A European Monetary Co-operation Fund (EMCF)[29] has responsibility to acquire reserves from the monetary authorities

and issue ECUs in exchange. These ECUs would be used as a means of settlement. Initially, participating members are to deposit 20 per cent of their gold holdings and 20 per cent of their gross reserves in US dollars in exchange for ECUs. Interest is paid (earned) by participants when their holdings fall below (are in excess of) the amounts received against their deposits.[30] At a later stage, ECUs may be created against domestic currencies.[31]

(5) Short-term as well as medium-term financial assistance has been substantially enlarged.

The steps taken are, in fact, quite modest. Exchange rate margins permitted (2.25 per cent) are twice those allowed under the old snake. There is also explicit provision for changes in central rates. Thus the scheme cannot be said to conform to even what we called a weak union. In some ways it has few of the advantages of the weak union while retaining much of the earlier instability in exchange rates, as well as the disruptive speculative movements. Nevertheless, it constitutes a most important development that could well lead eventually to the ideals of monetary unification. Whether the new initiatives will prove more successful than the previous experiment is going to depend on several considerations, including how stable the international system will be and the vigour with which they pursue co-ordinated monetary policies.

Theoretical Analysis Applied to the EEC

It is now possible to apply, briefly, our theoretical framework to the case of the EEC. What does our analysis have to say about the appropriateness of forming a monetary union composed of the nine existing members? First, Britain's rate of growth of labour productivity is relatively low, so Britain is perhaps disadvantaged in this respect. Second, Britain and Italy tend to have relatively high propensities to inflate as compared to, say, Germany; hence there would, at the least, be transitional costs of adjusting to a lower rate of inflation. Third, Britain's intra-trade is significantly lower than the other members, so her 'gains' as we have argued would tend to be diminished (see Table 27.3). Fourth, both Britain and Italy are reputed to have relatively unstable economies so in this respect they may actually gain from membership. Fifth, labour mobility is probably weaker between Britain and the other members than within the continental members of the EEC, so again the cost of adjustment may be relatively higher for Britain.

The only conclusion to be drawn from this brief application is that Britain (and perhaps Italy) may be a little at odds in the group. However, it is difficult to be dogmatic about this. There may be significant gains for Britain if joining the union acted to reduce her

Table 27.3 Major trade partners in intra-EEC trade (1972)

Country	*Exports to EEC % of total exports*	*Imports from EEC % of total imports*
Netherlands	74.0	62.3
Belgium–Luxembourg	74.0	71.3
Ireland	77.9	69.3
Denmark	43.2	46.0
United Kingdom	30.3	31.6
Germany	46.9	55.1
Italy	50.3	49.2
France	56.3	56.0

Source: L. Tsoukalis (1977), p. 44.

propensity to inflate and her potential domestic instability. Participation would itself lift Britain's intra-trade, her labour mobility and, possibly, her labour productivity.

Notes for Chapter 27

1 Useful references here are: W. M. Corden (1972); J. C. Ingram (1973); P. B. Kenen (1969); R. I. McKinnon (1963); G. Magnifico (1973); R. A. Mundell (1961); E. Tower and T. Willett (1976); L. Tsoukalis (1977); Y. Ishiyama (1975); J. M. Fleming (1971).

2 On some of these benefits see E. Tower and T. Willett (1976), Chapter 2.

3 It is also sometimes contended that money will become more efficient in its function as a store of value. The intuitive rationale here is that variance of inflation will be diminished with the use of a common currency because now the disturbance to the price of imports (or tradables) from exchange rate changes will be eliminated. See R. I. McKinnon (1963). For a criticism of this argument see W. M. Corden (1972). Even if the argument held, the practical benefit flowing from it would be very small; in effect the benefit would come from the saving of trips to banks.

4 To obtain some idea of the order of magnitude of these gains consider the case of Germany within a European monetary union. (See the discussion of this later in the chapter.) Germany's trade with the EEC is roughly one half of her total trade. Assuming that, in a strong union, half of her reserves were freed to invest long term and assuming, moreover, that she was able to earn an additional three percentage points, her gain would then amount to something like 0.1 per cent of her GNP.

5 For an evaluation of the potential gains accruing to a reserve currency country see Chapter 9.

6 See also, on this, Chapter 25.

7 See Chapter 24.

8 If the countries, say, shared a Phillips curve but had different preferences and they chose some intermediate common rate of inflation, then if the Phillips curves were non-linear the increase in unemployment in the 'high inflation' countries might be less than the reduction in unemployment in the low inflation country. On balance, unemployment within the union might fall under these conditions.

9 See J. M. Parkin (1972). See also the discussion in Chapters 12 and 24.

10 It is important to note than the money illusion here is quite different from the money illusion required to generate a long Phillips curve trade-off. In the case of the Phillips curve money illusion implies that the rate of change in wages is less than the rate of inflation. In the case of an assumed change in the exchange rate money illusion simply means that the level of wages does not fully adjust to a change in the price level. The latter is possible but the former, as we have already argued, is unlikely.
11 See the discussion of vicious circles in Chapter 25.
12 See R. A. Mundell (1961).
13 See, for example, W. M. Corden (1972).
14 P. B. Kenen (1969).
15 However, the more diversified, the less open will tend to be the economy and, hence, as we have seen, thus far at any rate, the weaker may be the case for the union.
16 The case of the domestic price shock turns out to be very complicated and ambiguous, so it is disregarded.
17 With the obvious exception of the money supply shock which disappears in the strong union.
18 For treatments of the two-country world see: R. A. Mundell (1964); A. Swoboda and R. Dornbusch (1973); S. W. Arndt (1973); V. Argy and J. Salop (1978).
19 See Chapter 22.
20 For a discussion of some of these issues see, again, Chapter 22.
21 This was the criterion proposed by McKinnon in a well-known contribution to the literature on monetary unions. McKinnon argued that the more open the economies the stronger the case for the union.
22 For details here see L. Tsoukalis (1977).
23 This was proposed in general terms. In the event it was a serious weakness of the original report that increased exchange rate stability was being proposed without putting forward a serious program for co-ordination of macro-policies.
24 There was, however, no commitment to proceed to the later stages. France opposed this and insisted on commitment only to the first stage.
25 Norway did not, in fact, join the EEC.
26 See the symposiums in *Euro Money*, June 1979 and *The Banker*, January 1979. Details are contained in IMF (1979).
27 Norway, which had been a member of the snake, did not join the new scheme.
28 This was an extension of the European unit of account which had been introduced in April 1975.
29 The EMCF was originally created in April 1973 to administer the payments mechanism and to promote the narrowing of exchange rate margins.
30 This is, of course, very similar to the SDR system.
31 When that happens new international reserves will be created. With the initial arrangements no new reserves are created since there is simply an exchange of one form of reserve against another.

Part Six

Macro-Policy

Chapter 28

Conventional Macro-Policy – Targets, Instruments and Assignments

Introduction

Thus far we have been concerned with exchange rate policy in isolation, focusing particularly on the choice between fixed and flexible rates. We now turn our attention to the question of the role of exchange rates within a broader macro-policy framework. The key issue, to which we will now address ourselves, is how the available macro-instruments of policy, which may or may not include exchange rates, are related to and are able to serve the aims of policy.

There are several approaches to macro-policy-making of which the more important are those of Meade, Tinbergen, Theil and Mundell.[1] Tinbergen advanced the important principle that if governments aimed at *n* independent targets of policy then they should also have *n* effective and unbounded instruments of policy if the targets are all to be met. Suppose, to illustrate Tinbergen's 'fixed targets' approach, governments had three targets and only two instruments. Then clearly, except by coincidence, the three targets could not be met and some choice among the targets would need to be made. On the other hand, if governments had three targets and as many as four instruments, one instrument would be 'redundant' since only three need to be manipulated to achieve the targets.

Theil's approach is different. He starts with the premise that governments have a welfare function, which includes both targets and instruments, with weights attaching to each component of the welfare function to reflect its relative importance. Thus, in this approach, there are no inherent limits to the number of targets accommodated. The welfare function would then be optimised subject to the constraints determined by the structure of the economy.

If governments were armed with detailed information about the structure of the economy (in the form, say, of a usable econometric model), Tinbergen's approach would be relatively simple to apply. It reduces, ultimately, to a mathematical exercise where the target values are plugged into the model, forecasts are made of the exogenous variables in the model (for example, exports, foreign interest rates and prices), values are placed on the lagged variables and the model is then solved for the appropriate values of the instruments. Within this framework, if there were insufficient instruments then targets would have to be dropped to ensure the equality of targets and instruments.

Theil, on the other hand, offers the important insight that some instruments need to be included in the welfare function to allow for the possibility that there are costs incurred in changing instruments, possible diminishing returns in the use of instruments and constraints on the magnitude of changes in the instruments. Examples of instruments assuming a role similar to targets abound. Three obvious ones are: interest rates, exchange rates and budget deficits.

Tinbergen's approach therefore is simpler than Theil's, which, though more realistic, is much more difficult to apply. Tinbergen's approach would lead one to believe that there are sufficient instruments available to meet macro-targets, while Theil's much broader approach suggests that there may be a problem of too many targets and an insufficient number of instruments. In practice Tinbergen's 'basic' approach has been much more widely used. However, it needs to be tempered by the awareness that there is no absolutely clear dividing line between instruments and targets and that frequently governments treat apparent instruments as targets.

Mundell's approach descends directly from Tinbergen. His major insight is that where the detailed structure of an economy is not known and/or where policy-making is decentralised, governments may be able to proceed, on the strength of only limited information, by assigning a policy instrument to that target for which it has a relative advantage.[2] In other words, in a simple two-instrument two-target framework, one instrument would be assigned to one target and the other instrument to the other target. The instrument would be altered, whenever its target variable was outside the acceptable range, in a way that would bring the variable closer to its targeted value.

On what basis would the assignment be made? Formally, again in a two-target two-instrument context, we ask how the two instruments must be varied conceptually to achieve the same change in one of the targets. Then given the required changes in the instruments we need to determine how the other target responds to those same changes in the instruments. The instrument that produces the largest absolute change in the other target is the one that ought to be assigned to that target. It has been shown that this ensures stability in the sense that assignment in this way will tend to move the economy closer to its targets. However, the reverse assignment need not be unstable; indeed it may also be stable.[3] So the Mundellian criterion for assignment ensures that the policy is stabilising while the reverse assignment may or may not be stabilising. This is essentially the approach we will be adopting to the assignment problem in the treatment that follows. The key question in applying the assignment approach is whether assignment is actually feasible on the basis of only limited information about relative effects or whether a good deal more detailed information is required to determine assignment.

Mundell's Assignment

Mundell's world is essentially a short-term fixed rate world where the exchange rate is either not available as a policy instrument or central banks do not choose to use it as an instrument over a short-term horizon. Governments are concerned over the level of employment (the internal balance target) and the state of the balance of payments (the external balance target) and have two instruments at their disposal: monetary and fiscal policies.

We assume fiscal policy takes the form of variations in government expenditure holding monetary policy neutral. Monetary policy can be defined in several alternative ways. The monetary authorities may manipulate the interest rate or the volume of money or finally their domestic assets.[4] In what follows we will define the monetary instrument as the volume of money.[5]

The underlying framework for our analysis is again the fixed price, fixed exchange rate version of the neo-Keynesian model, with the volume of money as the monetary policy instrument. From our standpoint now we need to remind ourselves of three key assumptions: that capital flows are influenced only by relative interest rates, that the current account is determined only by the level of output (given prices and exchange rates) and not by the composition of output and that the country is small. Each of these assumptions will be relaxed later, to demonstrate potential limitations in the Mundellian framework.

Recalling our assignment principle, suppose there is a monetary and fiscal expansion such that the increase in output is the same. The emerging deficit in the current account will by definition be the same; at the same time, if capital mobility is low, fiscal expansion and the associated higher interest rate will induce an inflow of capital that will serve to partially offset the deficit. Monetary expansion, on the other hand, and the associated lower interest rate will induce an outflow of capital that will come on top of the current account deficit. Hence, the absolute turnaround in the balance of payments will be larger for monetary than for fiscal expansion. It follows that in this case monetary policy should be assigned to the external target and fiscal policy to the internal target.

If capital mobility is high fiscal expansion will produce an overall surplus while monetary expansion will produce a deficit. In principle, the relative balance of payments outcome is indeterminate in this case and will depend on the extent of the drop in the interest rate for monetary expansion and the extent of the increase in the interest rate for fiscal expansion. If the latter is significantly larger, then the associated inflow may transform the current account deficit into a surplus which is larger than the overall deficit from monetary expansion. In this case, the assignment principle dictates the reverse assignment: monetary policy to internal balance and fiscal to external balance. These cases are illustrated in Figures 28.1 and 28.2.

Figure 28.1 *Money as instrument – low capital mobility*

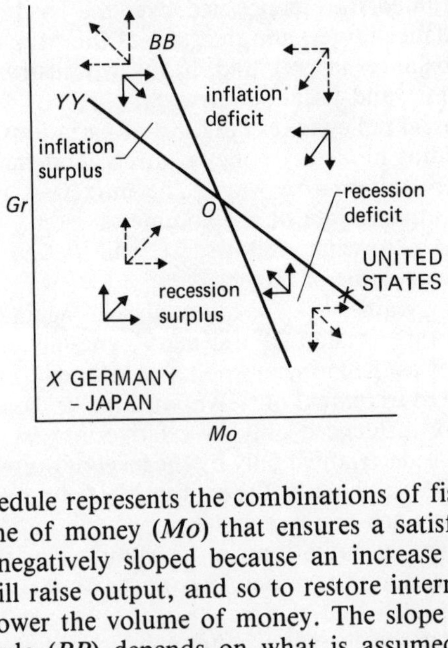

The *YY* schedule represents the combinations of fiscal policy (*Gr*) and the volume of money (*Mo*) that ensures a satisfactory level of output. It is negatively sloped because an increase in government expenditure will raise output, and so to restore internal balance it is necessary to lower the volume of money. The slope of the external balance schedule (*BB*) depends on what is assumed about capital mobility. If capital mobility is low, then an increase in government expenditure has an adverse effect on the overall balance of payments (because capital inflows associated with the higher interest rate are insufficient to offset the current account deficit) and so a reduction in the volume of money is required to restore external balance. In this case, the *BB* schedule is also negatively sloped. This case is shown in Figure 28.1. If, however, capital mobility is high an increase in government expenditure will improve the balance of payments (because now the capital inflows exceed the current account deficit)

Figure 28.2 *Money as instrument – high capital mobility*

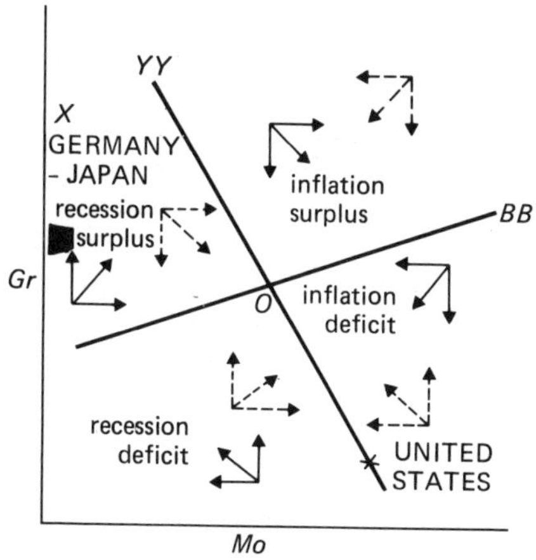

and an increase in the volume of money is needed to restore external balance. The *BB* schedule will now be positive, as in Figure 28.2.

In each case we can identify four segments, representing different combinations of internal and external disequilibria. The area to the right (left) of *YY* represents a situation where, given fiscal policy, the volume of money is too high (low) relative to the internal balance target; hence the economy has excess demand (is in recession). The area to the right (left) of *BB* represents a situation where, again given fiscal policy, the volume of money is too high (low) relative to the external balance target; hence there is an overall deficit (surplus).

The unbroken arrows show the simultaneous (Mundellian) assignment of the volume of money to external balance and fiscal policy to internal balance. For example, in Figures 28.1 and 28.2, in the regions labelled recession–surplus, the volume of money is allowed to increase to correct the surplus while government expenditure is allowed to increase to reduce the unemployment. Broken arrows, on the other hand, show the reverse assignment – money to internal balance, fiscal to external balance. For low capital mobility it is easily seen that the Mundellian assignment is stable but the reverse assignment is unstable. In other words, Mundell's assignment allows the economy to converge towards point *0* where the two targets are met while the reverse assignment drives the economy away from its target. For high capital mobility, both assignments turn out to be stable although the directness of the convergence may be different (see Figure 28.2 and Annex).

It seems, then, that so long as we limit ourselves to relatively simple models of this kind and without exact knowledge of the structure of the economy, the Mundellian assignment will be the appropriate one in the sense that it will ensure stability whatever the degree of capital mobility.

The position of the USA in late 1978 is located on the two figures. Then the USA had a very large deficit but was close to internal balance. The Mundellian analysis would prescribe a switch towards a tighter monetary policy and an easier fiscal policy (in other words, move along *YY*). In this way, economic activity would be maintained while, at the same time, the higher interest rate would secure some improvement in the capital account. By way of contrast, both Japan and Germany had large surpluses and were also in recession. They are located in that region. The Mundellian prescription here is to switch to easier monetary and fiscal policies. This would both lift economic activity and reduce the surplus.

How robust, however, is our result? To illustrate the potential limitations of the analysis we now proceed to relax each of the key assumptions mentioned earlier. Suppose that different components of expenditure make different demands on imports so that the same level of output attained through different components of expenditure need not have the same effect on the current account.[6] Again, suppose that the volume of money is increased and government expenditure increased so as to generate the same increase in income. Clearly, the private investment component of expenditure will be larger with monetary expansion while the government component will be larger with fiscal expansion. If the import component of private investment is less than the import component of government expenditure, then it is conceivable that the current account deficit will be smaller with monetary than with fiscal policy. In this case if, for example, the degree of capital mobility is not very high the overall deficit may be smaller for monetary than for fiscal policy. Hence, the reverse assignment may be appropriate.

Second, the model assumes that a change in the interest rate will generate a continuing flow of capital over time. By contrast, as we have seen (see Chapter 11), the stock theory of capital movements assumes that a change in the interest rate generates a once-over stock adjustment in the initial period but the flow of capital is not maintained in subsequent periods. Moreover, the flow theory underlying the model disregards the effects of capital movements on the subsequent flow of interest payments between countries. For example, an initial outflow of capital which is not sustained will result in a subsequent continuing addition to net interest receipts from overseas.

Now, in the light of this, consider again a policy of monetary and fiscal expansion which generates the same impact on income. The effect on the current account is the same in the two cases but now (disregarding the growth of wealth) there is no permanent effect on the capital account in either case; at the same time, for monetary policy the initial outflow of capital will permanently improve the net interest account which will offset, in part, the deficit in the current account. For fiscal expansion the net interest account will deteriorate because now the initial inflow will generate an outflow of interest payments in the future, so the current account deficit will actually be aggravated. Hence, the absolute effect on the balance of payments may be[7] smaller under monetary than under fiscal policy, so the reverse assignment may be appropriate.[8]

Third, the model disregards the possibility that income may also influence capital movements. As we saw in Chapter 22, a higher level of income, for example, may create more favourable expectations about the economy and encourage a flow of direct investment. Suppose, again, that we have a monetary and a fiscal expansion such that an equivalent increase in income occurs. The adverse effect on the current account will be the same. With monetary policy there will also be an outflow of capital due to the lower interest rate and an inflow due to the higher level of income. With fiscal policy there will be, in addition, an inflow due to the higher level of income. The absolute effect on the balance of payments may again be larger for fiscal than for monetary policy so the appropriate assignment may need to be reversed.

What the foregoing appears to point to is the important fact that a more detailed knowledge of the structure of the economy may be necessary before the correct assignment may be determined. Assignment, in other words, may not be feasible after all, on the basis of only very limited knowledge. In principle, this conclusion would have to be correct. Nevertheless, if we are concerned with relatively short-term assignment, the Mundellian assignment would still appear to be a relatively safer way to proceed than its reverse.[9]

How does the analysis apply to a multi-country world? Provided there are no inconsistencies in balance of payments targets the *n*th country's balance of payments will be automatically fulfilled, so in a two-target two-instrument world one of its two instruments will be redundant. The *n*th country is frequently taken to be the USA whose balance of payments would be the 'residual'; hence the USA, in our analytical framework, would require only one instrument to meet the internal balance target.[10]

A Swan-based Assignment[11]

In Swan's framework the targets remain those of internal and external balance but now it is assumed that the exchange rate may be used as an instrument. The two instruments are fiscal and exchange rate policies, with the interest rate now held fixed. The question then, is, how to manipulate the fiscal and exchange rate instruments to achieve internal and external balance.

Once again in our analysis we draw on the fixed price component of the neo-Keynesian model. How now ought fiscal and exchange rate policies to be assigned? Orthodoxy would assign the exchange rate to the balance of payments and fiscal policy to the level of employment. To evaluate this assignment we again apply the same procedure as previously. Consider the case where a devaluation and an increase in government expenditure produce the same increase in output. We then ask which change in policy instrument generates the larger absolute change in the balance of payments. The answer, as it happens, depends on several structural coefficients in the underlying model, so no a priori answer is possible. We show, in an Annex, that the appropriate assignment is the reverse of the orthodox one if the following expression is positive but is the orthodox one if the expression is negative:

$$\frac{ML[\alpha_9 - (1 - \alpha_1)]}{1 - \alpha_1 + \alpha_9}$$

where *ML* represents the Marshall–Lerner condition, α_1 is the marginal propensity to spend out of income and α_9 is the marginal propensity to import. Assuming the Marshall–Lerner condition holds, the expression states that the reverse assignment is appropriate if the marginal propensity to import exceeds the marginal propensity not to spend on consumption and investment. It is evident that the reverse assignment is more likely to be the appropriate one the higher is the marginal propensity to import (α_9) and the higher the marginal propensity to spend (α_1).[12] It is also evident that, within our framework, only limited (and, indeed, easily available) information is required.

For fiscal expansion a large marginal propensity to spend increases the output and hence the balance of payments effects; at the same time, the higher the marginal propensity to import the stronger will be the balance of payments effects, for given output changes. On the other hand, the higher the marginal propensity to spend and the larger the marginal propensity to import, the weaker will tend to be the balance of payments effects of a devaluation. Under these conditions there is a greater likelihood that the reverse assignment will be the appropriate one. This is effectively the argument advanced by the New Cambridge School who tend to assume that the marginal propensity to spend on consumption and investment is close to unity.[13] In this case, there are no domestic leakages and the increase in imports must be such as to completely offset any improvement in the balance of payments due to the devaluation.

These points may be illustrated graphically, again, with the help of internal and external balance schedules. These now trace combinations of the exchange rate and fiscal policy that will secure internal and external balance. The *YY* slope is negative because a devaluation (an increase in *E*) is assumed to increase domestic output; hence to restore internal balance the level of government expenditure needs to be reduced. This slope is shown in the Annex to be equal to $1/ML$, so it would be flatter (steeper) the larger is the Marshall–Lerner condition.

The slope of the external balance schedule (*EE*) depends on the underlying structure. We show in the Annex that the (positive) slope of the *EE* schedule is equal to $\alpha_9/[ML(1-\alpha_1)]$ so the schedule is steeper the larger is α_9 and α_1 and the smaller is ML. Two cases are shown in Figures 28.3 and 28.4, one (Figure 28.3) where *EE* is relatively horizontal and another (Figure 28.4) where *EE* is vertical, implying $\alpha_1 = 1$ (the extreme New Cambridge Case).

It is possible again to identify, on the diagrams, alternative combinations of internal and external disequilibria. Consider, for example, the area to the right of the *EE* schedule. Given the exchange rate, the area represents 'excessive' government expenditure relative to that level of government expenditure required to maintain external balance. Hence, within this area the external accounts must be in deficit. By analogous reasoning the area on the left of the *EE* schedule must represent a surplus in the external accounts. Now consider the area to the right of the *YY* schedule. This represents 'excessive' government expenditure and, hence, must correspond to situations of

Figure 28.3 *Orthodox assignment*

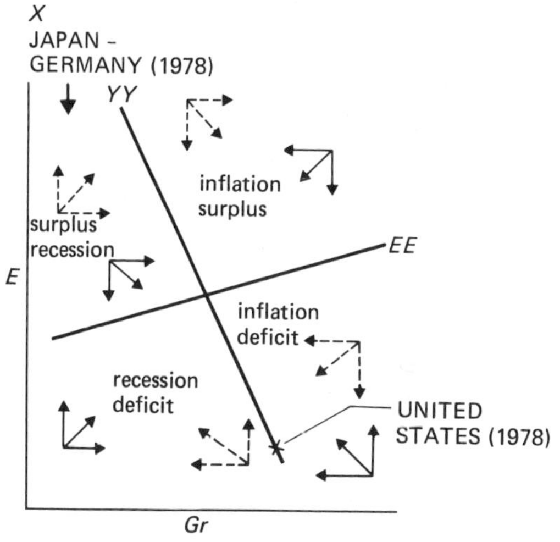

Figure 28.4 *New Cambridge assignment*

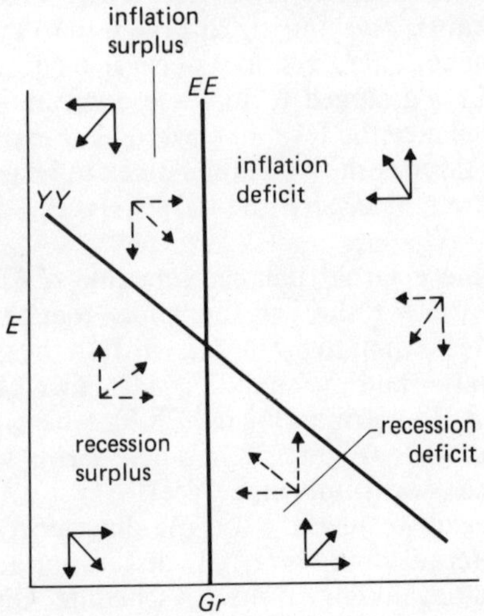

excess demand (inflation). The area to the left of the *YY* schedule represents situations of deficient demand (recession).

The unbroken arrows show the direction of change when the exchange rate is directed at external balance and government expenditure at internal balance. For example, in the deficit–recession zones the exchange rate is devalued in response to the deficit while government expenditure is increased in response to the recession. The reverse assignment – government expenditure for external balance and the exchange rate for internal balance – is demonstrated by the broken arrows. The analysis confirms the earlier verbal argument, that when *EE* is very steep the correct assignment is the reverse of the orthodox one. Figure 28.4 shows that if, for these conditions, the reverse of the orthodox assignment was followed convergence towards equilibrium would be more direct.

To illustrate the possible real world applicability of this framework consider, again, the position of the USA, Germany and Japan in late 1978. Assuming Figure 28.3 is the appropriate one, the analysis suggests that Japan and Germany with a surplus and a recession should have revalued and, at the same time, implemented an expansionary fiscal policy (keeping monetary policy – as defined – neutral). This combination of policies would have served, at one and the same time, to reduce the surplus and unemployment. The USA, on the other hand, with close to full employment but a large deficit should have implemented a restrictive fiscal policy together with a devaluation. These policies would now have served to maintain economic activity but, at the same time, to improve the balance of payments.

Figure 28.3 also illustrates the important point, emphasised by Swan himself, that in each quadrant there is always some change in a single policy instrument that will promote the two targets. In non-dilemma situations (inflation–deficit and surplus–recession) a change in government expenditure would be the appropriate policy. For example, with inflation–deficit (recession–surplus) a reduction (increase) in government expenditure would help to correct the internal and external imbalances. On the other hand, in 'dilemma' situations (inflation–surplus, recession–deficit) the change in the exchange rate would be appropriate. For example, with inflation–surplus (recession–deficit) a revaluation (devaluation) would help to correct the two imbalances. This also highlights, within this framework, the usefulness of having the exchange rate as an available instrument to cope with dilemma-type situations (where demand-management policies promote one target but at the expense of the other).

What kinds of criticism can be levelled at Swan-based assignments? An obvious one is that it disregards the price effects of exchange rate changes and assumes a considerable degree of money illusion. For a relatively short-term horizon of a year or so (before, say, labour markets have adjusted to any great extent) this is not perhaps too unrealistic. However, if the emphasis is on short-term (reversible) policy then there is the problem that over, say, the first six months or so exchange rate changes may have perverse effects[14] (for example, the sum of the demand elasticities will be less than 1). With perverse effects the analysis is considerably more complicated. We have also totally disregarded monetary policy and capital flows by making the convenient assumption that the interest rate is fixed. This allowed us to concentrate only on current account deficits; however, if (against the spirit of the Swan analysis) we had held the volume of money fixed, fiscal expansion might have improved the overall balance of payments, complicating the outcomes further.

Conclusions on the Assignment Strategy

Despite the vast literature on the assignment, confusion and uncertainty continue to reign supreme in this area. The sources of this uncertainty, as we have noted time and time again, are many. First, in general, the moment one introduces refinements to a model, the appropriate assignment begins to depend very much on one having a detailed structural knowledge of the economy. If, however, this structural knowledge were available assignment would then be unnecessary. Second, even if the appropriate assignment can be arrived at with relatively minimal information, this is not to say that the opposite assignment is necessarily unstable, which makes for difficulties in trying to reach firm conclusions. Third, most of the literature has focused on the two-by-two case. At the least, the analysis should be extended to the three-by-three case which would include the price level as a target. But, as it happens, this is very difficult to handle within this framework.

Fourth, there may be a conflict between short-term and long-term assignment. For example, as we have seen, the Mundellian assignment is likely to be appropriate to the short term but the opposite assignment may be more appropriate to the long term. Again, in the longer term, it may be more appropriate to assign the exchange rate to the price level than to either employment or external balance.[15] The reason is that, as we have seen, in the long run under certain conditions a change in the exchange rate only affects prices and leaves output and the balance of payments (the flow variable) unchanged. Yet another illustration of how assignment might have to be different in the long run is the following. In macro-models that allow for financial wealth it is known that long-run equilibrium is reached when the budget deficit is equal to the current account deficit. This is because the former adds to financial wealth while the latter reduces financial wealth and the economy can only reach equilibrium when there is no further change in financial wealth. In this case, it is evident that a change in the fiscal stance which, say, reduced the size of the budget deficit would in the very long run manifest itself in an equivalent reduction in the size of the current account deficit. Fiscal policy, then, in this context would need to be assigned to external balance, as in the New Cambridge Model.[16]

We therefore conclude that the marginal real productivity of this vast literature has been very small indeed and that the assignment strategy really does not provide a useful basis for policy-making.

Annex – Mundell's Assignment

Notation

B	=	balance of payments
E	=	exchange rate (units of domestic currency per unit of foreign currency)
edm	=	elasticity of demand for imports
edx	=	elasticity of demand for exports
Gr	=	real government expenditure
Mo	=	money supply
Yr	=	real GNP

For fixed prices and exchange rates we need a relationship between government expenditure and the volume of money such that the level of output is unchanged (the *YY* schedule). This is derived by rearranging the aggregate demand equation of the neo-Keynesian model (Equation 11.16) as follows:

$$\Delta Gr = -\frac{\alpha_3}{\alpha_6}\Delta Mo + \left(1 - \alpha_1 + \alpha_9 + \frac{\alpha_3\alpha_4}{\alpha_6}\right)\Delta Yr \qquad (28A.1)$$

so the slope of *YY* is negative and equal to α_3/α_6.

To derive the *BB* schedule we need first to write the balance of payments equation for the model in terms of the two instruments. This is:

$$\Delta B = -\frac{(\alpha_9\alpha_6 - \alpha_{12}\alpha_4)}{D1}\Delta Gr - \left(\frac{\alpha_3\alpha_9 + \alpha_{12}(1 - \alpha_1 + \alpha_9)}{D1}\right)\Delta Mo \qquad (28A.2)$$

where $D1 = \alpha_6(1 - \alpha_1 + \alpha_9) + \alpha_3\alpha_4$.

For a given balance of payments, the *BB* schedule is then:

$$\Delta Gr = -\left(\frac{\alpha_3\alpha_9 + \alpha_{12}(1 - \alpha_1 + \alpha_9)}{(\alpha_9\alpha_6 - \alpha_{12}\alpha_4)}\right)\Delta Mo \qquad (28A.3)$$

which may be positive or negative, as shown in the text, depending on the degree of capital mobility. Capital mobility is low (high) if $\alpha_9\alpha_6$ is greater than (less than) $\alpha_{12}\alpha_4$. (See Annex to Chapter 22.)

For low capital mobility ($\alpha_9\alpha_6 > \alpha_{12}\alpha_4$) it is easy to demonstrate, too, that the *BB* schedule is steeper than the *YY* schedule (that is, the negative slope of *BB* is larger than the negative slope of *YY*).

To determine the appropriate assignment we substitute in the balance of payments equation (Equation 28A.2) output equivalent changes in monetary and fiscal policies from Equation (28A.1).

The balance of payments effect of a given monetary expansion is (from Equation 28A.2):

$$-\left(\frac{\alpha_3\alpha_9 + \alpha_{12}(1 - \alpha_1 + \alpha_9)}{D1}\right)$$

For an equivalent fiscal expansion (Equation 28A.1) the balance of payments effect is:

$$-\frac{\alpha_3(\alpha_9\alpha_6 - \alpha_{12}\alpha_4)}{\alpha_6 D1}$$

For low capital mobility ($\alpha_9\alpha_6>\alpha_{12}\alpha_4$) the expression for monetary expansion is unambiguously larger, so the appropriate assignment is the orthodox one.

However, for high capital mobility the surplus from fiscal expansion less the deficit from monetary expansion is:

$$\frac{\alpha_3\alpha_{12}\alpha_4-2\alpha_3\alpha_6\alpha_9-\alpha_6\alpha_{12}(1-\alpha_1+\alpha_9)}{\alpha_6D1}$$

If this expression is positive the assignment rule prescribes that fiscal policy should be assigned to external balance and monetary policy to internal balance. At the same time, it can easily be shown that under these same conditions the slope of the (positive) *YY* schedule is steeper than the slope of the *BB* schedule. This is how the schedules are drawn in the text.[17]

The Swan-based Assignment

For the model, with the interest rate fixed, we can derive from the goods market Equation (11.7) of the basic model:

$$\Delta E=\frac{1-\alpha_1+\alpha_9}{ML}\Delta Yr-\frac{1}{ML}\Delta Gr \tag{28A.4}$$

where $ML=X(edx+edm-1)$ so the slope of the *YY* schedule is $1/ML$.

The equation for the balance of payments can be derived by combining Equations (11.7) and (11.14) and treating the interest rate as fixed:

$$B=\frac{ML(1-\alpha_1)}{1-\alpha_1+\alpha_9}\Delta E-\frac{\alpha_9}{1-\alpha_1+\alpha_9}\Delta Gr \tag{28A.5}$$

For a given balance of payments, the slope of the *EE* schedule $\Delta E/\Delta Gr$ is:

$$\frac{\alpha_9}{ML(1-\alpha_1)}$$

To determine the appropriate assignment we need to evaluate the relative balance of payments effects of exchange rate and fiscal policies for equivalent output changes.

Substituting equivalent output effects from Equation (28A.4) into Equation (28A.5) shows that the absolute balance of payments effect of an increase in government expenditure less the balance of payments effect of an equivalent output devaluation is:

$$\frac{ML[\alpha_9 - (1 - \alpha_1)]}{1 - \alpha_1 + \alpha_9} \qquad (28A.6)$$

It is evident that the larger is α_1 the greater the likelihood that this expression is positive, implying that the appropriate assignment is the unorthodox one.

Notes for Chapter 28

1 J. Meade (1951); J. Tinbergen (1952); H. Theil (1961); R. Mundell (1962). See also J. M. Fleming (1968).
2 See R. Mundell (1962); M.v. N. Whitman (1970); J. Helliwell (1969); J. Levin (1972); R. Jones (1968); S. C. Tsiang (1975).
3 See J. Levin (1972). Our analysis in the next section of the Mundellian assignment follows Levin fairly closely.
4 If capital is very mobile the only monetary instrument available to them is the last.
5 In Mundell's original contribution the monetary instrument was the interest rate. See also J. Levin (1972).
6 See R. Jones (1968) and J. Helliwell (1969).
7 This will be the case if capital mobility is low. With high capital mobility this need not follow as the additional surplus on invisibles may be so large as to convert the overall balance of payments into a surplus which is absolutely larger than the deficit under fiscal policy.
8 See J. Levin (1972).
9 For example, this would certainly be the case for near perfect capital mobility where the monetary instrument is the domestic assets of the Central Bank. In this case, monetary policy has no effect on economic activity and has to be assigned to external balance.
10 See R. Cooper (1969), p. 240.
11 See T. W. Swan (1955). Swan himself does not deal with assignment in the Mundellian sense but his basic analysis is easily adaptable to the assignment framework.
12 Also, of course, the lower the marginal propensity to tax, since this will raise the propensity to spend out of income.
13 The New Cambridge School tends to treat taxes as exogenous so a change in disposable income is equivalent to a change in total income. For a discussion of the New Cambridge School see: J. Spraos (1975); R. Smith (1976); J. Bispham (1975).
14 See Chapter 21.
15 R. J. Ball, T. Burns and J. S. E. Laury (1977).
16 R. McKinnon (1969).
17 For a rigorous demonstration of how the Mundellian assignment is also stable when capital mobility is high see J. Levin (1972).

Chapter 29

The New Economic Environment and its Policy Implications

Introduction

In retrospect, the economic situation in the industrial world in the 1950s and 1960s was very favourable. Real economic growth was unprecedented in recorded history, unemployment rates were the lowest on record and inflation, for most of that time, was not severe. There was no major recession, while the variations in real output growth, unemployment and in the rate of inflation were relatively small.

Already by the second half of the 1960s there were serious and increasing strains in the international monetary system. At the same time, the US inflation rate had by then risen significantly. Also in the late 1960s many industrial countries, notably France, Italy and the UK, experienced wage explosions with associated serious industrial unrest. By the early 1970s the inflation rate had accelerated throughout the industrial world while the international monetary system was increasingly threatened.

In early 1973 at a time when the industrial world was caught up in a global boom the monetary regime collapsed and was replaced by a managed float regime. Then, at the end of 1973, came the oil price shock with a quadrupling of oil prices. This shock and the policy stances at the time were together largely responsible for the collapse in economic activity some time in 1974.

These developments and others have dramatically transformed the economic environment of recent years and, also, the character of the policy debate. This chapter will try to identify these changes in the economies and some, at least, of their policy implications.

The Changed Environment in Industrial Countries

First, exchange rates have become more flexible since 1973. While there continues to be a good deal of official intervention in foreign exchange markets, nevertheless exchange rate movements are now principally determined by market forces.

Second, the rate of inflation is now higher, for most industrial countries, than in the 1960s and also more variable on a year to year basis. This appears to have two implications. One is that the economy is now located on a higher point on its presumed vertical Phillips curve; another is that its short-run trade-off at that point may be steeper than in the past because, with increased price consciousness, labour markets may now adjust more rapidly.[1]

Third, unemployment rates have also remained relatively high by historical standards. In evaluating this increase in unemployment, a useful distinction to make is between cyclical unemployment (attributable to a lack of effective demand) and structural unemployment (which is not readily removable by demand stimulus). While some of the unemployment that emerged in 1974/75 was cyclical, it is claimed that, beginning in the late 1960s, the structural component has also assumed considerably more importance. The precise reasons for this secular trend remain, however, a matter for debate. Suggested explanations include: the mismatching of labour due to structural changes in demand composition; the change in the net demand for labour associated with the change in the composition of production; demographic factors (an increased share in the labour force of women and teenagers); relatively high real unemployment benefits encouraging greater voluntary unemployment and search activity; inappropriate real wages for particular groups (for example, youth); a low rate of industrial investment in recent years; an economy-wide real wage rate which is too high and accelerated labour-saving technological change.[2]

What we have observed then in recent years is not only a sharp shift to the right in the short-run Phillips curve and a (possible) change in its slope but also, most importantly, an increase in the natural rate of unemployment, some of which is transitional but some of which may, in fact, be longer lasting.

Fourth, disturbances originating on the 'supply side' (for instance, from wages and commodity prices) have now assumed considerably more importance, creating new dilemmas for policy. For example, in the face of a supply shock, macro-policy can be accommodating, allowing the push in prices, or neutral, allowing now a more moderate rise in prices but at the cost of additional unemployment.[3]

Fifth, budget deficits in recent years have also been very high by historical standards, posing again new problems for policy (see later).

Table 29.1 shows how, for select industrial countries, the general government deficit as a percentage of GDP increased very substantially after 1974. The dominant reason, of course, was the sharp reduction in economic activity. Significantly, in the USA where economic growth was most rapid in the years 1976–78 the deficit, as a percentage of GNP, fell sharply over those three years.

Table 29.1 Financial surplus (+) or deficit (−) of general government – selected OECD countries percentages of GDP

	Average						
Country	*1964–69*	*1970–73*	*1974*	*1975*	*1976*	*1977*	*1978*
Australia	+1.5	+1.8	+0.4	− 0.8	−0.7	−1.8	− 2.5
Canada	+0.8	+0.6	+1.9	− 2.4	−1.8	−2.6	− 3.5
France	+0.4	+0.8	+0.6	− 2.2	−0.5	−1.3	− 2.4
Germany	−0.2	+0.3	−1.4	− 5.8	−3.6	−2.6	− 2.7
Italy	−2.8	−5.4	−5.9	−11.7	−9.1	−8.1	−10.6
Japan	−2.7	+0.9	+0.4	− 2.7	−3.6	−3.9	− 4.8
United Kingdom	−0.9	−0.7	−4.1	− 4.8	−5.0	−3.2	− 3.9
United States	0	−0.2	+0.5	− 3.5	−1.4	−0.3	+ 0.3

Source: OECD Economic Outlook (July 1979), Table 68, p. 143.

Sixth, in the wake of the oil price shock the industrial countries, as a group, have had to live with substantially larger current account deficits than in the pre-1974 era. For example, in the years 1970–73 the average current account surplus of the OECD as a whole was of the order of $8 billion, while the average for the years 1974–77 was a $19 billion deficit – a turnaround of some $27 billion. These developments have led policymakers to attach more importance to trends in the current account than they had in the past.

Seventh, the government sector is now substantially larger than in the 1960s (see Chapter 16). In most industrial countries the share of public expenditure in GNP rose between 1965–69 and 1974/75 by some five to ten percentage points. This, of course, has been associated with much higher rates of taxes and hence greater tax consciousness. At the same time that there has been an erosion of 'price' illusion there has also been some erosion of 'tax' illusion.

For example, in today's world, an increase in government expenditure exactly matched by an increase in income taxes might lead not to a balanced budget expansion, as in traditional Keynesian analysis, but to some stagflation (providing some rationale for a balanced budget contraction).[4] Again, the public will now resist attempts by governments to raise the burden of taxes as a means of

Table 29.2 Degree of openness – exports as percentage of GNP – select periods

Country	*1953–55*	*1963–65*	*1973–75*
Australia	20.3	16.4	16.3
Canada	20.2	19.5	24.7
France	14.8	13.4	20.2
Germany	18.8	19.6	27.6
Italy	10.7	15.0	21.7
Japan	11.2	10.2	13.2
United Kingdom	21.4	18.4	25.6
United States	4.3	4.8	7.9

Source: IMF, *International Financial Statistics* – National Accounts.

combating excess demand in the economy, so a large public sector renders it more difficult for governments to use variations in tax rates to fight inflation.

Eighth, it could also be argued that the industrial world is now more interdependent than in the past. For example, the economies are now more integrated trade-wise (see Table 29.2) and (possibly) capital-wise, a fact that needs to be taken into account in the formation of policy.[5] This contention, however, needs to be tempered by the important consideration that, with flexible exchange rates, the ways in which changes in one economy make an impact on the rest of the world have changed and have probably become more complex.

Ninth, there have been significant financial innovations in recent years, at least in some industrial countries, leading to a reassessment of the liquidity of different financial assets. For example, in the USA many banks and thrift institutions now offer services on interest bearing accounts, which closely parallel those offered by demand deposits.[6] This means that a particular concept of money that was appropriate in the past may now have become obsolete, creating special difficulties for the design of monetary policy and for monetary targeting. For example, in the USA, $M1$, defined in the traditional way, grew by some 5.1 per cent in 1979, well within the 3–6 per cent targeted. However, when these other forms of money are also included in $M1$ (as they now are) it turns out that $M1$ grew by some 13 per cent, at least, in 1979.

Tenth, in many industrial countries the household savings ratio increased significantly in recent years. Consistent and comparable data on savings are difficult to obtain but it does appear that of the seven large industrial countries the increase has been very large in Canada, Japan and the UK. In the UK, for example, whereas the savings rate was some 8.4 per cent on average in the years 1963–70 it has, in more recent years (1975–77), hovered around 14 per cent. In Japan it rose from some 18 per cent in 1963–70 to some 24 per cent in 1975–77. In Canada the increase was from 5.6 per cent in the early period to some 10.5 per cent in the later period.

In explaining the increase in the savings ratio most of the emphasis has been placed on the effects of accelerated inflation on consumer confidence and on the real value of nominal assets and, also, on the effects of the increased unemployment on the propensity to spend of the unemployed and on precautionary savings.[7]

The implications for policy of the increase are important. A higher savings ratio opens up a potentially larger deflationary gap which needs to be closed in some way by increased business investment, a reduced government surplus (increased government deficit) or a larger current account surplus.[8] At the same time, the higher savings ratio implies an accumulation of readily available liquid assets that could be converted, as economic conditions changed, into spending, with potentially disturbing effects.

Eleventh, there may have been a secular drop in the growth of productivity in many industrial countries. For example, in its December 1978 *Economic Outlook* the OECD notes that 'it is clear that for a number of countries, cyclical factors . . . cannot explain the entire slowdown in productivity growth since 1973–74. Thus, while more than two thirds of the observed slowdown in productivity growth could perhaps be accounted for by cyclical factors in Japan, Germany and France, only half of the observed slowdown could be explained in the USA and a third in the UK, Canada and Italy' (p. 15).[9] Several factors may explain the secular decline. These include: the effect of the oil price shock on potential GNP, the slower pace of capital formation, the increased weight of the service sector (where productivity is relatively low) and the absorption of some industrial investment to meet new environmental or safety regulations.

An important implication of the secular fall in productivity is that the inflationary struggle for shares in domestic real resources may intensify. In other words, with a decline in the growth in real incomes for the community as a whole attention may now be diverted towards securing real gains by redistribution.

Twelfth, there is evidence, in recent years, of a rise in protectionism in the West, not on the scale of the 1930s but nevertheless sufficient to create considerable concern around the world.[10] The new barriers to trade have assumed many subtle, non-tariff, forms; these include: anti-dumping pleas, voluntary restraints on exports, lame-duck rescues, subsidies-incentives, government procurement, countervailing duties against imports judged to have been subsidised, regional policies. This trend, coming on top of the effects of the oil price shocks and the secular decline in productivity growth, carries still further implications for the growth of real incomes.

The New Macro-policy Debate – Two Schools of Thought

There are, essentially, two schools of thought that have emerged in the macro-policy debate of the mid-late 1970s. One is the Liberal–Keynesian, the other is the Conservative–Monetarist school.

Several important issues divide these two schools. First, Conservative–Monetarists (Liberal–Keynesians) tend to attach relatively more (less) importance to the costs of inflation than to the costs of unemployment. Second, Conservative–Monetarists (Liberal–Keynesians) attach more (less) importance to the structural than to the cyclical influences on unemployment. Third, Conservative–Monetarists attach considerable importance to the continuing large budget deficits; at the same time, there is disagreement over the best means of reducing these deficits. Fourth, Conservative–Monetarists tend to stress that, in the new environment of the mid-late 1970s, traditional expansionary monetary and fiscal policies are likely to be ineffective in creating employment. Fifth, and finally, whereas the Liberal–Keynesian school tends to believe that it is possible to design policies (for example, a Prices and Incomes Policy, a changed monetary-fiscal mix, a marginal employment subsidy) that will reduce unemployment without aggravating inflation (or which will reduce both), the Conservative–Monetarist school tends to be very sceptical of such policies. (This particular issue is taken up in some detail in the next two chapters.)

The Relative Costs of Inflation and Unemployment

Whereas the social and economic losses associated with unemployment are well known and identifiable there continues to be considerable disagreement over the costs associated with inflation. In evaluating these costs economists make a sharp distinction between fully anticipated and unanticipated inflation. Suppose, to begin with, that inflation were fully anticipated and that there is universal indexation. For these conditions, what would be the real costs to the community of a higher rate of inflation? First, there are the welfare costs of economising on currency (demand deposits), on which interest cannot (may not) be paid (the so-called extra trips to the banks). Second, there are the resource costs of making (more frequent) price changes (the so-called menu costs). Third, the increase in the variance around the new mean rate increases uncertainty, making decision-making more difficult and less efficient. Fourth, since price adjustment will not be synchronised relative price disparities will emerge, misallocating resources and offering increased returns from additional search activity (to exploit these disparities).[11]

By contrast, if inflation were unanticipated the costs would then be much more substantial. These costs would flow from the redistribution in income and wealth, from the much more severe relative price distortions and from the real effects of the greater uncertainty about future inflation.

Conservative–Monetarists attach considerable importance to the costs of fully anticipated inflation while Liberal–Keynesians, on the other hand, concede that the costs of unanticipated inflation are serious but contend that for fully anticipated inflation rates of the order of 10–20 per cent the costs are small.

To illustrate the differences, consider a situation where inflation has accelerated from 5 per cent to 15 per cent and the economy is fully indexed at the now higher rate. At the same time, drawing on the monetarist expectations-augmented Phillips curve framework in Chapter 12, suppose that the economy is placed at a higher point on its vertical Phillips curve at its natural unemployment rate. Should the inflation rate be brought down? Conservative–Monetarists would argue that the benefits of a permanently lower rate of inflation are large and that they are likely to exceed the costs associated with additional, but only transitional, unemployment as well as the costs of the now (in part, at least) unanticipated reduction in the rate of inflation. The rational-expectations wing of this school would take the argument even further, contending that a deceleration in monetary growth would itself lead to a change in inflationary expectations and hence to a quick reduction in the rate of inflation, with little cost in terms of an increase in unemployment (see later). By contrast, Liberal–Keynesians argue that the benefits flowing from the lower rate of inflation are very small and would be overwhelmed by the protracted social and economic disruption associated with policies aimed at reducing the inflation rate.

Of course, in reality, the situation facing industrial countries in 1978/79 was much more complicated. Consider, for example, the situation where monetary growth had been allowed to decelerate and where economies were still in the throes of a protracted adjustment process. In other words, inflation had not fully adjusted while unemployment still exceeded the natural rate of unemployment. The choice here is between persisting with the restrictive policy or reversing it. It could be argued, in this context, that, since some of the costs had already been borne, the case for reversal is correspondingly weaker. The issues are clearly extremely complex and cannot be pursued here.

Cyclical and Structural Unemployment

Conservative–Monetarists also argue that there has been a substantial increase in the natural unemployment rate (for reasons already discussed), leaving little room for a significant reduction in cyclical unemployment. In the view of this school, priority should be given to policies aimed at reducing this natural unemployment rate (for example, by manpower policies, policies to correct real wage imbalances, investment subsidies to secure increased capacity). Also, they emphasise the uncertainty about the natural rate of unemployment and the serious risks associated with underestimating it (see Chapter 12). Liberal–Keynesians do not deny that policies to reduce the natural unemployment rate would be helpful but contend that there is still considerable room for a reduction in cyclical unemployment.

The Importance of the Budget Deficit

Conservative–Monetarists attach considerable importance to the large budget deficits, arguing that they need to be substantially reduced as a precondition for any sustained and secure recovery in the economy. They argue that large budget deficits need to be financed either by monetary growth, which they say is inflationary, or by the sale of government paper, which they say will raise interest rates and, at the same time, leave in its wake servicing as well as debt management problems for the future. They also tend to argue that the public are rational and will take account of their future tax liabilities, in which case their current expenditure will be reduced, making debt financing somewhat more analogous to tax financing.[12] Again, they contend that since large budget deficits are a major concern to business this fact of life must be taken into account in the formulation of policy.

Liberal–Keynesians, by contrast, are not nearly so concerned about the size of the deficits, arguing that the costs of conservative budgetary policies far outweigh any (small) costs associated with large budget deficits. They also reject the notion of tax discounting and argue that fiscal stimulus may so lift activity that the deficit may actually fall.

The Changed Effectiveness of Monetary and Fiscal Policies

There are two ways in which the effects of any given change in policy might now be different. The 'variance' surrounding an expected outcome may now be greater and, in addition, the 'expected' outcome may itself be different.

In today's world there may be greater uncertainty about the outcome of any policy change than in the past. At least three reasons might be adduced for this. First, the outcome of a policy change will depend very much on the ways in which households and businesses respond to the policy and, in turn, this depends on their 'state of expectation', which is now more volatile and unpredictable. Second, the outcome of a policy change will depend on how exchange rates respond and, in turn, on how the economy responds to the change in exchange rates. Since there is considerable uncertainty attaching to these two links in the chain the outcome of a policy change is bound to be highly unpredictable. Third, there is greater uncertainty about how prices and labour markets will respond.

In the face of increased uncertainty surrounding the effects of policy changes, it has been argued that policy-makers ought to adopt a more cautious approach[13] (in other words, the magnitude of the change in policy should be reduced). This would provide one rationale for constraining the range of variation in the rate of monetary growth (for example, by bands around a monetary target).

Fiscal Policy and Crowding Out – Conventional Analysis

The view that fiscal expansion cannot affect real output and leads to an offsetting reduction in private expenditure enjoyed a major resurgence in the mid-1970s.[14] This resurgence was due to two factors: first, the apparent lack of success attendant on the expansionary fiscal policies followed by many industrial countries at the onset of the recession in 1974/75; second, inspired by the changed environment, a new rationale was provided for crowding out.

The first contention can readily be dismissed. There are, to begin, very important differences in the extent (if at all) to which countries switched to expansionary policies, in the timing of the switch and the degree to which it was sustained (see Chapter 18). Of much greater importance, as we saw in Chapter 18, were the major deflationary influences at work in the industrial countries during 1974/75. It would be quite reasonable, therefore, to argue that fiscal expansion, where it occurred, was effective but that its effects were, in fact, overwhelmed by the other deflationary influences.

We now turn to the relevance of the changed environment to the crowding out thesis. It is convenient, in this context, to begin, first, with conventional mechanisms by which the private sector might be crowded out and then demonstrate how the changed environment can alter some of the conclusions we reach.

Suppose there is an increase in government expenditure financed by the sale of government paper. In what conditions will the private sector be crowded out? Two basic mechanisms can be identified here: first, through developments in the goods market; second, through associated price changes.

In dealing with the goods market, abstracting altogether from price developments, three mechanisms need to be distinguished: (1) the effects of associated changes in exchange rates or (for fixed rates) of incomplete sterilisation, (2) wealth effects and (3) financial effects.

(1) Some crowding out is possible if the exchange rate is flexible and capital is mobile. At the limit when capital is very mobile, so that the domestic interest rate cannot effectively depart from the foreign interest rate, something approximating complete real crowding out is possible.

Crowding out is also possible if the exchange rate is fixed, capital is relatively immobile and the monetary authorities allow the volume of money to respond to the balance of payments (there is incomplete sterilisation). At the limit, when capital is completely immobile (so the capital account does not respond to relative interest rates), output cannot increase since the current account must now be in balance. (See Chapter 22 for these results.)

(2) Under certain conditions, the associated wealth effects from fiscal expansion may also generate some real crowding out. The sale of public debt will add to private sector wealth. This, in turn, may increase household expenditure and, in addition, increase the demand for money. The former is expansionary while the latter is deflationary. If the latter effect is dominant, some real crowding out may occur.[15]

(3) Financial effects fall into two categories. A familiar 'Keynesian' effect and a less familiar 'asset composition' effect. Keynesian crowding out occurs because with a fixed volume of money an increase in real demand will tend (potentially) to raise interest rates. Complete real crowding out is possible here in only two extreme cases: where the demand for money is not interest sensitive (the *LM* schedule is vertical) or the interest sensitivity of investment is infinite (the *IS* schedule is infinitely elastic).

Changes in asset composition will also have effects on the demand for money and, in turn, on private expenditure.[16] Assume, for simplicity, that there are three types of financial assets: government bonds, money and private bonds. It is evident that, all other things being equal, a deficit will entail an accumulation of government bonds in private portfolios. What will a higher proportion of government bonds do to interest rates and private expenditure? The answer depends on the degree of substitution of different assets. If government bonds were closer substitutes for money than for private securities there would be an excess supply of liquidity and the cost of finance would fall. If, however, the bond issues were illiquid and were closer substitutes for private securities, there would be an excess supply of relatively illiquid assets and the cost of finance would rise. Debt issue, then, could provide additional stimulus or reverse part of the stimulus depending on the liquidity of the bonds issued by governments to finance the deficits. This effect would be felt immediately the bonds were sold.

To sum up, briefly, something like complete real crowding out through the goods market requires one of the following to hold:

(1) flexible exchange rates with very high capital mobility,
(2) fixed exchange rates with incomplete sterilisation and very low capital mobility,
(3) a very low interest sensitivity of the demand for money,
(4) a very high interest sensitivity of investment,
(5) strong wealth effects on the demand for money overpowering wealth effects on household consumption,
(6) strong asset composition effects, with government bonds viewed as relatively illiquid financial assets.

Since none of these extreme assumptions is at all likely to hold we may safely conclude that complete real crowding out through the goods market is of only academic interest in conventional analysis.

What happens when we allow wages and prices to adjust? More particularly, what happens ultimately to real output if we make the (realistic) assumption that the real wage rate is restored? Here much depends on (1) how the aggregate supply sector is represented, (2) the exchange rate regime, (3) the mobility of capital.

If an expectations-augmented Phillips curve, with zero money illusion, is used to represent the aggregate supply sector of the economy, real crowding out has to be complete in the long run. The economy, in other words, reverts to its natural rate of unemployment (NRU). At most, fiscal policy will simply serve to accelerate the move towards the NRU.

In our own neo-Keynesian model the distribution of effects between output and prices depends ultimately on the exchange rate regime and how mobile capital is (see Annex).[17] With fixed rates and sterilisation, there will be some increase in output and some increase in the price level. With exchange rates fixed, this will allow some drop in the real wage rate to producers while maintaining the real wage rate to suppliers of labour. With flexible rates the outcomes are much more complicated. Provided there is some capital mobility fiscal expansion will have favourable output effects. At the same time, the effects on domestic prices are ambiguous. For example, if capital mobility were high the associated revaluation would reduce import prices, while the excess demand would tend to push domestic prices up; under these conditions, with wages adjusting to the overall price level, the domestic price level could actually fall on balance.

Crowding Out – Some New Considerations

How would this analysis have changed in the new environment? First, there is the state of expectations. Fiscal expansion may be adversely received by the private sector (for instance, because it may entail a larger budget deficit) and, hence, may discourage investment or lift liquidity preference, in this way crowding out the private sector. Second, with a sustained large budget deficit, requiring continued large sales of government debt, the 'asset composition' effect may have assumed more importance. Third, with a larger component of structural unemployment fiscal expansion may not be capable of reducing unemployment significantly and may manifest itself in higher inflation. Fourth, in so far as labour markets adjust more rapidly some real crowding out may occur sooner than in the past. Fifth, in so far as the public are now more deficit conscious there is a greater likelihood that they will discount future taxes, so the potential for real crowding out would be greater. Fifth, the larger net global current account deficit acts as a dampener on fiscal expansion by individual countries. Sixth, even without a labour constraint there may be a capacity constraint on fiscal expansion. For example, if investment has been inadequate a substantial expansion in demand cannot be met with existing capacity and prices will be forced up rapidly.[18]

Monetary Policy, Inflation and Rational Expectations

A once-over increase in the volume of money (with fixed real wages) has, ultimately, no real effects but only price effects. This is as true for an adjustable peg regime as for a flexible rate regime. The difference between the two regimes is that in the former case the exchange rate adjusts with a (long) lag.

There are two reasons why monetary expansion may now, over a given short-term horizon, have larger price effects than in the past. First, with flexible rates monetary expansion leads to a devaluation which has immediate effects on import prices and, to a lesser extent, on prices of tradable goods. Second, to the extent that labour markets adjust more quickly, the early price effects will be more substantial.

By way of contrast, the real output effects of monetary expansion, again over a given short-term horizon, may now be larger or smaller, depending on a number of considerations. For example, if the initial price effects are substantial and, also, if the effects of exchange rate changes are initially perverse, output effects will also be weaker. If, however, a devaluation improved the trade balance the positive output effects may overwhelm the price effects.

Given the evidence we reviewed on Marshall–Lerner conditions in Chapter 21, a case could be made for the view that monetary expansion under flexible rates will lead to less output and more inflation in the short term. This in itself has the potential for a vicious circle. For example, with real effects relatively weaker monetary authorities may be encouraged to activate new rounds of monetary expansion.

The view that labour markets adjust more rapidly is represented in an extreme form in the application of the theory of rational expectations to monetary policy. In recent years, monetarists have mounted a new attack on discretionary monetary policy and its effectiveness, taking as their starting point the view that expectations are rationally formed. Although the theory of rational expectations has broader applications to macro-policy, including fiscal policy, its widest application has been made to monetary policy and there now exists a large and academically esoteric literature dealing with it.[19]

Assuming some variant of an expectations-augmented Phillips curve (EAPC) analysis these monetarists have been able to show that if monetary growth were fully anticipated, it would have no transitional real effects but would affect only prices. If the monetary authorities, for example, were to follow a discretionary monetary policy rule (for instance, where the rate of growth of money is geared to known policy targets) and this rule became known, so that the rate of growth of money that the monetary authorities will implement is fully anticipated, monetary policy will be ineffective and the monetary authorities will do better (since there will be less uncertainty) to follow a Friedmanite monetary rule (that is, allow the money supply to grow at a fixed rate). Only if the monetary authorities should have superior information, not accessible to the public, could they pursue a successful discretionary monetary policy.

This policy position will now be illustrated by drawing on our own presentation of the EAPC. Four key assumptions underly the monetarist argument. The first is that purchasing power parity holds. The second is that there is no money illusion. The third is that expectations are rationally based while the fourth is that changes in price expectations are quickly translated into changes in the actual rate of inflation.

Assuming PPP holds and there is no money illusion the key equations[20] are:

$$\dot{P} = \dot{W} \tag{29.1}$$

$$\dot{W} = \dot{P}e - b_{15}(U - UN) \tag{29.2}$$

$$U - U_{-1} = b_{21}(\dot{Y}c - \dot{Y}r) \tag{29.3}$$

$$\dot{Y}r = \dot{M}o - \dot{P} \tag{29.4}$$

Notation used in this chapter

Gr = real government expenditure
$\dot{M}e$ = expected rate of growth in the money supply
$\dot{M}o$ = rate of growth in the money supply

$\dot{P}$ = overall rate of inflation
$\dot{P}e$ = expected overall rate of inflation
U = unemployment rate
UN = natural unemployment rate
$\dot{W}$ = rate of change in wages
$\dot{Y}c$ = rate of change in full employment output
$\dot{Y}r$ = rate of change in real GNP

The solution for the rate of inflation is:

$$\dot{P} = \frac{1}{1+b_{15}b_{21}}\dot{P}e + \frac{1}{1+b_{15}b_{21}}\dot{P}_{-1} - \frac{1}{1+b_{15}b_{21}}\dot{P}e_{-1} + \frac{b_{15}b_{21}}{1+b_{15}b_{21}}\dot{M}o - \frac{b_{15}b_{21}}{1+b_{15}b_{21}}\dot{Y}c \quad (29.5)$$

If expectations are formed rationally in the sense that the structure of the economy, as represented by Equation (29.5), is known, that equation will also serve to explain the expected rate of inflation.

We can then write Equation (29.5) as:

$$\dot{P}e = \frac{1}{b_{15}b_{21}}\dot{P}_{-1} - \frac{1}{b_{15}b_{21}}\dot{P}e_{-1} + \dot{M}e - \dot{Y}c \quad (29.6)$$

To obtain 'rational expectations' solutions for the rate of inflation we now substitute Equation (29.6) into Equation (29.5). After substituting $-b_{15}(U_{-1} - UN)$ for $\dot{P}_{-1} - \dot{P}e_{-1}$ this yields:

$$\dot{P} = -\frac{1}{b_{21}}(U_{-1} - UN) + \frac{1}{1+b_{15}b_{21}}\dot{M}e + \frac{b_{15}b_{21}}{1+b_{15}b_{21}}\dot{M}o - \dot{Y}c \quad (29.7)$$

To obtain a solution for unemployment we substitute Equation (29.6) and Equation (29.7) into the equation

$$U - UN = -\frac{1}{b_{15}}(\dot{P} - \dot{P}e)$$

to yield:

$$U - UN = \frac{b_{21}}{1+b_{15}b_{21}}(\dot{M}e - \dot{M}o) \quad (29.8)$$

Equations (29.7) and (29.8) together reveal that if a change in monetary growth were fully anticipated (that is, $\dot{M}e = \dot{M}o$) it would have no effect on real output but would lead to an equivalent change in the rate of inflation. by contrast, an unanticipated change in monetary growth will have real effects and will increase the rate of inflation by something less than the change in monetary growth.

What do these results mean? Consider the neoclassical version of the model, which is most consistent with the spirit of the analysis.[21] We saw that when there is a change in the volume of money workers are 'fooled' into believing that their real wage rate has increased and so they are willing to supply more labour. This will happen, for example, if they deflated current wages on the basis of 'past' prices without observing that current changes in wages are being passed on in higher domestic prices. If, however, they were 'rational' and understood the mechanics of price determination they could not be fooled into believing that their real wage had risen. In these circumstances, wages and prices would increase in proportion to the increase in the volume of money, leaving real money balances and real demand, and hence employment, unchanged. Clearly, the speed of adjustment of prices to changes in the volume of money (which are anticipated) will now be very much quicker (indeed, virtually instantaneous).

The argument has a certain appeal but it is open to several objections. One (minor) objection is that PPP does not hold in the short run. With fixed exchange rates, a fully anticipated increase in the volume of money can increase the relevant real wage rate (because with domestic prices rising in proportion to wages, wages deflated by the overall price level will have risen). A more serious objection is that expectations are not rationally based. The counter argument here would be that monetarist thinking in recent years has made such an impact that there is now a vastly greater understanding of the close links between monetary changes and changes in prices. The most serious objection of all is that, whether or not expectations are rationally based, there are lags and rigidities in the system that delay the adjustment of wages to prices. These take the form, for example, of contracts or indexed agreements (which allow wages to adjust to preceding changes in prices). To conclude, then, while rational expectations may have speeded the adjustment process it is far from proven that only unanticipated changes in money can have real effects.

Annex – Effects on Output of an Increase in Government Expenditure with Real Wages Fixed

This Annex briefly demonstrates how output is affected, under fixed and flexible exchange rates, by an increase in government expenditure assuming the real wage rate and the volume of money are both held fixed. It provides a solution to the complete neo-Keynesian model of Chapter 11 for two exchange rate regimes MR and FR.

For the MR regime the solution is:

$$\Delta Yr = \frac{\alpha_6\alpha_{15}(1-\alpha_{14})}{\alpha_3\alpha_4\alpha_{15}(1-\alpha_{14}) + \alpha_3 Mo + \alpha_6\alpha_{15}(1-\alpha_{14})(1-\alpha_1+\alpha_9) + \alpha_6 ML}\Delta Gr \tag{29A.1}$$

which is positive indicating that fiscal expansion will unambiguously increase real output (see text).

For FR the solution for output is more complicated:

$$\Delta Yr = \alpha_{12}Mo\alpha_{15}(1-\alpha_{14})/\alpha_3\alpha_9 Mo\alpha_{15}(1-\alpha_{14}) + \alpha_3 Mo.ML + \alpha_{12}Mo\alpha_{15}(1-\alpha_{14})(1-\alpha_1+\alpha_9) + \alpha_{12}Mo.ML/\Delta Gr \tag{29A.2}$$

The solution for domestic prices (Pd) is:

$$\Delta Pd = \alpha_6\alpha_9\alpha_{15}(1-\alpha_{14}) + \alpha_6 ML - \alpha_4\alpha_{12}\alpha_{15}(1-\alpha_{14})/ \alpha_3\alpha_9 Mo\alpha_{15}(1-\alpha_{14}) + \alpha_3 Mo.ML + \alpha_{12}Mo\alpha_{15}(1-\alpha_{14})(1-\alpha_1+\alpha_9) + \alpha_{12}Mo.ML/\Delta Gr \tag{29A.3}$$

These results demonstrate the point made in the text that, provided there is some capital mobility ($\alpha_{12}>0$), fiscal expansion will increase output but the effect on domestic prices is ambiguous. Equation (29A.3) demonstrates that, if capital is sufficiently mobile, fiscal expansion may actually lower domestic prices (see text).

One particular result is worth highlighting. If capital mobility is perfect ($\alpha_{12}\rightarrow\infty$) Equation (29A.3) shows that the domestic price level must actually fall. The reason can easily be explained by reference to the equilibrium conditions in the money market. If capital mobility is perfect the domestic interest rate cannot change. At the same time, by assumption the volume of money is fixed; hence, if output increases this must be associated with a fall in domestic prices.

The results for output represent a striking contrast to the case where domestic prices are held fixed (see Chapter 22). With domestic prices fixed we saw that the effectiveness of fiscal policy weakens as capital mobility increases. Now Equation (29A.2) shows that the more mobile capital is the stronger is the effect on output.

The rationale for this result is the following. With zero capital mobility equilibrium in the foreign exchange market requires that the current account be in balance. This, in turn, would require that any increase in real output be offset by some improvement in the real exchange rate. By way of contrast, equilibrium in the labour market requires that any improvement in the real exchange rate be associated with a reduction in output. Hence, equilibrium, in this case, requires that the real exchange rate and output be unchanged.

However, as capital mobility increases, the balance of payments can be equilibrated with some deterioration in the real exchange rate as well as some improvement in real output. The key point here is that, as capital mobility increases, the currency strengthens (moving from devaluation to revaluation) and this allows the real wage rate to be maintained to workers while falling to employers.

We have seen that, in the face of fixed real wages, flexible exchange rates and mobile capital, fiscal policy can have some effectiveness. In sharp contrast, monetary policy under those same conditions will be totally ineffective. Fiscal policy, in other words, has some advantage over monetary policy in that it is able to exploit the effects on the exchange rate.

Notes for Chapter 29

1 The evidence for this comes from the widespread resort, in recent years, to indexation provisions. See: A. R. Braun (1976); N. Thygesen (1978); G. Richardson (1979). For a theoretical argument (and some evidence) that greater price variability leads to a steeper Phillips curve see R. E. Lucas, Jr. (1973); M. Friedman (1979b).
2 For evidence bearing on this and some discussion of the issues see OECD (1977a) and (1979b); F. H. Gruen (1978); OECD (1978c); S. Nickell (1979).
3 E. Gramlich (1979); R. Gordon (1975); E. Phelps (1978).
4 For a theoretical demonstration of this point see V. Argy and J. Salop (1979).
5 See Chapter 14.
6 J. Lovati (1977); J. Wenninger and C. Sivesind (1979); R. Porter, T. Simpson and E. Mauskopf (1979).
7 For a careful analysis see: D. H. Howard (1976); J. C. Townend (1976).
8 From the identity: $S=I+(G-T)+(X-M)$ where S=domestic savings, I=investment, G=government expenditure, T=taxes, X=exports and M=imports.
9 For a detailed exploration of this secular trend in the UK and the USA see: J. Sargent (1979); J. A. Tatom (1979).
10 IMF (1978); B. Balassa (1978).
11 S. Fischer and F. Modigliani (1978); M. Feldstein (1978); J. Parkin and A. Swoboda (1976). For recent attempts to evaluate empirically the costs of inflation and unemployment flowing from changes in policies see: E. Gramlich (1979) and F. Modigliani and L. Papademos (1978).
12 See N. Stevens (1979). Stevens concludes from a review of the evidence that 'the evidence does not appear strong enough for one to completely disregard the possibility of less than full discounting' (p. 19).
13 W. Brainard (1967).
14 See K. Carlson and R. Spencer (1975).

15 Very few econometric models allow for the effects of wealth accumulation on the demand for money. Allowing for these wealth effects will increase the degree of crowding out. For empirical evidence of this see: J. Butkiewicz (1979). See also A. Blinder and R. Solow (1973) for a discussion of stability problems in the context of a model that allows for wealth in expenditure as well as in the demand for money.

16 Much popular thinking about crowding out has roots in this case. This case is an important feature of a model of Stein's. See J. Stein (1976) and J. Tobin and W. Buiter (1976).

17 The econometric evidence (at least from the older models), briefly reviewed in Chapter 14, supports the view that there is little crowding out over, say, the first two years or so.

18 This argument was applied to the USA during 1979. O. Eckstein defined the downturn in 1979 as the 'first genuine supply recession in modern US history'. According to Eckstein the economy had reached its limits of industrial capacity. See O. Eckstein (1979).

19 See: S. Fischer (1977); R. Gordon (1976); B. T. McCallum (1977b); F. Modigliani (1977); R. Barro (1977); T. J. Sargent and N. Wallace (1976).

20 This is the model used in Chapter 12.

21 See, again, Chapter 12.

Chapter 30

Policies for Stagflation – I:

A Review of Some Proposals

Introduction

This chapter examines three policy proposals to deal with stagflation. The first is an employment subsidy. The second is a tax-based incomes policy. The third is a changed mix of monetary and fiscal policy.

An Employment Subsidy

In recent years many governments in industrial countries have been attracted by the idea of an employment subsidy, as one means of relieving a situation of stagflation.[1]

There are a large number of variations on this particular theme. First, a subsidy may be offered on the existing payroll (for example, in the form of a reduction in the payroll tax). Alternatively, the subsidy may be offered on new recruits, or on net additions to employment or on those who would otherwise be made redundant (to preserve existing jobs). Second, the subsidy may be for a specified duration or it may be more permanent. Third, the subsidy may be an absolute amount or it may be a percentage of the wage bill or wage rate. Fourth, it may be offered to select categories of labour (for example, to youth, or to those who have been unemployed over an extended period of time) or to regions or, again, for training in particular skills.

Table 30.1 provides an illustration of the kinds of schemes implemented in four industrial countries: France, West Germany, the UK and the USA. The table shows that in France and the UK the subsidy was a fixed amount while in West Germany and the USA it was proportionate to the wage bill. In all four cases the subsidy was a marginal one. A distinctive feature of the UK's scheme is that it was paid on workers 'declared to be redundant' (so as to preserve existing employment). In Germany, the eligible employee had to be unemployed for at least three months and, in addition, live in a region characterised by relatively high unemployment.

It is not possible, in this chapter, to evaluate these numerous permutations and their implications for the economy. All we can do here is to provide one illustration of a particular employment subsidy and then indicate the kinds of claims made on its behalf, as well as the kinds of objections that have been raised against it.

Suppose an employment subsidy, exactly equal to the relevant unemployment benefit, is offered to an enterprise on additions to its labour force beyond a defined base period. What kinds of benefits might flow from such a marginal employment subsidy?

First, by reducing the relevant real wage rate to employers these will now have an inducement to increase their level of employment. Second, by reducing costs at the margin the subsidy may put downward pressure on prices. Third, if the addition to employment is entirely attributable to the subsidy, the budget deficit may actually fall. The reason is that the subsidy paid exactly offsets the charge on the budget, represented by the payment of the unemployment benefits, that would otherwise be borne; at the same time, however, the additional incomes earned will be subject to tax and will yield extra revenue to the Treasury. Fourth, the employment subsidy also effectively represents an export subsidy; hence, the subsidy may also yield benefits in the form of an improvement in the trade balance.

These benefits appear substantial. Nevertheless, there has been considerable caution in using the subsidy and numerous reservations have been voiced. First, it is possible that, in anticipation of the introduction of the employment subsidy, employers would lay off workers, thus frustrating a major objective of the subsidy. Second, subsidies are paid on all increments to employment, including those that are due to influences other than the employment subsidy (for instance, when there is a reallocation of the labour force, or when aggregate employment would have expanded anyway). In these conditions, some of the claimed saving in net cost to the budget may not eventuate. Third, substitution effects may lead to 'hidden' reductions in other employment. For example, a subsidy of the kind being discussed (offered as a fixed amount) will favour some types of labour at the expense of others. Also, there may be a substitution of labour for capital. Again, the subsidy favours additions to the labour force at the expense of overtime by the existing labour force.

Fourth, the scheme may be inequitable in that it favours those enterprises that are relatively labour intensive as well as those leading the recovery in economic activity. Fifth, the employment subsidy may succeed in lowering the price level and, hence, the rate of inflation but this benefit cannot be sustained. In due course, other things being equal, the rate of inflation will return to its pre-subsidy level at least; indeed, with economic activity higher the rate of inflation may accelerate. It is also claimed (perhaps dubiously, in this context) that

Table 30.1 Temporary wage subsidies

Country and subsidy	*Method of payment*	*Amount and duration*
United States		
New jobs tax credit	Credit against income tax of eligible employers. The employer's deduction of wages is reduced by the amount of the credit.	Fifty per cent of the lesser of the following amounts: (1) the increase in the current year's wage bill subject to the Federal Unemployment Tax Act (FUTA) above 102 per cent of the previous year's FUTA wage bill. (2) the increase in the current year's total wage bill above 105 per cent of the previous year's total wage bill, and (3) 50 per cent of the wage bill subject to FUTA. The credit is limited to a yearly maximum of US$2, 100 per employee and US$100.000 per employer. Credit in excess of current tax liability can be carried back 3 years and forward 7 years.
France		
Incentive bonus for job creation	Cash grant (taxable) to eligible employers	F 500 per month per eligible worker during the initial 6 months of employment.

in major industrial countries

Eligible employer	Eligible employee	Effective dates
Any employer (other than certain tax-exempt organizations) who employs eligible workers, and whose wage bill subject to the Federal Unemployment Tax Act (FUTA) has increased above 102 per cent of the previous year's FUTA wage bill, and whose total wage bill has increased above 105 per cent of the previous year's level.	Any employee who is employed by an eligible employer and is covered by the Federal Unemployment Tax Act (FUTA) system, is an agricultural employee, or is a railroad employee.	Employment must take place between January 1, 1977 and December 31, 1978.
(1) Any employer who hires an eligible worker, for at least one year, without reduction for economic reasons in the establishment's work force below that of June 4, 1975. (2) Any craftsman or small employer (with less than 10 employees) who hires an eligible worker, for at least one year, without reduction for economic reasons in the establishment's work force below that of June 4, 1975. This base level of employment was subsequently brought forward to January 26, 1977.	(1) Any person who is hired by an eligible employer (other than a craftsman or small employer), and is either unemployed and registered for employment at least 6 months prior to being hired; or under 25 years of age seeking first employment; or discharged from active military duty and registered for employment. (2) Any person who is hired by an eligible craftsman or small employer, and is either unemployed and registered for employment; or under 25 years of age; or discharged from active military duty and registered for employment. Since January 26, 1977, eligibility has been restricted to any person who is hired by an eligible craftsman or small employer, and is either under 20 years of age seeking first employment or has been discharged from active military duty within 6 months prior to being hired.	(1) Hiring by an eligible employer (other than a craftsman or small employer) must take place between June 4 and November 30, 1975. (2) Hiring by an eligible craftsman or small employer must take place between June 4, 1975 and December 31, 1977.

Table 30.1 (cont.)

Country and subsidy	*Method of payment*	*Amount and duration*
Germany, Fed. Rep. Wage cost subsidy	Cash grant (taxable) to eligible employers.	Sixty per cent of the basic wage of eligible workers during the initial 6 months of employment.
United Kingdom Temporary employment subsidy	Cash grant (taxable) to eligible employers.	£10 per week per eligible full-time worker during the following 6 months of employment (excluding leave time); increased to 12 months of employment for applications made after February 12, 1976; and increased to £20 per week for applications made after April 6, 1976. Since March 30, 1977, a Supplementary Temporary Employment Subsidy equivalent to one half of the normal amount is provided to eligible employers for up to 6 months of additional employment. All payments are reduced by one half with regard to eligible part time workers.

Eligible employer	*Eligible employee*	*Effective dates*
Any employer who hires an eligible worker for permanent position, without reduction in the establishment's work force below its level of December 10, 1975, and declares that he would not have hired the worker in the absence of the subsidy.	Any person unemployed for at least 3 months prior to being hired and living in a region where the unemployment rate was above the average national unemployment rate by at least 0.5 per cent from September 1975 through November 1975.	Hiring must take place between December 10, 1974 and May 1, 1975.
Any employer who files jointly with the trade unions concerned an application for subsidy, after deciding to dismiss a number of workers whom he declares to be redundant. The minimum qualifying redundancy per employer was 50 workers prior to December 17, 1975, which was then lowered to 25 until February 12, 1976, and was thereafter lowered to 10 workers. Further, the employer must not be insolvent or about to become insolvent, and must abide by the Government's pay limit.	Any full-time worker (working at least 35 hours a week) or part-time worker (working between 21 and 35 hours a week) whose job is declared redundant by an eligible employer.	Application must be made between August 18, 1975 and March 31, 1978.

Source: G. F. Kopits (1978), p. 498.

the employment subsidy may place unions in a stronger bargaining position and so lead to bigger wage demands. Sixth, the 'export subsidy' element may invite protests or be repeated in other countries, in which case the benefit would be neutralised. Seventh, and finally, the eventual removal of the subsidy may recreate unemployment problems in the future.

It is evident, from the discussion, that an employment subsidy does have considerable merit; at the same time, it is open to some serious objections. This, then, calls for caution and care in implementing schemes of this kind.

A Tax-based Incomes Policy (TIP)

An interesting new proposal is the tax-based incomes policy (TIP), first advanced by Weintraub and Wallich.[2] The Weintraub and Wallich proposal contains two key elements. First, a norm for wage increases is set for a particular year. Second, if the increase in the wage bill or total employee compensation for an enterprise in that year exceeded the norm the enterprise would incur a penalty tax on its profits.[3]

It is argued, in favour of the TIP, that there would be minimal government involvement, no new bureaucracy and that it could be readily accommodated within existing tax regulations. It is also claimed that the penalty tax would effectively serve to discourage enterprises from paying wages in excess of the norm and, hence, to reduce inflation.

Critics of the TIP, however, have drawn attention to several possible difficulties associated with it. First, there might be serious problems in defining the base for the TIP. For example, if fringe benefits are left out of the 'wage bill' there might be scope for substituting these benefits for increases in wages, or if the wage bill increased because of a change in the skill-mix the enterprise involved might be unfairly penalised. Second, it has been suggested that in so far as the TIP is passed forward inflation might actually increase, with enterprises awarding wage settlements in excess of the norm and passing on the excess profits tax. This is conceivable when, for example, wage negotiations take place on an industry-wide basis and where, in addition, the demand for the industry's product is relatively inelastic. Third, if some enterprises pay no tax because they are not profitable there would then be no tax disincentive to pay excess wage increases – a situation that some unions may be able to exploit.[4] Finally, the fastest growing enterprises seeking additional labour might be unduly penalised by the tax penalty.

A Changed Monetary–Fiscal Mix

In Chapter 28 we focused our attention on the two-target two-instrument approach to policy-making. In that discussion, the two principal targets of policy were employment and the balance of payments. With the new environment in mind we now switch our attention to a different two-target framework where the two targets are inflation and unemployment. The two instruments on which our analysis will focus are the volume of money and the income tax rate, keeping the exchange rate fixed.[5] We will also, in the course of the discussion, have something to say about the current account effects of alternative policy mixes, in deference to the increased emphasis being placed on current account positions.

The question, then, is which policy mix is appropriate in a stagflation situation.[6] Once again we draw on our neo-Keynesian model to illustrate the analysis. The new element we introduce is the assumption that workers now bargain on the basis of post-tax incomes.[7] On this basis, a cut (an increase) in income taxes will reduce (increase) wage demands and, hence, reduce (increase) the costs of production.

We want to derive schedules that combine our monetary and fiscal instruments so as to maintain a given output level (*YY*) and, also, a given price level (*PP*). Consider the *YY* schedule. An increase in the tax rate, for a given volume of money, will reduce output for two reasons: first, the reduction in disposable incomes and second, the wage-pressure on domestic prices. In other words, both the aggregate demand and aggregate supply schedules will now shift to the left. On the other hand, an increase in the volume of money will raise output. The *YY* schedule, therefore, will be positively sloped because an increase in the tax rate will require an increase in the volume of money to restore the desired level of output. This is shown in Figure 30.1.

The *PP* schedule is more complicated. An increase in the tax rate may raise or lower the domestic price level depending on the relative importance of the demand pull effect, which tends to depress the price level, and the tax push effect which tends to lift the price level. Assume as a first possibility that, on balance, the price level is raised; then, in this case, an offsetting decrease in the volume of money is required to restore the original level of prices. This case is shown in Figure 30.1.

The area to the right of *PP* represents a situation where prices are too 'high' because, with a given volume of money, the tax rate is above that required to maintain a satisfactory level of prices. The area to the right of *YY* represents a situation where output is below the level judged to be satisfactory because, again, with a given volume of

Figure 30.1 *Policy mix for stagflation – increased taxes raise prices*

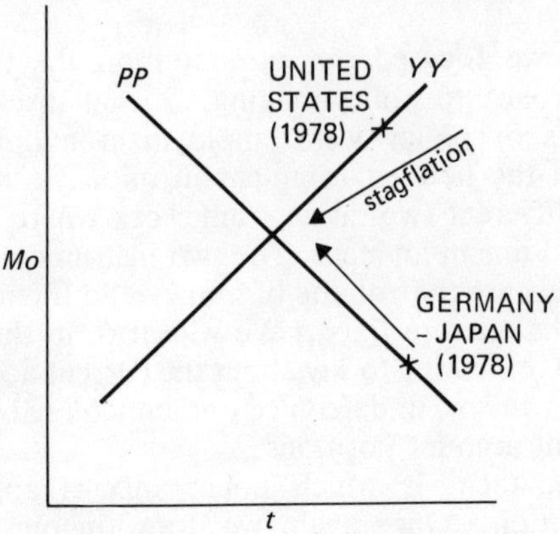

money, the tax rate is higher than that required to maintain the satisfactory level of output. We can therefore identify the quadrant where prices are too high and also where output is below its desired level (stagflation).

What policy mix then would be called for in this case? If a country is close to its output target but its inflation is still too high (placing it in the upper range of the stagflation quadrant), the appropriate policy mix is to reduce taxes and to simultaneously reduce the volume of money. The reduction in the volume of money is intended to temper the effects on output of the tax cut but to reinforce the price effects of the tax cut. The change in policy mix will both reduce (significantly) the price level and lead to some (small) improvement in the level of economic activity. If, on the other hand, a country were close to its desired level of inflation but some distance from its output target (placing it in the lower end of the quadrant), the appropriate policy would be to reduce taxes again but now, however, to increase the volume of money. The rationale is that the increase in the volume of money is needed to reinforce the effects on output of the cut in taxes; at the same time, it will temper the effects of the tax cut on the price level. A tax cut, therefore, is always the appropriate policy in this quadrant but the direction of change in monetary policy is ambiguous.[8] The cases discussed correspond roughly to the positions of the USA, on the one hand, and Germany–Japan, on the other, in late 1978. Then the USA was near its full employment but had a high rate of inflation while Germany–Japan had a low inflation rate but still considerable unemployment.

We may now ask what effect these policy mixes are likely to have on the current accounts of the balance of payments. To see this we need

Figure 30.2 *Policy mix for stagflation – allowing for current account effects*

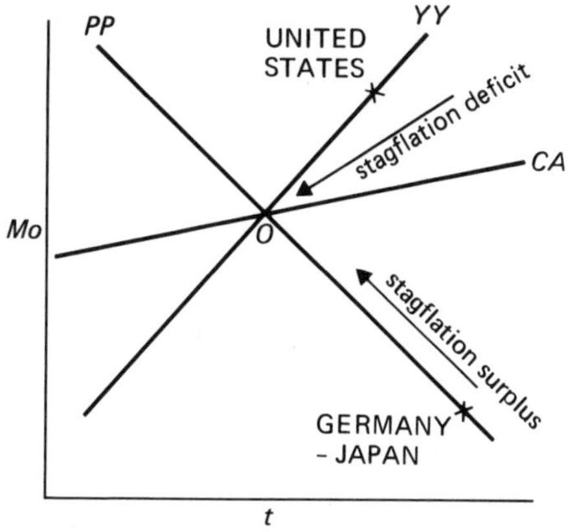

to determine what combinations of monetary and tax policies will leave the current account position (assumed to be satisfactory) unchanged. Suppose an increase in the tax rate improves the current account (the reduction in output dominating the increase in prices) so that some increase in the volume of money is required to restore the current account position. Then the current account schedule (*CA*) will be positively sloped, but somewhat flat. This is shown in Figure 30.2. For example, starting from point *0* an increase in taxes and an increase in the volume of money, so as to maintain the level of output, is bound to open up a current account deficit because domestic prices will now be higher. On the other hand, a movement, from *0*, downward along the *PP* schedule is bound to open up a surplus because now with the same price level the level of output will have dropped.

It is easily seen that the appropriate policy mixes for inflation and output will also be those that will tend to correct the disequilibrium in the current account. The country that focuses on reducing its prices while (marginally) lifting output will also tend to reduce its current account deficit. In late 1978 the USA had, at one and the same time, high inflation, a high level of activity and a large current account deficit. This policy mix might, therefore, have served to reduce inflation and the current account deficit without, at the same time, interfering with the level of activity. At the other end of the spectrum, the country that focuses on increasing its output while (marginally) reducing its inflation will tend to reduce any surplus it enjoys on its current account. Germany and Japan in late 1978 had low inflation rates, low levels of economic activity and large current account

Figure 30.3 *Policy mix for stagflation – allowing for current account effects*

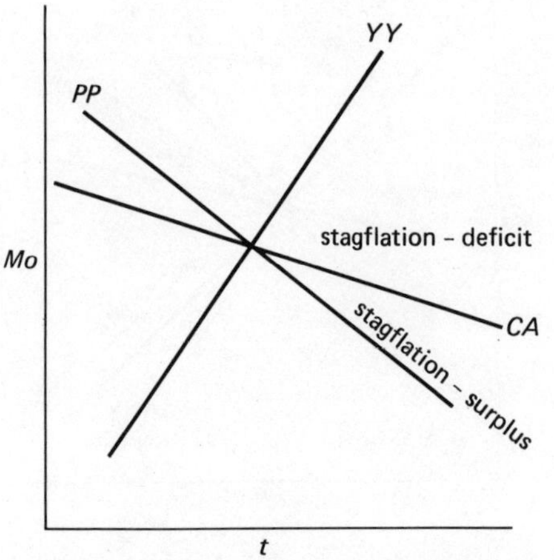

surpluses; the policy mix in that situation would have served to reduce the surplus and increase economic activity without, at the same time, raising the rate of inflation.

If the *CA* schedule were negatively sloped (because the increase in the tax rate adversely affects the current account – now the increase in the price level dominating the drop in output), it is easily shown that it would have to fall to the right of the *PP* schedule within the stagflation area.[9] This case is shown in Figure 30.3. Interestingly, the analysis and outcomes are very similar.

We now turn to the other case, where the *PP* schedule is positively sloped (because an increase in the tax rate lowers the price level, requiring an increase in the volume of money to restore the price level). This case is shown in Figure 30.4. The slope of *YY* must now be steeper than the slope of *PP*. The reason is that if taxes and the volume of money are raised in such a way as to maintain the level of output the price level will have to be higher because the increase in the volume of money raises prices by more than an equivalent output increase in taxes.[10] In this case, the appropriate policy mix for stagflation is unambiguous: a tax cut is required together with a restrictive monetary policy.

The *CA* schedule is also unambiguous (see Figure 30.4). An increase in the tax rate must improve the current account (with output decreasing and prices falling) so an increase in the volume of money is required to maintain the current account. It is again seen that the policy mix implemented will help to correct the disequilibria in the current account.

Figure 30.4 *Policy mix for stagflation – increased taxes lower prices*

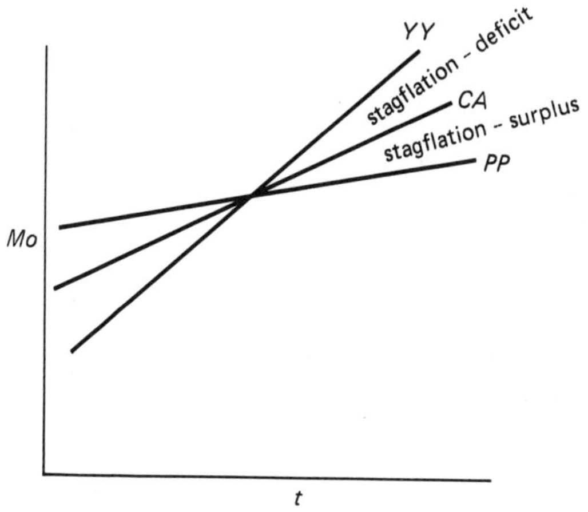

Useful as the analysis is, it needs to be emphasised that we have had to overlook several other concerns of policy-makers (for example, the effects of the policy mixes on the budget deficit or on interest rates). More important, it is evident that the types of policy changes discussed are designed to lower the level of prices within a given period below what it otherwise would have been. This is useful in itself and may provide a useful breathing space; however, as in the case of the employment subsidy, the rate of inflation will subsequently be at least as high and possibly higher (if the level of output were higher) than it was before the policy was implemented.

Annex – A Changed Monetary Fiscal Mix for Stagflation

Notation

Ar = real absorption
Gr = real government expenditure
Mo = money supply
P = overall price level
Pd = domestic price level
r = domestic interest rate
t = tax rate
Tr = real taxes
W = nominal wage rate
Yr = real GNP

The neo-Keynesian model of Chapter 11 can now be amended to accommodate the cases discussed in the text.

The key wage equation is:

$$\frac{W(1-t)}{P} = No \qquad (30A.1)$$

where *No* is a constant which can be set at unity. This equation states that it is the after-tax real wage rate that is maintained; so that wages are allowed to adjust fully not only to prices but also to changes in tax rates. Differentiating this equation and setting the initial price level and *No* at unity yields:

$$\Delta W = \frac{1}{1-t}\Delta P + \frac{1}{(1-t)^2}\Delta t \qquad (30A.2)$$

To accommodate the possibility of only partial adjustment (either because of some money illusion or because of a limited time horizon) this equation is amended as follows:

$$\Delta W = \frac{n}{1-t}\Delta P + \frac{n}{(1-t)^2}\Delta t \qquad n>0<1 \qquad (30A.3)$$

where n is the partial adjustment coefficient. If $n = 1$ there is complete adjustment as in Equation (30A.2). With $n = 0$ we have the Keynesian fixed wage case.

The new relevant aggregate supply equation is:

$$\Delta Yr = -\frac{\alpha_{15}n}{(1-t)^2}\Delta t + \frac{\alpha_{15}}{1-t}(1 - n\alpha_{14})\Delta Pd \qquad (30A.4)$$

We also allow for the effects of changes in tax rates on real absorption. Assuming, for simplicity, that only real consumption is related to real income, Equation (11.3) of the basic model can be written as follows:

$$Ar = \alpha_{1A}(Yr - Tr) - \alpha_3 r + Gr \qquad (30A.5)$$

where $Yr - Tr$ represents real disposable income and α_{1A} the marginal propensity to consume out of real disposable income.

Real taxes are a function of real income:

$$Tr = t.Yr \qquad (30A.6)$$

Then, differentiating Equation (30A.5) we have:

$$\Delta Ar = \alpha_{1A}(1-t)\Delta Yr + \alpha_{1A} Yr\Delta t - \alpha_3 \Delta r + \Delta Gr \qquad (30A.7)$$

The relevant aggregate demand equation is now:

$$\Delta Yr = \frac{\alpha_3}{D1}\Delta Mo - \frac{\alpha_6\alpha_{1A} Yr}{D1}\Delta t - \frac{\alpha_6 ML + \alpha_3 Mo}{D1}\Delta Pd \qquad (30A.8)$$

where

$$D1 = \alpha_6[1-\alpha_{1A}(1-t)+\alpha_9]+\alpha_3\alpha_4$$

$$ML = X(edx + edm - 1)$$

To obtain the *PP* schedule we eliminate real output from the two equations (Equations 30A.4 and 30A.8) and then take the ΔPd to be zero. The *PP* schedule will thus be:

$$\Delta Mo = \left[\frac{[-\alpha_{15}n/(1-t)^2] + (\alpha_6\alpha_{1A} Yr/D1)}{\alpha_3/D1}\right]\Delta t \qquad (30A.9)$$

which may be positive or negative depending on the relative importance of demand ($\alpha_6\alpha_{1A} Yr/D1$) and tax push [$\alpha_{15}n/(1-t)^2$]. The larger the coefficient of adjustment, n, the greater the likelihood that the slope will be negative. If $n=0$ (the neo-Keynesian case when wages are fixed) the slope is, of course, unambiguously positive.

To obtain the *YY* schedule we eliminate *Pd* from the equations and take $\Delta Yr = 0$. The solution is:

$$\Delta Mo = \frac{\alpha_6\alpha_{1A} Yr(1-t)(1-n\alpha_{14}) + n(\alpha_6 ML + \alpha_3 Mo)}{\alpha_3(1-t)(1-n\alpha_{14})}\Delta t \qquad (30A.10)$$

which is unambiguously positive.

It is worth noting that if $n=0$, with no wage adjustment, the two slopes are identical ($\alpha_6\alpha_{1A} Yr/\alpha_3$), so there is no way of discriminating between price and output effects. However, so long as $n>0$, the two slopes are different. It is also easily verifiable that if the slope of *PP* is positive, the slope of *YY* must be greater than the slope of *PP*.

Notes for Chapter 30

1 For a review of the issues and an evaluation of the experience in particular countries see: G. Kopits (1978); J. Burton (1977); S. Nickell (1979); V. Argy and J. Salop (1979); J. Bishop and R. Haveman (1979); J. Perloff and M. Wachter (1979).

2 S. Weintraub (1971); H. Wallich and S. Weintraub (1971). See A. Okun and G. Perry (1978); L. Seidman (1978); L. Dildine and E. Sunley (1978); G. Ackley (1978); F. Modigliani (1978); A. Rees (1978); N. A. Jianakoplos (1978); R. Slitor (1979).

3 Alternative methods of penalising these enterprises would be by increasing the payroll tax or by not allowing the deduction of excessive wages in taxable income.

4 See A. Rees (1978), p. 457.

5 For a more complicated case where exchange rates are flexible see: V. Argy and J. Salop (1979).

6 See T. Dernburg (1974); R. Dornbusch and P. Krugman (1976); J. Perkins (1979); A. Blinder (1973); V. Argy and J. Salop (1979). Although all these papers deal in one way or another with some of the issues in this section, it is Perkins's book that is nearest to the analysis undertaken.

7 The evidence supporting this has already been reviewed in Chapter 16.

8 We have emphasised the effects of tax cuts on wages and prices. The effects of tax cuts on allocation, tax avoidance and incentives are also emphasised in J. Perkins (1979).

9 Because again a movement upward along *YY* must generate a deficit while a movement downward along *PP* must generate a surplus.

10 This is demonstrated in the Annex.

Chapter 31

Policies for Stagflation – II:

Prices and Incomes Policies (PIP)

Introduction

Over the years, and in several industrial countries, governments have resorted to some form of direct control over prices and incomes, with the principal aim of securing an improved relationship between unemployment and inflation.[1] Other objectives of a prices and incomes policy (PIP) have included an improved distribution of factor incomes, an improved allocation of resources and an improved productivity performance.

In the most general terms, a PIP sets out criteria for both wage and price changes. These policies are either statutory (enforceable by law) or voluntary. In the case of wages a guideline, representing the allowable rate of growth of wages in the economy as a whole, is laid down. Frequently some exceptions to the general rule are permitted. In the case of prices, price changes are generally allowable on the basis of a mark-up over costs or subject to a net profit constraint.

In this chapter we review, in some detail, the experience of both the UK and the USA with a PIP. We then summarise the benefits and costs that may flow from such policies and try and evaluate these in the light of the available evidence, principally for the UK and the USA.

The UK's Experience (1965–1978)

The UK's experience between 1965 and 1978 has been rich and wide-ranging and serves well to demonstrate many of the inherent problems associated with a PIP.[2] The UK has, in the post-war years, felt a continuing need to implement a PIP for reasons to do with her relatively militant trade unions, her relatively high inflation and her persistent balance of payments deficits.

It is possible to identify three cycles in the use of a PIP in the UK, corresponding to the experience of, first, a Labour government

(1964–70), then a Conservative government (1970–74) and last a Labour government (1974–78). As we will note, subsequently, there are certain common patterns in each of these cycles.

The Labour Government (1964–1970)

The Labour Party came into power at the end of 1964. Its first serious effort at a PIP was to create, in April 1965, a National Board for Prices and Incomes (NBPI). This Board had the task of examining claims for increases in wages and prices referred to it by the government and making relevant recommendations in the light of various norms dictated by the government. Initially, the Board had no statutory powers, hence there was no obligation to accept its recommendations.

The first 'norm' for wage increases applicable over the period May 1965 to June 1966 was 3–3.5 per cent, corresponding roughly to the expected national growth of productivity, but there were several exceptions allowed. These so-called gateways were very important and are worth setting out in full:[3]

(1) Where the employees concerned, for example, by accepting more exacting work or a major change in working practices, make a direct contribution towards increasing productivity in the particular firm or industry. Even in such cases some of the benefit should accrue to the community as a whole in the form of lower prices.
(2) Where it is essential in the national interest to secure a change in the distribution of manpower (or to prevent a change which would otherwise take place) and a pay increase would be both necessary and effective for this purpose.
(3) Where there is general recognition that existing wage and salary levels are too low to maintain a reasonable standard of living.
(4) Where there is widespread recognition that the pay of a certain group of workers has fallen seriously out of line with the level of remuneration for similar work, and needs in the national interest to be improved.

The first two exceptions were based on considerations of economic efficiency while the last two were based on grounds of equity.

In mid-1966 with inflation continuing high and the balance of payments in deficit the government switched to a statutory policy. Between July 1966 and January 1967 a general statutory freeze was enforced, followed by a six-month period of severe restraint during which the norm was zero, while exceptions were now defined more tightly.[4] From the end of June 1967, the norm effectively continued to be zero but the exceptions were looser and defined as in 1965. The last phase ran from April 1968 to the end of 1969 when the norm was again zero but now, for the exceptional cases, the maximum allowable increase was 3.5 per cent. All these provisions were embodied in a succession of Acts in 1966, 1967 and 1968, which gave the Board delaying powers ranging from six to twelve months. By the end of 1969, the PIP had effectively collapsed, as reflected in the wage explosions of 1969/70. The powers given to the government under the 1968 Act were not then renewed.

The Conservative Government (1970–1974)

After an unsuccessful early attempt to implement a voluntary PIP the Conservative government enforced a statutory freeze on wages and prices from the end of November 1972 to the end of April 1973. During Phase II, which followed, from April to November 1973, the government assumed new statutory powers to regulate wages and prices and established two new agencies, a Price Commission and a Pay Board,[5] to operate the new rules. The price and wage norms were to be administered by the Price Commission and the Pay Board, respectively. For prices three categories of undertakings were defined: the largest and more dominant had to give prior notification of price increases and these needed the agreement of the Commission; the second largest were required to report regularly, while the smallest simply had to keep records to produce if needed. Rules were laid down for increases in costs that were allowed to be passed on in price increases and for net profit margins permitted.

A similar three-tier system operated for pay claims: major settlements required prior notification and approval, smaller settlements had to be reported but could be implemented, while the smallest settlements were required to be formally recorded. The formula for permissible increases in pay was a limit of £1 a week plus 4 per cent of the average pay bill per head for the group over the previous year, excluding overtime, with a maximum of £250 a year for any one individual. Moreover, the interval between settlements was to be at least twelve months (in other words, no increase in pay was allowable earlier than twelve months from the last previous increase). The only exceptions allowed in this phase were for settlements deferred by the freeze and for moves to equal pay.

Phase III, which followed from November 1973, was somewhat more flexible and relaxed than Phase II but it continued to be compulsory. Pay increases were limited to £2.25 a week or 7 per cent whichever was higher; in addition there were complicated 'threshold' clauses permitting a pay increase for increases in prices in excess of 7 per cent.[6] Also, the exception relating to productivity agreements was revived. But, with mounting trade union opposition, an explosion in commodity prices, a rapidly growing money supply and severe problems in interpreting the new regulations, Phase III of the PIP broke down completely and a new wage explosion followed. In March 1974 the Conservatives were voted out of office.

The Labour Government (1974–1978)

After attempts by the two previous administrations to implement a statutory PIP, the Labour government abandoned all statutory controls on wages, relying entirely on voluntary controls. At the same time, it retained the Prices Commission and the Statutory Price Code.

It began by experimenting with a Social Contract, trading wage restraint by the unions for a number of undertakings, including continuing price and rent control, public transport and housing subsidies, improvements in social welfare provisions, the fostering of industrial democracy and the repeal of the Tories' Industrial Relations Act. Wage restraint was understood to mean that wage deals would aim at maintaining real incomes and no more, while all major increases would be twelve months apart. There were, however, numerous exclusions, including again for productivity deals, for lower paid workers and to improve the status of women.

This experiment by the Labour Party failed for a number of reasons. The Trade Union Congress (TUC) did not have the power to vet agreements, the guidelines were not observed while the loopholes–exceptions proved, in the end, too generous and loose.

After its initial failure the Labour Party, in August 1975, proposed that wage increases for the succeeding year be voluntarily restricted to £6 a week (with those earning over £8500 receiving no rise at all). The only exception allowed was for equal pay. An increasing feature here was that wage increases that exceeded the norm were not allowable in entirety as cost increases. In Phase II, which followed from August 1976 to July 1977, a 5 per cent increase in basic pay was allowed subject to a minimum of £2.50 and a maximum of £4, with no exceptions this time. Also the Price Code was relaxed to assist investment and the cash position of enterprises. Phase III, from July 1977 to July 1978, proposed a 10 per cent ceiling on pay increases while Phase IV, beginning July 1978, proclaimed a 5 per cent limit on pay increases. But already during Phase III there was considerable unrest and opposition to the policies; the situation deteriorated further later in 1978 when there was a new upsurge in wage claims, during which the PIP effectively collapsed. In May 1979 the Labour government was ousted.

Summary of the UK Experience

Several features of the UK experience are especially worth noting. First, both the Labour and the Conservative parties have felt a need, when in power, to institute some form of control over wages. Second, in two of the three cycles summarised above, there was some resort, after an attempt at voluntary controls, to a statutory freeze, followed by looser and more flexible rules. Third, each of the three cycles ended in increasing restlessness and a wage explosion, which, as it happened, contributed to the downfall of the government in power at the time. Fourth, exceptions to pay policies, for reasons of economic efficiency and equity, were frequently allowed but with varying degrees of vigour. Fifth, a most important element in many of the pay policies was the intent to improve the position of the low paid workers. This was achieved either directly by treating the low paid as exceptions (as in the 1960s) or by norms which provided for bigger percentage increases for those in lower income brackets (as in the 1970s).

The US Experience (1971–1974)

In the post-war years the USA tried two experiments with a PIP policy. The first was in the years 1962–66 when a voluntary guideline policy (with exceptions) was followed. This ran for some three to four years, after which it was abandoned.[7] The second, and more important from our point of view, was the PIP implemented in the years 1971–74 (see Table 31.1). This preceded the UK experience in 1972–74 and was, in fact, its inspiration.

The persistence of inflationary pressures, notwithstanding the politically unacceptable rates of unemployment, forced the Nixon Administration to implement a statutory PIP which began with a statutory freeze (Phase I) which ran from August to November 1971. Phase II, after the freeze, created a number of new agencies to administer a statutory program of controls: a Cost of Living Council to review policy, a Pay Board to vet pay claims and a Price Commission to vet claims for price increases. Phase III, which followed, was basically voluntary but had some statutory features. The Price Commission and Pay Board were both abolished in this phase and the rules were now largely self-administered, although still subject to vetting by the Cost of Living Council. Phase III was followed by a second freeze from June to August 1973 while Phase IV, which fell between the tough Phase II and the easier Phase III, ran from August 1973 to April 1974, during which there was mounting discontent with the PIP. After Phase IV ran its course controls were abandoned. The full details of Phases II, III and IV are provided in Table 31.1.

Potential Benefits of a PIP

Recalling the design of a typical PIP, as above, several potential

Table 31.1 Regulations of the control program – phases II, III and IV – United States

Program	*Phase II:* *14 November 1971 to 11 January 1973*	*Phase III:* *11 January 1973 to 13 June 1973*	*Phase IV:* *12 August 1973 to 30 April 1974*
General standards			
Price increase limitations	Percentage pass-through of allowable cost increases since last price increase, or Jan. 1, 1971, adjusted for productivity and volume offsets. Term limit pricing option available.	Self-administered standards of Phase II.	In most manufacturing and service industries dollar-for-dollar pass-through of allowable cost increase since last fiscal quarter ending prior to Jan. 11, 1973.
Profit margin limitations	Not to exceed margins of the best 2 of 3 fiscal years before Aug. 15, 1971. Not applicable if prices were not increased above base level, or if firms "purified" themselves.	Not to exceed margins of the best 2 fiscal years completed after Aug. 15, 1968. No limitation if average price increase did not exceed 1.5 percent.	Same years as Phase III, except that a firm that had not charged a price for any item above its base price, or adjusted freeze price, whichever was higher, was not subject to the limitation.
Wage increase limitations	General standard of 5.5 percent. Exceptions made to correct gross inequities, and for workers whose pay had increased less than 7 percent a year for the last 3 years. Workers earning less than $2.75 per hour were exempt. Increases in qualified fringe benefits permitted raising standard to 6.2 percent.	General Phase II standard self-administered. Some special limitations. More flexibility with respect to specific cases. Workers earning less than $3.50 per hour were exempt after May 1.	Self-administered standards of Phase III. Executive compensation limited.

Program	*Phase II: 14 November 1971 to 11 January 1973*	*Phase III: 11 January 1973 to 13 June 1973*	*Phase IV: 12 August 1973 to 30 April 1974*
Prenotification			
Prices	Prenotification required for all firms with annual sales above $100 million, 30 days before implementation, approval required.	After May 2, 1973, prenotification required for all firms with sales above $250 million whose price increase had exceeded a weighted average of 1.5 percent.	Same as Phase II except that prenotified price increases could be implemented in 30 days unless CLC required otherwise.
Wages	For all increases of wages for units of 5,000 or more; for all increases above the standard regardless of the number of workers involved.	None.	None.
Reporting			
Prices	Quarterly for firms with sales over $50 million.	Quarterly for firms with sales over $250 million.	Quarterly for firms with sales over $50 million.
Wages	Pay adjustments below standard for units greater than 1,000 persons.	Pay adjustments for units greater than 5,000 persons.	Same as Phase III.
Special areas	Health, insurance, rent, construction, public utilities.	Health, food, public utilities, construction, petroleum.	Health, food, petroleum, construction, insurance, executive and variable compensation.
Exemptions	Raw agricultural commodities, import prices, export prices, firms with 60 or fewer employees.	Same as Phase II plus rents.	Same as Phase III plus public utilities, lumber, copper scrap, and long-term coal contracts, initially with sector-by-sector decontrol of prices and wages until April 30, 1974.

Source: US Cost of Living Council.

benefits might flow in general from such policies. First, there is the possible benefit from a lower rate of inflation and/or a higher level of economic activity. Second, there is a possible benefit from an improved distribution of factor incomes. Third, in so far as monopoly prices or profits are controlled there may be an improved allocation of resources. Fourth and finally, there may be gains in productivity.

The Effects on Inflation and Economic Activity

In what circumstances will the first benefit be realised? Several possibilities present themselves. Suppose, to begin, we were in a fixed rate world and a country had an unfavourable Phillips curve because it had militant trade unions; then it might have to endure an unsatisfactory unemployment rate. Under these conditions, an incomes policy that shifted the Phillips curve to the left would serve to reduce the country's unemployment rate while keeping its own rate of inflation in line with the rest of the world. Another way of putting this is that, in the absence of an incomes policy, the country may have to live with a relatively higher rate of inflation and then endure regular balance of payments crises and severe stop–go demand-management policies.

Alternatively, if a country has a relatively high rate of inflation, a slowing down in the rate of growth of money combined with an incomes policy which succeeded in changing expectations might diminish the transitional (unemployment) costs or, again, the prospect of a successful incomes policy might actually encourage a government to reduce the rate of growth in the volume of money, when otherwise, faced with transitional costs, it would not have. Again, with the same rate of growth in the volume of money, a successful incomes policy might reduce the rate of inflation, raise the rate of growth of real money balances and so permit some increase in the level of economic activity in that period. Finally, an incomes policy might succeed in disallowing price shocks (for example, due to changes in food and energy prices or to changes in exchange rates) from flowing into wages.

What is the evidence on these benefits? There is a vast econometric literature that attempts to evaluate the degree to which an incomes policy served independently to reduce the rate of inflation or the rate of growth in wages. For the UK there now appears to be a growing consensus which is best summarised in the most recent of numerous econometric studies for the UK over the years.[8]

> Our results indicate that whilst some incomes policies have reduced the rate of wage inflation during the period in which they operated this reduction has only been temporary. Wage increases in the period immediately following the ending of the policies were higher than they would otherwise have been, and these increases match losses incurred during the operation of the incomes policy.

The conclusion for the UK is a most important one. It suggests that in the longer run any short-term gains are lost or reversed when the PIP is relaxed or abandoned. As we have seen, every attempt at a PIP in the UK since 1965 ended in a wage explosion. How, then, can one rationalise a wage explosion? First, if an incomes policy is successful in initially reducing real wages (say, because commodity or import prices have risen without compensation) there may be subsequent attempts to restore the real income position. Second, there may be an element of money illusion in that workers bargain for rates of increase in nominal wages and so after an incomes policy phase they revert to larger nominal wage claims. Third, a PIP allows little scope for the exercise of trade union initiative or militancy in wage claims; when the policy is abandoned trade union leaders reassert themselves and recover the initiative with exorbitant wage claims. Fourth, the expectation that the relaxation of a PIP will lead to an upsurge in prices encourages a scramble by individual unions to keep ahead of price increases. Fifth, relative positions do, and indeed, as we have seen, are intended to, change. A relaxation of controls will then encourage the disadvantaged groups to try to restore their relative positions, creating new inflationary pressures. Sixth, Stevenson and Trevithick[9] showed that there is evidence, for the UK, that the growth of income velocity slows down during a PIP but increases rapidly when the PIP is relaxed, suggesting, to these authors, that the build-up of excess liquidity during a PIP is released subsequently.

For the USA the position is less clear. J. Pohlman,[10] summarising the results of the US studies, finds them difficult to interpret but, however, concludes that 'it appears quite likely that the controls program did play a significant role in calming wage-push inflation'.[11] But another survey of the econometric evidence by Kraft and Roberts[12] concluded, 'An examination of this evidence should generally result in a no-decision conclusion; the problems of measurement and specification have prevented a concensus opinion'.[13]

An interesting calculation of the benefits, for the USA, is made in Lanzillotti, Roberts and Hamilton.[14] They first calculate, econometrically, the reduction in inflation due to the PIP (in force in 1971–73). Then assuming the growth of money (and hence nominal income) were unchanged they figure that GNP would have been some $14 billion to $21 billion higher over a six-quarter period (which is about 1.8 per cent of 1972 GNP).

The Effects on the Distribution of Incomes

Do incomes policies improve the distribution of factor incomes – the second potential benefit? There are two direct ways to test this: one is to look at wage differentials to see if they have tended to narrow during a PIP. Another is to look at the share of income from employment in gross domestic product.[15] Let us look at each of these. A careful study of differentials for the UK concluded, surprisingly, that there was not much evidence of any narrowing,[16] despite the explicit intent in the guidelines to achieve this objective.[17] (The author of the study does concede, though, that the data is inadequate to test the hypothesis.) J. M. Parkin[18] found that, over the period 1951–72, a PIP was in force on four of the five occasions when labour's share fell suggesting that, if anything, labour's relative position may actually have deteriorated during a PIP. One has to conclude, then, that there appears to be little evidence to support the notion either that a PIP narrows differentials or that it improves labour's relative position, at least in the UK.[19] An even more important question, which will not be dealt with here, is whether, in any event, it is appropriate to redistribute income through a PIP or whether it is not more efficient to redistribute through the tax system (showing up in a redistribution in post-tax rather than in pre-tax incomes).

The Effects on the Allocation of Resources and on Productivity

It is very difficult to obtain evidence on the third potential benefit – that monopoly prices and profits might be contained. In any event, it would be hard to justify the use of a PIP in these terms when there are, in fact, more efficient direct ways of dealing with monopolistic practices (for example, by tariff policies, anti-monopoly legislation, etc.).

Finally, there is the fourth benefit flowing from improvements in productivity. Here again hard evidence is extremely difficult to come by. We need to know what would have happened in the absence of a PIP. It is true, for example, in the case of the UK, that, by allowing productivity agreements as exceptions to the norm for pay increases, substantial encouragement was being given to enter into such agreements. For example, Hunter[20] reports that while productivity bargaining had been growing in importance in the years 1960–66, productivity agreements mushroomed, with some 4000 of these approved, between 1967 and 1969. However, there is a question as to how real and lasting these were.[21]

Potential Costs of a PIP

In many ways the potential costs of a PIP are far more difficult to identify because these will vary depending on the form of the PIP implemented. In general, it is useful to distinguish four types of costs associated with a PIP. The first is the direct regulatory cost. The second is represented by the side effects associated with the realisation of the purposes and terms of the PIP. The third is the cost of evasion of the regulations, and the fourth is the cost of economic mismanagement of the PIP.

The Regulatory Costs

The direct regulatory costs include the cost of the government bureaucracy as well as the direct costs of compliance (for example, conforming to regulations, legal costs, recording costs) on the part of enterprises and unions. These costs will, of course, be much more substantial when the PIP is statutory than when it is voluntary. An interesting calculation of this for the (statutory) US PIP (Phases I and II in 1971–73) was made by Lanzillotti, Roberts and Hamilton,[22] who estimate that public and private costs totalled something like $1.2 billion (which is roughly 0.1 per cent of the 1972 GNP).

Some Side Effects of a PIP

There are several costs associated with a PIP which is successful by its own terms. If enterprises are constrained from raising their prices some may be able to lower the quality of their product.[23] Thus, instead of raising prices in line with costs, unit costs are lowered. Also a PIP may, in some circumstances, actually create additional unemployment. For example, a PIP directed at narrowing differentials, as in the UK (1972–74), may price some (low-paid) categories of labour out of the market while creating shortages in other categories. J. Fleming argues,[24] on the basis of plausible assumptions about substitution elasticities, that the narrowing of differentials might have led to something like 1.5 per cent of the working population becoming unemployed. However, as we have seen, the effects on differentials are uncertain. Still another way in which a PIP might lead to more unemployment is by encouraging productivity agreements that entail some reduction in manpower.[25]

Again, a PIP is bound to create several different kinds of inequities. For example, the timing of a PIP may affect adversely those groups who have not settled. Or the regulations may bear down harder on the larger unions or enterprises than on the smaller ones.[26] Also, as was the case in the UK, the productivity agreement exception favoured those unions in industries that offered scope for changes in methods of production. Finally, exceptions (which were particularly important in the UK in 1965–68) allow governments to accommodate those unions with political muscle in order to avoid confrontation.

Again, a badly administered or designed price control programme may result in shortages of particular goods. There are several instances of this in the later stages of the US PIP.[27] It is also sometimes alleged that a price control programme may reduce profits and investment or reduce the incentives to greater efficiency (insofar as the increased efficiency is not allowed to be translated into larger profits). It has been argued,[28] too, that a bargain struck with the trade union movement to win their support for a PIP may not be in the best interests of the community as a whole. (An example of this is the Social Contract episode in the UK in 1974/75.)

The Costs of Evasion

There may also be a cost associated with a PIP that is ineffective in whole or in part. Consider, at one extreme, a PIP that is completely ineffective, leaving everyone's real and relative positions exactly as they would have been without controls. Even in this case there may be costs (for instance, of challenging the government's authority, associated social frictions). More realistically, however, there will be partial evasion arbitrarily allowing some groups to benefit at the expense of others and hence generating considerable social frictions and loss of respect for the law. The devices used for evading the letter (or spirit) of the regulations are well known: 'spurious' productivity agreements (UK, 1967/68), renaming a product, reclassifying a position, spurious promotion or overtime, manipulation of inventory or asset valuations, payment in other forms (for example, free lunches, welfare), the provision of 'token' services to lift book costs, avoiding price control by 'arranging' the import of a domestically-produced good.[29]

The Costs of Economic Mismanagement

As indicated above an incomes policy will only succeed if it is competently designed in such a way that it will be consistent with the thrust of demand-management policies. A PIP that aimed at reducing the rate of inflation while allowing monetary policies to be too expansionary is bound to fail. For example, with money supply (*M*3) in the UK growing at an average of 25 per cent in 1972/73 (two and one-half times the rate in 1970/71) it is not surprising that the pay policy broke down during 1973.[30] A PIP may actually accelerate inflation if, for example, governments are lulled into a false sense of security, allowing them to overexpand in the belief that the rise in prices will be restrained.[31] A good example of this may have occurred in the USA in 1971/72 when both monetary and fiscal policies became expansionary during the early phases of the controls.[32] Controls may also encourage the continuation of a lax macro-policy by disguising the effects of these policies.[33]

Conclusions on PIP

It is possible to draw several conclusions from our review of a PIP. The most important one is that while, in principle, it has an important role to play under certain conditions, in practice it has been very difficult to design and implement a successful PIP over a period of several years. On balance, it is fair to say that the benefits, if any, have been modest while, on the other hand, the costs in toto may have been more substantial. None the less, one may yet want to argue that something has been learnt from the experience, possibly enabling an improved performance in the future.

If a PIP is to be successful a number of minimal conditions would appear to be necessary. First, the policy must have the endorsement of both the Trade Union movement and Employers Organisations.[34] Ideally, a 'social contract' involving the government, the trade unions and the employers must be at the basis of any PIP. Such an arrangement is more likely to succeed in countries where there are relatively few trade unions, where negotiations are more centralised, where claims tend to be more synchronised and where there is little plant bargaining.[35] Second, voluntary schemes are unlikely, in general, to be effective: the pressures on individual trade unions, for example, to secure some relative advantage will, in the end, be too strong.[36] Third, a PIP must be so designed as to appear equitable, in the sense that there will be no arbitrary redistribution of income towards particular groups. Fourth, a PIP will fail and indeed will be discredited if governments pursued inconsistent demand-management policies. Fifth, while there will always be loopholes and scope for evasion (a point that is notoriously true of any area of government regulation), these ought to be minimised and regulations carefully drafted and tightened.

Notes for Chapter 31

1 Useful general references on PIP are: A. R. Braun (1975); J. Parkin and M. Sumner (1972); A. R. Braun (1978); L. Ulman and R. Flanagan (1971); D. Robinson (1973).
2 The UK's experience with a PIP dates back to 1948–50. This chapter, however, concentrates only on the more recent developments. For some discussion and evaluation of the UK experience see: J. Parkin, M. Sumner and R. Jones (1972); H. Clegg (1971); A Jones (1973); S. Brittan and P. Lilley (1977); R. Tarling and F. Wilkinson (1977).
3 White Paper (1967).
4 See Hugh Clegg (1971) for details.
5 The NBPI was abolished by the Conservatives.
6 For details of these clauses see: A. Braun (1976). Braun demonstrates the risks associated with allowing wage indexation in the face of steep increases in import prices.
7 For a detailed analysis of this phase see G. P. Schultz and R. Z. Aliber (eds) (1966).
8 S. Henry and P. Ormerod (1978). An earlier paper reviewing the econometric literature to that point arrives at much the same conclusion. See J. Parkin, M. Sumner and R. Jones (1972).

9 A. Stevenson and J. Trevithick (1977). Their analysis clearly begs a number of questions which cannot be pursued here.

10 J. Pohlman (1976), Chapter 12.

11 J. Pohlman (1976), p. 225.

12 J. Kraft and B. Roberts (1975), Chapter 9.

13 J. Kraft and B. Roberts (1975), p. 149.

14 R. Lanzillotti, B. Roberts and M. Hamilton (1975).

15 The first may be intended, the second may be an unintended by-product. In reality an incomes policy may seek to reduce rather than raise the share of wages.

16 A. J. H. Dean (1978). A similar conclusion is reached by L. Hunter (1975).

17 Dean finds that when overtime is taken out of earnings some narrowing was noticeable.

18 J. Parkin (1978).

19 For the USA the results are mixed. See J. Kraft and B. Roberts (eds) (1975), Chapter 9 (conclusions); A. Rees (1978).

20 L. Hunter (1973).

21 See L. Hunter (1973); Hugh Clegg (1971), esp. Chapter 5; Aubrey Jones (1973), esp. Chapter 5.

22 R. Lanzillotti, B. Roberts and M. Hamilton (1975).

23 For a discussion of this and instances for the USA see M. Darby (1978); W. Poole (1973).

24 J. Flemming (1976). See also P. Lilley (1977).

25 See L. Hunter (1973), p. 25.

26 C. Jackson–Grayson (1978), Chapter 6.

27 M. H. Kosters (1974), Chapter 4.

28 P. Lilley (1977), p. 29.

29 W. Poole (1973) gives a very good illustration from the USA of the last form of evasion. In his own words, 'Since the Price Commission could not control foreign producers, and import prices were thus uncontrolled, producers in the Pacific North-West exported lumber to Canada and reimported it at substantially higher prices. In some cases the transactions involved dummy exports: export and import papers were processed while the lumber sat in a US warehouse' (p. 292).

30 J. Williamson and G. Wood (1976).

31 P. Lilley (1977), p. 23; M. H. Kosters (1974), pp. 174–5.

32 M. H. Kosters (1974), pp. 174–5.

33 This is the argument in Stevenson and Trevithick (1977) and M. H. Kosters (1974).

34 For example, trade unions in the UK were bitterly opposed to Phase III in 1973 and became increasingly dissatisfied with the Labour government's PIP during 1978. In the USA, too, the AFL-CIO voiced increasing opposition in the later stages of the PIP.

35 See F. Blackaby (1978). For a review of the European experience with social contracts see O. Kuntze (1978).

36 F. Blackaby (1978).

Chapter 32

A Framework for Macro-Policy

Introduction

In thinking about macro-policy it is important to know the aims governments are pursuing and the instruments which are available to them in seeking out these aims. It is also important to have some idea of the kinds of disturbances to which an economy might be exposed, and against which policy action might have to be directed.

Table 32.1 Macro-policy framework

Macro-targets	*Macro-instruments*	*Disturbances*
Primary: Inflation, unemployment and balance of payments (or reserve position) *Secondary:* Size of budget deficit, interest rate, exchange rate	Money supply Fiscal policy Incomes policy Capital controls Interest rate structure Exchange rates	Domestic demand Demand for money Foreign interest rates Domestic price (wage) Foreign real demand Foreign prices including an oil price shock

Table 32.1 lists these aims and instruments as well as types of disturbances. The table makes a distinction between a primary macro-target such as inflation, unemployment and the balance of payments and a secondary target to which governments, for a variety of reasons, attach some (albeit generally lesser) importance, such as budget deficits, interest rates and exchange rates. Six macro-instruments are listed and six types of disturbances are identified. For example, a domestic demand disturbance means that over the policy-making horizon (of, say, a year or so) real private demand is changing at a rate that was unanticipated at the time policy was determined, while a

demand for money disturbance means that the demand for money (at given interest rates, real output, prices) is changing at a rate that had not been anticipated.

Long-run Strategy

It is useful to make a distinction between longer-run macro-policy and macro-policy directed at managing the economy on a year to year basis. In the longer run, few economists would quarrel with the proposition that the rate of inflation can be controlled by appropriately controlling the rate of growth in the volume of money. Once the long-term real rate of growth of the economy is known and some estimate is made of the long-term percentage change in velocity the required rate of growth of money to secure the desired inflation rate is easily derived. For example, if the percentage increase in velocity is expected to be 1 per cent, in the real output growth 4 per cent and in the 'feasible' rate of inflation 5 per cent, then the required rate of growth in the volume of money is 8 per cent. This ought then to be the government's long-term monetary growth target (which can, of course, be adjusted downwards over time as governments seek to bring down gradually the rate of inflation).[1] Given a country's desired inflation rate the exchange rate should then be used to correct for the effective difference between that country's inflation rate and that of the rest of the world (for example, if the 'world' inflation rate is 10 per cent and the country's rate is 5 per cent the country would revalue at an annual rate of some 5 per cent).

Short-run Strategy

Policy Directed at Counteracting Disturbances

Over the shorter-term horizon of a year or so policy is considerably more complicated. What we propose here is an approach that focuses not so much on assigning instruments to particular targets but rather on assigning instruments to sources of disturbances. The basic idea is very simple: each disturbance is now paired with one or a combination of instruments. The source of disturbance is paired to a 'like' instrument(s) that will most effectively serve to counteract that disturbance, in the sense that, on balance, the net disturbance to the economy is minimised. The number of instruments need not be equal to the sources of disturbances and, moreover, more than one instrument may be invoked to cope with a particular disturbance.

In the short term the rate of growth in the volume of money will be allowed to depart from its long-term target within a band of, say, two to three percentage points. All the other instruments are manipulable, subject to the constraint that the secondary targets are not significantly 'disturbed' (in the sense that they will not be allowed to move outside, say, a prescribed range).

A Domestic Real Disturbance

The most logical pairing for a domestic real disturbance is fiscal policy. If fine tuning is going to be undertaken a real disturbance ought to be counteracted by a 'like' instrument of policy, which in this case is government expenditure (or less appropriately, tax policy). If the signs are clear, fiscal changes ought to be made quickly enough to offset the disturbance from the private sector. The objection that may be raised that fiscal policy might be ineffective would, in fact, be hard to sustain in this context, provided fiscal policy had effects on the economy that are similar, in the main, to changes in private expenditure.

A Demand for Money Disturbance

A change in the demand for money ought to be counteracted by a 'like' instrument which, in this case, is the volume of money. Such changes in the demand for money ought to be fully accommodated by changes in the rate of growth of money within the prescribed band. If this were implemented sufficiently promptly it would ensure that there would be virtually no net disturbance to the domestic economy.

A Foreign Interest Rate Disturbance

Now consider how policy ought to be directed at counteracting changes in foreign interest rates. In a highly integrated world, changes in foreign interest rates are disruptive to the domestic economy by provoking changes in inflows or outflows of capital that affect not only a country's international reserve position but also (possibly) its domestic money supply. Several possibilities present themselves here. First, the monetary authorities may allow the exchange rate to change freely. For a rise in foreign interest rates this would lead to a devaluation in the currency to counteract the potential outflow of capital. For several reasons this would be an inappropriate policy in the circumstances. To begin with, in the very short term, during which asset (financial) markets adjust the exchange rate change required might be intolerably large (and indeed may well go outside the 'prescribed range' for exchange rates). For example, during this phase, the devaluation may have to be large enough to induce expectations of a subsequent revaluation, sufficient to offset the incentives to send capital overseas. Then, in due course, 'real' markets (trade and domestic demand) will adjust, with complex lags, to the exchange rate change and this will be highly disruptive to the economy.

A second way of dealing with changes in foreign interest rates is to sterilise the effects on the volume of money of the associated capital movements. In this case the country's international reserve position would bear the brunt of the adjustment. This policy is appropriate provided the policy does not have to be sustained too long and provided, too, the country's capital markets are not too highly integrated with the rest of the world. If the economy is highly integrated or if the policy is maintained for long the outflows (inflows) may put intolerable strains on the country's international reserves, which may make it difficult, in fact, to sustain a given exchange rate.

A third approach is to invoke capital controls to regulate the flows of capital. This serves the dual purpose of securing management of both the volume of money and the reserve position. Indeed, this method has been widely used in industrial countries in the last decade to control the movement of disruptive capital. Techniques of control have varied widely while their effectiveness has been extensively debated. These controls, it must be admitted, are administratively cumbersome, their incidence may be inequitable and in the longer run they lead to initiatives to bypass them. Nevertheless, they remain a useful arm of policy and ought on occasion to be used, together with sterilisation policies, to deal with disruptive changes in foreign interest rates.

A fourth approach is to try and alter the term structure of interest rates. For example, if foreign (short-term) interest rates are rising, domestic monetary policy might be directed at matching, partially or fully, foreign interest rates while, at the same time, minimising the disruption to the domestic economy by allowing long-term interest rates to fall or at least remain unchanged. This debt-management policy would entail the selling of securities at the short end and the buying of securities at the long end. If short-term rates affected capital flows predominantly and had very little effect on economic activity and if long-term rates affected economic activity predominantly and capital flows only weakly, the intended effects (of minimising both outflows and disturbances to the domestic economy) might be realised; but it is far from clear that short and long rates do have these significant differential impacts.

Fifth, the monetary/fiscal mix may be changed. For example, if foreign interest rates are rising and suppose sterilisation, capital controls and changes in the interest rate structure are all (or in combination) not feasible, then monetary policy might be tightened (the monetary target, say, would be kept at the lower end of the band) while fiscal policy would become more expansionary to counteract the effects on domestic activity. In principle, a policy mix of this kind could maintain economic activity, without any pressure on reserves. The higher interest rate can match the foreign rate, so there are no disruptive capital flows; at the same time, fiscal expansion could ensure that domestic activity is unaffected. Appealing as this policy mix might be it would in fact be a difficult one to manage. Differences in monetary–fiscal lags, interest rate and budget deficit implications pose obvious problems.

Sixth, and finally, a dual exchange rate arrangement could allow the exchange rate on capital transactions to bear the brunt of the adjustment without any associated real disturbances. For example, an outflow would lead to a devaluation of the exchange rate on the capital account which is sufficient to generate an offsetting expectation of a subsequent revaluation. In principle, this solution is a good one; however, there are serious administrative difficulties in managing a dual exchange rate scheme.[2]

A Domestic Price Disturbance

Now consider the case of a domestic price shock (for instance, a change in food prices, indirect taxes or public utility prices). It is useful to consider this in two stages: the direct impact on the price level and the secondary effects of the change in the price level on wages. How should this be dealt with? The direct effect ought to be accommodated by an appropriate change in the volume of money. This allows the price rise but ensures that there are no changes in real money balances, which would have disruptive effects on employment and real demand. The potential secondary effects are more difficult to deal with. Ideally an incomes policy ought again to be invoked here; in its absence, however, a difficult decision has to be taken as to whether the secondary effects ought to be accommodated by the monetary authorities. In our judgement they should be. One has to recall that here one is dealing with once-over changes in the rate of inflation, not a sustained upward change in the inflation rate. In general, too, upward movements will tend to be offset by downward movements.

There may also be unanticipated short-term changes in wages. More :ontroversially, these may be countered by combining two policy :hanges: an accommodating change in the volume of money and an)ffsetting change in the exchange rate.

A Real Foreign Demand Disturbance

Ve now turn to the case of change in real foreign demand. Of the everal instruments the only two that might be appropriate would be he exchange rate and fiscal policy. Suppose, for example, there were n upsurge in the real demand for exports and the exchange rate were llowed to adjust to market forces. If the revaluation was thought to e temporary, the expectation of a devaluation and the associated utflow of capital would leave the balance of payments unchanged ut, however, at the expense of some disruption to the domestic economy in the form of an improvement in the current account. Again, even if the revaluation left the current account unchanged (the revaluation exactly offsetting the rise in real demand abroad), this would still entail significant shifts in resources within the domestic economy.

A restrictive fiscal policy in the face of an increase in real foreign demand would allow reserves to change (improve) while resources would have to move out of consumer goods (say, if household taxes were raised) into the export sector to maintain economic activity. We conclude, then, that for a real disturbance originating abroad there is no one policy or policy combination that is exactly tailored to counteract it.

A Foreign Price (Non-Oil) Disturbance

Consider, now, a disturbance flowing from a change in (non-oil) foreign prices. Realistically, in dealing with changes in world prices we need to at least distinguish between world prices of manufactured goods and world prices of non-oil commodities (for example, farm products, minerals). Typically, over a cycle the amplitude of price fluctuations tends to be greater for the latter than for the former. In the face of these differential price changes and given different weights attaching to these commodity groups in imports and exports, a change in the exchange rate will not typically be able to fully insulate the economy from these foreign disturbances.

To illustrate, suppose that 'commodities' made up some 50 per cent of a particular developed country's imports while that country's exports were made up predominantly of manufactured goods. Suppose, too, that world prices of manufactured goods accelerated by some 10 per cent, while world prices of commodities accelerated by some 20 per cent. Import prices would be rising by an additional 15 per cent while export-competing prices would be rising by an additional 10 per cent. Suppose the country were to revalue its currency by 12.5 per cent. What would happen to the overall price level? Import prices would rise by some 2.5 per cent but if export prices of manufactured goods were determined by domestic costs the net revaluation of 2.5 per cent would not lower export prices. In this instance, then, there might be some rise in the overall price level. At the same time, the trade effects will depend on the relative elasticities of demand for manufactured goods and commodities. Hence, neither prices nor trade would be fully insulated, by exchange rate changes from world price changes. Or, again, a developed country's exports could be predominantly mineral or rural while its imports could be predominantly of manufactured goods (as in Australia). Attempts to offset foreign price developments by exchange rate changes will, again, confront similar potentially disruptive effects. Nevertheless and despite these qualifications, the exchange rate instrument remains the most appropriate one to deal with disturbances from foreign price changes.

An Oil Price Disturbance

Finally, we come to an oil price shock which, given its large domestic and international repercussions, is easily the most difficult to cope with. In dealing with it it is helpful to distinguish four distinct aspects of the adjustment process. First, there is the problem of financing the associated deficit. Second, given the emerging current account deficit, there is the problem of how to sustain domestic demand and, at the same time, mitigate the inflationary impact. Third, again given the emerging deficit, there is the intertemporal problem of the distribution of the needed reduction in real consumption over time. Fourth, there is the problem of the 'optimal' distribution of the global current account deficits over the oil-consuming countries.

The problem of 'financing' is relatively straightforward. For the world, as a whole, the OPEC surplus will be equal to the sums of the current account deficits of the rest of the world. Assuming fixed exchange rates, for an individual oil-consuming country the required borrowing (or running down of reserves) is equal to the increase in the expenditure on oil less the sum of the increase in OPEC imports from that country and autonomous capital flows from the OPEC. In countries with highly developed capital markets and/or which specialise in exports wanted by the OPEC, the overall surplus (deficit) may actually increase (decrease). On the other hand, in countries that have less attractive investment opportunities and financial markets and cannot sell more exports to the OPEC some borrowing will be required.

With exchange rates more flexible the 'surplus' countries will appreciate while the deficit countries will devalue. The initial current account deficits of the surplus (deficit) countries will then increase (reduce). With freely flexible exchange rates, by definition the problem of financing is, with time, eliminated (in the sense that it is automatically financed by OPEC inflows).[3] In reality, individual countries may have a policy choice between, say, an exchange rate adjustment and/or induced borrowing to meet the overall deficit. This choice is essentially an intertemporal one: borrowing as against exchange rate flexibility may permit more current real consumption at the expense of future consumption.

An oil price shock means first that real expenditure overseas increases, thus reducing demand for domestic goods (which may be partly offset by additional OPEC imports), and second, that there is a direct effect on the price level. Can domestic demand be sustained for these conditions? An expansionary fiscal policy combined with an accommodating monetary policy (so as to avoid changes in real money balances) will tend to minimise the domestic disturbance. However, there are bound to be major structural adjustments to the domestic economy that are certain to impose strains (for instance, in the form of additional structural unemployment). Moreover, the direct effect on the price level may well provoke some wage adjustments accentuating the price effects. An incomes policy to prevent price changes from translating into wage changes, in this context, therefore assumes particular importance.[4]

The oil price shock imposes a loss of real income on the oil-consuming countries. The loss of real income will have to entail, in time, a reduction in real consumption. It is, however, open to governments to alter the time distribution of this loss by, say, choosing between borrowing and exchange rate flexibility, as we have seen, and also by influencing the time pattern of the composition of output between consumption and investment. An example will make this clear. Suppose, to take an extreme case, exports to OPEC increased to the same extent as the increase in oil imports. Then, clearly, the country's command over real resources will fall off immediately. Governments, however, may be able to mitigate the loss in current consumption by a fiscal policy that cut back on investment and encouraged more consumption. (The policy would then gradually be reversed over time.) At the other extreme, current command over resources may remain unchanged (for instance, if there is no change in exports to OPEC) but, in this case, governments may wish to encourage investment at the expense of current consumption, so as to alleviate the loss in real consumption in future years.

Clearly, acute dilemmas are posed by an oil price shock. It might appear on the face of it that one way the oil-consuming countries could avoid the real income loss is, in fact, by inflating sufficiently to restore the original real price of oil. To some extent this is what happened during 1975–78 when the real price of oil actually fell significantly. In the end, however, the oil-producing countries will set in motion a new oil price shock, so as to regain a real-price advantage (as they did in 1978/79). This will then trigger a new price spiral, the source of which is the battle over the share of the world's real resources. The difference between this price spiral and the classic domestic wage–price spiral over claims on domestic real resources is simply that the former originates externally while the latter originates domestically.

It is evident that the domestic adjustment by an individual country to an oil price shock is very complex. What is clear is that, in the face of a major disturbance of this kind, many arms of policy need to be invoked, including changes in monetary policy, exchange rate adjustment, foreign borrowing and finally fiscal policy, with particularly careful attention in the latter case to the effects on the composition of output. Moreover, countries ought to co-ordinate their macro-policies. For example, if one country were to sustain demand while the rest of the world allowed some unemployment the country might have to borrow heavily or to devalue, with further repercussions on intertemporal incomes and/or domestic prices.

There is also the question of the optimal distribution of the current account deficits among the oil-consuming countries. Taking, for example, the OECD countries as a group how ought they to distribute a larger OECD deficit?[5] Several suggestions have been made. These include distribution on the basis of (1) the increase in oil payments less OPEC imports, (2) real income per capita (the country with the lower standard of living being allowed the 'larger' deficit so as to mitigate the loss in command over real resources), (3) relative GNP (the larger GNP being allowed a larger deficit) and (4) the social rate of return on capital (the country with the higher social rate of return being allowed a larger current account deficit and, hence, a bigger command over resources, which could be allocated to the more profitable investment opportunities). It is, however, difficult to see how agreement could ever be reached on any such criteria or, even if agreement were reached, exactly how it would be implemented. We must conclude, therefore, that while there are important issues here they remain, largely, of academic interest.

Summary

To sum up, our analysis suggests that when foreign prices or real foreign demand are changing changes in exchange rates are appropriate. When the demand for money or domestic prices is changing, a change in the volume of money is appropriate. For unanticipated changes in wages, an accommodating change in the volume of money combined with an exchange rate adjustment would be the appropriate policy. When domestic real expenditure is changing fiscal policy may be appropriate. When foreign interest rates are changing, under normal circumstances, the combination of capital flow regulations and sterilisation policies ought to be capable of minimising the disturbance to the domestic economy. Finally, for an oil price shock several arms of policy need to be invoked and then, international co-ordination becomes particularly important.

A final comment about the policy strategy proposed is in order. Our emphasis on counteracting different disturbances by invoking different policy instruments brings into sharp focus the need to identify dominant disturbances. Clearly considerably more research is needed here. Two promising lines of attack are worth pursuing. First, policy strategy over, say, a year is generally based on some assumption about likely trends in domestic expenditure, domestic money demand, wages and foreign developments. Deviations from these trends provide hints of disturbances in one direction or another. In principle, policy, on balance, can then be reoriented to counter these disturbances.

Second, one might be able to identify dominant sources of disturbances in terms of combinations of outcomes in certain key variables in the economy. For example, each disturbance produces a unique combination of changes in a range of endogenous variables such as domestic interest rates, economic activity, the current and capital accounts of the balance of payments, domestic prices. To take the simplest possible illustration of this, consider the distinction between a domestic expenditure disturbance and a demand for money disturbance. An increase in domestic expenditure leads to a rise in activity and a rise in domestic interest rates while a fall in the demand for money leads to a rise in activity but now a fall in interest rates. So, all other things being equal, rising economic activity associated with rising interest rates might be indicative of a 'real' disturbance, while rising economic activity associated with falling interest rates might indicate a monetary disturbance.

Notes for Chapter 32

1 The appropriate long-run rate of inflation must take account of institutional conditions (principally wage-setting arrangements, trade union militancy) and, also, the rate of inflation in the immediately preceding years. Whatever the rate of inflation determined, clearly something like a long-run incomes policy will be needed.

2 See A. Lanyi (1975).

3 Assuming, of course, the exchange rate change is effective. See, however, Chapter 25.

4 An expansionary fiscal policy which took the form of a cut in household or indirect taxes might serve the dual purpose of moderating the impacts on wages and prices and sustaining aggregate demand.

5 For a discussion of these issues see A. Crockett and D. Ripley (1975); R. Solomon (1975).

Bibliography

Acheson, A. L. K., Chant, J. F. and Prachowny, M. F. J. (1972) *Bretton Woods Revisited* (University of Toronto Press).

Ackley, G. (1978) 'Implications for policy: a symposium', *Brookings Papers on Economic Activity*, 2nd quarter, pp. 507–10.

Aliber, R. Z. (1964) 'The cost and benefits of the US role as a reserve currency country', *Quarterly Journal of Economics*, vol. LXXVIII, August, pp. 422–56.

Aliber, R. Z. (1976) 'The firm under pegged and floating exchange rates', *Scandinavian Journal of Economics*, vol. 78, pp. 309–22.

Argy, V. (1969) 'Monetary variables and the balance of payments', *International Monetary Fund Staff Papers*, vol. XVI, July, pp. 267–88.

Argy, V. (1975) 'The dynamics of monetary policy under flexible exchange rates: an exploratory analysis', in *Papers in Monetary Economics* (Sydney: Reserve Bank of Australia).

Argy, V. (1978) 'Monetarist models of open economies', *Economies et Societes*, vol. XII, nos. 10–12, pp. 1707–40.

Argy, V. (1979) 'Monetary stabilisation and the stabilisation of output in select industrial countries', *Banca Nazionale del Lavoro Quarterly Review*, no. 129, June, pp. 155–66.

Argy, V. and Carmichael, J. (1976) 'Models of imported inflation for a small country – with particular reference to Australia', in *International Money – Experiments and Experience: Papers and Proceedings of the Port Stephens Conference*, W. Kasper (ed.) (Canberra: Department of Economics, Research School of Social Sciences, Australian National University).

Argy, V. and Clements, K. W. (1980) 'The forward rate as a predictor of the spot rate – an analysis of four major currencies', paper presented at *Centre for Studies in Money, Banking & Finance*, Macquarie University, Sydney, Australia – Seminar June 27, 1980.

Argy, V. and Hodjera, Z. (1973) 'Financial integration and interest rate linkages in the industrial countries: 1958–1971', *International Monetary Fund Staff Papers*, vol. XX, March, pp. 1–77.

Argy, V. and Kouri, P. J. K. (1974) 'Sterilisation policies and the volatility in international reserves', in *National Monetary Policies and the International Financial System*, R. Z. Aliber (ed.) (University of Chicago Press).

Argy, V. and Porter, M. G. (1972) 'The forward exchange market and the effects of domestic and external disturbances under alternative exchange rate systems', *International Monetary Fund Staff Papers*, vol. XIX, November, pp. 503–32.

Argy, V. and Salop, J. (1978) 'Monetary and fiscal expansion in a two-country world under flexible exchange rates and variable wage rates' (Washington DC: International Monetary Fund), December.

Argy, V. and Salop, J. (1979) 'Price and output effects of monetary and fiscal policy under flexible exchange rates', *International Monetary Fund Staff Papers*, vol. XXVI, June, pp. 224–56.

Arndt, S. W. (1973) 'Joint balance: capital mobility and the monetary system of a currency area', in *The Economics of Common Currencies*, H. G. Johnson and A. K. Swoboda (eds) (London: Allen & Unwin), Chapter 11.

Artus, J. R. (1976) 'Exchange rate stability and managed floating: the experience of the Federal Republic of Germany', *International Monetary Fund Staff Papers*, vol. XXIII, July, pp. 312–33.

Artus, J. R. (1977) 'Measures of potential output in manufacturing for eight industrial countries', *International Monetary Fund Staff Papers*, vol. XXIV, March, pp. 1–35.

Artus, J. R. (1978) 'Methods of assessing the long-run equilibrium value of an exchange rate', *Journal of International Economics*, vol. 8, pp. 277–99.

Artus, J. R. and Crockett, A. D. (1978) 'Floating exchange rates and the need for surveillance', *Essays in International Finance No. 127*, Princeton University, Princeton, N.J.

Artus, J. R. and Young, J. H. (1979) 'Fixed and flexible rates: a renewal of the debate', unpublished (Washington DC: International Monetary Fund), May.

Bacon, R. W. and Eltis, W. A. (1976) 'How growth in public expenditure has contributed to Britain's difficulties', in *The Dilemmas of Government Expenditure* (The Institute of Economic Affairs).

Bacon, R. W. and Eltis, W. A. (1978) 'The non-market sector and the balance of payments', *National Westminster Bank Quarterly Review*, May, pp. 65–9.

Bacon, R. W. and Eltis, W. A. (1979) 'Britain's economic problem: the growth of the non-market sector? – an interchange', *The Economic Journal*, vol. 89, June, pp. 392–415.

Balassa, B. (1964) 'The purchasing power parity doctrine: a re-appraisal', *Journal of Political Economy*, vol. 72, December, pp. 584–96.

Balassa, B. (1978) 'The "new protectionism" and the international economy', *Journal of World Trade Law*, vol. 12, September/October, pp. 409–36.

Ball, R. J., Burns, T. and Laury, J. S. E. (1977) 'The role of exchange rate changes in balance of payments adjustment – the United Kingdom case', *The Economic Journal*, vol. 87, March, pp. 1–29.

Bank for International Settlements (BIS), *Annual Reports*, Basle.

Bank of England, *Quarterly Bulletin*, London.

Barro, R. (1977) 'Unanticipated money growth and unemployment in the US', *The American Economic Review*, vol. 67, March, pp. 101–15.

Basevi, G. and De Grauwe, P. (1977) 'Vicious and virtuous circles: a theoretical analysis and a policy proposal for managing exchange rates', *European Economic Review*, vol. 10, pp. 277–301.

Baxter, J. L. (1973) 'Inflation in the context of relative deprivation and social justice', *Scottish Journal of Political Economy*, vol. 20, February, pp. 263–82.

Bell, G. (1974) *The Euro-Dollar Market and the International Financial System* (London: Macmillan).

Bernstein, E. M. (1963) 'A radical proposal for international monetary reserves', *Model, Roland and Company Quarterly Review*, 4th quarter.

Bernstein, E. M. *et al.* (1976) 'Reflections on Jamaica', *Essays in International Finance No. 115*, Princeton University, Princeton, N.J.

Bilson, J. F. O. (1978) 'The monetary approach to the exchange rate: some empirical evidence', *International Monetary Fund Staff Papers*, vol. XXV, March, pp. 48–75.

Bilson, J. F. O. (1979a) 'The "vicious circle" hypothesis', *International Monetary Fund Staff Papers*, vol. XXVI, March, pp. 1–37.

Bilson, J. F. O. (1979b) 'The deutsche mark/dollar rate – a monetary analysis', *Journal of Monetary Economics – Supplement*, vol. 11, pp. 59–102.

Bishop, J. and Haveman, R. (1979) 'Selective employment subsidies: can Okun's Law be repealed?', *The American Economic Review*, vol. 69, May, pp. 124–30.

Bispham, J. A. (1975) 'The new Cambridge and "Monetarist" criticisms of "conventional" economic policy-making', *National Institute Economic Review*, No. 74, November, pp. 39–55.

Black, S. W. (1976) 'Comment on J. Williamson "Exchange rate flexibility and reserve use"', *Scandinavian Journal of Economics*, vol. 78, pp. 340–45.

Black, S. W. (1978) 'Policy responses to major disturbances of the 1970s and their transmission through international goods and capital markets', *Weltwirtschaftliches Archiv*, Band 114, pp. 614–41.

Blackaby, F. T. (1978) 'The reform of the wage bargaining system', *National Institute Economic Review*, No. 85, August, pp. 49–54.

Blinder, A. S. (1973) 'Can income tax increases be inflationary?: an expository note', *National Tax Journal*, vol. 26, June, pp. 259–301.

Blinder, A. S. and Solow, R. M. (1973) 'Does fiscal policy matter?', *Journal of Public Economics*, vol. 2, November, pp. 319–37.

Bloomfield, A. (1959) *Monetary Policy under the International Gold Standard 1880–1914* (Federal Reserve Bank of New York).

Bloomfield, A. (1963) 'Short-term capital movements under the pre-1914 gold standard', *Princeton Studies in International Finance No. 11*, Princeton University, Princeton, N.J.

Boyer, R. (1975) 'Commodity markets and bond markets in a small fixed-exchange rate economy', *Canadian Journal of Economics*, vol. VIII, February, pp. 1–23.

Brainard, W. (1967) 'Uncertainty and the effectiveness of policy', *The American Economic Review*, vol. 57, May, pp. 411–25.

Branson, W. H., Halttunen, H. and Masson, P. (1977) 'Exchange rates in the short run: the dollar deutsche mark rate', *European Economic Review*, vol. 10, pp. 303–24.

Branson, W. H. and Hill, R. (1971) 'Capital movements in the OECD area: an econometric analysis', *OECD Occasional Studies*, December.

Braun, A. R. (1975) 'The role of incomes policy in industrial countries since World War II', *International Monetary Fund Staff Papers*, vol. XXII, March, pp. 1–36.

Braun, A. R. (1976) 'Indexation of wages and salaries in developed economies', *International Monetary Fund Staff Papers*, vol. XXIII, March, pp. 226–71.

Braun, A. R. (1978) 'Incomes policies in industrial countries since 1973', unpublished (Washington DC: International Monetary Fund), January.

Brechling, F. and Wolfe, J. N. (1965) 'The end of stop–go', *Lloyds Bank Review*, No. 75, January, pp. 23–30.

Brinner, R. E. (1977) 'The death of the Phillips Curve reconsidered', *Quarterly Journal of Economics*, vol. LXXXXI, August, pp. 389–418.

Brittan, S. (1971) *Steering the Economy*, revised edition (Harmondsworth: Penguin).

Brittan, S. and Lilley, P. (1977) *The Delusion of Incomes Policy* (Temple Smith).

Brown, W. A. (1940) *The International Gold Standard Reinterpreted: 1914–1934*, 2 vols (National Bureau of Economic Research).

Brunner, K. (ed.) (1978) 'Keynesian policies, the drift into permanent deficits and the growth of government – a symposium', *Journal of Monetary Economics*, vol. 4, pp. 569–636.

Buchanan, J. and Wagner, R. (1977) *Democracy in Deficit* (London and New York: Academic Press).

Burton, J. (1977) 'Employment subsidies – the cases for and against', *National Westminster Bank Quarterly Review*, February, pp. 33–43.

Butkiewicz, J. L. (1979) 'Outside wealth, the demand for money and the crowding out effect', *Journal of Monetary Economics*, vol. 5, pp. 249–58.

Cagan, P. (1956) 'The monetary dynamics of hyperinflation', in *Studies in the Quantity Theory of Money*, M. Friedman (ed.) (University of Chicago Press).

Carlson, K. M. and Spencer, R. W. (1975) 'Crowding out and its critics', *Federal Reserve Bank of St Louis Monthly Review*, vol. 57, December, pp. 2–17.

Casas, F. R. (1977) 'Capital mobility and stabilization policy under flexible exchange rates: a revised analysis', *Southern Economic Journal*, vol. 43, April, pp. 1528–37.

Chrystal, K. A. (1978) 'International money and the future of the SDR', *Essays in International Finance No. 128*, Princeton University, Princeton, N.J.

Claasen, E. M. (1976) 'World inflation under flexible exchange rates', *Scandinavian Journal of Economics*, vol. 78, pp. 346–65.

Claasen, E. M. and Salin, P. (eds) (1972) *Stabilization Policies in Interdependent Economies* (Amsterdam: North-Holland).

Clark, C. (1945) 'Public finance and changes in the value of money', *The Economic Journal*, vol. LV, December, pp. 371–89.

Clark, C. (1976) 'Paying for inflation', *Quadrant*, February, pp. 31–4.

Clark, P. B. and Grubel, H. G. (1972) 'National monetary sovereignty under different exchange rate regimes', *The Bulletin*, New York University, nos. 78–79.

Clarke, S. V. O. (1977a) 'Exchange rate stabilization in the mid-1930s: negotiating the Tripartite Agreement', *Princeton Studies in International Finance No. 41*, Princeton University, Princeton, N.J.

Clarke, S. V. O. (1977b) 'The influence of economists on the Tripartite Agreement of September 1936', *European Economic Review*, vol. 10, pp. 375–89.

Clegg, H. (1971) *How to Run an Incomes Policy and Why We Made Such a Mess of the Last One* (London: Heinemann).

Clements, K. and Frenkel, J. A. (1980) 'Exchange rates, money and relative prices: the dollar–pound in the 1920s', *Working Paper No. 429*, National Bureau of Economic Research Inc. (*Journal of International Economics*, forthcoming).

Clements, K. and Nguyen, P. (1979) 'Estimating the price deflator for nominal cash balances', *Economics Letters*, 3, pp. 175–8.

Cohen, B. J. (1971) 'The seignorage gain of an international currency: an empirical test', *Quarterly Journal of Economics*, vol. LXXXV, August, pp. 494–507.

Cohen, S. D. (1970) *International Monetary Reform 1964–1969: The Political Dimension* (New York: Praeger).

Commission of the European Communities (1977) *Inflation and Exchange Rates: Evidence and Policy Guidelines for the European Community* (Brussels).

Connors, T. A. (1979) 'The apparent effects of recent IMF stabilization programs', *International Finance Discussion Paper No. 135*, Federal Reserve System, Washington DC.

Cooper, R. N. (1968) 'The balance of payments', in *Britain's Economic Prospects*, R. E. Caves and Associates (eds) (Washington DC: The Brookings Institution; London: Allen & Unwin).

Cooper, R. N. (1969) 'Comment', in *Monetary Problems of the International Economy*, R. A. Mundell and A. K. Swoboda (eds) (University of Chicago Press).

Cooper, R. N. (1972) 'Euro-dollars, reserve dollars and asymmetries in the international monetary system', *Journal of International Economics*, vol. 2, pp. 325–44.

Cooper, R. N. (1975) 'Prolegomena to the choice of an international monetary system', in *World Politics and International Economics*, C. F. Bergsten and L. B. Krause (eds) (Washington DC: The Brookings Institution).

Corden, W. M. (1972) 'Monetary integration', *Essays in International Finance No. 93*, Princeton University, Princeton, N.J.

Corden, W. M. (1977) *Inflation, Exchange Rates and the World Economy – Lectures on International Monetary Economics* (Oxford: Clarendon Press).

Cornell, W. B. (1977) 'Spot rates, forward rates and exchange market efficiency', *Journal of Financial Economics*, vol. 5, pp. 55–65.

Cornell, W. B. and Dietrich, J. K. (1978) 'The efficiency of the market for foreign exchange under floating exchange rates', *The Review of Economics and Statistics*, vol. LX, February, pp. 111–20.

Crockett, A. D. and Goldstein, M. (1976) 'Inflation under fixed and flexible exchange rates', *International Monetary Fund Staff Papers*, vol. XXIII, November, pp. 509–44.

Crockett, A. D. and Ripley, D. (1975) 'Sharing the oil deficit', *International Monetary Fund Staff Papers*, vol. XXII, July, pp. 284–312.

Darby, M. R. (1978) 'The U.S.A. – 1971–1974: how many matzo balls in the soup?', in *Wage-Price Control – Myth and Reality* (The Center for Independent Studies).

Dean, A. J. H. (1978) 'Incomes policies and differentials', *National Institute Economic Review*, No. 85, August, pp. 40–8.

Dernburg, T. (1974) 'The macro-economic implications of wage retaliation against higher taxation', *International Monetary Fund Staff Papers*, vol. XXI, November, pp. 758–88.

Deutsche Bundesbank, *Monthly Report of the Deutsche Bundesbank*, Frankfurt am Main.

De Vries, M. G. (1976) *The IMF 1966–1971 – The System Under Stress, Volume 1: Narrative* (Washington DC: International Monetary Fund).

Di Calogero, R. G. (1977) 'A note on the integration of short-term financial markets', unpublished (Washington DC: International Monetary Fund), August.

Dildine, L. L. and Sunley, E. M. (1978) 'Administrative problems of tax-based incomes policies', *Brookings Papers on Economic Activity*, 2nd quarter, pp. 363–400.

Dooley, M. P. and Isard, P. (1978) 'A portfolio-balance rational-expectations model of the dollar-mark rate: May 1973 to June 1977', *International Finance Discussion Paper No. 123*, Federal Reserve System, Washington DC.

Dooley, M. P. and Shafer, J. (1976) 'Analysis of short-run exchange rate behaviour: March 1973 to September 1975', *International Finance Discussion Paper No. 76*, Federal Reserve System, Washington DC.

Dornbusch, R. (1973) 'Devaluation, money and non-traded goods', *The American Economic Review*, vol. 63, December, pp. 871–83.

Dornbusch, R. (1975) 'Alternative price stabilization rules and the effects of exchange rate changes', *Manchester School of Economic and Social Studies*, no. 3, September, pp. 275–92.

Dornbusch, R. (1976) 'Expectations and exchange rate dynamics', *Journal of Political Economy*, vol. 84, December, pp. 1161–76.

Dornbusch, R. (1978) 'Monetary policy under exchange-rate flexibility', in *Managed Exchange-Rate Flexibility: The Recent Experience* (Federal Reserve Bank of Boston, Conference Series No. 20).

Dornbusch, R. and Krugman, P. (1976) 'Flexible exchange rates in the short run', *Brookings Papers on Economic Activity*, 3rd quarter, pp. 537–75.

Dufey, G. and Giddy, I. H. (1978) *The International Money Market* (Englewood Cliffs, N.J.: Prentice-Hall).

Eckes, A. E. (Jr) (1975) *A Search for Solvency: Bretton Woods and the International Monetary System – 1941–1971* (University of Texas Press).

Eckstein, O. (1979) 'Why supply-side economics is suddenly popular', *Business Week*, September 17.

Emminger, O. (1977) 'The D-mark in the conflict between internal and external equilibrium – 1948–1975', *Essays in International Finance No. 122*, Princeton University, Princeton, N.J.

Emminger, O. (1979) 'The exchange rate as an instrument of policy', *Lloyds Bank Review*, no. 133, July, pp. 1–22.

Ethier, W. and Bloomfield, A. I. (1975) 'Managing the managed float', *Essays in International Finance No. 112*, Princeton University, Princeton, N.J.

Ethier, W. and Bloomfield, A. I. (1978) 'The reference rate proposal and recent experience', *Banca Nazionale del Lavoro Quarterly Review*, no. 126, September, pp. 211–32.

Fase, M. G. (1976) 'The interdependence of short-term interest rates in the major financial centres of the world: some evidence for 1961–72', *Kyklos*, vol. 29, fasc. 1, pp. 63–96.

Feldstein, M. (1978) 'The private and social costs of unemployment', *The American Economic Review*,vol. 68, May, pp. 155–8.

Fieleke, N. S. (1979) 'Foreign exchange speculation by US firms: some new evidence', *New England Economic Review*, Federal Reserve Bank of Boston, March/April, pp. 5–17.

Fischer, S. (1977) 'Long-term contracts, rational expectations and the optimal money supply rule', *Journal of Political Economy*, vol. 85, February, pp. 191–205.

Fischer, S. and Modigliani, F. (1978) 'Towards an understanding of the real effects and costs of inflation', *Weltwirtschaftliches Archiv*, Band 114, pp. 810–33.

Fitzgerald, C. and Higgins, C. (1977) 'Inside RBA-76', in *Conference in Applied Economic Research* (Sydney: Reserve Bank of Australia).

Fleming, J. M. (1962) 'Domestic financial policies under fixed and under flexible exchange rates', *International Monetary Fund Staff Papers*, vol. IX, November, pp. 369–80.

Fleming, J. M. (1968) 'Targets and instruments', *International Monetary Fund Staff Papers*, vol. XV, November, pp. 387–404.

Fleming, J. M. (1971) 'On exchange rate unification', *Economic Journal*, vol. 81, September, pp. 467–88.

Flemming, J. S. (1976) *Inflation* (Oxford University Press).

Ford, A. G. (1962) *The Gold Standard 1880–1914 – Britain and Argentina* (Oxford University Press).

Fraser, H. F. (1933) *Great Britain and the Gold Standard: A Study of the Present World Depression* (London: Macmillan).

Freedman, C. (1977) 'The euro-dollar market – a review of five recent studies', *Journal of Monetary Economics*, vol. 3, pp. 467–78.

Frenkel, J. A. (1978) 'Purchasing power parity – doctrinal perspective and evidence from the 1920s', *Journal of International Economics*, vol. 8, pp. 169–91.

Frenkel, J. A. and Clements, K. (1978) 'Exchange rates in the 1920s: a monetary approach', unpublished, June.

Frenkel, J. A. and Johnson, H. G. (eds) (1976) *The Monetary Approach to the Balance of Payments* (London: Allen & Unwin).

Frenkel, J. A. and Levich, R. M. (1977) 'Transaction costs and interest arbitrage: tranquil versus turbulent periods', *Journal of Political Economy*, vol. 85, December, pp. 1209–26.

Fried, E. R. and Schultze, C. L. (eds) (1975) *Higher Oil Prices and the World Economy: The Adjustment Problem* (Washington DC: The Brookings Institution).

Fried, J. (1973) 'Inflation unemployment trade-offs under fixed and floating exchange rates', *Canadian Journal of Economics*, vol. VI, February, pp. 43–52.

Friedman, M. (1953) 'The case for flexible exchange rates', in *Essays in Positive Economics* (University of Chicago Press).

Friedman, M. (1968) 'The role of monetary policy', *The American Economic Review*, vol. 68, March, pp. 1–17.

Friedman, M. (1969) 'The euro-dollar market: some first principles', *Morgan Guaranty Survey*, October, pp. 4–14.
Friedman, M. (1979a) 'Volcker's inheritance', *Newsweek*, August 20.
Friedman, M. (1979b) 'Inflation and jobs', *Newsweek*, November 12.
Frisch, H. (1977) 'Inflation theory 1963–1975: a second generation survey', *Journal of Economic Literature*, vol. XV, December, pp. 1289–317.
Fromm, G. and Klein, L. R. (1973) 'A comparison of eleven econometric models of the United States', *The American Economic Review*, vol. 63, May, pp. 385–93.
Gardner, R. (1975) 'Bretton Woods', in *Essays on J. M. Keynes*, M. Keynes (ed.) (Cambridge University Press).
Gayer, A. D. (1935) *Monetary Policy and Economic Stabilisation – A Study of the Gold Standard* (New York: Macmillan).
Gold, J. (1970) 'Special drawing rights – character and use', *International Monetary Fund Pamphlet Series No. 13*, second edition, Washington DC.
Gold, J. (1971) 'The Fund's concepts of convertibility', *International Monetary Fund Pamphlet Series No. 14*, Washington DC.
Gold, J. (1977) 'International capital movements under the law of the International Monetary Fund', *International Monetary Fund Pamphlet Series No. 21*, Washington DC.
Gold, J. (1978a) 'The Second Amendment of the Fund's Articles of Agreement: a general view I', *Finance and Development*, vol. 15, March, pp. 10–3.
Gold, J. (1978b) 'The Second Amendment of the Fund's Articles of Agreement: a general view II', *Finance and Development*, vol. 15, June, pp. 15–8.
Gold, J. (1978c) 'Some first effects of the Second Amendment', *Finance and Development*, vol. 15, September, pp. 24–9.
Goldstein, H. N. (1965) 'Does it necessarily cost anything to be the "World Banker"?', *The National Banking Review*, vol. 2, March, pp. 411–15.
Goldstein, H. N. (1979) 'Floating exchange rates and modified purchasing power parity: evidence from recent experience using an index of effective exchange rates', in *Proceedings of 1978 West Coast Academic Federal Reserve Economic Research Seminar* (Federal Reserve Bank of San Francisco).
Goldstein, M. (1977) 'Downward price inflexibility, ratchet effects and the inflationary impact of import price changes: some empirical tests', *International Monetary Fund Staff Papers*, vol. XXIV, November, pp. 569–612.
Gordon, R. J. (1975) 'Alternative responses of policy to external supply shocks', *Brookings Papers on Economic Activity*, 1st quarter, pp. 183–204.
Gordon, R. J. (1976) 'Recent developments in the theory of inflation and unemployment', *Journal of Monetary Economics*, vol. 2, pp. 185–219.
Gordon, R. J. (1977) 'World inflation and monetary accommodation in eight countries', *Brookings Papers on Economic Activity*, 2nd quarter, pp. 409–77.
Gordon, R. J. (1978) 'What can stabilization policy achieve?', *The American Economic Review*, vol. 68, May, pp. 335–41.
Gramlich, E. M. (1979) 'Macro-policy responses to price shocks', *Brookings Papers on Economic Activity*, 1st quarter, pp. 126–66.
Gregory, T. (1925) *The Return to Gold* (London: Ernest Penn).

Grubel, H. G. (ed.) (1963) *World Monetary Reform* (Stanford University Press).

Grubel, H. G. (1964) 'The benefits and costs of being the World Banker', *The National Banking Review*, vol. 2, December, pp. 197–205.

Grubel, H. G. (1972) *The International Monetary System*, second edition (London: Penguin Modern Economics).

Gruen, F. H. (1978) 'Structural unemployment as a rival explanation – a survey of an inconclusive argument: international and Australian aspects', *Australian National University Working Paper No. 63*, July.

Haas, R. D. (1974) 'More evidence on the role of speculation in the Canadian forward exchange market', *Canadian Journal of Economics*, vol. VII, August, pp. 496–501.

Haas, R. D. and Alexander, W. E. (1979) 'A model of exchange rates and capital flows: the Canadian floating rate experience', *Journal of Money, Credit and Banking*, vol. XI, November, pp. 467–82.

Haberler, G. (1976) *The World Economy, Money and the Great Depression 1919–1939* (Washington DC: American Enterprise Institute for Public Policy Research).

Haberler, G. (1977) 'How important is control over international reserves?', in *The New International Monetary System*, R. A. Mundell and J. J. Polak (eds) (New York: Columbia University Press).

Hadjimatheou, C. G. and Skouras, A. (1979) 'Britain's economic problem: the growth of the non-market sector? – an interchange', *The Economic Journal*, vol. 89, June, pp. 392–415.

Hagemann, H. A. (1969) 'Reserve policies of central banks and their implications for U.S. balance of payments policy', *The American Economic Review*, vol. 59, March, pp. 62–71.

Halm, G. N. (1965) 'The "band" proposal: the limits of permissible exchange rate variations', *Special Papers in International Economics No. 6*, Princeton University, Princeton, N.J.

Halm, G. N. (1969) 'Towards limited exchange rate flexibility', *Essays in International Finance No. 73*, Princeton University, Princeton, N.J.

Harris, S. E. (ed.) (1961) *The Dollar in Crisis* (New York: Harcourt Brace & World).

Harrod, R. F. (1965) *Reforming the World's Money* (New York: Macmillan/St Martin's Press).

Hawtrey, R. G. (1931) *The Gold Standard in Theory and Practice* (London: Longman).

Heilperin, M. A. (1963) 'The case for going back to gold', in *World Monetary Reform*, H. G. Grubel (ed.) (Stanford University Press).

Heller, H. R. and Khan, M. S. (1978) 'The demand for international reserves under fixed and floating exchange rates', *International Monetary Fund Staff Papers*, vol. XXV, December, pp. 623–49.

Helliwell, J. F. (1969) 'Monetary and fiscal policies for an open economy', *Oxford Economic Papers*, vol. XXI, March, pp. 35–55.

Helliwell, J. F. *et al.* (1971) 'The structure of RDX2', *Staff Research Studies No. 7*, Bank of Canada, Ottawa.

Helliwell, J. F., Maxwell, T. and Waslander, H. E. (1979) 'Comparing the dynamics of Canadian macromodels', *Canadian Journal of Economics*, vol. XII, May, pp. 181–94.

Henry, S. G. B. and Ormerod, P. A. (1978) 'Incomes policy and wage inflation: empirical evidence for the U.K. 1961–1977', *National Institute Economic Review*, No. 85, August, pp. 31–9.

Herring, R. J. and Marston, R. C. (1977) 'Sterilisation policy: the trade-off between monetary autonomy and control over foreign exchange reserves', *European Economic Review*, vol. 10, pp. 325–43.

Hewson, J. (1975) *Liquidity Creation and Distribution in the Euro-Currency Markets* (Lexington Books).

Hewson, J. and Sakakibara, E. (1974) 'The euro-dollar deposit multiplier: a portfolio approach', *International Monetary Fund Staff Papers*, vol. XXI, July, pp. 307–28.

Hewson, J. and Sakakibara, E. (1975) 'The impact of U.S. controls on capital outflows on the U.S. balance of payments: an exploratory study', *International Monetary Fund Staff Papers*, vol. XXII, March, pp. 37–60.

Hodgson, J. (1972) 'An analysis of floating exchange rates: the dollar-sterling rate 1919–1925', *Southern Economic Journal*, vol. 39, October, pp. 249–57.

Hodgson, J. and Phelps, P. (1975) 'The distributed impact of price-level variation on floating exchange rates', *Review of Economics and Statistics*, vol. LVII, February, pp. 58–64.

Hodjera, Z. (1973) 'International short-term capital movements: a survey of theory and empirical analysis', *International Monetary Fund Staff Papers*, vol. XX, November, pp. 683–740.

Hodjera, Z. (1976) 'Alternative approaches in the analysis of international capital movements: a case study of Austria and France', *International Monetary Fund Staff Papers*, vol. XXIII, November, pp. 598–623.

Hodrick, R. J. (1978) 'An empirical analysis of the monetary approach to the determination of the exchange rate', in *The Economics of Exchange Rates: Selected Studies*, eds J. A. Frenkel and H. G. Johnson (Reading, Mass.: Addison-Wesley).

Horsefield, J. K. (ed.) (1969) *The I.M.F. 1945–1965: Twenty Years of International Monetary Co-operation*, vols 1–3 (Washington DC: International Monetary Fund).

Howard, D. H. (1976) 'Personal saving behavior in five major industrialised countries', *International Finance Discussion Paper No. 90*, Federal Reserve System, Washington.

Humphrey, T. and Lawler, T. (1977) 'Factors determining exchange rates: a simple model and empirical tests', *Economic Review*, Federal Reserve Bank of Richmond, vol. 63, May/June, pp. 10–15.

Hunter, L. C. (1973) 'Some lessons from the failure of British incomes policies', in *Incomes Policy: What Can We Learn from Europe?*, W. Galenson (ed.) (Ithaca, N.Y.: Cornell University Press).

Hunter, L. C. (1975) 'British incomes policy 1972–1974', *Industrial and Labour Relations Review*, vol. 29, October, pp. 67–84.

Ingram, J. C. (1973) 'The case for European monetary integration, *Essays in International Finance No. 98*, Princeton University, Princeton, N.J.

International Monetary Fund (IMF), *Annual Report*, Washington DC.

International Monetary Fund (IMF), *International Financial Statistics*, Washington DC.

International Monetary Fund (IMF), *IMF Survey*, Washington DC.

International Monetary Fund (IMF) (1968) *Articles of Agreement of the International Monetary Fund*, Washington DC.

International Monetary Fund (IMF) (1969) 'Quantitative criteria for the assessment of reserve needs', reprinted in IMF, *International Reserves: Needs and Availability*, Washington DC, 1970.

International Monetary Fund (IMF) (1970a) *International Reserves: Needs and Availability*, Washington DC.

International Monetary Fund (IMF) (1970b) *The Role of Exchange Rates in the Adjustment of International Payments – A Report by the Executive Directors*, Washington DC.

International Monetary Fund (IMF) (1972) *Reform of the International Monetary System – A Report by the Executive Directors*, Washington DC.

International Monetary Fund (IMF) (1974a) *International Monetary Reform – Documents of the Committee of Twenty*, Washington DC.

International Monetary Fund (IMF) (1974b) 'Guidelines for countries authorized to adopt floating rates', *IMF Survey*, vol. 3, pp. 181–3.

International Monetary Fund (IMF) (1977) *The Monetary Approach to the Balance of Payments*, Washington DC.

International Monetary Fund (IMF) (1978) 'The rise in protectionism', *International Monetary Fund Pamphlet Series No. 24*, Washington DC.

International Monetary Fund (IMF) (1979) 'The European monetary system', *IMF Survey Supplement*, 19 March.

Isard, P. (1977) 'How far can we push the law of one price?', *The American Economic Review*, vol. 67, December, pp. 942–8.

Isard, P. (1978) 'Exchange rate determination: a survey of popular views and recent models', *Princeton Studies in International Finance No. 42*, Princeton University, Princeton, N.J.

Ishiyama, Y. (1975) 'The theory of optimum currency areas: a survey', *International Monetary Fund Staff Papers*, vol. XXII, no. 2, July, pp. 344–83.

Jackson, D., Turner, H. and Wilkinson, F. (1975) *Do Trade Unions Cause Inflation?*, second edition (Cambridge University Press).

Jackson–Grayson, C. (1978) 'Is prostitution a service industry or a regulated utility? – dilemma of a price controller', in *Wage-Price Control – Myth and Reality* (Center for Independent Studies).

Jianakoplos, N. A. (1978) 'A tax-based incomes policy (TIP): what's it all about?', *Federal Reserve Bank of St Louis Monthly Review*, vol. 60, February, pp. 8–12.

Jones, A. (1973) *The New Inflation: The Politics of Prices and Incomes* (Penguin – in association with André Deutsch).

Jones, R. (1968) 'Monetary and fiscal policy for an economy with fixed exchange rates', *Journal of Political Economy*, vol. 76, Part II, July/August, pp. 921–43.

Jonson, P. D. (1973) 'Our current inflationary experience', *The Australian Economic Review*, 2nd quarter, pp. 21–6.

Jonson, P. D. and Kierzkowski, H. (1975) 'The balance of payments: an analytic exercise', *Manchester School of Economic and Social Studies*, no. 2, June, pp. 105–33.

Jonson, P. D., Moses, E. and Wymer, C. (1977) 'The RBA-76 Model of the

Australian Economy', in *Conference in Applied Economic Research* (Sydney: Reserve Bank of Australia).
Karlik, J. R. (1968) 'The costs and benefits of being a reserve-currency country: a theoretical approach applied to the U.S.', in *The Open Economy: Essays on International Trade and Finance*, P. B. Kenen and R. Lawrence (eds) (New York: Columbia University Press).
Katz, S. I. (1972) 'Devaluation – bias and the Bretton Woods system', *Banca Nazionale del Lavoro Quarterly Review*, no. 101, June, pp. 178–98.
Kenen, P. B. (1969) 'The theory of optimum currency areas: an eclectic view', in *Monetary Problems of the International Economy*, R. A. Mundell and A. K. Swoboda (eds) (University of Chicago Press).
Kenen, P. B. (1976) 'Capital mobility and financial integration: a survey', *Princeton Studies in International Finance No. 39*, Princeton University, Princeton, N.J.
Kern, David (1979) 'Neither alarm nor complacency', *Euromoney*, April, pp. 110–16.
Kesselman, J. (1971) 'The role of speculation in forward rate determination: the Canadian flexible dollar – 1953–1960', *Canadian Journal of Economics*, vol. IV, August, pp. 279–97.
Kindleberger, C. P. (1973) *The World in Depression 1929–1939* (Berkeley, Calif.: University of California Press).
King, D. T. (1977) 'The performance of exchange rates in the recent period of floating: exchange rates and relative rates of inflation', *Southern Economic Journal*, vol. 43, April, pp. 1582–7.
Kirschen, E. (1974) 'The American external seignorage: origins, cost to Europe and possible defences', *European Economic Review*, vol. 5, pp. 355–78.
Klopstock, F. (1968) 'The euro-dollar market: some unresolved issues', *Essays in International Finance No. 65*, Princeton University, Princeton, N.J.
Klopstock, F. (1970) 'Money creation in the euro-dollar market: a note on Professor Friedman's views', *Federal Reserve Bank of New York Monthly Review*, vol. LII, January, pp. 12–15.
Kohlhagen, S. W. (1979) 'The identification of destabilising foreign exchange speculation', *Journal of International Economics*, vol. 9, pp. 321–40.
Komiya, R. and Suzuki, Y. (1977) 'Inflation in Japan', in *Worldwide Inflation*, L. B. Krause and W. S. Salant (eds) (Washington DC: The Brookings Institution).
Kopits, G. F. (1978) 'Wage subsidies and employment: an analysis of the French experience', *International Monetary Fund Staff Papers*, vol. XXV, September, pp. 494–527.
Kosters, M. H. (1974) *Controls and Inflation: An Overview* (New York: National Bureau of Economic Research), November.
Kouri, P. J. K. (1976) 'The exchange rate and the balance of payments in the short run and the long run: a monetary approach', *Scandinavian Journal of Economics*, vol. 78, pp. 280–304.
Kouri, P. J. K. and Porter, M. G. (1974) 'International capital flows and portfolio equilibrium', *Journal of Political Economy*, vol. 82, May/June, pp. 443–67.
Kraft, J. and Roberts, B. (1975) 'Wage and price controls: success or failure',

in *Wage and Price Controls: The U.S. Experiment*, J. Kraft and B. Roberts (eds) (New York: Praeger).

Krause, L. B. and Salant, W. S. (eds) (1977) *Worldwide Inflation* (Washington DC: The Brookings Institution).

Kravis, I. B. and Lipsey, R. E. (1971) *Price Competitiveness in World Trade* (New York: National Bureau of Economic Research).

Kravis, I. B. and Lipsey, R. E. (1978) 'Price behaviour in the light of balance of payments theories', *Journal of International Economics*, vol. 8, pp. 193–246.

Kreinin, M. E. and Officer, L. H. (1978) 'The monetary approach to the balance of payments: a survey', *Princeton Studies in International Finance No. 43*, Princeton University, Princeton, N.J.

Krueger, A. O. (1965) 'The impact of alternative government policies under varying exchange systems', *Quarterly Journal of Economics*, vol. LXXIX, May, pp. 195–208.

Kuntze, O. E. (1978) 'Social contracts in Europe as a means of incomes policy', *IFO Digest*, March, pp. 14–18.

Laidler, D. E. W. (1973) 'The influence of money on real income and inflation: a simple model with some empirical tests for the U.S.: 1953–1972', *Manchester School of Economic and Social Studies*, no. 4, December, pp. 367–95.

Laidler, D. E. W. (1976a) 'Inflation in Britain: a monetarist perspective', *The American Economic Review*, vol. 66, September, pp. 485–500.

Laidler, D. E. W. (1976b) 'Inflation – alternative explanations and policies: tests on data drawn from six countries', *Journal of Monetary Economics – Supplement*, vol. 4, pp. 251–305.

Laidler, D. E. W. and Parkin, J. M. (1975) 'Inflation: a survey', *The Economic Journal*, vol. 85, December, pp. 741–809.

Lanyi, A. (1969) 'The case for floating exchange rates reconsidered', *Essays in International Finance No. 72*, Princeton University, Princeton, N.J.

Lanyi, A. (1975) 'Separate exchange markets for capital and current transactions', *International Monetary Fund Staff Papers*, vol. XXII, November, pp. 714–49.

Lanzillotti, R., Roberts, B. and Hamilton, M. (1975) *Phase II in Review: The Price Commission Experience* (Washington DC: The Brookings Institution).

Laury, J. S. E., Lewis, G. R. and Ormerod, P. A. (1978) 'Properties of macro-economic models of the U.K. economy: a comparative study', *National Institute Economic Review*, no. 83, February, pp. 52–72.

Lee, B. (1973) 'The euro-dollar multiplier', *Journal of Finance*, vol. XXVIII, September, pp. 867–74.

Levich, R. M. (1979a) 'On the efficiency of markets for foreign exchange', in *International Economic Policy: Theory and Evidence*, R. Dornbusch and J. A. Frenkel (eds) (Baltimore, Md.: Johns Hopkins University Press).

Levich, R. M. (1979b) 'Analysing the accuracy of foreign exchange advisory services: theory and evidence', manuscript, February.

Levin, J. H. C. (1972) 'International capital mobility and the assignment problem', *Oxford Economic Papers*, vol. XXIV, March, pp. 54–67.

Lilley, P. (1977) 'Incomes policies: a cost-benefit analysis', *National Westminster Bank Quarterly Review*, May, pp. 19–31.

Lindert, P. (1969) 'Key currencies and gold: 1900–1913', *Princeton Studies in International Finance No. 24*, Princeton University, Princeton, N.J.

Little, J. S. (1975) *Euro-Dollars: The Money-Market Gypsies* (New York: Harper & Row).

Little, J. S. (1977) 'The euro-currency market and the growth of international reserves', *New England Economic Review*, Federal Reserve Bank of Boston, May/June, pp. 9–23.

Little, J. S. (1979) 'Liquidity creation by euro-banks: 1973–1978', *New England Economic Review*, Federal Reserve Bank of Boston, January/February, pp. 62–72.

Lovati, J. M. (1977) 'The growing similarities among financial institutions', *Federal Reserve Bank of St Louis Monthly Review*, vol. 59, October, pp. 2–11.

Lucas, R. E. (Jr) (1973) 'Some international evidence on output–inflation trade-offs', *The American Economic Review*, vol. 63, June, pp. 326–34.

Lutz, F. A. (1963) 'The problem of international liquidity and the multiple-currency standard', in *World Monetary Reform*, H. G. Grubel (ed.) (Stanford University Press).

McCallum, B. T. (1977a) 'The role of speculation in the Canadian forward exchange market: some estimates assuming rational expectations', *Review of Economics and Statistics*, vol. LIX, May, pp. 145–51.

McCallum, B. T. (1977b) 'Price level stickiness and the feasibility of monetary stabilization policy with rational expectations', *Journal of Political Economy*, vol. 85, June, pp. 627–34.

McCloskey, D. N. and Zecher, J. R. (1976) 'How the gold standard worked 1880–1913', in *The Monetary Approach to the Balance of Payments*, J. A. Frenkel and H. G. Johnson (eds) (London: Allen & Unwin).

McKinnon, R. I. (1963) 'Optimum currency areas', *American Economic Review*, vol. 53, September, pp. 712–25.

McKinnon, R. I. (1969) 'Portfolio balance and international payments adjustment', in *Monetary Problems of the International Economy*, R. A. Mundell and A. K. Swoboda (eds) (University of Chicago Press).

McKinnon, R. I. (1971) 'Monetary theory and controlled flexibility in the foreign exchanges', *Essays in International Finance No. 84*, Princeton University, Princeton, N.J.

McKinnon, R. I. (1976a) 'The limited role of fiscal policy in an open economy', *Banca Nazionale del Lavoro Quarterly Review*, no. 117, June, pp. 95–117.

McKinnon, R. I. (1976b) 'Floating exchange rates 1973–74: the emperor's new clothes', in *Institutional Arrangements and the Inflation Problem*, K. Brunner and A. Meltzer (eds) (Amsterdam: North-Holland).

McKinnon, R. I. (1977) 'The euro-currency market', *Essays in International Finance No. 125*, Princeton University, Princeton, N.J.

Machlup, F. (1966) *International Monetary Economics – Collected Essays* (London: Allen & Unwin).

Machlup, F. and Malkiel, B. (1964) *International Monetary Arrangements: The Problem of Choice* (Department of Economics, International Finance Section, Princeton University, Princeton, N.J.).

Magnifico, G. (1973) *European Monetary Unification* (London: Macmillan).

Manser, W. (1971) *Britain in Balance: The Myth of Failure* (Harmondsworth:

Penguin).
Mayer, H. W. (1976) 'The BIS concept of the euro-currency market', *Euro-Money*, May, pp. 60–6.
Maynard, G. W. (1978) 'Keynes and unemployment to-day', *The Three Banks Review*, no. 120, December, pp. 3–20.
Meade, J. E. (1951) *The Balance of Payments: The Theory of International Economic Policy*, Vol. 1 (Oxford University Press).
Meade, J. E. (1955) 'The case for variable exchange rates', *The Three Banks Review*, no. 27, September, pp. 3–28.
Mikesell, R. F. and Goldstein, H. N. (1975) 'Rules for a floating-rate regime', *Essays in International Finance No. 109*, Princeton University, Princeton, N.J.
Minot, W. G. (1974) 'Tests for integration between major western European capital markets', *Oxford Economic Papers*, vol. XXVI, November, pp. 424–39.
Modigliani, F. (1977) 'The monetarist controversy, or should we forsake stabilization policies?. *The American Economic Review*, vol. 67, March, pp. 1–19.
Modigliani, F. (1978) 'Implications for policy: a symposium', *Brookings Papers on Economic Activity*, 2nd quarter, pp. 514–8.
Modigliani, F. and Papademos, L. (1978) 'Optimal demand policies against stagflation', *Weltwirtschaftliches Archiv*, Band 114, December, pp. 736–82.
Modigliani, F. and Tarantelli, E. (1977) 'Market forces, trade union action and the Phillips Curve in Italy', *Banca Nazionale del Lavoro Quarterly Review*, no. 120, March, pp. 3–36.
Moggridge, D. E. (1972) *British Monetary Policy 1924–1931: The Norman Conquest of $4.86* (Cambridge University Press).
Morgan Guaranty Trust Company of New York, *World Financial Markets* (New York).
Morgenstern, O. (1959) *International Financial Transactions and Business Cycles* (Princeton, N.J.: Princeton University Press).
Mundell, R. A. (1961) 'A theory of optimum currency areas', *The American Economic Review*, vol. 51, September, pp. 657–65.
Mundell, R. A. (1962) 'The appropriate use of monetary and fiscal policy for internal and external stability', *International Monetary Fund Staff Papers*, vol. IX, March, pp. 70–9.
Mundell, R. A. (1963) 'Capital mobility and stabilisation policy under fixed and flexible exchange rates', *Canadian Journal of Economics and Political Science*, vol. XXIX, November, pp. 475–85.
Mundell, R. A. (1964) 'A reply: capital mobility and size', *Canadian Journal of Economics and Political Science*, vol. 30, August, pp. 421–31.
Mundell, R. A. (1968) *International Economics* (London: Macmillan).
Mussa, M. (1979) 'Empirical regularities in the behavior of exchange rates and theories of the foreign exchange market', *Journal of Monetary Economics – Supplement*, vol. 11, pp. 9–57.
Neumann, M. J. M. (1978) 'Offsetting capital flows: a re-examination of the German case', *Journal of Monetary Economics*, vol. 4, pp. 131–42.
Nevile, J. W. (1975) *Fiscal Policy in Australia: Theory and Practice*, second edition (Melbourne: Cheshire).

Nevile, J. W. (1976) 'Government expenditure and inflation', *Bank of New South Wales Review*, no. 17, March.

Nevile, J. W. (1977) *Tax Cuts as an Anti-Inflationary Weapon* (Sydney: University of New South Wales, Centre for Applied Economic Research), November.

Nickell, S. (1979) 'Unemployment and the structure of labor costs', *Journal of Monetary Economics – Supplement*, vol. 11, pp. 187–222.

Niehans, J. (1975) 'Some doubts about the efficacy of monetary policy under flexible exchange rates', *Journal of International Economics*, vol. 5, pp. 275–81.

Niehans, J. and Hewson, J. (1976) 'The euro-dollar market and monetary theory', *Journal of Money, Credit and Banking*, vol. VIII, February, pp. 1–27.

Niskanen, W. (1978) 'Deficits, government spending and inflation', *Journal of Monetary Economics – Supplement*, vol. 4, pp. 591–602.

Nordhaus, W. D. (1972) 'The world-wide wage explosion', *Brookings Papers on Economic Activity*, 2nd quarter, pp. 431–65.

Nurkse, R. (1944) *International Currency Experience* (Princeton, N.J.: League of Nations).

Officer, L. (1976) 'The purchasing power parity theory of exchange rates: a review article', *International Monetary Fund Staff Papers*, vol. XXIII, March, pp. 1–60.

Okun, A. M. (1962) 'Potential GNP: its measurement and significance', in *Proceedings of the Business and Economic Statistics Section* (American Statistical Association), pp. 98–104.

Okun, A. M. and Perry, G. L. (eds) (1978) 'Special issue – innovative policies to slow inflation', *Brookings Papers on Economic Activity*, 2nd quarter.

Organisation for Economic Co-operation and Development (OECD), *OECD Economic Outlook*, Paris.

Organisation for Economic Co-operation and Development (OECD), *OECD Observer*, Paris.

Organisation for Economic Co-operation and Development (OECD) (1972) 'Monetary policy in Japan', *OECD Monetary Studies Series*, Paris.

Organisation for Economic Co-operation and Development (OECD) (1973) 'The international transmission of inflation', *OECD Economic Outlook*, July, Paris.

Organisation for Economic Co-operation and Development (OECD) (1976a) *National Accounts of OECD Countries*, Paris.

Organisation for Economic Co-operation and Development (OECD) (1976b) 'Public sector budget balances', *OECD Economic Outlook – Occasional Studies*, July, Paris.

Organisation for Economic Co-operation and Development (OECD) (1977a) *Structural Determinants of Employment and Unemployment – Experts' Meeting, Paris, 7–11 March 1977*, Vol. 1, Paris.

Organisation for Economic Co-operation and Development (OECD) (1977b) 'Towards full employment and price stability', *The McCracken Report – A Report to the OECD By a Group of Independent Experts*, Paris.

Organisation for Economic Co-operation and Development (OECD) (1978a) 'Budget indicators', *OECD Economic Outlook – Occasional Studies*, July, Paris.

Organisation for Economic Co-operation and Development (OECD) (1978b) 'The international competitiveness of selected OECD countries', *OECD Economic Outlook – Occasional Studies*, July, Paris.

Organisation for Economic Co-operation and Development (OECD) (1978c) *Employment Policies, Incomes and Growth in the Medium Term – Preparatory Documents and Conclusions of a Trade Union Seminar Convened by the OECD, Paris, 12–14 October 1977*, Paris.

Organisation for Economic Co-operation and Development (OECD) (1978d) 'Public expenditure trends', *Studies in Resource Allocation No. 5*, Paris.

Organisation for Economic Co-operation and Development (OECD) (1978e) *Revenue Statistics of OECD Member Countries 1965–76*, Paris.

Organisation for Economic Co-operation and Development (OECD) (1979a) 'Monetary targets and inflation control', *OECD Monetary Studies Series*, Paris.

Organisation for Economic Co-operation and Development (OECD) (1979b) *Structural Determinants of Employment and Unemployment – Experts' Meeting, Paris, 7–11 March 1977*, Vol. 2, Paris.

Palyi, M. (1972) *The Twilight of Gold 1914–1936: Myths and Realities* (Henry Regnery).

Panic, M. (1978) 'The origin of increasing inflationary tendencies in contemporary society', in *The Political Economy of Inflation*, F. Hirsch and J. H. Goldthorpe (eds) (Oxford: Martin Robertson).

Parkin, J. M. (1972) 'An overwhelming case for European monetary union', *The Banker*, vol. 122, September, pp. 1139–42.

Parkin, J. M. (1978) 'Britain 1951–1972 – the lessons unlearned', in *Wage–Price Control – Myth and Reality* (The Center for Independent Studies).

Parkin, J. M. and Sumner, M. T. (eds) (1972) *Incomes Policy and Inflation* (Manchester University Press).

Parkin, J. M., Sumner, M. T. and Jones, R. A. (1972) 'A survey of the econometric evidence of the effects of incomes policy on the rate of inflation', in *Incomes Policy and Inflation*, J. M. Parkin and M. T. Sumner (eds) (Manchester University Press).

Parkin, J. M. and Swoboda, A. K. (1976) 'Inflation: a review of the issues', *Discussion Paper No. 10*, Graduate Institute of International Studies.

Parkin, J. M. and Zis, G. (eds) (1976) *Inflation in Open Economies* (Manchester University Press and University of Toronto Press).

Payer, C. (1974) *The Debt Trap: The I.M.F. and the Third World* (New York: Monthly Review Press).

Peacock, A. and Ricketts, M. (1978) 'The growth of the public sector and inflation', in *The Political Economy of Inflation*, F. Hirsch and J. H. Goldthorpe (eds) (Oxford: Martin Robertson).

Perkins, J. O. N. (1979) *The Macroeconomic Mix to Stop Stagflation* (Melbourne: Macmillan).

Perloff, J. M. and Wachter, M. L. (1979) 'The New Jobs Tax Credit: an evaluation of the 1977–78 wage subsidy program', *The American Economic Review*, vol. 69, May, pp. 173–7.

Perry, G. L. (1975) 'Determinants of wage inflation around the world', *Brookings Papers on Economic Activity*, 2nd quarter, pp. 403–47.

Phelps, E. S. (1968) 'Money–wage dynamics and labour market equilibrium', *Journal of Political Economy*, vol. 76, August, pp. 678–711.

Phelps, E. S. (1978) 'Commodity-supply shock and full-employment monetary policy', *Journal of Money, Credit and Banking*, vol. X, May, pp. 206–21.

Phillips, A. W. (1958) 'The relationship between unemployment and the rate of change of money wage rates in the U.K.: 1861–1957', *Economica*, vol. 25, November, pp. 283–399.

Pohlman, J. (1976) *Inflation Under Control?* (Reston).

Polak, J. J. (1971) 'Some reflections on the nature of special drawing rights', *International Monetary Fund Pamphlet Series No. 16*, Washington DC.

Polak, J. J. (1974) 'Valuation and rate of interest of the SDR', *International Monetary Fund Pamphlet Series No. 18*, Washington DC.

Polak, J. J. and Argy, V. (1971) 'Credit policy and the balance of payments', *International Monetary Fund Staff Papers*, vol. XVIII, March, pp. 1–24.

Pollack, G. A. (1975) 'Are the oil payments deficits manageable?', *Essays in International Finance No. 111*, Princeton University, Princeton, N.J.

Pollard, S. (ed.) (1970) *The Gold Standard and Employment Policies Between the Wars* (London: Methuen).

Poole, W. (1970) 'Optimal choice of monetary policy instruments in a simple stochastic macro-model', *Quarterly Journal of Economics*, vol. LXXXIV, May, pp. 197–216.

Poole, W. (1973) 'Wage price controls: where do we go from here?', *Brookings Papers on Economic Activity*, 1st quarter, pp. 285–99.

Porter, M. G. (1974) 'The interdependence of monetary policy and capital flows in Australia', *The Economic Record*, vol. 50, March, pp. 1–20.

Porter, M. G. (1977) 'The exchange rate and portfolio equilibrium', unpublished.

Porter, R. D., Simpson, T. D. and Mauskopf, E. (1979) 'Financial innovations and the monetary aggregates', *Brookings Papers on Economic Activity*, 1st quarter, pp. 213–29.

Posner, M. (1972) 'The world monetary system: a minimal reform program', *Essays in International Finance No. 96*, Princeton University, Princeton, N.J.

Quirk, P. J. (1977) 'Exchange rate policy in Japan: leaning against the wind', *International Monetary Fund Staff Papers*, vol. XXIV, November, pp. 642–64.

Reddaway, W. B. (1970) 'Was $4.85 inevitable in 1925?', *Lloyds Bank Review*, no. 96, April, pp. 15–28.

Rees, A. (1978) 'New policies to fight inflation: sources of skepticism', *Brookings Papers on Economic Activity*, 2nd quarter, pp. 453–77.

Rhomberg, R. (1976) 'Indices of effective exchange rates', *International Monetary Fund Staff Papers*, vol. XXIII, March, pp. 88–112.

Richardson, G. (1979) 'The prospects for an international monetary system', *Bank of England Quarterly Bulletin*, vol. 19, September, pp. 290–7.

Ripley, D. (1978) 'The transmission of fluctuations in economic activity: some recent evidence', in *Managed Exchange-Rate Flexibility: The Recent Experience* (Federal Reserve Bank of Boston, Conference Series No. 20).

Robbins, L. (1934) *The Great Depression* (London: Macmillan).

Robertson, J. (1943) 'The post-war monetary plans', *The Economic Journal*, vol. LIII, December, pp. 352–60.

Robinson, D. (1973) *Incomes Policy and Capital Sharing in Europe* (New York: Barnes & Noble).

Robinson, J. (1943) 'The international currency proposals', *The Economic Journal*, vol. LIII, June–September, pp. 161–75.

Roosa, R. V. (1965) *Monetary Reforms for the World Economy* (New York: Harper & Row).

Rowan, D. (1974) 'The rate structure and capital movements: a note on Operation Twist', *Banca Nazionale del Lavoro Quarterly Review*, no. 111, December, pp. 294–318.

Rueff, J. (1961) 'The west is risking a credit collapse', *Fortune*, vol. LXIV, July, pp. 126–7.

Rushing, P. (1972) 'The reciprocal currency arrangements', *New England Economic Review*, Federal Reserve Bank of Boston, November/December, pp. 3–15.

Sacchetti, U. (1972) 'Mechanico – discretionary tools for parity changes', *Banca Nazionale del Lavoro Quarterly Review*, no. 103, December, pp. 364–95.

Salant, W. S. (1964) 'The reserve currency role of the dollar: blessing or burden to the U.S.', *Review of Economics and Statistics*, vol. XLVI, May, pp. 165–72.

Salant, W. S. (1977) 'International transmission of inflation', in *Worldwide Inflation: Theory and Recent Experience*, L. B. Krause and W. S. Salant (eds) (Washington DC: The Brookings Institution).

Salop, J. (1974) 'Devaluation and the balance of trade under flexible wages', in *Trade, Stability and Macroeconomics – Essays in Honor of L. A. Metzler*, G. Horwich and P. A. Samuelson (eds) (New York and London).

Santomero, A. M. and Seater, J. J. (1978) 'The inflation–unemployment trade-off: a critique of the literature', *Journal of Economic Literature*, vol. XVI, June, pp. 499–544.

Sargent, J. (1979) 'Productivity and profits in U.K. manufacturing', *Midland Bank Review*, Autumn, pp. 7–13.

Sargent, T. J. and Wallace, N. (1976) 'Rational expectations and the theory of economic policy', *Journal of Monetary Economics*, vol. 2, pp. 169–83.

Schadler, S. (1977) 'Sources of exchange rate variability: theory and empirical evidence', *International Monetary Fund Staff Papers*, vol. XXIV, July, pp. 253–96.

Schultz, G. P. and Aliber, R. Z. (eds) (1966) *Guidelines – Informal Controls and the Market Place* (University of Chicago Press).

Seidman, L. S. (1978) 'Tax-based incomes policies', *Brookings Papers on Economic Activity*, 2nd quarter, pp. 301–48.

Slitor, R. E. (1979) 'Implementation and design of tax-based incomes policies', *The American Economic Review*, vol. 69, May, pp. 212–15.

Smith, D. (1975) 'Public consumption and economic performance', *National Westminster Bank Review*, November, pp. 17–30.

Smith, R. P. (1976) 'Demand management and the "new school"', *Applied Economics*, vol. 6, pp. 193–205.

Sobol, D. M. (1979) 'A Substitution Account – precedents and issues', *Federal Reserve Bank of New York Quarterly Review*, Summer, pp. 40–8.

Sohmen, E. (1961) *Flexible Exchange Rates* (University of Chicago Press).

Sohmen, E. (1966) 'The theory of forward exchange', *Princeton Studies in International Finance No. 17*, Princeton University, Princeton, N.J.

Solomon, R. (1975) 'The allocation of "oil deficits"', *International Finance Discussion Paper No. 62*, Federal Reserve System, Washington DC.

Solomon, R. (1977) *The International Monetary System: 1945–76: – An Insider's View* (New York: Harper & Row).

Spitaeller, E. (1971) 'Prices and unemployment in selected industrial countries', *International Monetary Fund Staff Papers*, vol. XVIII, November, pp. 528–69.

Spitaeller, E. (1976) 'Some annual wage equations for the manufacturing sectors in six major industrial countries: 1957 (1) to 1972 (2)', *Weltwirtschaftliches Archiv*, Band 112, pp. 300–37.

Spraos, J. (1972) 'The arbitrage function', in *Le Change a Terme – Technique, Theorie, Politique*, P. Coulbois (ed.) (Paris: Editions Cujas).

Spraos, J. (1975) 'New Cambridge macro-economics, assignment rules and interdependence', in *The Political Economy of International Monetary Reform*, R. Z. Aliber (ed.) (University of Chicago Press).

Stein, J. L. (1963) 'The optimum foreign exchange market', *The American Economic Review*. vol. 53, June, pp. 384–402.

Stein, J. L. (1976) 'Reply: a Keynesian can be a monetarist', in *Monetarism*, vol. 1, J. L. Stein (ed.) (Amsterdam: North-Holland).

Stem, C., Makin, J. and Logue, D. (eds) (1976) *Euro-Currencies and the International Monetary System* (Washington DC: American Enterprise Institute for Public Policy Research).

Stern, R. M. (1973) *The Balance of Payments: Theory and Economic Policy* (London: Macmillan).

Stern, R. M., Francis, J. and Schumacher, B. (1976) *Price Statistics in International Trade – An Annotated Bibliography* (London: Macmillan).

Stevens, N. (1979) 'Government debt financing – its effects in view of tax discounting', *Federal Reserve Bank of St Louis Monthly Review*, vol 61, July, pp. 11–19.

Stevenson, A. A. and Trevithick, J. A. (1977) 'The complementarity of monetary policy and prices and incomes policy: an examination of recent British experience', *Scottish Journal of Political Economy*, vol. 24, February, pp. 19–31.

Stoll, H. (1968) 'An empirical study of the forward exchange market under fixed and flexible exchange rate systems', *Canadian Journal of Economics*, vol. I, February, pp. 55–78.

Suss, E. C. (1976) 'A note on reserve use under alternative exchange rate regimes', *International Monetary Fund Staff Papers*, vol. XXIII, July, pp. 387–94.

Swan, T. W. (1955) 'Longer run problems of the balance of payments', in *The Australian Economy: A Volume of Readings*, H. W. Arndt and W. M. Corden (eds) (Melbourne: Cheshire Press).

Sweeney, R. J. and Willett, T. D. (1977) 'Euro-dollars, petro-dollars and world liquidity and inflation', *Journal of Monetary Economics – Supplement*, vol. 5, pp. 277–310.

Swoboda, A. K. (1968) 'The euro-dollar market: an interpretation', *Essays in International Finance No. 64*, Princeton University, Princeton, N.J.

Swoboda, A. K. (1972) 'Equilibrium, quasi-equilibrium and macro economic policy under fixed exchange rates', *Quarterly Journal of Economics*, vol. LXXXVI, February, pp. 162–71.

Swoboda, A. K. (1977) 'Monetary approaches to worldwide inflation', in *Worldwide Inflation: Theory and Recent Experience*, L. B. Krause and W. S. Salant (eds) (Washington DC: The Brookings Institution).

Swoboda, A. K. (1978) 'Gold, euro-dollars and the world money stock under fixed exchange rates', *The American Economic Review*, vol. 68, September, pp. 625–42.

Swoboda, A. K. and Dornbusch, R. (1973) 'Adjustment, policy and monetary equilibrium in a two-country model', in *Inter-Trade and Money*, M. Connolly and A. Swoboda (eds) (London: Allen & Unwin), Chapter 12.

Tarling, R. and Wilkinson, F. (1977) 'The social contract: postwar incomes policies and their inflationary impact', *Cambridge Journal of Economics*, vol. 1, pp. 395–414.

Tatom, J. (1978) 'Economic growth and unemployment: a reappraisal of the conventional view', *Federal Reserve Bank of St Louis Monthly Review*, vol. 60, October, pp. 16–22.

Tatom, J. (1979) 'The productivity problem', *Federal Reserve Bank of St Louis Monthly Review*, vol. 61, September, pp. 3–16.

Theil, H. C. (1961) *Economic Forecasts and Policy*, second revised edition (Amsterdam: North-Holland).

Thirwall, A. P. (1978) 'The U.K.'s economic problem: a balance of payments constraint?', *National Westminster Bank Quarterly Review*, February, pp. 24–32.

Thomas, L. (1973) 'Behavior of flexible exchange rates: additional tests from the Post World War I episode', *Southern Economic Journal*, vol. 40, October, pp. 167–82.

Thygesen, N. (1978) 'Inflation and exchange rates: evidence and policy guidelines for the European community', *Journal of International Economics*, vol. 8, pp. 301–17.

Tinbergen, J. (1952) *On The Theory of Economic Policy* (Amsterdam: North-Holland).

Tobin, J. and Buiter, W. (1976) 'Long-run effects of fiscal and monetary policy on aggregate demand', in *Monetarism*, Vol. 1, J. L. Stein (ed.) (Amsterdam: North-Holland).

Tosini, P. A. (1977) 'Leaning against the wind: a standard for managed floating', *Essays in International Finance No. 126*, Princeton University, Princeton, N.J.

Tower, E. and Courtney, M. M. (1974) 'Exchange rate flexibility and macro-economic stability', *Review of Economics and Statistics*, vol. LVI, May, pp. 215–24.

Tower, E. and Willett, T. (1976) 'The theory of optimum currency areas and exchange rate flexibility' in *Special Papers in International Economics No. 11* (Princeton, N.J.: Princeton University Press), Chapter 2.

Townend, J. C. (1976) 'The personal saving ratio', *Bank of England Quarterly Bulletin*, vol. 16, March, pp. 53–73.

Triffin, R. (1959) 'Tomorrow's convertibility: aims and means of international policy', *Banca Nazionale del Lavoro Quarterly Review*, no. 49, June, pp. 131–200.

Triffin, R. (1960) *Gold and the Dollar Crisis* (New Haven, Conn.: Yale University Press).

Triffin, R. (1964) 'The evolution of the international monetary system: historical reappraisal and future perspectives', *Princeton Studies in International Finance No. 12*, Princeton University, Princeton, N.J.

Tryon, R. (1979) 'Testing for rational expectations in foreign exchange markets', *International Finance Discussion Paper No. 139*, Federal Reserve System, Washington DC.

Tsiang, S. C. (1959) 'The theory of forward exchange and effects of government intervention on the forward exchange market', *International Monetary Fund Staff Papers*, vol. VII, April, pp. 75–106.

Tsiang, S. C. (1975) 'The dynamics of international capital flows and internal and external balance', *Quarterly Journal of Economics*, vol. LXXXIX, May, pp. 195–214.

Tsoukalis, L. (1977) *The Politics and Economics of European Monetary Integration* (London: Allen & Unwin).

Turnovsky, S. J. (1976) 'The relative stability of alternative exchange rate systems in the presence of random disturbances', *Journal of Money, Credit and Banking*, vol. VIII, February, pp. 29–50.

Ulman, L. and Flanagan, R. (1971) *Wage Restraint – A Study of Incomes Policies in Western Europe* (Berkeley, Calif.: University of California Press).

Underwood, T. (1973) 'Analysis of proposals for using objective indicators as a guide to exchange rate changes', *International Monetary Fund Staff Papers*, vol. XX, March, pp. 100–17.

Vanderkamp, J. (1975) 'Inflation: a simple Friedman theory with a Phillips Twist', *Journal of Monetary Economics*, vol. 1, pp. 117–22.

Viner, J. (1943) 'Two plans for international monetary stabilisation', *The Yale Review*, September, pp. 77–107.

Viner, J. (1951) *International Economics – Studies* (Glencoe, Ill.: The Free Press).

Wallich, H. and Weintraub, S. (1971) 'A tax-based incomes policy', *Journal of Economic Issues*, vol. 5, June, pp. 1–19.

Ward, R. and Zis, G. (1974) 'Trade union militancy as an explanation of inflation: an international comparison', *Manchester School of Economic and Social Studies*, no. 1, March, pp. 46–65.

Weintraub, S. (1971) 'An incomes policy to stop inflation', *Lloyds Bank Review*, no. 99, January, pp. 1–12.

Wenninger, J. and Sivesind, C. M. (1979) 'Defining money for a changing financial system', *Federal Reserve Bank of New York Quarterly Review*, vol. 4, Spring, pp. 1–8.

White Paper, *Prices and Incomes After 30th June 1967* (London: HMSO Cmnd. 3255).

Whitman, M. v. N. (1970) 'Policies for internal and external balance', *Special Papers in International Economics No. 9*, Princeton University, Princeton, N.J.

Whitman, M. v. N. (1974) 'The current and future role of the dollar: how much symmetry?', *Brookings Papers on Economic Activity*, 3rd quarter, pp. 539–91.

Whitman, M. v. N. (1975) 'Global monetarism and the monetary approach to the balance of payments', *Brookings Papers on Economic Activity*, 3rd quarter, pp. 491–536.

Willett, T. D. (1977) *Floating Exchange Rates and International Monetary Reform* (Washington DC: American Enterprise Institute for Public Policy Research).

Willett, T. D. and Lancy, L. O. (1978) 'Monetarism, budget deficits and wage push inflation: the cases of Italy and the U.K.', *Banca Nazionale del Lavoro Quarterly Review*, no. 127, December, pp. 315–31.

Willett, T. D. and Officer, L. H. (1970) 'The covered-arbitrage schedule: a critical survey of recent developments', *Journal of Money, Credit and Banking*, vol. II, May, pp. 247–57.

Williamson, J. (1963) 'Liquidity and the multiple key currency proposal', *The American Economic Review*, vol. 53, June, pp. 427–33.

Williamson, J. (1965) 'The crawling peg', *Essays in International Finance No. 50*, Princeton University, Princeton, N.J.

Williamson, J. (1975) 'The future exchange rate regime', *Banca Nazionale del Lavoro Quarterly Review*, no. 113, June, pp. 127–44.

Williamson, J. (1976) 'Exchange rate flexibility and reserve use', *Scandinavian Journal of Economics*, vol. 78, pp. 327–39.

Williamson, J. (1977) *The Failure of World Monetary Reform: 1971–1974*, (New York University Press).

Williamson, J. and Wood, G. E. (1976) 'The British inflation: indigenous or imported', *The American Economic Review*, vol. 66, September, pp. 520–31.

Wonnacott, P. (1963) 'A suggestion for the revaluation of gold', *Journal of Finance*, vol. XVIII, March, pp. 49–55.

Yeager, L. B. (1976) *International Monetary Relations: Theory, History and Policy*, second edition (New York: Harper & Row).

Zolotas, X. (1961) 'Towards a reinforced gold exchange standard', *Bank of Greece Papers and Lectures No. 7*, Athens. [Reprinted in *World Monetary Reform*, H. G. Grubel (ed.) (Stanford University Press), 1963.]

Index